Today's Chicago Blues

Karen Hanson

First Edition

Chicago
www.lakeclaremont.com

Today's Chicago Blues
Karen Hanson

Published January 2007 by:

P.O. Box 25291
Chicago, IL 60625
773/728-1600
lcp@lakeclaremont.com
www.lakeclaremont.com

Publisher's Cataloging-In-Publication Data
(Prepared by The Donohue Group, Inc.)

Hanson, Karen, 1956-
    Today's Chicago blues / Karen Hanson. — 1st ed.

    p. : ill. ; cm.

    Includes index.
    ISBN-13: 978-1-893121-19-5
    ISBN-10: 1-893121-19-4

    1. Blues (Music)—Illinois—Chicago—Guidebooks. 2. Nightclubs—Illinois—Chicago—Guidebooks. 3. Musical landmarks—Illinois—Chicago—Guidebooks. 4. Chicago (Ill.)—Guidebooks. I. Title.

ML3521 .H36 2006
781.643/09773/11   2006925492

10 09 08 07   8 7 6 5 4 3 2 1

Table of Contents

Chapter 5   91
Down-Home Blues:
Chicago Record Labels

Alligator Records
Delmark Records
Earwig Music

Chapter 6   101
Just Wanna Play My Axe:
Blues Jams

Jam Tips for Musicians
Jam Tips for the Audience
Blues Jams

Rob Stone and the C-Notes
Big Time Sarah Streeter
Bob Stroger
Hubert Sumlin
Tail Dragger
Eddie Taylor Jr.
Koko Taylor
Larry Taylor
Melvin Taylor
Nellie "Tiger" Travis
Maurice John Vaughn
Carl Weathersby
James Wheeler
Artie "Blues Boy" White
Jody Williams
Zora Young

Publisher's Credits

Cover design by Timothy Kocher.

Editing by Laura R. Gabler.

Interior design and layout by Michael Wykowski.

Proofreading by Elizabeth Daniel, Diana Runge, and Sharon Woodhouse.

Indexing by Diana Runge and Elizabeth Daniel.

Acknowledgments

Research was the most enjoyable part of this project, but it was also the hardest part. For that reason I am grateful for the assistance of many people in the Chicago blues community who supplied me with information and pointed me in the right direction to find more.

My thanks especially to the blues artists whom I interviewed formally and informally: Koko Taylor, Lonnie Brooks, Jimmy Burns, Eddy Clearwater, John Primer, Joanna Connor, Nora Jean Bruso, Fruteland Jackson, Zora Young, Gloria Shannon, Liz Mandville Greeson, Michael Coleman, Fernando Jones, Willie "Big Eyes" Smith, Chico Banks, Nick Moss, Bob Stroger, Deitra Farr, David "Chainsaw" Dupont, Tom Holland, Bonnie Lee, Billy Branch, Vance Kelly, Big Time Sarah Streeter, and Artie "Blues Boy" White. It was a pleasure and privilege to speak with all of you.

My appreciation also goes to club owners for their hospitality and for taking time to talk with me. Special thanks to Tony Mangiullo of Rosa's Lounge; Gino Battaglia and the staff of Blue Chicago, especially Lorenzo Grant and Jeff at the Blue Chicago Store; Stanley Davis of Lee's Unleaded Blues; Rob Hecko of B.L.U.E.S.; Thel Davis of Genesis Lounge; the Bossman; Ken Zimmerman of the Harlem Avenue Lounge; Bill FitzGerald of FitzGerald's Nightclub; and Donna from Kingston Mines.

For helping to arrange interviews with artists, I am grateful to Bruce Iglauer, Marc Lipkin, and Chris Levick of Alligator Records; and to Ken Zimmerman, Kate Moss, Bettie White, Karen Leipziger, Lisa Becker, Sharon Pomaville, Mark Bruso, Steve Pasek, Manuel Arrington, Paul Singer, and Scott Robinson.

Thanks also to record label owners Bob Koester of Delmark

Records, Michael Frank of Earwig Music, and, again, Bruce Iglauer of Alligator Records, for their incredible knowledge of the history of Chicago blues clubs, labels, and music and for sharing with me the vast resources of biographical information about Chicago-area artists. I appreciate your encouragement and support in this undertaking.

For information and assistance in research, I would like to thank Barry Dolins and the staff at the City of Chicago Mayor's Office of Special Events; the staff of the Harold Washington Library eighth-floor music department; and Gregg Parker and Stefanie Mielke of the Chicago Blues Museum. Special thanks to Gregg and Stefanie for their generosity in allowing the use of images owned by the Chicago Blues Museum and Chicago Jazz Museum.

Thanks also to other knowledgeable folks in the blues community, especially Tony Bagdy, Steve Balkin, Buzz Kilman, and Steve Cushing. Additionally, I'd like to acknowledge the amazing collective knowledge of the Blues-L online discussion group, especially Scott Dirks, Dick Waterman, Tom Holland, Twist Turner, Dave Markovits, Greg Freerksen, and Chuck Winans. Special thanks to Dave and Greg for their viewpoints.

For encouragement and moral support, thanks goes to my friends at the Brainstorms online community. I would especially like to thank Richard J. Lee for generously sharing his expertise.

I'd like to thank Derek Hanson for his editorial assistance and organizational skills. Finally, I am eternally grateful to my husband, Brian, who for the past decade has driven me places and carried my stuff.

Today's Chicago Blues

Introduction

Sweet Home Chicago:

Today's Chicago Blues

In 1936, when legendary slide guitarist Robert Johnson recorded "Sweet Home Chicago," Chicago already had a flourishing blues scene with such stars as Big Bill Broonzy, Tampa Red, Lonnie Johnson, Memphis Minnie, and Sonny Boy (John Lee) Williamson I. After World War II, Chicago blues became a worldwide force with the arrival of Muddy Waters, Little Walter, Jimmy Reed, Howlin' Wolf, and other innovative musicians from the Mississippi Delta area.

In Chicago the rural blues of the South was amplified and took on the hard sounds of the big city. Shuffling rhythms, electrified slide guitar, wailing harmonica, and gritty vocals constituted the characteristic Chicago blues sound. Within a few years other blues styles emerged in Chicago: the guitar-focused West Side sound of Magic Sam and Otis Rush, the soulful blues of Etta James and Otis Clay, the distinctive pop rhythms of Bo Diddley and Chuck Berry. Not only were these sounds influential within the blues, but they sparked a new musical genre, rock and roll. Blues radio shows, along with record labels like Chess and Vee-Jay, spread the music beyond the African-American community, throughout America, and overseas.

In fact, Chicago-made blues was responsible for launching one of the greatest rock-and-roll bands of all time. As the story goes, Keith Richards struck up a conversation with Mick Jagger in 1960 at a train station when he noticed Jagger was carrying two Chess albums, *The Best of Muddy Waters* and *Rockin' at the Hops* by Chuck Berry. The band they formed took its name from Muddy Waters's song "Rollin' Stone." On their first trip to the United States, the Rolling Stones visited Chicago so they could record in the famous Chess Studios.

Now, in the twenty-first century, Chicago is still the center of the blues world. Only in Chicago can you hear live blues music seven days a week, 365 days a year, by musicians who helped create the Chicago blues sound and today carry it forward into the future. In Chicago more clubs are devoted entirely to the blues than in any other metropolitan area. Blues bands also play regularly at numerous restaurants and lounges in the city and suburbs.

Likewise, more blues musicians live and work steadily in the Chicago area than in any other city in the world. Many, like Buddy Guy and Koko Taylor, are famous internationally, even to nonblues fans. Still other musicians are known and respected by blues aficionados. Chicago remains the place where aspiring blues musicians come to learn the blues and get their big breaks. Guitarists, harp players, drummers, and vocalists have relocated to Chicago from all over the United States, Europe, and Asia just to play the blues.

Every year thousands of fans visit Chicago specifically to see the living legends of the blues. On any given night, a half dozen different languages can be heard in Chicago blues clubs. But the blues is not just for tourists. Blues bands play in neighborhood bars where the clientele are local residents out for a good time. And Chicago is home to the largest free blues festival in the world. Each June a half million people or more flock to Grant Park to indulge in four days of wailing guitars, boogie-woogie piano, plaintive blues harp, and soulful vocals.

Three active and influential blues record labels call Chicago home, and blues programming appears on both commercial and public radio stations. In addition, Chicago boasts more places of significance in blues history than anyplace else north of the Mississippi Delta.

But even in Sweet Home Chicago, the blues often happens off the mainstream radar. Most popular media either overlook the blues or treat the genre as a relic from the past. Current information about the blues is hard to find unless you know where to look for it. Even then, it's scattered, incomplete, or outdated.

Today's Chicago Blues brings together everything fans will need to know about the blues in Chicago. Here you will find descriptions of clubs and lounges where live bands play, a directory of blues radio shows, a listing of blues jams, information about historical blues sites, a guide to the Chicago Blues Festival, and profiles of numerous blues musicians who live and perform in the Chicago area. In addition, each chapter provides historical and cultural context so that novice fans might be inspired to learn more. While you may enjoy listening to the Chicago blues strictly for entertainment, you will find your appreciation deepen if you understand the roots of the music.

Visitors to Chicago will find here a more comprehensive look at the Chicago blues scene than found in typical guidebooks, which usually lump the blues in with tourist attractions like Navy Pier and the Sears Tower. *Today's Chicago Blues* takes you to places that tourists don't know about.

Chicago-area residents will also be able to use *Today's Chicago Blues* as a valuable resource for exploring the rich cultural treasure that's right in their own backyards. Chicagoans should take pride in living in the home of the blues. Attending a blues show is a great way to celebrate a special occasion, have fun with friends, or top off an evening in the city.

Wherever you're from, *Today's Chicago Blues* can help you discover that the blues is more than a feeling of sadness and melancholy, as the name suggests. The blues began as party music, and it remains so today. Go to the clubs, and you'll hear the rollicking roll of a Chicago-style shuffle, the upbeat tempo of a boogie-woogie piano, and the swooping melodies of the blues harp. You'll find that the music will draw you in, make you move, and reach deep into your soul.

Muddy Waters, Jimmy Rogers, James Cotton, Otis Spann, and Junior Wells were among the blues artists who performed at Smitty's Corner, located at 35th Street and Indiana.
Copyright and courtesy of the Chicago Blues Museum. The Chicago Blues Museum is a registered trademark.

Colorful posters advertised show dates at clubs like the 708 Club on 47th Street.
Copyright and courtesy of the Chicago Blues Museum. The Chicago Blues Museum is a registered trademark.

Chapter 1

Put on Your High–Heeled Sneakers:

Blues Clubs in the City

In the 1950s, Chicago's blues clubs were clustered on the South and West sides of the city. Patrons were African-Americans, typically recent arrivals in Chicago from the southern states who were looking for those down-home blues. They found it at places like Silvio's, Pepper's Lounge, Club Zanzibar, the 708 Club, Ross and Ma Bea's, Curley's, the Avenue Lounge, Smitty's, and more.

The stretch of 43rd Street where the old Checkerboard Lounge was located is now known as Honorary Muddy Waters Drive.

Many of today's blues artists started out by playing in those historic clubs. Guitarist Eddy Clearwater, who came to Chicago in 1950, recalls that people from the South naturally drifted together to play the music they had grown up with. "It became like having a big house party every weekend," says the Mississippi-born Clearwater.

One of the most famous clubs on the West Side during the 1960s was Silvio's, first located at Lake and Oakley and later at Lake and Kedzie. The club booked the most famous blues acts, like Howlin' Wolf and Muddy Waters. Sometimes both bands were booked on the same night, recalls Bob Koester, founder of Delmark Records. Because both Muddy and the Wolf were on the road so much, it was uncertain which band would show up. Koester explains, "Silvio would say, 'I've got to hire two bands to make sure I have one.'"

By the 1970s, however, the sounds of R&B, soul, and Motown were outpacing the blues in popularity among African-American fans, and many clubs were closing. Those that remained open, like Theresa's Lounge on the South Side, were still gathering places for working and aspiring blues musicians. Theresa Needham opened her club in 1949 in the basement of a three-flat at 4801 S. Indiana. Throughout the 1950s and '60s, bluesmen like Little Walter, Otis Rush, and Earl Hooker would hang out at Theresa's on nights they didn't have gigs. In the 1970s and into the early '80s, harmonica great Junior Wells was the star attraction at Theresa's. By then the club had gained leg-

Several blues musicians have tried their hands at club ownership. Eddie Shaw owned the 1815 Club on Roosevelt Road. Eddy Clearwater and Koko Taylor both opened clubs in the late 1990s and early in the new century. Artie "Blues Boy" White owned four different clubs on the South Side.

endary status around the world, says John Primer, who once played in the house band. It wasn't uncommon for internationally known artists like B.B. King and Johnny Winter to drop by, Primer recalls.

Pepper's Lounge also made the transition from the 1950s to the '70s. Johnny Pepper opened the club at 503 E. 43rd Street in 1956. In 1971 the club moved to 1321 S. Michigan Avenue. Entertainer Manual Arrington emceed at Pepper's starting in 1963, when Muddy Waters and Howlin' Wolf performed there. Arrington's job was to keep the crowd happy while the bands took a break or set up their gear. Arrington describes Pepper's as "nothing fancy, real raw." It was like a Mississippi joint inside the city of Chicago, only with a concrete instead of a dirt floor, Arrington says. The cover charge was 50¢ and drinks cost 30¢. Arrington remembers Jimmy Reed, Lefty Dizz, Buddy Scott, B.B. Odom, John Primer, and Buddy Guy playing at Pepper's.

The demographics of blues fans started to shift in the 1970s due to the "rediscovery" of the blues by British rock bands. Increasingly, white fans who listened to the Rolling Stones, Led Zeppelin, and Fleetwood Mac began searching for the blues. South Side clubs like the Checkerboard Lounge, which was opened in 1972 by Buddy Guy and his partner L.C. Thurman, became popular destinations for white fans from all over the world.

The Checkerboard opened at 423 E. 43rd Street in the historic African-American neighborhood Bronzeville, within blocks of Pepper's, Theresa's, and the 708 Club. A bright red-and-white checkerboard pattern with primitively drawn images of a guitar and a cocktail glass adorned the exterior. Inside, the bar was dingy, smoky, and dark, with long skinny tables and a small stage.

In its 30-year existence, the Checkerboard hosted historic moments. Perhaps the most famous occurred in 1981, when the Rolling Stones sang backup to the great Muddy Waters. Mick Jagger joined in while Muddy sang

"I'm a Man" and "Hoochie Coochie Man." Later, Keith Richards and Buddy Guy traded licks. On another occasion in the early 1980s, Eric Clapton jammed with Buddy Guy, and Stevie Ray Vaughan visited the Checkerboard. In 1989 a scene for the movie *Next of Kin*, starring Patrick Swayze, was filmed at the Checkerboard. In 1999 Hillary Rodham Clinton, then the first lady, visited the club.

Buddy Guy sold his interest in the Checkerboard in 1985, and four years later he opened Buddy Guy's Legends in the South Loop. But Thurman continued the Checkerboard, and the club became popular with students from the nearby University of Chicago. The club had also gained fame worldwide, and people came from all over the world to see the blues at Checkerboard.

After the turn of the century, the Checkerboard ran into problems. Although Thurman owned the business, he did not own the building. The landlord substantially raised the rent, but the building was falling into disrepair. The next several months were tumultuous, with various factions—Thurman, the University of Chicago, Hyde Park activists, Bronzeville proponents, and a group called the Friends of the Checkerboard Lounge—all weighing in with their opinions about the fate of the historic club. In the end Thurman made the final decision. On his 65th birthday, in March 2003, he held a combination birthday and farewell party at the Checkerboard. A few days later, he closed the club. The following month, city building inspectors determined the building was unsafe. The New Checkerboard Lounge, at 52nd Street and Harper Avenue in Hyde Park, opened in late 2005 and presents both blues and jazz.

One South Side club to successfully make the transition to the present day is the Queen Bee, now called Lee's Unleaded Blues, on South Chicago Avenue at 74th Street. Other former club buildings have been demolished or converted for other uses. Silvio's burned to the ground in the riots following the assassination of the Reverend Martin Luther King Jr. in April 1968. It reopened for a few more years, but the site where Howlin' Wolf once reigned is today an empty lot. The 708 Club at 708 E. 47th Street, where Memphis Minnie performed with Little Son Joe, now houses a furniture store. Only the sign remains of Turner's Blue Lounge, on South Indiana under the L tracks, where Sonny Boy Williamson II (Rice Miller) and Little Walter used to shoot pool. Theresa's Lounge is also gone. When Theresa Needham lost her lease in the building on South Indiana in 1983, the club moved to 43rd Street, just east of the Checkerboard. But old magic was never recaptured in the new location; it closed in 1986, and Theresa died in 1992.

Today's Blues Clubs

In the 1970s blues clubs began opening on the North Side, specifically in the Lincoln Park neighborhood. The Elsewhere Club, Wise Fool's Pub, Kingston Mines, and B.L.U.E.S. were within blocks of each other, earning the area the nickname of Blues Alley. Most patrons of these North Side clubs were white, young, and middle-class. Most bands consisted of blues musicians who, by now, had gained fame, such as Koko Taylor, Son Seals, Willie Dixon, and Lonnie Brooks.

Today the Elsewhere has long been closed. Wise Fool's Pub, after changing hands a few times, still hosts musical acts but rarely books blues bands. Kingston Mines and B.L.U.E.S., however, survived through ups and downs in the blues and the economy and remain popular with tourists and Chicago residents.

But the North Side doesn't hold a monopoly on blues clubs. The two Blue Chicago clubs, the House of Blues, and Buddy Guy's Legends are all located downtown in the Loop. Rosa's Lounge is on Armitage Avenue just west of the Bucktown–Wicker Park area.

Blues can still be found in clubs on the South and West sides. Many of these clubs are tiny bars known only to locals. They don't advertise in the large newspapers, but shows are promoted through word of mouth, signs in the windows, or flyers delivered by hand, person to person. The blues in the African-American community often incorporates soul, funk, jazz, and R&B, and musical heroes are Little Milton, Tyrone Davis, Denise LaSalle, Z.Z. Hill, and Bobby Rush.

Chicago's blues clubs vary in size, atmosphere, and amenities. For some, the main focus is on the blues; others are restaurant lounges that feature occasional live entertainment. Most larger clubs collect a cover charge, but smaller clubs often do not. Some places offer ticket sales online, but except for special events and big headliners, it usually isn't necessary to buy advance tickets. Arrive early, pay the cover at the door, and save yourself the service charge.

Blues clubs tend to be casual and intimate. In between sets, it's common for band members to hang out at the bar, give autographs, and chat with fans. Musicians often have their latest CD available for purchase. It's also common to see famous blues musicians "in the house" on days they don't have gigs themselves.

To find club schedules, or to look for a favorite band or artist, pick up the *Chicago Reader* (a free newspaper distributed every Thursday) or visit the paper's Web site (www.chicagoreader.com). Weekend schedules are also printed in the Friday entertainment section of the *Chicago Tribune* and the *Chicago Sun-Times*. Most club Web sites also post calendars.

If you're not familiar with the club, call ahead or check its Web site. Business conditions can vary, and clubs may change their hours or days of operation without notice. It's also possible that clubs may have opened, closed, or changed since the information for this book was collected.

Backporch Stage at the House of Blues

329 N. Dearborn Street
312/923-2000
www.hob.com/venues/clubvenues/chicago/

Don't look for blues on the main stage of the House of Blues. That venue is used for hip-hop, rock, and pop bands. Instead, blues bands play seven nights a week at the Backporch Stage in the restaurant portion of the club.

As the name suggests, the Back Porch Restaurant is casual and relaxed, although it is far from rustic (the restrooms have attendants). Hoodoo candles illuminate the wooden booths and tables. Folk art paintings cover the walls, part of a collection of more than 1,000 original pieces owned by the House of Blues, Inc. On the ceiling are

Photo by Karen Hanson.

bas relief portraits of blues legends, everyone from Charley Patton and Blind Lemon Jefferson to B.B. King and Albert King to Elvis Presley and Johnny Winter.

The House of Blues is based on the fictional legend of Jake and Elwood Blues, portrayed by John Belushi and Dan Aykroyd in the 1980 *The Blues Brothers* movie. Although the movie was filmed on location in Chicago, the first House of Blues didn't open in Chicago but in Cambridge, Massachusetts, in the fall of 1992.

The House of Blues, along with the House of Blues Hotel, is located in the Marina Towers complex near the Chicago River. Other hotels, restaurants, and entertainment attractions are within blocks.

Note

Several Chicago-area artists appeared in The Blues Brothers *movie. Big Walter Horton, Pinetop Perkins, Willie "Big Eyes" Smith, Luther "Guitar Junior" Johnson, and Calvin "Fuzz" Smith all performed in the film. Junior Wells, Lonnie Brooks, and Koko Taylor appeared in the sequel,* Blues Brothers 2000.

*Every Sunday the **House of Blues** offers a buffet-style brunch and a gospel performance. Two seating times are available, at 10 A.M. and 12:30 P.M. On holidays a third seating time of 2:30 P.M. may be added. Tickets for the Gospel Brunch must be purchased in advance through the HOB box office (312/923-2000). Tickets for children ages six to 12 are discounted, and younger kids are admitted free.*

Hours: Open for lunch 11:30 A.M. to 5 P.M. Dinner served 5 to 10 P.M. Music begins: 10 P.M.

Cover: $7 on Sunday through Thursday; $10 on Friday and Saturday. Diners who stay for the show don't have to pay the cover.

Parking: Street parking is not easy to find. Lots and garages are nearby but cost a minimum of $12 to $14 for a few hours. Valet parking is available.

Public transportation: Blue Line stops at Clark; Brown, Green, Orange, and Purple lines stop at State; Red Line stops at Lake. Taxis are plentiful.

Food: Full menu of Southern cuisine. Reservations are available (call 312/923-2007).

Blue Chicago

536 N. Clark Street (at Ohio)
312/661-0100
www.bluechicago.com

736 N. Clark Street (at Superior)
312/642-6261

Blue Chicago consists of two clubs a couple of blocks apart on Clark Street in the River North entertainment district. Within walking distance from many hotels and restaurants, the clubs are popular stops for out-of-town visitors curious to sample the Chicago blues.

Situated amid tourist attractions like the Hard Rock Café, the supersized McDonald's, and the Rainforest Café, Blue Chicago may seem at first glance like just another pop-culture replica of real life. But entertaining inside these clubs are veteran bluesmen like John Primer, who once played in Muddy Waters's band. Blue Chicago is also the only club in Chicago that regularly spotlights female vocalists like Shirley Johnson, Big Time Sarah, and Patricia Scott.

John Primer and the Real Deal Band take the stage at Blue Chicago, 736 N. Clark Street.
Photo by Karen Hanson.

"The blues really started with women like Ma Rainey and Bessie Smith," says Gino Battaglia, who owns the club with his wife, Bernadette. Battaglia decided long ago that he would pair popular guitar players with female singers, who have a genuine way of telling the story of the blues. "We felt that women weren't getting the exposure they deserved," Battaglia explains. "We have a lot of talent here in Chicago."

Battaglia, who was born in Italy and grew up on Chicago's South Side, opened Blue Chicago in 1985 on State and Walton Streets. The demand for the blues was great enough that he opened an additional club on Clark Street in 1991. The original club moved to the second Clark Street location in 1995.

Blue Chicago has had some remarkable visitors over the years. Once two tribesmen from the Indonesian rain forests visited the club as a university cultural exchange. The men had never seen a big city like Chicago, and they had never heard the blues.

"They came to the club, and they loved it so much, they came back the second night," Battaglia recalls. The tribesmen would have come a third night, but they had an early-morning flight to catch. They honored Battaglia with a parting gift he still treasures: a traditional drawing they had made on the inside of a section of tree bark.

The smaller club, at 536 N. Clark, is a long, narrow, 1920s-era building with wooden floors and an Art Deco–style bar. There's an elevated seating area and room for dancing near the small corner stage.

The Blue Chicago club up the street at 736 N. Clark is larger in all respects. It has a rectangular center bar, more tables, comfortable booths, and a spacious dance floor.

"Blues music touches everyone, regardless of culture, language, or background."

—Gino Battaglia,
Owner of Blue Chicago

The exposed-brick walls lend a hard urban edge to the atmosphere.

If you're up for a short walk, you can pay one cover charge and visit both clubs in one night. Performance schedules are synced so you won't miss out on the music.

The artwork of John Carroll Doyle adorns the walls at both Blue Chicago locations. Prints are available at the Blue Chicago store.
Photo by Karen Hanson.

Spotlight

Mojo Mama *and the other paintings and prints you see at Blue Chicago are the creation of artist John Carroll Doyle of Charleston, South Carolina. Doyle created eight blues-themed paintings at the request of Blue Chicago owner and art aficionado Gino Battaglia. Reproductions of Doyle's work appear on T-shirts, mugs, posters, and other items available at the Blue Chicago store. Doyle owns an art gallery in Charleston.*

Spotlight

To enter Blue Chicago, you first must go through Lorenzo Grant, the ever-vigilant doorman. Lorenzo's been collecting cover charges and keeping order at Blue Chicago since the club opened the 536 N. Clark location in 1991. Although his considerable physical presence may seem intimidating, Lorenzo has an easy, affable manner with the guests, who often chat and ask him questions about Chicago and the club.

Lorenzo Grant greets all who enter the Blue Chicago club at 536 N. Clark Street.
Photo by Karen Hanson.

Lorenzo has been immortalized in a giant replica of the John Carroll Doyle painting Sweet Home Chicago *on the north outside wall of Blue Chicago. In the painting, Lorenzo sits at a piano, with a cigarette dangling from his mouth and hands poised to strike a chord. Lorenzo doesn't really play a musical instrument, but he does accept his fame with a certain flair. Just ask, and he'll be happy to sell you a postcard of himself standing in front of Blue Chicago and personally autograph it for you.*

Hours: Sunday through Friday, 8 P.M. to 2 A.M.; Saturday, 8 P.M. to 3 A.M. 536 N. Clark: closed Monday. 736 N. Clark: closed Sunday.
Music begins: 9 P.M.
Cover: $6 to $8. Visit both clubs for one cover charge. Two-drink minimum at each club.
Parking: Street parking is difficult to find. Expect to pay upwards of $14 for a few hours in a parking garage. Valet parking is available.
Public transportation: Red Line stops at Grand. Taxis are available. Both clubs are within walking distance from many hotels.

Down in the Basement

Blue Chicago Store
534 N. Clark Street
312/661-1003

Every Saturday night, Gloria Shannon entertains fans of all ages in a family-friendly environment in the Blue Chicago store basement.
Photo by Karen Hanson.

Down in the Basement at Blue Chicago hosts the only regular alcohol-free, smoke-free, family-friendly blues show in the city. The shows begin at 8:20 P.M. every Saturday in the unfinished basement of the Blue Chicago store. This cozy, casual arrangement is the perfect environment for families and kids of all ages to become acquainted with the blues.

Gloria Shannon and her blues band have been entertaining and educating the basement crowds since 1998. Gloria, a Chicago native, introduces her songs with a short history lesson about Bessie Smith, Howlin' Wolf, B.B. King, and other blues greats. In the second set, kids are invited to jam with the band. Some bring their own instruments, but a guitar is available.

"I tell them, they don't have to play the blues. They can play whatever they want," Gloria says.

Down in the Basement attracts a lot of school groups who are visiting Chicago, but families are welcome, as are adults who don't care for the smoking or alcohol found in bars. Cover charge is $5 for adults. Kids under 12 get in free.

B.L.U.E.S.

2519 N. Halsted Street
773/528-1012
www.chicagobluesbar.com

The tiny B.L.U.E.S. club, located on Halsted Street in Blues Alley, has operated seven days a week, 365 days a year, since 1979.

B.L.U.E.S. was founded when current owner Rob Hecko teamed up with former owner Bill Gilmore (who had operated the Elsewhere Club on Lincoln Avenue). With assistance from pianist Erwin Helfer, Hecko and Gilmore began booking big names like Jimmy Walker and Sunnyland Slim. In fact, it was Sunnyland Slim, along with Big Time Sarah, who performed the very first show at B.L.U.E.S. Sunnyland became a regular fixture at the club, where he played every weekend for years, and later, just on Sunday nights. New Orleans pianist Dr. John came to Chicago every year on Sunnyland's birthday to play with him. Though he died in 1995, Sunnyland still has a presence at B.L.U.E.S. A photo of Sunnyland hangs on the wall behind the stage near the old upright grand he used to play.

Photo by Karen Hanson.

B.L.U.E.S. has been the scene of many memorable nights, but the one that stands out most in Hecko's mind is the benefit for harmonica player Big Walter Horton, who died in 1981. Horton had no insurance, and funds were needed to pay his burial costs. Word about the benefit quickly spread among the blues musicians, and everyone from Koko Taylor to Jimmy Johnson, Son Seals, and Magic Slim showed up. Still rather new in the blues bar business, Hecko was impressed. "People I hardly knew at all came," he says. The benefit raised nearly all the money needed.

Autographed photos of numerous celebrities who have visited B.L.U.E.S. hang over the entrance door. One of the most remarkable visits came from country singer Wynonna Judd and her actress sister, Ashley Judd. Hecko was surprised to find out that Wynonna was very shy, and when invited onstage to sing, she was reluctant. Finally she took the off-stage mike used for introductions and sang an amazing gospel duet with singer Joe Barr.

In 1987 Hecko opened a second club, B.L.U.E.S. Etcetera, on Belmont Avenue. The larger club featured big-name acts like Buddy Guy, Bo Diddley, and Koko Taylor. Due to changing market conditions, the club was closed in 1999.

B.L.U.E.S. is decidedly a no-frills club. Seating consists of beat-up, backless bar stools, some patched with duct tape. The main floor has just five bistro tables, but an additional elevated seating area is situated across from the bar. There's some standing room by the stage and in a small room near the restrooms. The stage, a two-foot-tall platform in the back corner, is just large enough for a four-piece band if the bass player cozies up against Sunnyland Slim's piano.

Fans cheer as Michael Coleman entertains at B.L.U.E.S. on Halsted.
Photo by Karen Hanson.

B.L.U.E.S. is located in Lincoln Park on Halsted just north of Fullerton amid specialty restaurants, snack shops, movie theaters, night-clubs, and pubs. Kingston Mines is one block north and across the street.

Hours: Sunday through Friday, 8 P.M. to 2 A.M.; Saturday, 2 P.M. to 3 A.M. **Music begins:** 9:30 P.M.

Cover: Averages $8 on weekdays; $10 on weekends. Tuesday night is Good Neighbor Night—anyone living in zip codes 60614, 60657, or 60610 gets in free.

Parking: Park free Sunday through Thursday, with paid admission, in the Children's Memorial Hospital garage on the corner of Lincoln and Fullerton Avenues. On Friday and Saturday parking costs $3 in the hospital garage. The doorman or waitstaff can validate your parking receipt. Valet parking is available on Friday and Saturday nights for $7. Street parking is nearly impossible to find.

Public transportation: Red, Brown, and Purple lines stop at Fullerton. Taxis are plentiful.

Bossman Blues Center

3500 W. Lake Street
773/722-1153; 773/772-8744

It's common at the Bossman Blues Center for guests in the house to sit in with the band. Lynn Lane, daughter of classic blues singer Mary Lane, belts out a tune to a spellbound audience.
Photo by Karen Hanson.

Bossman Blues Center may be the closest thing to a Mississippi juke joint that you can find on the West Side. Many of the regular customers originally hail from the Mississippi Delta, including the Bossman himself.

The music is spontaneous, raw, and unpredictable. Bands play nearly every night, and there's no telling who else will show up. The audience sits right in the midst of the band, and everyone's expected to clap, dance, and sing along.

In many ways, Bossman's is more like a house party than a blues show. Inside the tiny establishment, the atmosphere is homey and casual. Seating consists of a hodgepodge of kitchen and folding chairs. The bar seats about ten; on the opposite wall are a drink shelf and additional bar stools. Murals of Bossman's blues heroes are painted at either end of the bar. The band performs in front of the window by the front door.

Bossman himself usually works the bar, pouring drinks and serving ice cold beer in bottles. He says his place plays only two kinds of blues: gutbucket and monkey grip. Gutbucket is the down-home blues, the blues brought to Chicago from the Delta. But what's the monkey grip blues?

Bossman's isn't big, but there's room enough to dance if you're in the mood.
Photo by Karen Hanson.

"It's when you fall in love with somebody and want to hold on forever," explains Bossman, who opened the West Side club in 2002.

Bossman grew up in the town of Marks, just east of Clarksdale, in the Delta region of Mississippi. On weekends people from miles around would come to Marks. "It only had one red light back then, but it was bigger than the other towns," Bossman recalls. Legends of the blues like John Lee Hooker, Jimmy Reed, and Howlin' Wolf would come into town and perform for the crowds.

Bossman got his nickname at the age of ten after he got a job at a shoe store shortly after he moved to Chicago. He claims that even his best friends don't know his real name. (You can ask him his real name, but he won't tell you. A lot of the performers at the Bossman's club aren't called by their real names either.) Bossman has also worked as a promoter, booking such big names as Tyrone Davis, Little Milton, and Bobby Rush. All three have performed at Bossman's.

Local performers are the usual entertainment at Bossman's, which is a gathering spot for West Side blues talent, both young and veteran players. It's the kind of club where young musicians can hone their chops with seasoned bluesmen. A little soul and R&B make their way into the music, but Bossman doesn't like rap, hip-hop, rock, or pop.

Bossman Blues Center is located in the shadow of the L tracks near Garfield Park on Chicago's West Side. Call Bossman for directions.

At Bossman's, current musicians like singer L.T. McGee and guitarist Tony Bagdy play in the presence of legends like Tyrone Davis, Bobby Rush, B.B. King, Muddy Waters, and Ray Charles, as depicted in murals by Scott Robinson.
Photo by Karen Hanson.

Spotlight

Bossman's "Wall of Fame" showcases images of his favorite bluesmen: Tyrone Davis, Bobby Rush, B.B. King, and Muddy Waters. A second section features Ray Charles and Humphrey Bogart. Why Bogart? Bossman always liked the movie Casablanca, *especially the scene in which Bogart's character tells the piano man to "play it again." Pairing the actor with Ray Charles seemed the right thing to do. The floor-to-ceiling black-and-white murals were painted by artist Scott Robinson.*

Hours: Tuesday through Thursday, 5 P.M. to 1 A.M.; Friday, 5 P.M. to 2 A.M.; Saturday, noon to 3 A.M.; Sunday, noon to 1 A.M.
Music begins: About 9 P.M.
Cover: None. Two-drink minimum. The band may have a tip jar.
Parking: Street parking is available under the L tracks.
Public transportation: Green Line stops at Conservatory–Central Park.

Photo by Karen Hanson.

Mt. Bluesmore, featuring the images of Muddy Waters, Howlin' Wolf, Little Walter, and Sonny Boy Williamson II, was painted by Dan Bellini, a former guitarist and harp player with the band Howard and the White Boys. The talented Bellini also created portraits of Willie Dixon, Lightnin' Hopkins, and Stevie Ray Vaughan.
Photo by Karen Hanson.

Buddy Guy's Legends

754 S. Wabash Avenue
312/427-0333
www.buddyguys.com

Buddy Guy's star power shines at Legends. Four larger-than-life photos of Buddy form the backdrop of the stage. A showcase by the front door holds his many Grammy and Handy awards, as well as his newest award, the trophy marking his induction into the Rock and Roll Hall of Fame.

Out-of-towners are often surprised and thrilled to see Buddy walking in the crowd, greeting people, and signing autographs. When he's not on the road touring, Buddy nearly always hangs out in his club. And on occasions when the spirit moves him, he's been known to jump onstage to join an old friend's band for a song or two. But don't expect a full show from Buddy Guy. He plays his own club only once a year, for a couple weeks in January.

Since Legends opened in 1989, a parade of blues and rock legends has taken the stage, including Willie Dixon, Albert Collins, Luther Allison, Junior Wells, Bo Diddley, Jimmy Rogers, ZZ Top, David Bowie, Jeff Beck, Gregg Allman, Billy Corgan, and the Black Crowes. The Rolling Stones jammed with Buddy Guy on the Legends stage, and Eric Clapton played a three-day gig to promote his *From the Cradle* CD in 1994. Other celebrities, such as Sting, Mel Gibson, Kathleen Turner, and Bruce Springsteen, have dropped by. The club still draws famous visitors, who often sit in the VIP section to the right of the stage.

The walls of Legends resemble a museum of blues history. Take a walk around and you'll see a sequined dress once worn by Koko Taylor, a contract signed by Howlin' Wolf in 1959, and a 78 Checker single by Little Walter. There's Sonny Rhodes's red-and-white polka-dot outfit, Johnnie Johnson's hat, and a shirt belonging to Sunnyland Slim. Photos of legends like Honeyboy Edwards, Willie Dixon, and Jimmy Rogers and guitars autographed by John Lee Hooker, B.B. King, Lonnie Brooks, Jeff Beck, Jimmie Vaughan, and more hang on the walls. Junior Wells's hat and harps can be found near the tiny Harp Bar in the back corner, along with memorabilia from harmonica players Jerry Portnoy, Charlie Musselwhite, and James Cotton.

Fridays and Saturdays begin with free acoustic sets at 5:30 P.M. The cover charge is collected at about 9 P.M. Expect a well-known Chicago-area band for the opening act, followed by the headliner, often a nationally known blues artist. Weekdays and Sundays spotlight the best of Chicago-area blues musicians. Monday is the blues jam.

Legends has more seating than most blues bars, about 25 tables each seating four, but arrive by 8 P.M. if you want to sit down. Saving seats is not allowed, so if you come as a single or couple, feel free to take any available chair. There's plenty of standing room, but watch the marks on the floor—aisles are set aside for the waitstaff to maneuver through the crowds. On busy nights, the four pool tables are covered and pushed back to accommodate the crowds.

Legends is located in the revitalized South Loop, just behind the Chicago Hilton and Towers, in a neighborhood of brand-new residential condos, retail and service businesses, and university student apartment buildings.

Hours: Monday through Friday, 11 A.M. to 2 A.M.; Saturday, 5 P.M. to 3 A.M.; Sunday, 6 P.M. to 2 A.M.

Music begins: 9 or 9:30 P.M. for the opening act; 11 P.M. for the main show.

Cover: Ranges from $10 on weekdays to $15 on Friday and Saturday; covers may be higher for selected artists and events. No cover for Friday and Saturday acoustic sets.

Parking: Some street parking is available on Wabash, State, and other side streets. Look for parking lots on Wabash and State. Lot rates average $10; garages run a bit more.

Public transportation: Red, Green, and Orange lines stop at Roosevelt; Red Line stops at Harrison and State. Taxis are plentiful. The club is within walking distance from some hotels.

Food: Cajun and Louisiana cuisine. Lunch menu is available on weekdays from 11 A.M. to 4 P.M. Kitchen closes at midnight.

Note

Buddy Guy's Legends welcomes blues fans of all ages, cover free, until 8 P.M., when the club prepares for the main show of the evening. The acoustic show starts at 5:30 P.M. on Friday and 6 P.M. on Saturday. Legends is also open for lunch from 11 A.M. to 4 P.M. every day. Acoustic acts occasionally entertain at lunch, and kids and their parents can browse the memorabilia and photos on the walls. Reservations aren't necessary.

Kingston Mines

2548 N. Halsted Street
773/477-4646
www.kingstonmines.com

Photo by Karen Hanson.

Kingston Mines is Chicago's late-night party spot for the blues. Bands play on two stages in two adjacent rooms, filling the Lincoln Park bar with music until 4 or 5 A.M. nightly.

But when the Mines opened in 1968 at its original location on Lincoln Avenue, it wasn't a blues club. Instead, the former trolley barn hosted coffeehouse-style entertainment like poetry readings, folk music, and small theater productions. In fact, in 1971 the original version of *Grease* premiered at Kingston Mines. Titled *Grease Lightning*, the musical about high school life in the 1950s was the creation of Chicago writers Jim Jacobs and Warren Casey. Within a year, the play was revised, retitled *Grease*, and moved to Broadway, where it became an instant hit.

The Mines continued on Lincoln Avenue into the early 1980s, until, after a night of heavy rain, the roof caved in. The club moved temporarily to an old disco on the corner of Clark and Ontario Streets (now the site of the huge downtown McDonald's). It stayed there for about six months, until moving to its present site at 2548 N. Halsted.

Through the years, the best of Chicago's blues artists have per-

The music of Vance Kelly and the Backstreet Band gets people out of their seats and onto the dance floor.
Photo by Karen Hanson.

formed on the stages of Kingston Mines. John Belushi and Dan Aykroyd put on a show to promote their 1980 movie, *The Blues Brothers*. Other Hollywood celebrities and rock stars who have dropped in or jammed with the bands are Mick Jagger, David Bowie, Gregg Allman, Ted Nugent, Robert Plant, John Candy, Patrick Swayze, Harrison Ford, Vince Vaughn, and Nicolas Cage.

The stages at the Mines are designed to resemble the front porch of an old farmhouse. The two rooms are spacious with numerous long skinny tables and plenty of standing room. The walls are painted with murals of riverboats and cotton fields.

The bands alternate playing; when one band takes a break, the other begins. Patrons can easily go from one room to the next, but it isn't necessary. Live video feed of the performing band is broadcast on television screens in both rooms.

Waitstaff serve drinks, but they don't take food orders. Instead, there's a window in the rear of the Mines where you can order and pick up barbecue, fish, and other hearty fare. Don't forget to clean up after yourself, and stay clear of the marked aisles on the floor for waitstaff. If you want to smoke cigars, you have to step outside.

You'll be asked to buy tickets at a window before you go in. Be prepared to show ID: everyone is carded.

Kingston Mines is located in the Lincoln Park neighborhood near restaurants and other entertainment venues. Nearby is DePaul University; the bar attracts many students (especially since student discounts are available) and other young singles. However, you'll find blues fans of all ages. B.L.U.E.S. is located across the street and a block to the south.

Hours: Sunday through Friday, 8 P.M. to 4 A.M.; Saturday, 2 P.M. to 5 A.M. **Music begins:** 9:30 P.M.

Cover: Averages $12 to $15. Weekday discounts are available for college students (over 21) and faculty; ID required. Blues fans age 50 or older can also get a discount card.

Parking: Street parking and lots are nearly impossible to find. Valet parking is available for under $10.

Public transportation: Red, Brown, and Purple lines stop at Fullerton. Taxis are plentiful.

Food: Doc's Rib Joint offers a full menu, from appetizers to entrees. Specialties include wild wings, ribs, catfish, chicken, and sandwiches.

Lee's Unleaded Blues

7401 S. South Chicago Avenue
773/493-3477

Lee's Unleaded Blues has been a South Side hot spot for the blues since the 1970s, when it was known as Queen Bee's Lounge. Now owned by Stanley Davis, a retired police officer, the corner

Photo by Karen Hanson.

club is as active as ever. Duke, the doorman, greets guests and makes them feel welcome. Stan sits at the far end of the bar, using a wireless microphone to announce the arrival of well-known guests, introduce the band, and encourage the patrons to enjoy themselves. "It makes me feel good to see people coming in and having a good time," he explains.

The club showcases local blues bands, but in Chicago that includes internationally known recording artists like Johnny Drummer. Musicians also drop by to hang out and sit in with the bands as musical guests.

"Guests get insulted if you don't call them up," Stan says.

Lee's Unleaded Blues has been featured in *National Geographic*, and *Men's Journal* magazine named it one of the six best juke joints in the country. Davis is proud to call his place a juke joint. The juke joint is an African-American creation, he says. In the rural South, black people had no clubs, so people would gather in houses or barns or wherever they could find space. Today places like Lee's Unleaded Blues continue that tradition.

> *"Blacks are coming back to the blues, slowly but surely, realizing what they've been missing on the live entertainment circuit."*
>
> —Stanley Davis,
> Owner of Lee's Unleaded Blues

Club patrons are mostly South Side residents, but devoted blues fans regularly find their way to Lee's Unleaded to take in the music and the friendly atmosphere. The club has had visitors from China, Japan, Argentina, and Sweden. "They all got up danced," Stan says.

People accustomed to the traditional 12-bar shuffles they might hear in North Side clubs will hear a different sound on the South Side, according to Stan. On the South Side, the blues has echoes of soul, R&B, and jazz. "South Side blues have a lot more vocals than North Side blues," Stan explains.

For a juke joint, Lee's Unleaded Blues has a classy style. The red-topped bar makes an undulating profile along one wall. Overhead, a rope light bounces off and on with the beat of the music. On the other side, there are a few tall tables and stools, all in black. Rows of chairs are set up, theater-style, directly in front of the stage.

But the classiest parts of the club are the impeccably clean restrooms, which are equipped with shiny black fixtures. Before Stan took over Lee's Unleaded Blues in 2002, he researched clubs to see what people wanted. Clean restrooms were high on the list.

Stan was no stranger to the entertainment business when he bought Lee's Unleaded Blues. In addition to his full-time job as a police officer with the Illinois Secretary of State, Stan worked part-time for 20 years as a bodyguard for musicians at concerts. He worked with such legends as the Rolling Stones, Prince, the Grateful Dead, and Earth, Wind and Fire. As a result, he became interested in the entertainment business, and when he retired in 2001, he looked around for the right establishment. He had good timing; the former owners of Lee's Unleaded were also getting ready to retire and wanted to sell.

Johnny Drummer and the Starliters have been the weekend entertainment at Lee's Unleaded Blues since the 1990s. On this night, Gaylord the Arkansas Belly Roller sang with the band and Calvin "Kadakie" Tucker played the African drums. *Photo by Karen Hanson.*

After he bought the club, Stan redecorated the club and moved the stage from the far corner to front and center. Johnny Drummer helped design the new stage.

Many patrons of Lee's are dressed up for a night on the town, but Stan says there's no dress code. "Everything from jeans to your finery, whatever you want to wear," he says.

Lee's Unleaded Blues is located in a quiet area of warehouses and service businesses a few blocks east of the Dan Ryan Expressway.

> **Hours:** 8 P.M. to 2 A.M.
> **Music begins:** 9 P.M.
> **Cover:** None.
> **Parking:** Free street parking is available. There is a small lot in back.
> **Public transportation:** Red Line stops at 69th Street, or take the #30 South Chicago bus.

The New Checkerboard Lounge

5201 S. Harper Avenue
773/684-1472

Located in a shopping center behind the Dixie Kitchen restaurant, the New Checkerboard Lounge carries on the blues tradition in a new location and with an expanded musical lineup that includes jazz.

The historic Checkerboard Lounge first opened in 1972 at 423 E. 43rd Street, founded by Buddy Guy and L.C. Thurman. For 30 years, the Checkerboard hosted the biggest names in the blues. Guy and Junior Wells often performed there together, and blues legends such as Muddy Waters, Howlin' Wolf, and Jimmy Reed also took the stage. World-famous rock stars and other celebrities, including the Rolling Stones and Eric Clapton, visited the Checkerboard.

When Guy sold his interest in the club in 1985, Thurman continued to operate the Checkerboard, which became a popular spot for college students and tourists. But deteriorating building conditions and landlord disputes led Thurman to close the club in 2003.

The New Checkerboard Lounge opened in November 2005 in the Hyde Park neighborhood, not far from the University of Chicago. The new lounge is roomy and modern with comfortable wooden tables and chairs. Those who want a reminder of the old Checkerboard can see a padded tan bench and a skinny table covered with peeling Contact paper that were salvaged from the former building.

Bands entertain every night of the week. The majority are blues bands, but jazz acts also play regularly. No smoking is permitted inside the club.

Hours: Daily, 6 P.M. to 2 A.M.
Music begins: 9:30 P.M.
Cover: Ranges from $5 to $20, depending on the act.
Parking: Metered lot. Walking distance from the University of Chicago.
Public transportation: CTA Bus #28 stops at Hyde Park Boulevard and Lake Park Avenue.

Rosa's Lounge

3240 W. Armitage Avenue
773/342-0452
www.rosaslounge.com

Since the early 1980s, Rosa's Lounge has been the home for everything from the Delta blues of Honeyboy Edwards to the Chicago-style blues of James Wheeler to the cutting-edge blues of Melvin Taylor and Carlos

Photo by Karen Hanson.

Johnson. "Our ambition is to cover the whole spectrum of the blues," says Tony Mangiullo, who owns the club with his mother, Rosa. For Tony, the blues is more than just music. "It's also an instrument of education for us," he explains. Listening to the blues, the music fan can hear the bridges that connect the blues to rock, R&B, jazz, and hip-hop, he says.

Rosa's Lounge advertises itself as "Chicago's Friendliest Blues Lounge." Tony, ever present in the lounge, introduces the bands, checks the equipment, chats with the musicians, and greets the guests. An accomplished drummer, he also plays occasionally with some of the bands. Rosa—everyone calls her Mama—tends the bar nearly every night.

A picture of Mama Rosa as a young woman graces the backdrop of the stage at the far end of the lounge. Most nights there's ample seating at tables and at the bar, but there's also enough room to comfortably stand

Spotlight

Tony Mangiullo's favorite picture at Rosa's is a photo of Junior Wells and Billy Branch. Junior is standing, "in a teaching mode," looking down at a young Billy, seated with a harmonica in his mouth, ready to play. Tony says the photo symbolizes what Rosa's is all about: creating the opportunity for experienced blues players to pass on what they know to a younger generation. The photo comes from the book Down at Theresa's... Chicago Blues *(2000), a collection of photographs taken by Marc PoKempner at Theresa's during the 1960s. Several photos from the book are blown up bigger than life and hang on the walls at Rosa's. Photos by Susan Greenberg are also on display.*

Tony Mangiullo, owner, introduces the night's entertainment at Rosa's Lounge. That's James Wheeler on guitar, Willie "Big Eyes" Smith on drums, and Ariyo on piano. *Photo by Karen Hanson.*

when the room fills up. While waiting for the music to start, patrons can play a game of pool or look at the historic photos of blues legends that cover almost every inch of wall space.

Tony Mangiullo was a long-haired, skinny 20-year-old kid from Milan, Italy, when he first arrived in Chicago on August 15, 1978. He came in search of the blues, and the first person he looked for was blues harp player Junior Wells. Tony left the airport and went straight to the South Side home of Junior Wells, whom he had met a few months earlier backstage at a jazz concert in Italy. Junior had told him, "You come to Chicago, and I'll be responsible for you." He gave Tony his home address and the address of Theresa's Lounge, the legendary blues club on South Indiana Avenue. Tony wasn't sure what he meant, but he knew then that he had to get to Chicago.

"Coming to Chicago was a dream," Tony recalls. "Knowing that Junior Wells and Buddy Guy and all the people we used to listen to, and never had a chance to see, were there."

In Italy, American records were rare, but Tony had heard enough blues to know it was the music he loved. The music on *Fleetwood Mac in Chicago*, a double album featuring guitarist Peter Green and bluesmen Otis Spann, Willie Dixon, Honeyboy Edwards, Walter "Shakey" Horton, and S.P.

Leary, had a profound influence on him. "There was something about that sound," he says. "How it touched me directly . . . I cannot express it, necessarily. It was so direct. The music seemed aesthetically so simple, yet it expressed so much emotion, that I became attached immediately."

Once in Chicago, Theresa's became Tony's second home. "The musicians, the people, everybody was so friendly," he remembers. Theresa Needham, owner of Theresa's Lounge, welcomed the young Italian who aspired to be a blues musician.

"At Theresa's, the people were participating," Tony says. "They were almost like part of the band. They were interacting with the musicians so it was hard to say, 'whose music is this? Is it the band's? Is it the people's?' It was everybody's music."

Soon he found himself sitting in with the bands. "Theresa would give me some eggs and beer and some smokes," he says. "To me I was living a dream."

A year later, Tony's mother, Mama Rosa, arrived. In August 1984, without having much of a plan, Tony and Rosa bought the building at 3240 W. Armitage on the Near Northwest Side. A month later, Rosa's Lounge opened. The grand opening featured Billy Branch and the Sons of Blues.

Since then nearly every great blues name in Chicago has appeared at Rosa's. But while Tony has always honored and respected the older generation, he's a firm believer in encouraging younger players and new styles.

"We like to think it's an instrument of education for us," he says. "Here we have this great potential for interaction with musicians, old and young, and it's very valuable."

The atmosphere at Rosa's is reminiscent of Theresa's, cool and laid back, with the musicians hanging out at the bar between sets, and the audience an important part of the musical experience. Tony didn't plan it that way—it just happened. "It was the only reference that I had," Tony says.

And just like back at Theresa's, the spirit of Junior Wells is never far away. "I consider him to be my spiritual father," Tony says. "He's the one that gave me strength to be here."

Hours: 8 P.M. to 2 A.M. Closed Sunday and Monday (reserved for private parties).
Music begins: 9:30 or 10 P.M.
Cover: Ranges from $5 to $15; covers are higher on weekends.
Parking: Street parking is available, on Armitage and side streets.
Public transportation: Blue Line stops at California.

Smoke Daddy

1804 W. Division Street
773/772-6656
www.thesmokedaddy.com

The Smoke Daddy has offered free live music seven nights a week year-round since 1994. The bands appearing at this barbecue restaurant aren't exclusively blues, but most of the music is roots based. Billy Flynn, Jimmie Lee Robinson, Bo Diddley, Billy Boy Arnold, Kim Wilson, Willie "Big Eyes" Smith, and Jerry Portnoy are some of the well-known blues artists who have performed here.

The Smoke Daddy is located amid other restaurants and nightspots on Division Street in the Wicker Park neighborhood. Side streets are packed with newly constructed residential condos.

Hours: Monday through Wednesday, 11:30 A.M. to midnight; Thursday and Sunday, 11:30 A.M. to 1 A.M.; Friday, 11:30 A.M. to 2 A.M.; Saturday, 11:30 A.M. to 3 A.M.
Music begins: 9 P.M. on weekdays; 10 P.M. on weekend.
Cover: None.
Parking: A small parking lot on the west side of the club holds six to eight vehicles. There's a lot of competition for the metered spaces on Division Street. Side streets are residential.
Public transportation: Blue Line stops at Division.
Food: Barbecue, ribs, and lots of side dishes and desserts.

Voodoo Lounge at the Redfish

400 N. State Street
312/467-1600
www.redfishamerica.com

Blues bands play Friday and Saturday nights at the Voodoo Lounge at the Redfish, a Louisiana-themed restaurant in Chicago's River North area.

The restaurant and lounge share a common entrance, but the rooms are separate. In the nonsmoking restaurant, people can dine on catfish, crawfish étouffée, and other Cajun-style cuisine for lunch and dinner daily. Food is also available in the lounge, where patrons can also enjoy a cold drink and watch a game on TVs.

Photo by Karen Hanson.

The roomy lounge is dominated by a large rectangular bar in the center. Tables and booths ring the perimeter. Mardi Gras masks, voodoo dolls, cartoon alligators, and other faux swamp kitsch decorate the walls and hang from the ceiling.

You may not find the big names at the Voodoo Lounge, but you have a good chance of hearing some excellent music. Performers represent the full spectrum of blues, in addition to jazz, Cajun, zydeco, and R&B.

The River North area, which encompasses some of Chicago's best hotels and restaurants, is hopping with nightlife every day of the week. You'll find a mixture of tourists, young singles, and people out for dinner or a drink after work. Park once and make it a blues doubleheader: the House of Blues is only about a block away.

Hours: Friday and Saturday, open until 2 A.M. Restaurant also open Sunday through Thursday, 11 A.M. to 11 P.M.; and Friday and Saturday, 11 A.M. to 2 A.M.

Music: Live music (mostly blues) every Friday and Saturday night.

Music begins: 9:30 P.M.

Cover: None.

Parking: Valet parking is available and may be cheaper than nearby lots. Street parking is free after 9 P.M. but may be hard (though not impossible) to find.

Public transportation: Red Line stops at Grand.

Food: Louisiana-style menu. There is also a separate dining room.

Blues Nights

A number of other Chicago-area clubs regularly or occasionally book blues bands. Schedules change, so call ahead or check the Web sites.

7313 Club

7313 S. Halsted Street
773/723-0592

This South Side juke joint is owned by vocalist Fred Johnson, who performs with his band, the Checkmates, every weekend.

Andy's Jazz Club

11 E. Hubbard Street
312/642-6805

Pianist Dave Specter and singer Sharon Lewis play a regular Friday-night gig.

Artis's

1249 E. 87th Street
773/734-0491

Billy Branch has performed every Monday night at Artis's for more than 15 years. The club also features Tré and the Blue Knights on Sundays.

City Lights Bar and Grill

3809 N. Harlem Avenue
773/777-9500

The Michael Charles blues band performs regularly.

Flamingo
6644 S. Cottage Grove Avenue
773/684-0600

Jimmy Pryor and the Double J Band play at this South Side club on Monday nights.

The Hideout
1354 W. Wabansia Avenue
773/227-4433
www.hideoutchicago.com

The folk-blues band Devil in a Woodpile plays a regular gig on Tuesdays.

HotHouse
31 E. Balbo Drive
312/362-9707
www.hothouse.net

Jazz and world music predominate at the HotHouse, but the non-profit cultural venue sometimes showcases blues and blues-inspired bands. Look for special presentations during the Chicago Blues Festival. The HotHouse, located on Balbo and Wabash in the heart of the South Loop, is just a few blocks from Buddy Guy's Legends.

Hugo's Frog Bar
1024 N. Rush Street
312/640-0999
www.hugosfrogbar.com

Blues bands often perform in the bar area of this upscale seafood restaurant on Rush Street. Hugo's Naperville location also books blues bands.

Joe's Be-Bop Cafe
700 E. Grand Avenue on Navy Pier
312/525-5299
www.joesbebop.com

A blues-inspired jazz band may play onstage in the middle of this restaurant, which offers a Southern-style menu including barbecue.

Katerina's
1920 W. Irving Park Road
773/348-7592
www.katerinas.com

Blues acts like Erwin Helfer and Dave Weld have appeared at this café/coffeehouse that advertises itself as "an eclectic club with its soul in the arts."

Lilly's
2513 N. Lincoln Avenue
773/525-2422

Lilly's, in the Lincoln Park area, books all kinds of trendy music and the occasional blues band.

Linda's Place
1044 W. 51st Street
(Phone unavailable)

This tiny club on the South Side is the regular home of the Fantastic L-Roy and the Bulletproof Band.

Mitchell's Lounge
2005 W. 69th Street
773/434-8469

Blues bands play on Sunday nights from 4 P.M. to 10 or 11 P.M.

My Friend's Place

10815 S. Michigan Avenue

773/264-6336

Elmore James Jr. and his Broom Dusters play on Thursdays.

New Apartment Lounge

504 E. 75th Street

773/483-7728

Jazz saxophonist Von Freeman plays at this South Side club every Tuesday night.

Nick's Beer Garden

1516 N. Milwaukee Avenue

773/252-1155

www.nicksbeergarden.com

A blues, soul, R&B, or funk band plays in this Wicker Park–area bar on Friday and Saturday nights. No cover.

Chainsaw Dupont entertains at Nick's Beer Garden in Wicker Park.
Photo by Steve Pasek, Big Productions.

Nick's Uptown

4015 N. Sheridan Road

773/975-1155

www.nicksuptown.com

Blues bands play on Friday and Saturday nights. No cover.

Shaw's Crab House

21 E. Hubbard Street

312/527-2722

www.shawscrabhouse.com

Blues bands like Mississippi Heat and the Chicago Bound Band have performed here.

Some Place Else Cocktail Lounge

11043 S. Ashland Avenue

773/239-4010

Vance Kelly plays at this South Side club on Tuesday nights.

Underground Wonder Bar

10 E. Walton Street

312/266-7761

www.undergroundwonderbar.com

On-the-edge type blues, jazz, and other musical acts play at this bar that was founded by singer-songwriter Lonie Walker. Open until 4 A.M.

Chapter 2

Key to the Highway:

Clubs in the Suburbs

While the city of Chicago has had a thriving and continuous blues scene since the 1930s, the suburbs have emerged as a venue for blues bands only in the last couple of decades. Today the demand for the blues transcends municipal boundaries, generation, race and ethnicity, socioeconomic status, and lifestyle.

Although only a few suburban clubs are devoted strictly to the blues, blues bands play regularly at numerous bars and restaurants. Suburban clubs often serve as venues for local semiprofessional blues bands, but several clubs also host nationally known bands and pretty big stars.

Compared to city blues clubs, suburban clubs have some distinct advantages. Many don't charge a cover, and the drinks tend to be cheaper. They are usually patronized by local residents and loyal blues fans instead of curious tourists. Plus clubs in the suburbs almost always have plenty of free parking.

Nick Moss and the Flip Tops perform at Bill's Blues in Evanston.
Photo by Karen Hanson.

Bill's Blues Bar

1029 Davis Street
Evanston
847/424-9800
www.billsbluesbar.com

"The nice thing about Chicago is the local acts are the nationals acts."

—Bill Gilmore

The blues at Bill's Blues Bar is as eclectic as it comes. You might hear the acoustic rhythms of Li'l Ed, the sultry vocals of Liz Mandville Greeson, or the hard electric sounds of Melvin Taylor.

Bill's Blues began in August 2003 when Bill Gilmore, a former owner of B.L.U.E.S. on Halsted and the Elsewhere Club, relocated his family to the north shore suburb of Evanston. Recognizing a vast void of blues between Chicago's Lincoln Park neighborhood and the city of Milwaukee, Gilmore opened the bar and started booking blues bands.

The bands perform on a small stage in front of the storefront window, which glows with blue and orange neon beer signs. The long narrow lounge area is clean and comfortable with a high wood ceiling and brick walls. Original paintings by local artists hang on the walls. A half dozen tables line one side of the room; a long bar, seating 12 to 15 people, takes up most of the other side. There are extra chairs and standing room in back.

In addition to blues, Bill's devotes some nights to folk, jazz, comedy, movies, karaoke, and other special events.

Bill's Blues Bar is located on a one-way street amid the bustling specialty shops, boutiques, and restaurants of downtown Evanston. Patrons tend to be suburbanites of all ages and students from nearby Northwestern University.

Hours: Monday through Thursday; 6 P.M. to 2 A.M.; Friday and Saturday, 6 P.M. to 3 A.M.; Sunday, 4 P.M. to midnight.
Music begins: 8 P.M.
Cover: None on Monday though Thursday; $5 to $7 on Saturday and Sunday.
Parking: Street parking is available; no meter feeding necessary after 9 P.M.
Public transportation: Purple Line stops at Davis. Metra Union Pacific North Line stops at Davis.

Chord on Blues

106 S. 1st Avenue
St. Charles
630/513-0074
www.chordonblues.com

In 2006 Chord on Blues was the recipient of the Blues Foundation's Keeping the Blues Alive Award.

Chord on Blues is a fine dining restaurant where you can enjoy a steak dinner, a bottle of fine wine, and pleasant conversation with friends. But after 10 P.M. on Fridays and Saturdays, the lights go down, the curtain goes up, and the restaurant becomes the biggest blues club in the Chicago suburbs.

Since 1996 Chicago's best blues bands and nationally known acts have taken the stage here at the largest blues venue in the western suburbs. The 14,000 square foot main room at Chord on Blues opens on Friday and Saturday nights only. You can have dinner only (reservations are recommended), or after dinner, you can pay the cover charge, and stay for the show. Alternately you can hang out in the bar area, pay the cover, and enjoy the music.

Adjacent to the dining room is the Grille, a casual lounge area open seven days a week. You can't hear or see the main act from the Grille, but you can order from a modified menu, shoot a game of pool on one of four tables, play a game of darts, or watch sports on TV. The Grille has its own sound system, and live music is featured in the covered beer garden during summer months.

Hours: Friday and Saturday, 5:30 P.M. to 2 A.M. The Grille is open Sunday through Thursday, 3:30 P.M. to 1 A.M.; and Friday and Saturday, 3:30 P.M. to 2 A.M.
Music begins: 10 P.M.
Cover: Averages $10.
Parking: Ample parking is available on the street and in nearby lots.
Food: Full menu on Friday and Saturday in the main dining room. Burgers and sandwiches served daily in the Grille.

Dell Rhea's Chicken Basket

645 Joliet Road
(Interstate 55 at Route 83)
Willowbrook
630/325-0780
www.chickenbasket.com

The famous song "Get Your Kicks on Route 66" was written by Bobby Troupe and was first recorded by Nat King Cole in 1946. More than 200 artists have recorded it since then.

If you want to get your kicks—and your blues—on Route 66, then Dell Rhea's Chicken Basket is the place to go. The historic restaurant has been serving its famous fried chicken since the 1940s, when it was a favorite stop for travelers on the legendary Route 66. These days the Chicken Basket is a popular local eatery, but it also draws tourists who are seeking Route 66 nostalgia.

On weekends the Blue Rooster Lounge features live entertainment. Acoustic acts play on Fridays and Saturdays. Once a month there's a full blues band. Sundays are open jam nights.

Bands perform alongside tables covered in red-and-white checkered tablecloths. The lounge is decorated with Route 66 signs, chicken images and figurines, and posters of Louis Armstrong. The full menu is available in the lounge.

The Chicken Basket is located on a winding road behind hotels and retail businesses at the intersection of Route 83 and Interstate 55. In 1992 Dell Rhea's Chicken Basket was inducted into the Route 66 Hall of Fame.

Hours: The Blue Rooster Lounge is open Tuesday through Thursday, 11 A.M. to 10 P.M.; Friday and Saturday, 11 A.M. to 1 A.M.; and Sunday, 11 A.M. to midnight. The restaurant closes at 9 P.M. on Tuesday, Wednesday, Thursday and Sunday; and at 10 P.M. on Friday and Saturday.

Music begins: 7 P.M. on Friday and Saturday.

Cover: None.

Parking: There is a parking lot.

Food: Chicken, seafood, steak, sandwiches, and so on.

FitzGerald's

6615 Roosevelt Road
Berwyn
708/788-2118
www.fitzgeraldsnightclub.com

The historic FitzGerald's nightclub in the near western suburb of Berwyn specializes in roots-based blues, folk, jazz, zydeco, rockabilly, bluegrass, and big band music. Famous acts that have appeared at the club include Bo Diddley, Big Mama Thornton, Koko Taylor, Luther Allison, Stevie Ray Vaughan, Albert Collins, Robert Cray, Marcia Ball, Charlie Musselwhite, Li'l Ed, Lonnie Brooks, Ronnie Baker Brooks, Pinetop Perkins, and Hubert Sumlin.

Built in the 1920s, the facility was first called the Deer Lodge and served as a hunting club. Next, as the Hunt Club, it was a popular jazz spot that booked big names like Lil Armstrong, wife of jazz trumpeter Louis Armstrong.

"It was a pretty hoppin' place back in the early 1950s with jazz," says Bill FitzGerald, whose family bought the club in 1980. The FitzGeralds expanded the musical offerings with other musical genres.

Koko Taylor recorded her Grammy-nominated CD *Live from Chicago: An Audience with the Queen* (Alligator) at FitzGerald's in 1987. In 1989 guitarist Lonnie Mack and his band recorded *Live! Attack of the Killer V*, which Alligator released in 1990.

Spotlight

Four Hollywood movies have used FitzGerald's for location shots. In The Color of Money *(1986), the club was transformed into a pool hall for a scene starring Paul Newman and Tom Cruise. FitzGerald's became a 1940s-style dance hall for a scene in* A League of Their Own *(1992), in which Madonna danced the jitterbug. In* Blink *(1994), Madeleine Stowe took the FitzGerald's stage to portray a violin player with the Drovers, a real Chicago Irish band. Albert Collins and Billy Branch played there together in the fictional Tear Drop Lounge in* Adventures in Babysitting *(1987).*

Note

Author David Whitaker and photographer Blair Jensen teamed up for the book Live from FitzGerald's: Songs and Stories of an American Music Club *(Uppercase Books, 2004). The companion CD features tracks recorded live at FitzGerald's by 16 different performers, including Marcia Ball, C.J. Chenier, Devil in a Woodpile, and Joe Ely. The book's Web site is:*

www.livefromfitzgeralds.com.

The stage occupies one end of a large entertainment room with a small bar to the side. For big events the few tables and chairs are removed to make room for standing and dancing. A large tent accommodates crowds for festivals and special events.

FitzGerald's American Music Festival, held each year since 1981 around the July 4th weekend, presents more than 30 bands on three stages over a period of four days. Children are welcome each day until 10 P.M. Other special parties are held on New Year's Eve, St. Patrick's Day, and Mardi Gras. Occasional fall festivals are also held.

The club was renovated in 2001 and expanded to add the Sidebar and the Roosevelt Grill, which specializes in New Orleans–style cuisine.

Hours: Tuesday through Saturday, opens at 7 P.M.; Sunday, opens at 5 P.M. Closed Monday.

Music begins: Anywhere from 7 to 10 P.M.

Cover: $6 to $15 or more, depending on the act or event. Tickets are available in advance or at the door.

Parking: Street parking is available on Roosevelt Road and side streets.

Food: Sandwiches and appetizers are served in the bar, except on Friday and Saturday nights. The Roosevelt Grill next door offers a full dinner menu.

Genesis Lounge
4838 W. 183rd Street
Country Club Hills
708/647-0509

The Genesis Lounge, which opened in 2004, spotlights top-notch blues bands two nights a week in a friendly, casual atmosphere, with no cover charge. Billy Branch and the S.O.B.s play every Wednesday. On Sunday the show is Vance Kelly and the Backstreet Band.

Singer, comedian, and former radio host Manual Arrington serves as emcee. During breaks he introduces the bands, welcomes people, announces the birthdays and anniversaries of patrons, sings, and tells jokes. Other musicians in the house often join the band for a song or two.

Billy Branch and the Sons of Blues play every Wednesday night at Genesis.
Photo by Karen Hanson.

Genesis is located, in true suburban style, at the end of a strip mall on 183rd Street just west of Cicero (Route 50). The exterior is plain and unimposing; inside, the large rectangular room is roomy and comfortable. The long L-shaped bar seats about 20 people. The main floor has numerous tables for two and for six.

A large rug at the far end of the room serves as the stage. Posters of Billie Holiday and Muhammad Ali hang on the back wall. In back are a pool table, video games, and a DJ booth often manned by a dancing DJ named "Rock."

Sandwiches, chicken wings, catfish, and other foods are served informally in baskets with fries and a couple of napkins.

Hours: Sunday, 2 P.M. to 2 A.M.; Monday through Thursday, noon to 2 A.M.; Friday, noon to 3 A.M.; Saturday, 5 P.M. to 3 A.M.

Music begins: 7:30 or 8 P.M.

Cover: None. Two-drink minimum.

Parking: There is a large lot.

Food: Wings, catfish, shrimp, beef sandwiches, hamburgers, and more.

Harlem Avenue Lounge

3701 S. Harlem Avenue
Berwyn
708/484-3610
www.harlemavenuelounge.com

Tom Holland and the Shuffle Kings perform at the Harlem Avenue Lounge.
Photo by Karen Hanson.

The first clue that the Harlem Avenue Lounge offers more than the average neighborhood bar are the posters of blues legends like W.C. Handy and Robert Johnson on the wood-paneled walls. Since 1990 the sounds of the blues have been heard four nights a week at this unassuming bar along busy Harlem Avenue in Berwyn. Tuesday, Friday, and Saturday feature blues bands ranging from well-known names to more local performers. Thursday is the popular jam night.

Well off the beaten path, Harlem Avenue Lounge isn't a place where you'll find many curious tourists or conventioneers. Although some devout out-of-town blues fans find their way to the suburban bar, most regular patrons live and work in nearby towns. That's part of the appeal, says owner Ken Zimmerman. "This is a neighborhood place where people can come to see the blues," explains Zimmerman, who also manages guitarist Joanna Connor.

Zimmerman has been operating the lounge since 1978. As business grew, he saw the potential for offering blues shows. These days he books bands with sounds ranging from cutting-edge blues rock to more traditional Chicago blues, plus the occasional solo act. Twice a year the lounge hosts the Old Town School of Folk Music harmonica graduation.

The lounge is dominated by a center rectangular bar that seats about 30. Another dozen chairs with a few tables are located in front of the stage at the far end. There's a drink shelf on one side and plenty of standing room near a pool table in back. The entrance to the bar is at the rear door by a small parking lot.

> **Hours:** Monday, 2 P.M. to 2 A.M.; Tuesday through Sunday, noon to 2 A.M.
> **Music begins:** 8:30 P.M. on Tuesday; 9:30 P.M. on Friday and Saturday.
> **Cover:** About $6 on Friday and Saturday; none on Tuesday and Thursday.
> **Parking:** There is a tiny lot behind the building. More parking is available across Harlem Avenue at the White Fence Farm. Posted signs will warn you repeatedly not to park in the White Castle lot—if you park there, you'll get towed.

Slice of Chicago
36 S. Northwest Highway
Palatine
847/991-2150
www.sliceofchicago.com

Slice of Chicago serves up the occasional blues band along with pizza, pasta, and beer. Bands set up on a small stage in the lounge area of this Italian-themed restaurant on Tuesdays, Fridays, and Saturdays.

Slice of Chicago opened in 1989. Owner Joe Barrutia, original owner of the Blue Chicago club, founded the club to bring "a little slice of Chicago to the suburbs."

> **Hours:** Restaurant is open 11 A.M. to 4 A.M. every day.
> **Music begins:** 10:30 P.M. on Friday and Saturday.
> **Cover:** $5.
> **Parking:** There is a parking lot.
> **Food:** Italian-style menu with pasta, pizza, sandwiches, and other entrees. Food is available in the bar until 3 A.M.

More Blues in the 'Burbs

A number of other suburban restaurants and bars regularly or occasionally book blues bands. Schedules change, so call ahead or check the Web sites.

Curly's Bar and Grill
499 Pennsylvania Avenue
Glen Ellyn
630/790-4878

This restaurant often hosts local blues bands on the weekends.

Frankie's Blue Room
16 W. Chicago Avenue
Naperville
630/416-4898
www.frankiesblueroom.com

Koko Taylor, Lonnie Brooks, Li'l Ed, Ronnie Baker Brooks, and Phil Guy have all played at one time or another at Frankie's Blue Room.

Geno's
12401 S. Ashland Avenue
Calumet Park
708/385-3100

Located near the Best Western hotel, Geno's sports bar offers soul food and the occasional jazz or blues show.

Hugo's Frog Bar
55 S. Main Street
Naperville
630/548-3764
www.hugosfrogbar.com

Jazz or blues bands are among the nightly musical offerings in the bar.

Molly Malone's
7652 W. Madison Street
Forest Park
708/366-8073
www.themollymalones.com

Only around Chicago will you find the occasional blues band at an Irish pub.

Muldoon's
133 W. Front Street
Wheaton
630/668-8866

Here's another Irish pub where you might find a blues band.

Orazio Pub
333 Center Street
Naperville
630/357-4350
www.oraziopub.com

Blues bands entertain on weekends at this bar and grill famous for its sandwiches.

Pete Miller's Steak and Seafood
1557 Sherman Avenue
Evanston
847/328-0399
www.petemillers.com

412 N. Milwaukee Avenue
Wheeling
847/243-3700

Pete Miller's advertises live jazz every night, but on occasion the performers are blues bands. To some people, it's all the same. No cover.

Porter's Oyster Bar

446 Virginia Street (Route 14)
Crystal Lake
815/477-0340
www.portersoysterbar.com

This seafood restaurant decorated in 1940s Art Deco style features live bands on Wednesday, Friday, and Saturday.

The Satisfied Frog

29 W. 012 Butterfield Road
Warrenville
630/393-2300
www.thesatisfiedfrog.com

Blues bands are among the live weekend entertainment offered by this frog-themed sports bar and grill.

Shaw's Crab House

1900 E. Higgins Road
Schaumburg
847/517-2722
www.shawscrabhouse.com/schaumburg

The Red Shell Lounge serves up seafood and the occasional blues show. Dave Specter and Matthew Skoller have played here.

Stage 83

10900 Archer Avenue
Lemont
630/257-9800
www.stage83.com

Bands of all genres play here. All-ages shows are sometimes held earlier in the evening.

Walter Payton's Roundhouse

205 N. Broadway

Aurora

630/264-BREW

www.walterpaytonsroundhouse.com

In 1995 Chicago Bears great Walter Payton and his partners bought this railroad station and train repair shop, built in 1856, and redeveloped it into a microbrewery, restaurant, and entertainment venue. Shows run Thursday through Sunday and vary from comedy acts to rock bands to blues bands. The Walter Payton Museum includes Payton's NFL Hall of Fame bust, his Super Bowl XX ring, and other memorabilia.

Chapter 3

Lake Michigan Blues:

The Chicago Blues Festival

Each June hundreds of thousands of people from all over the world gather in Grant Park in Chicago for the largest free blues festival in the world. Over the four-day fest, these fans can hear more than 70 musical acts and some of the biggest names in the blues. Performers represent the full spectrum of blues, from traditional Delta and Chicago-style blues to soul-blues, blues-rock, and everything in between. Fans can also sample food from some of Chicago's favorite restaurants and browse through displays by festival sponsors and local blues organizations.

The Chicago Blues Festival usually takes place on the second weekend in June, but blues season begins each year on May 1 with the birthday celebration of the late harmonica great "Little Walter" Jacobs. Throughout the month of May, leading up to the festival, there are special concerts, panel discussions, workshops, exhibits, and other events all over the city.

The Chicago club scene burns red-hot during festival weekend. Most clubs book high-profile artists and hold special events or parties.

The fest is organized by the City of Chicago Mayor's Office of Special Events. The festival grounds are located in Grant Park at Jackson Boulevard and Columbus Drive. Parts of both streets are closed for the duration of the fest, which runs from 11 A.M. to 9:30 P.M. each day. Festival details are available through the City of Chicago Web site (www.cityofchicago.org).

Making Blues History:
The Chicago Blues Festival

A combination of several factors led to the creation of the Chicago Blues Festival in 1984, according to Barry Dolins, who has coordinated the fest since its beginning. To start with, Harold Washington had become Chicago's first African-American mayor, on April 29, 1983. Then the next day, the city lost its premier bluesman when Muddy Waters passed away. Chicagoans were thinking about the blues and the contributions of African-Americans to the city.

At the same time, the city's biggest summer festival, ChicagoFest, had come to an end. The festival started in 1978, when Michael Bilandic was mayor, and had grown to a 12-day festival of food and entertainment. By the time it ended in 1983, blues stars like Muddy Waters, Koko Taylor, Lonnie Brooks, Willie Dixon, and Son Seals had all appeared on the ChicagoFest blues stage. In fact, city officials realized the blues stage had always been the most popular stage at the fest.

"It opened the eyes of the city fathers that blues is important in the city," Dolins says. The time was ripe for the blues to step out on its own.

Back in 1984 Dolins was an instructor at Loyola University in Chicago. He studied folklore and history and had written his master's thesis on blues piano from 1913 to 1927. Now Dolins had the idea for a series of six blues events called "Chicago Blues: An Urban Experience." The mini-festivals were sponsored through Loyola's Office of Continuing Education and a grant from the National Endowment of the Arts. To organize the events, Dolins coordinated with the Mayor's Office of Special Events.

The first two concerts, in honor of Martin Luther King Jr.'s birthday and Black History Month, were held indoors. The third was an outdoor event at the Maxwell Street Market organized as a Memorial Day tribute.

Note

The musicians who performed at the first Chicago Blues Festival, in 1984, signed waivers allowing their performances to be taped for the Chicago Blues Archives at the Chicago Public Library. While some artists, like Magic Slim (Morris Holt), signed their stage names, others used their real names. Sunnyland Slim signed Albert Luandrew; Junior Wells signed Amos Wells, Jr., and Jr. Wells; and Homesick James signed his real name, John William Henderson. Today the waivers and film footage—along with documents, video, audio, photographs, programs, and other items from every subsequent festival—are stored as part of the Blues Archives.

The event was advertised as an "all day blues and gospel program" featuring a "soul food jamboree" supplied by residents in the neighborhood. Snooky Pryor and Homesick James, both veterans of World War II, were honored.

The fourth concert, an outdoor concert, was slated for Grant Park. As it happened, Bruce Iglauer, founder of Alligator Records, was also thinking about the possibility of a blues festival. When he brought his idea to Lois Weisberg, the mayor's director of special events, she asked him to put together a committee to plan the event. Thus the first Chicago Blues Festival was born.

"We booked the first festival with the help of someone in her office who admitted that he knew nothing about the blues," Iglauer says. "We told him whom to book and gave him an idea about prices."

The one-stage festival was scheduled for June 8, 9, and 10 and was dedicated to the memory of Muddy Waters. To open the festival, Mayor Washington signed an official proclamation extolling the blues as "the heart and soul of the Chicago experience." Friday night featured a lineup of people who had worked with Muddy over the years: James Cotton, Willie Dixon, Carey Bell, Junior Wells, Jimmy Rogers, Sammy Lawhorn, and Johnny Winter, who, with Koko Taylor and the Legendary Blues Band, closed out the night.

Spotlight

Fifteen years before the first official Chicago Blues Festival, on August 30, 1969, an all-day concert called "Bringing the Blues Back Home" was held at the old Grant Park band shell on 11th Street. The ten-hour show drew more than 10,000 people.

Legendary bandleader and producer Willie Dixon wanted Chicago to host a festival similar to the folk and blues festivals taking place in the eastern United States and in Europe, so he approached Mayor Richard J. Daley's office and persuaded Assistant Mayor David Stahl to sponsor the event through the city's Reach Out program for young people.

Radio DJ Big Bill Hill of WOPA in Oak Park emceed the festival. The all-star lineup included Luther Allison, Fred Below, Jimmy Dawkins, Bo Diddley, Sleepy John Estes, Buddy Guy, Homesick James, John Lee Hooker, Lightnin' Hopkins, Big Walter Horton, Sam Lay, Lafayette Leake, Johnny Littlejohn, Robert Lockwood, Jr., Little Milton, Little Brother Montgomery, Otis Spann, Hound Dog Taylor, Koko Taylor, Big Mama Thornton, Muddy Waters, Junior Wells, Johnny Young, and Mighty Joe Young. Howlin' Wolf was invited but did not perform.

Muddy Waters closed the concert by playing "Got My Mojo Working."

Saturday's lineup showcased hometown talent: Magic Slim and the Teardrops, Homesick James, Snooky Pryor, Eddie Taylor, and brothers Jimmy and Syl Johnson. John Lee Hooker and Bobby "Blue" Bland headlined.

On Sunday the "Young Generation" took the stage. Led by Billy Branch and the Sons of Blues, the lineup consisted of Valerie Wellington, Gloria Hardiman, Johnny B. Moore, Lurrie Bell, Sugar Blue, Li'l Ed, Erwin Helfer, and Big Time Sarah. After Mama Yancy, Buckwheat Zydeco, and Bobby Rush performed, the evening was capped off with a "Texas Guitar Showdown" featuring Clarence "Gatemouth" Brown, Albert Collins, and Johnny "Clyde" Copeland.

By the end of the festival, an estimated 140,000 people had attended. No previous blues festival anywhere in the world had drawn crowds so big.

Following the success of the blues festival, Dolins became festival coordinator with the Mayor's Office of Special Events.

The second Chicago Blues Festival, held June 7 to 9, 1985, was more than a concert. Food and other vendors were added. Headlining the festival were Otis Rush and Etta James. Buddy Guy, Lonnie Brooks, Fenton Robinson, Lowell Fulson, Eddie "Cleanhead" Vinson, Big Joe Turner, Koko Taylor, and Stevie Ray Vaughan also performed.

Over the next several years, the festival showcased stars like Robert Cray, Chuck Berry, Bo Diddley, Dr. John, John Lee Hooker, Memphis Slim, Sunnyland Slim, Hubert Sumlin, Tyrone Davis, Albert Collins, Syl Johnson, Little Milton, Rufus Thomas, Denise LaSalle, Carl Perkins, Koko Taylor, Buddy Guy, Otis Rush, Son Seals, Honeyboy Edwards, Albert King, Etta James, Lonnie Brooks, Charles Brown, B.B. King, Bobby "Blue" Bland, Willie Dixon, James Cotton, Pinetop Perkins, and Irma Thomas.

In 1991 the Chicago Blues Festival marked the 80th anniversary of the birth of Robert Johnson. Since then all festivals have honored centennials and special birthdays of blues icons, both living and dead. In 1994 the festival honored the centennial of Bessie Smith and the 70th birthday of Jimmy Rogers. The following year, the festival celebrated Generation 1915, the group of blues legends born in 1915, which included the late Willie Dixon, Muddy Waters, Memphis Slim, Johnny Shines, Eddie Boyd, and Josh White. Living legends of that generation—Brownie McGhee, Robert Lockwood, Jr., Honeyboy Edwards, and Floyd McDaniel—performed. In 1999 the 16th festival celebrated "The Golden Age of the Blues" and marked the centennials of Sonny Boy Williamson II (Rice Miller), Sleepy John Estes, and Thomas A. Dorsey. The 2000 festival celebrated the 90th birthday of Howlin' Wolf and marked the centennials of Tampa Red and Pink Anderson.

The centennial celebrations honor the men and women who created the blues and place the music within its cultural and historical context, Dolins believes. "We are remembering icons and keeping them in the memory bank of the public," Dolins explains. "This music is not just a flash in the pan like pop musicians, but it has a history and culture."

Other festival themes have also been advanced. Blues Festival 13 in 1996 was titled "I Ain't Superstitious, Black Cat Cross My Trail," after lyrics from a Willie Dixon song. The 1991 festival commemorated the 20th anniversary of Alligator Records.

As its popularity grew, the fest was expanded from three to four days in 1997. The Juke Joint stage was added in 1996, and the Route 66 stage was added in 2000.

The Chicago Blues Festival has had many memorable moments over the years. In 1986 Rolling Stones guitarist Keith Richards surprised crowds by appearing onstage to jam with Chuck Berry. The great Ray Charles performed, backed by his Raelettes, in 1998. In 2000 the "Lone Star Shootout" featured Lonnie Brooks, Long John Hunter, and Phillip Walker.

Dolins fondly remembers the late Little Milton headlining the Petrillo stage, winding up the night singing, "Hey, Hey, the Blues Are All Right." He left the stage, and the audience stayed, still singing, still chanting: "The blues are all right."

"There are always these little things that happen that make blues history," he says.

Planning Your Day

The Chicago Blues Festival is laid out like a big plus sign, with the intersection of Columbus and Jackson as the center. The six stages are placed far enough apart that the music doesn't overlap but close enough to walk from one to another in just a couple of minutes. During the day, acts on all stages (except Petrillo) run simultaneously, but the sets are long enough, and the stages close enough together, that you can easily see a little bit of everything if you plan wisely.

Free pamphlet-sized schedules are available at the information booths at the festival. If you want to mark your itinerary ahead of time, most major newspapers publish the schedule. It's also available at the City of Chicago Web site (www.cityofchicago.org).

Numerous mature trees surround the Front Porch stage, and small groves of trees stand on either side of the Crossroads stage. Other than that, everything's pretty much in the open, so bring plenty of sunscreen, a hat, and, if rain seems possible, an umbrella. Because June weather in Chicago can be unpredictable, you may also want to pack a sweatshirt or windbreaker. Remember that "cooler near the lake" is not just a catchphrase for weather forecasters. Lake Michigan is just across the street from festival grounds, and temperatures may be several degrees cooler than farther inland.

Portable lawn chairs or camping stools will come in handy because seating is scarce at most stages. A downside to this is that toting a chair around may pose a dilemma once evening falls and the shows begin at the Petrillo band shell: you are not allowed to bring your own chair inside the fenced-in seating area. However, you may set up your chair in the lawn area outside the fence, where you will be able to hear, but not see, the bands.

Parking

As far as garage parking goes, the Grant Park and Millennium Park garages are closest to the festival. Rates range from $10 to $16 per day. You may be able to save a few dollars by parking in one of the open lots on Wabash and State streets, south of Congress Parkway. Rates range from $8 to $12 for the entire day. Another benefit is that parking there puts you in a good position for after-fest events at the HotHouse and Buddy Guy's Legends.

Grant Park is also convenient to public transportation, including Metra, the L, and buses. (For information, see www.transitchicago.com or call 888/YOURCTA.) An abundance of taxis run through downtown Chicago around the clock.

You can enter the festival grounds on foot from any direction. Because the festival is free, there are no gates or fences.

Food and Beverages

If you like a little barbecue with your blues, you'll find barbecued ribs, sandwiches, and turkey legs at the booths on Jackson Street. Most vendors are Chicago hometown favorites such as Robinson's Ribs, Connie's Pizza, and the Billy Goat Tavern. If you're a vegetarian or watching your diet,

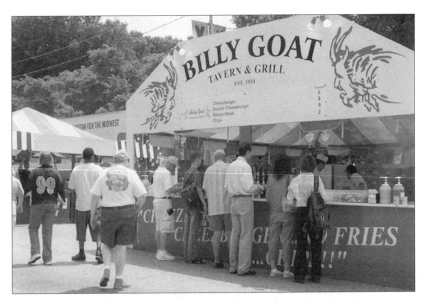

The food booths at the Chicago Blues Festival showcase Chicago-area restaurants like the Billy Goat Tavern.
Photo by Karen Hanson.

you can choose from such fare as pad thai noodles, corn on the cob, fresh fruit, or pickle on a stick. Soft drinks are sold in 20-ounce plastic bottles. To buy beer or alcoholic drinks, you must show ID. You can buy bottled water, but you can also fill your own bottles at continuously flowing water fountains located just beyond the trees north of the Crossroads stage.

Food and drinks can be purchased only with tickets, which are sold by the strip. You may also bring your own food and non-alcoholic drinks into the festival area. Competition for picnic tables is fierce, so many people spread out with a blanket on the ground at the Front Porch stage or, in the evenings, on the lawn area of the Petrillo band shell. Keep in mind that you will not be able to bring coolers into the fenced-in Petrillo seating area. Off the festival grounds, on nearby streets, are many restaurants, ranging from fast foot to sit-down dining to bar and grill.

Rows of portable toilets are situated in various locations on the festival grounds. Permanent public facilities are only a short walk away at Buckingham Fountain. The toilets flush, plus there's running water and a baby-changing table. Most stores and businesses on Michigan Avenue either do not have public restrooms or will not allow you to use them unless you are a paying customer.

Souvenirs

Official Chicago Blues Festival T-shirts, sweatshirts, hats, and other items can be purchased at the City of Chicago booths. It's an unofficial tradition for blues fans to collect festival T-shirts and wear their favorites from year to year. Some like to have T-shirts and hats autographed by blues artists.

The Blues Heaven Foundation or Koko Taylor's Celebrity Aid Foundation may also have booths where you can purchase T-shirts and other souvenirs, with the funds collected

Many blues clubs and associations have booths at the festival. Here, Tony Mangiullo, owner of Rosa's Lounge, vends T-shirts, hats, and other souvenirs. *Photo by Chuck Winans (pipphotography.com).*

used to benefit the work of these groups. Other sponsor booths may sell souvenirs or hand out giveaways ranging from stickers and buttons to posters and water bottles.

Stages

Front Porch

The Front Porch stage hosts traditional blues and folk-blues ranging from solo acts to hard-shuffling Chicago-style ensemble blues. Buddy Guy and Junior Wells played an acoustic set at the Front Porch in 1989, and Otha Turner and the Rising Star Fife and Drum Band performed here in 1996.

In 1988 Sunnyland Slim played on the Front Porch stage with fellow pianists Jimmy Walker, Erwin Helfer, and Big Moose Walker. Since Sunnyland's death in 1995, the Front Porch opens the festival with a Sunnyland Slim Memorial set of well-known piano players.

It's also traditional on the first day for the Blues in the Schools kids to make an appearance on the Front Porch stage. Led by Billy Branch, Katherine Davis, Eric Noden, and others, the kids sing and play harmonica, kazoo, and sometimes guitar and drums. Proud parents cheer them on, but the shows also have non-relatives crooning, "Aw, isn't that cute!"

Located in a grassy area just south of Jackson and west of Columbus, the Front Porch stage has lots of tall shade trees, a few picnic tables, and plenty of space for children to play. Many people bring folding chairs or blankets and settle in for the afternoon.

The grassy lawn and shady trees near the Front Porch stage invite fans to relax and enjoy an afternoon of music.
Photo by Karen Hanson.

Crossroads

The Crossroads stage is billed as the place where "acoustic meets electric," but it's also frequently the place where blues meets rock. The bands tend to be bigger, louder, and tougher than those on the other stages. Yet there's room for the traditional as well. Artists who have appeared on the Crossroads stage are Melvin Taylor, Joanna Connor, Lurrie Bell, Ronnie Baker Brooks, Shirley Johnson, Michael Coleman, Robert Jr. Lockwood, and Saffire: The Uppity Blues Women.

With Lake Michigan in the background, the Crossroads stage presents electric blues in an urban street setting.
Photo by Karen Hanson.

The Crossroads stage is set up on the pavement at the point where Jackson intersects with Lake Shore Drive. For best sight lines, most people stand in the street in front of the stage. The music can be heard well from the shady spots on both sides of the street, but from there it's difficult (or impossible) to see the performers onstage.

Juke Joint

The Juke Joint stage presents solo acts or duets in an intimate setting. Small and low to the ground, the Juke Joint offers the opportunity for fans to see the musicians up close.

Added in 1996, the Juke Joint is ideal for acoustic-type acts like Corey Harris, Harmonica Hinds, Fruteland Jackson, Guy Davis, and Honeyboy Edwards, all of whom have performed here in the past. But artists who usually play electric blues with a full band, like Jimmy Johnson and Carl Weathersby, have also performed at the Juke Joint.

At the Juke Joint stage, fans can hear the blues in an informal, intimate atmosphere. Here, Fernando Jones entertains at the 2005 Chicago Blues Festival.
Photo by Karen Hanson.

The stage has also thrown together some interesting combinations. In 2000 John Primer teamed up with Steve Bell, the harmonica-playing son of Carey Bell, and Little Milton sang accompanied by his former guitarist Eddie Cusic. Later, Lonnie Brooks and his two sons, Wayne Baker Brooks and Ronnie Baker Brooks, performed as a trio of guitars. In 2005 Hubert Sumlin and Bob Margolin played together.

The Juke Joint is located on Columbus north of Jackson near the School of the Art Institute of Chicago. Rows of benches provide lots of seating in front of the stage, but there's no shade.

Route 66 Roadhouse

The Route 66 stage has changed focus and locations since it began in 2000. At first the tented stage featured performances by lesser-known traditional artists, but in recent years the stage has been a site for presentations and discussions about issues in the blues. Panels have consisted of blues musicians, family members of blues legends, record producers, journalists, photographers, and others.

Petrillo

Entertainment begins in the early evening at the Petrillo stage, the largest stage of the festival. The huge lawn beyond the inside seating area accommodates hundreds of fans who like to picnic and party as they listen to the blues.
Photo by Karen Hanson.

The biggest names in the blues appear at Petrillo. Buddy Guy, Koko Taylor, Otis Rush, Lonnie Brooks, and Pinetop Perkins have each headlined more than once on the Petrillo stage. Ray Charles and his Raelettes entertained in 1998. In 2000 it was Little Milton and the "Lone Star Shootout" with three guitarists from Texas: Lonnie Brooks, Long John Hunter, and Phillip Walker. Bo Diddley performed in 2002, and Bonnie Raitt headlined in 2003. In 2005 Petrillo performers included John Mayall and Mavis Staples. Other artists to perform here are Artie "Blues Boy" White, Etta James, Magic Slim, Bobby Bland, and Albert King

The stage features three acts per night, the first beginning at 5 P.M. and the last finishing up at 9:30 P.M. Fans begin lining up hours prior to the 4 P.M. opening of the fenced-in seating area. You are not permitted to bring bottles, cans, coolers, or lawn chairs inside the fenced-in area. As you enter, your bags will be inspected for video or audio recording equipment. If you want to venture out for food or drink, you will need a hand stamp to reenter.

On the lawn beyond the fence, families and friends stake out areas with blankets, chairs, umbrellas, and tents. Groups often identify their spots by putting up tall flags or banners. A large-screen TV allows fans to see as well as hear the performances.

Chapter 4

Chicago Bound:

Blues Historical and Cultural Sites

Blues fans are often motivated to seek out the historical and cultural background of the blues. They want to see for themselves the places where their heroes performed, recorded, and lived.

Most old clubs where blues legends performed have closed or have been torn down, but fans can still visit many of the spots where blues history was made. You can hear the blues at the Maxwell Street Market, though the market isn't on Maxwell Street anymore. The Blues Heaven Foundation offers tours of the Chess Studios building, and Jazz Record Mart, although in a new location, still has the biggest collection of blues records anywhere in the city. The Chicago Blues Museum presents blues history in multimedia and offers an extensive collection of blues memorabilia. In the suburbs you can visit Westmont, where Muddy Waters once lived, or take a trip to Aurora, where the Bluebird Beat was born.

Chess Studios

2120 S. Michigan Avenue
www.bluesheaven.com

When the Rolling Stones made their first trip to Chicago, in June 1964, their destination was the building at 2120 S. Michigan Avenue, Chess Studios. In a two-day session, Mick Jagger, Keith Richards, and the rest of the Stones recorded such hits as "It's All Over Now," "Confessin' the Blues," and the song that immortalized the address of Chess: "2120 S. Michigan Ave."

Through the 1950s nearly every major blues musician in Chicago— Muddy Waters, Little Walter, Willie Dixon, Jimmy Rogers, Sonny Boy Williamson II, Bo Diddley, and more—recorded for the label created by brothers Leonard and Phil Chess. But until 1957, when the Chess brothers moved their headquarters to Michigan Avenue, all songs were recorded off-site, most often at the studios of Universal Recording on West Ontario Street.

The Chess label began in 1947 when Leonard and Phil Chess, then nightclub owners, purchased Aristocrat Records, located at 71st Street and Phillips. In 1950 the brothers moved the label to 49th and Cottage Grove and changed the name to Chess Records. In 1951 the Checker label was added. The label grew rapidly on the strength of a series of hit records, like Little Walter's "Juke" and Howlin' Wolf's "Moanin' at Midnight," plus the song-writing and production talents of Willie Dixon, who signed on with Chess in 1951. In response Chess soon established its song publishing company, Arc Music, in 1954, and Argo (later called Cadet), a jazz-oriented subsidiary, in 1956.

In 1957 the Chess brothers bought the Michigan Avenue building, which had once housed a furniture slipcover factory. They remodeled the interior and installed state-of-the-art recording equipment. The studio, later known as Tel-Mar, was acoustically designed to retain the characteristic Chess echo sound.

Over the next decade, the Chess/Tel-Mar studio recorded hit records like "My Babe" by Little Walter and "Seventh Son" by Willie Mabon (both written by Willie Dixon). New artists signing on with Chess were Buddy Guy, Etta James, Chuck Berry, and John Lee Hooker. In addition to blues, Chess continued to record R&B, gospel, and jazz.

But the 2120 S. Michigan address wouldn't be the last for Chess. In 1966 the brothers moved their offices to a larger facility at 320 E. 21st Street and expanded their R&B and gospel offerings. After Leonard Chess died in

The building at 2120 S. Michigan Avenue once housed the Chess Recording Studios. It's now the home of the Blues Heaven Foundation, established by Willie Dixon in the 1990s. In summer the gated garden area is often used for blues concerts.
Photo by Karen Hanson.

1969, the label was sold to General Recorded Tape (GRT). The label folded in 1974. MCA Records obtained the Chess masters in 1985 and reissued most of the songs on CD.

Blues Heaven Foundation

The City of Chicago recognized the historic significance of the Chess Studios building by naming it a landmark on May 16, 1990, but to Willie Dixon, the building also had deep personal meaning. Throughout the 1950s and '60s Dixon was the prime creative force at Chess Studios. He wrote hundreds of songs, such as Muddy Waters's hit "Hoochie Coochie Man" and Howlin' Wolf's incomparable "Evil." He also arranged music, rehearsed bands, produced records, and played bass on many of the songs. He was responsible for bringing in new talent, such as Koko Taylor, for whom he wrote "Wang Dang Doodle" in 1955. In the late 1950s Dixon left

Chess to work for a time at Cobra Records. There he helped along the careers of Buddy Guy, Otis Rush, and Magic Sam before returning to Chess in 1959.

Dixon founded the Blues Heaven Foundation in the early 1980s to promote the blues, assist musicians, and educate young people. He wanted to purchase the Chess building, which had lain vacant for years, for the foundation's headquarters, but he died in 1992, before seeing his dream become reality. The following year Marie Dixon fulfilled her late husband's vision by buying the Michigan Avenue building and donating it to the Blues Heaven Foundation. The building was restored and opened to the public in 1997.

The Blues Heaven Foundation provides emergency funds to help senior blues musicians with medical costs, conducts workshops designed to educate musicians about the business side of music, and assists musicians with legal issues and in recovering unpaid royalties. Blues Heaven annually awards the Muddy Waters Scholarship to a full-time college student in Chicago majoring in such subjects as history, music, journalism or African-American studies. The foundation sponsors American Blues Children, a Blues in the Schools program.

Touring Chess Studios

You can tour the 2120 S. Michigan building from noon to 3 P.M. Monday through Friday and from noon to 2 P.M. on Saturday. The cost is $10 per person. Groups should make arrangements in advance. If no one appears to be around when you arrive, ring the doorbell, and you'll be buzzed in.

The tour starts in the main recording studio on the second floor, now used for workshops. Tour-goers may view a film or examine the photos, documents, artwork, and memorabilia on the walls. A knowledgeable tour guide is on hand to tell the stories of Chess Records and Willie Dixon and to answer any questions. Also on the second floor are the rehearsal studio and the control room, filled with memorabilia donated by such artists as Koko Taylor, Lonnie Brooks, and Willie Dixon.

The tour then proceeds down the narrow back staircase used by musicians to transport their instruments and equipment to the studio. On the first floor are the shipping room and the offices of Leonard and Phil Chess. The front office is a gift shop. Concerts and other special events are held in the Blues Heaven Garden, adjacent to the building.

The Chess Studios building is only a few blocks south of the Loop in an area of rapid redevelopment. Parking is available in metered spaces on the street.

Chicago Blues Archives
Chicago Public Library
Harold Washington Library
400 S. State Street
312/747-4850

The Chicago Blues Archives holds a collection of audio and video recordings, books, magazines, photographs, files, and other items documenting the blues in Chicago and around the world. Highlights of the collection are posters, contracts, press kits, images, and sound recordings from Chicago Blues Festivals dating back to 1984; CDs, LPs, tapes, and 78 records of blues musicians, past and present; and recordings of performances from *Soundstage*, a WTTW public television production. Located on the eighth floor of the Harold Washington Library, the archives may be viewed under carefully controlled conditions by researchers, scholars, and those interested in blues history.

The archives began in 1981 when radio station WXRT donated recordings from its *Blues Breakers* specials, which includes performances by blues musicians such as Willie Dixon, Buddy Guy, John Lee Hooker, Lonnie Brooks, Taj Mahal, and Johnny Winter, recorded live in Chicago clubs. The collection has grown through donations from musicians, collectors, businesses, and fans. The City of Chicago Mayor's Office of Special Events donates all materials related to the annual Chicago Blues Festival. The eighth floor also uses an exhibit space to display blues-related memorabilia. Past exhibits have included a tribute to Delmark Records and a display of blues photography.

The Chicago Blues Archives produces a series of free programs called "Speakin' of the Blues," which feature live interviews and performances in the Harold Washington Library by Chicago blues musicians. These performances are recorded and preserved in the archives.

If you go: Call first and tell the librarians exactly what you are looking for. They will prepare the materials for your viewing. The materials are being catalogued and shelved and cannot be casually browsed. If you don't have a Chicago Public Library card, you will need to show a valid photo ID, such as a driver's license. Materials cannot be checked out.

Chicago Blues Museum

3636 S. Iron Street

773/828-8118

www.chicagobluesmuseum.com

Imagine seeing the Regal Theater as it might have looked in the days when Duke Ellington, Louis Armstrong, Ray Charles, and B.B. King performed there, listening to jazz from the bandstands of the Club DeLisa, or strolling among the booths and tables from the old Checkerboard Lounge. With exhibits like these, the Chicago Blues Museum brings to life the city's thriving center of musical entertainment from the 1930s through the 1960s. The multimedia displays trace the history of blues, jazz, R&B, soul, and gospel music through historic photographs, rare film footage, artifacts, memorabilia, and recordings.

Since 1992 fans have enjoyed the sights and sounds of the Chicago Blues Museum under a tent at the Chicago Blues Festival. This annual event has been only part of the museum's activities. The museum has had traveling exhibits at the DuSable Museum of African American History, the Chicago Jazz Festival, the Chicago Cultural Center, Navy Pier, and various Chicago Park District locations. The Chicago Blues Museum also lent numerous artifacts, photos, and film footage to "Sweet Home Chicago: Big City Blues," a special exhibit at the Museum of Science and Industry in 2004.

Now the Chicago Blues Museum at long last has a permanent home, a 100-year-old former warehouse in an industrial park in Bridgeport, just a few blocks west of U.S. Cellular Field, home of the White Sox. The museum will eventually spread out to fill three of the five floors, each measuring about 8,200 square feet of space. Additional areas will be filled with fine art galleries, recording studios, video production studios, and rehearsal space.

Chicago native Gregg Parker, a musician, producer, and historian, founded the museum in 1991. Parker grew up on the South Side just blocks away from soul singer Sam Cooke. Freddye Cole Bates, a star dancer at the Club DeLisa, was Parker's aunt, and guitarist Lefty Bates was his uncle. Parker toured more than 20 years as a rock guitarist, playing in the bands of Santana, Isaac Hayes, Buddy Miles, and Ringo Starr, as well as in his own band, Ozz. After returning to Chicago in the early 1990s, Parker took on the museum project with

The Chicago Blues Museum showcases photos, memorabilia, and live performance film footage of blues and jazz artists from the 1920s to the present. *Copyright and courtesy of the Chicago Blues Museum. The Chicago Blues Museum is a registered trademark.*

Muddy Waters and virtually every other blues artist in Chicago during the 1950s and '60s walked through this door at Muddy's house on South Lake Park Avenue. *Copyright and courtesy of the Chicago Blues Museum. The Chicago Blues Museum is a registered trademark.*

a few artifacts and a big vision: he wanted to preserve and promote the people, places, and sounds of African-American music in Chicago.

Parker has collected more than 350,000 photos depicting musicians, political figures, and sports players. He owns the publicity photos from Chess Records, news photos from the *Chicago Defender* and other newspapers, original ledgers from the Regal Theater, a turntable once used by DJ Big Bill Hill, and the doors from the Chicago home of Muddy Waters. Working with the families of blues musicians, Parker has also gathered objects such as musical instruments, sheet music, and personal items once owned by music legends. Many of these items had been stored in people's basements or were about to be thrown away.

Along with his partner, designer Stefanie Mielke, Parker has arranged the displays so that visitors will be able to learn the blues by experiencing the music in its historical and cultural context. Parker also plans art exhibits, educational programs, musical performances, and other special events designed to teach people about the blues and to provide a creative outlet for Chicago's present-day artistic community. In addition to this, Parker heads up the Chicago Jazz Museum and the Record Row Foundation.

If you go: Call first to check on hours of operation and other details. Closed Monday.

Gravesites

Many famous blues musicians from the past have been laid to rest in cemeteries in the Chicago area. For fans a visit to the gravesites of their favorite bluesmen and women is a way to honor and show appreciation for their musical legacy. If you would like to visit a gravesite, call the cemetery first to check for the hours and any regulations.

Restvale Cemetery
117th Street and Laramie Avenue
Worth Township (near Alsip)
708/385-3506

Just southwest of the Chicago city limits, between the suburbs of

The graves of numerous blues legends can be found in the Restvale Cemetery in the south suburbs. Many blues fans pay their respects to their musical heroes by visiting the gravesites.
Photo by Karen Hanson.

Worth and Alsip, lies Restvale Cemetery, a modest but well-kept cemetery primarily serving the African-American community. It's an active cemetery, where family members adorn the graves of their loved ones with flower arrangements that spell out "Mom" and "Dad."

Restvale is also the final resting place for more than a dozen legendary blues musicians who are known the world over. Although the cemetery may be hard to find for many out-of-towners, it's not unusual to find fans paying their respects to the memories of Muddy Waters, Magic Sam, Hound Dog Taylor, Clarence "Pinetop" Smith, and many more.

Cemetery caretakers are accustomed to visits by blues fans. At the office near the entrance, visitors can pick up a list telling the locations of famous graves. Each cemetery section is clearly marked, and cemetery workers are happy to give directions. Most gravestones are simple rectangular stones placed flat to the ground, yet these stones pay tribute to the deceased's contributions to the musical world with engravings of guitars or harmonicas. The grave marker of McKinley Morganfield (a.k.a. Muddy Waters), for example, depicts his signature Telecaster guitar and the phrase "The mojo is gone . . . the master has won."

John Henry Barbee (Nov. 14, 1905 – Nov. 3, 1964)
Jazz Gillum (William McKinley Gillum) (Sept. 11, 1904 – March 29, 1966)
Earl Hooker (Jan. 15, 1929 – April 21, 1970)
Big Walter Horton (April 6, 1918 – Dec. 8, 1981)
J.B. Hutto (April 26, 1926 – June 12, 1983)
Little Johnny Jones (Nov. 1, 1924 – Nov. 19, 1964)
Magic Sam (Sam Maghett) (Feb. 2, 1937 – Dec. 12, 1969)
Charles "Papa Charlie" McCoy (May 26, 1909 – July 26, 1950)
Kansas Joe McCoy (May 11, 1905 – Jan. 28, 1950)
Jimmy Rogers (James A. Lane) (June 3, 1924 – Dec. 19, 1997)
Clarence "Pinetop" Smith (June 11, 1904 – March 15, 1929)
St. Louis Jimmy (James Oden) (June 26, 1903 – Dec. 30, 1977)
Eddie Taylor (Edward Taylor) (Jan. 29, 1923 – Dec. 25, 1985)
Hound Dog Taylor (Theodore Roosevelt Taylor) (April 12, 1915 – Dec. 17, 1975)
Luther Tucker (Jan. 20, 1936 – June 17, 1993)
Muddy Waters (McKinley Morganfield) (April 4, 1915 – April 30, 1983)
Johnny "Guitar" Watson (Feb. 3, 1935 – May 17, 1996)
Valerie Wellington (Nov. 14, 1959 – Jan. 2, 1993)

Burr Oak Cemetery
4400 W. 127th Street
Alsip
773/233-5676

James "Kokomo" Arnold (Feb. 15, 1901 – Nov. 8, 1968)
Willie Dixon (July 1, 1915 – Jan. 29, 1992)
Otis Spann (March 21, 1930 – April 24, 1970)
Dinah Washington (Aug. 29, 1924 – Dec. 14, 1963)

Homewood Memorial Gardens
600 Ridge Road
Thornton Township
708/798-0055

Frank "Son" Seals (Aug. 13, 1942 – Dec. 20, 2004)

Lincoln Cemetery

11900 Kedzie Avenue
Blue Island
773/445-5400

Big Bill Broonzy (June 26, 1893 – Aug. 15, 1958)
Jimmy Reed (Sept. 6, 1925 – Aug. 29, 1976)

Oak Ridge Cemetery

4301 W. Roosevelt Road
Hillside
708/344-5600

James Carter (1926 – Nov. 26, 2003)
Howlin' Wolf (Chester A. Burnett) (June 10, 1910 – Jan. 10, 1976)

Oak Woods Cemetery

1035 E. 67th Street
Chicago
773/288-3800

Thomas A. "Georgia Tom" Dorsey (July 1, 1899 – Jan. 23, 1993)
Eurreal Willford "Little Brother" Montgomery (April 18, 1906 – Sept. 6, 1985)
Roebuck "Pops" Staples (Dec. 28, 1915 – Dec. 19, 2000)
Amos "Junior" Wells (Amos Blackmore) (Dec. 9, 1934 – Jan. 15, 1998)

St. Mary's Catholic Cemetery

87th Street and Hamlin Avenue
Evergreen Park
708/422-8720

Little Walter (Jacobs) (May 1, 1930 – Feb. 15, 1968)

Washington Memorial Gardens

701 Ridge Road
Homewood
708/798-0645

Luther Allison (Aug. 17, 1939 – Aug. 12, 1997)

Jazz Record Mart

27 E. Illinois Street
312/222-1467
www.jazzmart.com

Jazz Record Mart boasts the largest collection of blues, jazz, gospel, R&B, and world music CDs, vinyl LPs, books, magazines, videos, posters, and T-shirts in Chicago. For nearly a half century, the store has drawn blues fans from all over the world in search of hard-to-find recordings and other resources.

"It's a rare day that I don't hear an accent in the store," says owner Bob Koester, who still often works in the store. Koester is also founder of Delmark Records.

Several people who came to Chicago to work at Jazz Record Mart pursued a future in the blues. Mike Bloomfield, guitarist for the Paul Butterfield Blues Band, used to hang around the store. Harmonica player Charlie Musselwhite worked there for a time. Both Michael Frank, founder of Earwig Music, and Bruce Iglauer, founder of Alligator Records, also worked for Koester.

Jazz Record Mart evolved from a record store called Seymour's Jazz Mart, which Koester bought in 1959, a year after moving to Chicago from St. Louis. The store was located at 439 S. Wabash Avenue, in the rear of Roosevelt University's Auditorium building. Koester operated the Delmark label in the basement.

In 1962 Koester moved the store to 7 W. Grand Avenue and changed the store name to Jazz Record Mart. As with the previous building, he used the basement space for offices and storage for Delmark Records. It was in this basement that country blues guitarist Big Joe Williams used to sleep on occasion.

Jazz Record Mart offers the city's largest collection of blues CDs, audiocassettes, LPs, books, magazines, videocassettes, and DVDs.
Photo by Karen Hanson.

Jazz Record Mart has moved several times since Bob Koester bought the store in 1959. The latest location is 27 E. Illinois Street.
Photo by Karen Hanson.

"He had a key to the place," Koester explains. "He'd park his car on Grand and stay in the basement whenever he was in town." Other people, including punk-rock star Iggy Pop, claimed to have slept in the basement of JRM, but Koester says if it happened, he didn't know about it.

During the 1960s Jazz Record Mart became a magnet for white blues fans, who came to Chicago from all over the country. Koester and his friends would take carloads of fans out to clubs on the South and West sides to see Howlin' Wolf, Magic Sam, Otis Rush, and other blues greats.

"A tremendous percentage of the people were from out of the country," recalls Koester. "They were almost never from Chicago." Once Koester led a caravan of six cars out to the West Side; the blues fans were from four or five different countries.

In the mid-1970s Jazz Record Mart moved two doors down to a larger store at 11 W. Grand. By that time the Delmark part of the business had moved to its own building, and the entire store space was taken up by records and other inventory.

Jazz Record Mart moved again in 1995, to an even larger, more modern facility at 444 N. Wabash. The store had a back room, the perfect space for in-store performances and the annual blues brunch during the Chicago Blues Festival.

The last move came in 2005, when the store moved around the corner to 27 E. Illinois Street, its present location. There's no performance space in the smaller facility, so the blues brunch and other events are held at the bookstore next door.

If you go: Jazz Record Mart hours are 10 A.M. to 8 P.M., Monday through Saturday, and noon to 5 P.M. on Sunday.

Leland Hotel

7 S. Stolp Avenue
Aurora

From 1937 to 1938 the top floor (the Sky Club) of the 22-story Leland Hotel in downtown Aurora was used as a recording studio for some of the most influential blues in prewar Chicago. There Sonny Boy (John Lee) Williamson I, Big Joe Williams, Robert Nighthawk, James "Yank" Rachell, Tampa Red, Big Bill Broonzy, Bill "Jazz" Gillum, Henry Townsend, Washboard Sam, and others all cut records for RCA Victor's Bluebird label.

Among the songs made at the Leland was Sonny Boy Williamson's

"Good Morning, Little Schoolgirl," which continues to influence blues harp players today. The music created at the Leland became known as the Bluebird Beat, considered to be the precursor of the urban Chicago blues.

It wasn't unheard of in those days to make blues records in hotels. In 1936 legendary bluesman Robert Johnson cut his first songs for Vocalion in a hotel room in San Antonio, Texas. Because RCA Victor did not have its own recording studios in Chicago, the Leland was used instead. No one is certain why RCA Victor or producer Lester Melrose selected the Leland; some speculate that a location outside of Chicago was chosen to avoid union conflicts. Others say that the Sky Club had good acoustics. Whatever the reason, the Leland was an attractive choice: at the time, it was the tallest building outside of Chicago. On the top floor, the Sky Club was a spacious ballroom where jazz-inspired big bands often played to all-white audiences.

The makeshift recording studio consisted of a couple of chairs and a couple of microphones, according to Henry Townsend in an interview given in 2000. The records were cut on wax, he said, because magnetic

Now an apartment building, the Leland Hotel was a hot nightspot in the 1930s and '40s.
Photo by Karen Hanson.

A plaque commemorating the historic Bluebird recordings was placed on the building in 1997. The Fox Valley Blues Society led the effort to draw attention to the historical significance of the Leland.
Photo by Karen Hanson.

tape and reel-to-reel recorders were not yet in widespread use.

Lester Melrose would bring several musicians into the studio at once, thereby producing a number of sides in a minimum amount of time. Each musician would take a turn as lead performer and then back the others on their recordings. On May 4, 1937, when Sonny Boy cut "Good Morning, Little Schoolgirl," "Blue Bird Blues," and four other tracks, he was accompanied by Big Joe Williams and Robert Lee McCoy on guitars. Later, Sonny Boy and Big Joe backed McCoy as he recorded six songs, including "Prowling Night Hawk," from which he took his nickname, Robert Nighthawk. Then Big Joe Williams recorded eight songs, including "Rootin' Ground Hog" and "Brother James," with McCoy on guitar and Sonny Boy on harp.

This method was used during several other times in 1937 and 1938 in sessions that combined the talents of Sonny Boy, McCoy, Townsend, Walter Davis, Yank Rachell, Jazz Gillum, Big Bill Broonzy, Washboard Sam, and Speckled Red.

RCA opened a recording studio in Chicago in 1940. However, Bluebird used the Leland at least one more time. In 1941 Robert Lockwood, Jr. recorded four songs in a session in which he also backed Doc Clayton.

The historical significance of the Leland Hotel went largely unrecognized until the late 1990s, when the Fox Valley Blues Society (FVBS) brought it to the attention of the city of Aurora. The Leland is now listed on the National Register of Historic Buildings. During the 1997 Blues on the Fox festival, the FVBS organized the dedication of a plaque commemorating the 60th anniversary of the first Bluebird recordings. T.W. Utley, Sonny Boy Williamson's half brother, attended the ceremony. The part of Stolp Avenue in front of the building has been renamed Blues Alley. In 1999 the FVBS was honored with the Blues Foundation's Keeping the Blues Alive Award for Blues Organization of the Year.

In 1997 the Sky Cub room was used once again to record the blues. On August 2 of that year, Earwig Music arranged for David "Honeyboy" Edwards to use the room to record *The World Don't Owe Me Nothing*, the CD released in conjunction with his autobiography of the same title.

Today the Leland Tower is still the tallest building in Aurora, but it's no longer a hotel. It has been converted into an apartment building with retail businesses on the bottom floor. The Sky Club room remains empty.

Spotlight
Blues on the Fox
City of Aurora
630/844-3640
www.aurora-il.org

The Blues on the Fox festival in downtown Aurora was founded in 1997 by the Fox Valley Blues Society. At its peak the festival ran four stages over a two-day period and drew as many as 20,000 visitors. For its efforts the FVBS received the 1999 Keeping the Blues Alive Award from the Blues Foundation as Blues Organization of the Year.

Now Blues on the Fox has been folded into the "Downtown Alive!" program operated by the City of Aurora's Mayor's Office of Special Events. The two-evening event takes place from 6 to 10:30 P.M. on the Friday and Saturday nights before Father's Day. The festival offers free parking, free admission and an area for children's activities. Food and beverages are available.

The Historic Maxwell Street Market

Near the corner of the intersection of Maxwell and Halsted Streets, in front of a coffeehouse and upscale condos, is a sign depicting a red circle with a line across the words *No Peddling*. It's an irony that escapes many of the young students who attend the nearby University of Illinois at Chicago. Few of them probably know that, for decades, this intersection was the nexus of the Maxwell Street Market, a huge open-air market and the creative cradle of the Chicago blues.

Each Sunday since the early years of the twentieth century until the market was closed in 1994, blues musicians took their guitars, harmonicas, washboards, kazoos, and homemade instruments to the market to play for tips. At one time or another, Memphis Minnie, Bo Diddley, John Lee Hooker, Muddy Waters, Jimmy Rogers, Howlin' Wolf, Snooky Pryor, Carey Bell, Jimmy Reed, Billy Boy Arnold, Honeyboy Edwards, and Hound Dog Taylor all played on Maxwell Street.

Harmonica virtuoso Little Walter played on Maxwell Street when he first arrived in Chicago in the late 1940s. He cut his first record, "I Just Keep Loving Her," for the Ora Nelle label of the Maxwell Radio Record

The corner of Maxwell and Halsted Streets, once the center of the bustling Maxwell Street Market, has been redeveloped into an upscale shopping area and is closed to peddlers these days. The market has moved a few blocks to the east. *Photo by Karen Hanson.*

Company, owned by Maxwell Street merchant Bernard Abrams. Even after becoming a star, Walter often headed to Maxwell Street to make a quick buck, sometimes playing guitar to avoid union conflicts.

Many musicians were Maxwell Street regulars for years: Floyd Jones and his cousin, Moody Jones, Daddy Stovepipe (Johnny Watson), Eddie "Pork Chop" Hines, Johnnie Mae Dunson Smith, Johnny Young, Blind Arvella Gray, Big John Wrencher, John Lee Granderson, Jimmie Lee Robinson, and "Maxwell Street" Jimmy Davis.

Bands would plug their amplifiers into businesses such as Jim's Original Hot Dog Stand and Johnny Dollar's Thrift Store. "Maxwell Street was the birthplace of urban electric blues," says Steve Balkin, a professor of economics and supporter of the Maxwell Street Markets. According to Balkin, the market and the blues were the perfect fit. "It's a music from the front porches and from the streets," he explains.

The blues thrived on Maxwell Street from the 1930s until a little more than a decade ago, when the market began to decline. The old Maxwell Street Market had never been orderly, but it became even less so in the mid-1980s. Conditions deteriorated and garbage accumulated. At the same time, the University of Illinois was looking to expand its campus. In 1994 the city closed down the Maxwell Street Market and moved it a few blocks east to Canal Street, where it operates today.

Although the market officially moved, the traditions of Maxwell Street weren't about to fade away easily. In 1992 the Maxwell Street Historical Preservation Association was formed. The group wanted to save as much of the old Maxwell Street as they could.

The association hoped that UIC would use a few empty lots for dormitories but would leave the older buildings untouched. The group held demonstrations and rallies, but the land was valuable, and the city used eminent domain to acquire the property. The buildings were closed and the people—some of whom had done business on Maxwell Street for generations—left. Gone now are Jim's Original Hot Dog Stand, famous for its polish sausage; Johnny Dollar's Thrift Store, where blues bands played every Sunday; and Nate's Deli, the storefront used in *The Blues Brothers* movie.

As for the new Maxwell Street Market, Balkin calls it "Maxwell Street Lite," a mere shadow of the old market. But that's not meant entirely as a criticism. "The old market was so great and so vibrant that even a shadow is still exciting," Balkin says.

The new market has about 400 vendors, enough to cover six blocks of Canal Street. The old market, however, had 1,200 vendors. "I could never see the entire market in one day," Balkin says.

The new market has also been gentrified, just like the area around it. At the old market, many vendors were poor and homeless and sold used and scavenged merchandise. But the increase in vendor fees—from $25 a year to $35 a day—has pushed poor people out of the market. Vendors today tend to be professionals selling mostly new merchandise.

The market has also changed culturally. The vendors and customers at the old market were a mix of African-Americans, Mexicans, Italians, and Jews, mostly of Eastern European heritage. (Black blues musicians often referred to Maxwell Street as "Jewtown.") But today most vendors and customers have little connection with the blues.

"There are blues musicians with historic ties to the old market," Balkin says. "Problem is, the market has become mostly Mexican and Mexican-American. But they're not a blues culture, so it's a struggle for the musicians to come there and get enough money put in the basket."

It's also harder for blues musicians to get the power they need for amplification. There are no small shops on the streets that will allow bands to tap into their electricity. The musicians must bring their own generators.

Still, a handful of blues bands still play regularly at the market. Piano C. Red used to play in front of Johnny Dollar's Thrift Store at the old market. Until recently he and his bandmates set up every week, weather permitting, at the south end of the market near 16th Street.

"On the one hand, a great travesty was done in getting rid of the old market and setting up the new market," Balkin said. "Never again should that happen. But no matter how much I complain about what they did, the new market is still worth going to. It's still an authentic place and the blues can come back. What it needs is for people to come out and support it."

The New Maxwell Street Market

On Canal Street between Taylor and 16th Streets
Every Sunday, 7 A.M. to 3 P.M.
312/744-4006

Blues bands such as Piano C. Red (right) and his band still perform each week at Canal and 16th Streets. (In early 2006, Piano C. Red was injured in a shooting and continues to recover.)
Photo by Karen Hanson.

The blues tent at the new Maxwell Street Market can be found on the south end of the market on Canal Street near 16th Street. Piano C. Red, along with many band members and guest musicians, started performing

The original Blues Bus, a weekly fixture at the old market, has been retired and replaced by a newer Blues Bus, where you can still buy CDs, cassettes, and other musical merchandise.
Photo by Karen Hanson.

years ago at the old market on Maxwell Street. These days you might see Frank "Little Sonny" Scott Jr. (with his handmade instrument made from house keys), harp player "Mr. H," singer Bobby Too Tough, or many others who play the blues much the same as you might have heard 30, 40, or 50 years ago.

In the midsection of the market is the Blues Bus, where you can purchase blues, R&B, and soul CDs, among others, at bargain prices. The Blues Bus is still operated by Reverend John Johnson and his family, just as it was years ago, but the vehicle itself is relatively new. The original Blues Bus has been retired and is used as a traveling exhibit to entertain and educate people about Maxwell Street.

Note

In the last few years of his life, guitarist and bass player Jimmie Lee Robinson became a spokesman for the Maxwell Street preservation movement. He wrote the song "Maxwell Street Tear Down Blues" in 1997, and he made public appearances on behalf of the cause. He also conducted two hunger strikes to draw media attention to the issue.

Throughout the rest of the market, you can hear music, but it's usually not the blues. Some booths play CDs of Latin music, hip-hop, rock, or pop. There are a few musicians, perhaps a fiddler or a flute player.

Just as in the old days, you can buy nearly anything under the sun at the new Maxwell Street Market. Food vendors sell mostly Mexican food, like tacos, burritos, flautas, tamales, and fajitas, but you will still be able to find a beef sandwich or a Polish sausage.

All kinds of new and used merchandise can be purchased at bargain prices at the new Maxwell Street Market.
Photo by Karen Hanson.

Canal Street, especially near the intersection with Roosevelt Road, is a busy commercial area that has recently undergone redevelopment with large chain stores. Lots of free parking can be found on the side streets near Canal.

For the latest information about Maxwell Street, see www.maxwellstreet.org or www.maxwellstreetfoundation.org.

Muddy Waters Home

4339 S. Lake Park Avenue
Chicago

When Muddy Waters lived in the two-story brick home at 4339 S. Lake Park Avenue, the house was filled with music and musicians. Muddy used the basement for rehearsals and impromptu jams whenever musicians like Mike Bloomfield, Howlin' Wolf, and Chuck Berry visited. Muddy's band members pianist Otis Spann and harp player Paul Oscher actually lived in the basement for a time.

Muddy Waters (McKinley Morganfield) and his family moved into the house at 4339 S. Lake Park Avenue in 1954. A distinctive feature of the house was the double front door, which was covered with a decorative wrought-iron grate depicting metal figures of flamingos. Inside the living room was a small spinet piano, on which Muddy kept photos of his family along with a prominently displayed picture of Little Walter. Muddy lived in the house until 1974, when he moved his family to suburban Westmont. The day he moved out, his drummer, Willie "Big Eyes" Smith, moved in. Smith lived in the home until 1980, when he moved to a house a few doors down.

By the mid-1990s the Lake Park Avenue house had fallen into disrepair and was quietly scheduled by the City of Chicago for demolition. When Gregg Parker, founder and director of the Chicago Blues Museum, discovered that the house would be razed, he called a friend at City Hall and set in motion efforts to save it. Parker had long wanted to use the house for museum headquarters but was unable to acquire the property. Working with the Morganfield family, Parker salvaged doors, windows, and other architectural features. In the end the house was spared.

In 1999 Muddy Waters's house was marked as a culturally significant site with a Chicago Tribute Marker of Distinction. The Chicago Tribute Markers are a joint effort by the Chicago Cultural Center Foundation, the Chicago Tribune Foundation, and the Chicago Department of Cultural Affairs.

If you go: Drive by and take a look, but remember that the home is on private property.

Chicago Blues Tour

Tickets: About $25 to $30.
866/LIVEBLUES
www.chicagobluestour.com
www.bluesu.com

The Chicago Blues Tour offers fans the opportunity to tour five or six blues clubs in one evening without the worry of driving, parking, or getting lost. The bus tours venture into the South and West sides to visit clubs that may be unknown to all but the most ardent fans. These bars, like the New Apartment Lounge and the 7313 Club, usually draw their customers from the immediate neighborhood. The entertainers may be local favorites or famous names in the blues world. As always in Chicago blues clubs, it's not unusual for surprise guests to sit in with the band.

The Chicago Blues Tour meets at a central location, in this case the HotHouse. Tour-goers board the bus and may visit a half dozen different clubs in one night. *Photo by Karen Hanson.*

The tours are operated during the spring, in the pre-Chicago Blues Festival season, and in the winter, during the city's Winter Delights weekends.

Steve Pasek (a.k.a. Mr. Big) started the tours in 1990. It was his feeling that the blues clubs located outside of downtown Chicago don't always get the support they need. "We felt there was a need to support the West and South side clubs because they're the cradle of where the music's coming from," Steve explains.

Chicago Blues Tour participants are split between out-of-town tourists and Chicago-area residents and consist of couples, groups of friends, and singles. Like most blues fans, the majority are older than 30.

Tour Tips

The buses leave and return from a centrally located club designated as the hub. The HotHouse and the House of Blues have served as hubs in the past.

You will receive a map of the bus routes and pickup times. The first bus leaves at about 8 P.M. Theoretically, the buses run every 15 minutes or so until 2 A.M., but schedules are loose. You should take a few minutes to familiarize yourself with the routes to decide which clubs or acts you really want to see. It's easy to get caught up in the excitement at one club while leaving little time to spend at the others.

The Chicago Blues Tour takes fans to small clubs on the South Side, such as the 7313 Club.
Photo by Karen Hanson.

You can get off or board the bus at any club along the route. A tour guide will enter the club with a sign to announce the arrival of a bus. The ticket price includes transportation and admission to clubs. Bring extra money for drinks, tips, and souvenirs. Eat before you go. Some clubs offer a bit of catered-in food. Others have restaurants nearby, but you may not have time for a restaurant stop.

Village of Westmont

In 1974 Muddy Waters moved out of his house at 4339 S. Lake Park Avenue in Chicago and headed for the suburbs. He settled in a house at 16 W. Adams Street in Westmont. He lived here until his death in 1983.

Though smaller than his house in Chicago, Muddy's new home was just as active. As Muddy's fame spread throughout the world, he often had noted guests from both the blues and rock worlds, such as Eric Clapton, Johnny Winter, and members of the Rolling Stones.

The Village of Westmont is located south of U.S. 34 (Ogden Avenue) at Cass Avenue. The house is now a private residence.

Muddy Waters Park

Muddy Waters Park consists of a fishing pond (catch and release) on four acres of shaded, grassy land on the corner of 63rd and Williams Streets. The park was named after Muddy Waters in the early 1990s after the Westmont Park District held a naming contest. The park district selected the suggestion to name the park in honor of Muddy Waters.

Citizens of Westmont chose the name Muddy Waters Park for this four-acre fishing park.
Photo by Karen Hanson.

Honorary Muddy Waters Way

Cass Avenue, one of the main streets in Westmont, was dedicated as Honorary Muddy Waters Way in 2005. The ceremony was attended by Muddy Waters's widow, Marva, and other members of the Morganfield family.

Taste of Westmont— Muddy Waters Blues Night

The annual Taste of Westmont, a festival of food, music, and a carnival, has been held in early July since 1995. In 2005 the village officially named the final night of the festival Muddy Waters Blues Night.

The Village of Westmont has honored its most famous musical resident by naming part of Cass Avenue, the main street through town, as Honorary Muddy Waters Way.
Photo by Karen Hanson.

Chapter 5

Down-Home Blues:

Chicago Record Labels

Chicago has played a key role in blues recording since the early 1930s. Chicago was a logical place for the development of so-called race records, those labels specializing in African-American music such as gospel, jazz, and blues. Here was a significant concentration of African-Americans, both as musical talent and as a potential market for records. One of the first blues labels was

In the mid-1960s the headquarters of a dozen or more recording-industry companies—such as Chess, Vee-Jay, Crash, One-derful, ABC/Paramount, United, Bamboo, and Constellation—were located on a 15-block stretch of Michigan Avenue south of Roosevelt Road that became known as Record Row.

Bluebird, a subsidiary of RCA Victor. Beginning in 1932 producer Lester Melrose recorded Tampa Red, Big Bill Broonzy, Sonny Boy (John Lee) Williamson, and many more.

After World War II blues record labels sprang up as the demand grew. In the late 1940s and early 1950s, several small labels started up in Chicago, some of them short-lived and others destined to become powerhouses. Ora Nelle, owned by Maxwell Street merchant Bernard Abrams, recorded Little Walter, Jimmy Rogers, and Johnny Young during its brief existence in 1947. Aristocrat Records was also founded in that year, by Charles and Evelyn Aron and their partners. Within months Leonard Chess bought an interest in Aristocrat and recorded Muddy Waters's first hit, "I Can't Be Satisfied." In 1950 Leonard and his brother Phil took complete ownership of the label and renamed it Chess Records. Chess operated until 1974, during which time it (and its Checker subsidiary) issued the greatest number of significant blues recordings by any single label and contributed to the creation of rock and roll.

The J.O.B. label, founded in 1949 by Joe Brown and bluesman St. Louis Jimmy (James Oden), became one of the first African-American–owned blues labels. Brown and Oden had briefly owned Opera Records, which issued only a handful of records, including one by the ubiquitous Sunnyland Slim. J.B. Lenoir, Sunnyland Slim, John Brim, and Snooky Pryor all recorded for J.O.B. in the 1950s. The label's biggest claim to fame was Eddie Boyd, whose 1952 recording of "Five Long Years" hit number one on the R&B charts. Another significant label in the early 1950s was Chance, founded in 1950 by record maker Art Sheridan. Chance released records by Homesick James and J.B. Hutto, among others, before folding in 1954.

Ewart Abner worked on the business side of Chance from 1952 to 1954. When Chance dissolved, Abner joined the fledging Vee-Jay label. Vee-Jay (sometimes known as VJ) was founded in 1953 by Vivian Carter and her husband, Jimmy Bracken (the label was named for the initials of their first names). Vivian had been working as a DJ for a radio station in Gary, Indiana, a position she had won in a contest run by legendary Chicago blues DJ Al Benson. She and Jimmy also owned a record store in Gary. The label's first releases were of a Gary singing group called the Spaniels and by harp player Jimmy Reed. Reed, usually accompanied by guitarist Eddie Taylor, became a big seller for Vee-Jay, producing multiple hit records including "High and Lonesome," "You Don't Have to Go," and "Big Boss Man."

Abner eventually became president of Vee-Jay, and Vivian's brother, Calvin Carter, was hired on as A&R man, or producer. Through the 1960s they recorded Floyd Jones, Eddie Boyd, Billy Boy Arnold, Snooky Pryor, Big Joe Williams, and others. The label also released gospel and R&B songs, including sides by Betty Everett, the Dells (a singing group from south suburban Harvey), the Staple Singers and the Impressions, starring Jerry "Iceman" Butler (who later became a Cook County commissioner) and the young Curtis Mayfield. By the 1960s the label was crossing over into the pop charts with hits like Gene Chandler's "Duke of Oil" and the Four Seasons' "Sherry."

Vee-Jay is also famous for being the first American label to issue songs by the Beatles. The popularity of the Fab Four was just starting to spread in England in 1962 but hadn't yet made it to America. EMI, a British recording company, offered some Beatles recordings to its U.S. affiliate, Capitol, but Capitol declined. At the same time, Vee-Jay was negotiating with another EMI associate for a contract on Frank Ifield. A contract for the Beatles was thrown in with Ifield's contract. Vee-Jay released "Please, Please

Me" in 1963. While the song had been a hit in England, it didn't do much on U.S. charts. It would take some time for the Beatles to catch on in America. Meanwhile Vee-Jay was having troubles. The Four Seasons sued for nonpayment of royalties, and Ewart Abner left the company. When the Beatles finally ignited, Vee-Jay and Capitol became embroiled in a legal battle, which was settled out of court. Capitol became the Beatles' new label. Vee-Jay rehired Abner in 1965, but the label was already going down for the count. The company's finances were in disarray, and in 1966 the company declared bankruptcy.

Al Benson, DJ with WGES radio, also entered the recording industry. His first label, the Old Swing-Master, had only a brief life after its 1949 start. His second try, in 1952 with Parrot Records, was more successful. The label recorded Willie Mabon, J.B. Lenoir, John Brim, Lowell Fulson, Snooky Pryor, Dusty Brown, and Albert King. Parrot's sister label, Blue Lake, which was formed in 1954, released singles by Sunnyland Slim, Jody Williams (as Little Papa Joe), jazz pianist Ahmad Jamal, and jazz singer Joe Williams, among others. Benson sold the labels in 1956. A decade later he started yet another label, Crash, which released a single by Magic Sam and a few other songs.

Cobra Records hit the charts in 1956 with a hit record by West Side guitarist Otis Rush, "I Can't Quit You Baby." Between 1956 and 1958 the label issued singles by Rush, Magic Sam, Big Walter Horton, and Ike Turner. Louis Myers and the Aces and Morris Pejoe recorded for Cobra's ABCO subsidiary. In 1958 Buddy Guy cut his first singles, "Sit and Cry the Blues" and "Try to Quit You Baby," for Cobra's Artistic label. Cobra went out of business in 1959.

While Chess and Vee-Jay dominated the blues market through the 1960s, another Chicago blues and jazz label was coming on the scene— Delmark Records, founded by Bob Koester, who also owned the Jazz Record Mart. Two of Koester's employees, Bruce Iglauer and Michael Frank, eventually went on to create their own blues labels, Alligator Records and Earwig Music, respectively. Through the last several decades, these three labels adapted to changes in technology from vinyl to audiocassette to CD and MP3s; to shifts in the demographics of blues audiences; through ups and downs in the economy; and to the inevitable loss, one by one, of the first generation of bluesmen and women. But Delmark, Alligator, and Earwig have each played important roles in discovering new blues talent, in recording previously underrepresented artists, and in documenting and preserving the legends of the blues.

Alligator Records
www.alligator.com

Bruce Iglauer was just 23 years old when he started Alligator Records in 1971. A few years earlier, as a college student in Wisconsin, Iglauer became hooked on the blues when he saw a performance by Mississippi Fred McDowell. Soon he began hosting a blues show on his college radio station. During that time he made several trips to Chicago, where he saw blues artists like Muddy Waters, Magic Slim, Otis Rush, and Carey Bell. He also arranged a show at his college starring Howlin' Wolf and Luther Allison.

In 1970 Iglauer moved to Chicago to take a job as a shipping clerk with Delmark Records. At night he hung out at the blues clubs and soon became a fan of Hound Dog Taylor and the HouseRockers. He wanted to record Hound Dog on Delmark, but label owner Bob Koester declined. Iglauer decided to take matters into his own hands, using a $2,500 inheritance to finance the project. He brought Hound Dog Taylor, guitarist Brewer Phillips, and drummer Ted Harvey into the studio. The recording session was "fast and furious," Iglauer says. "We recorded live to two-track, mixing as we went," he recalls. "We recorded almost every song that I heard the band play live, a couple of takes each. It was cut in two nights in the studio, fueled by immense amounts of Canadian Club."

The result, *Hound Dog Taylor and the HouseRockers*, was the first record to bear the Alligator name. Iglauer made 1,000 copies and delivered them by hand to radio stations and distributors. The response was good, and on the strength of his newfound fame, Hound Dog Taylor performed festivals and colleges all over the country until his death in 1974.

Iglauer's success with his first album encouraged him to quit Delmark to devote himself full-time to Alligator, which he operated out of his apartment. Finances were tough at first. For a while he was able to produce only one album a year. A big break came in 1975, when Koko Taylor's first album for Alligator, *I Got What It Takes*, was nominated for a Grammy award. In 1976 the label received a second Grammy nomination, for *Beware of the Dog*, a Hound Dog Taylor album released shortly after his death.

The next big step for Alligator was the signing of Albert Collins in 1978. His first album for the label, *Ice Pickin'*, won a Grammy nomination. That year Alligator also began the "Living Chicago Blues" series. The four-album series of compilations boosted the careers of established artists such as Jimmy Johnson, Carey Bell, Lonnie Brooks, Eddie Shaw, Pinetop Perkins,

Detroit Junior, Luther "Guitar Jr." Johnson, and Magic Slim to national prominence and gave young harp player Billy Branch widespread exposure. *Living Chicago Blues, Vol. 1* received a Grammy nomination.

In 1982 Clifton Chenier's zydeco album, *I'm Here*, received Alligator's first Grammy win. A few years later Alligator signed several artists with a blues-rock sound, such as Roy Buchanan, Lonnie Mack, and Johnny Winter. Winter, who already had a strong rock following, sought out Alligator because he wanted to record the blues.

"I think Johnny in particular had a lot of effect bringing rock fans to the blues, but that was when he first started out on Columbia," Iglauer says. "When he came to Alligator, his motive was to make pure blues records not intended to cross over."

Iglauer downplays the idea of blues benefiting from crossing over to the rock world. "To me, crossover happens only when an artist reaches heavy radio exposure," he says. "I don't think the exposure received by our artists has brought a lot of rock fans to the blues. I think a whole lot of people have discovered our artists and have fallen in love with them because they are soulful and bluesy."

By 1985 Alligator had moved out of Iglauer's house and into its own offices. The label, by this time producing about ten albums a year, had seven employees and its own promotion, publicity, and marketing departments. It also had international distribution to Europe, South America, and Japan.

Alligator celebrated its 20th anniversary in 1991 by issuing a compilation, *The Alligator Records 20th Anniversary Collection*, featuring songs by Hound Dog Taylor, James Cotton, Koko Taylor, Kenny Neal, Albert Collins, Johnny "Clyde" Copeland, and more. Two years later the label released its first CD by Luther Allison, *Soul Fixin' Man*. Through the remainder of the 1990s and into the new century, Alligator continued to add new artists, such as Shemekia Copeland, Coco Montoya, John Jackson, the Holmes Brothers, Marcia Ball, and Mavis Staples.

After more than 30 years in business, Alligator Records has grown to become one of the largest blues labels in the world. To date the label has issued more than 200 albums by most of the major contemporary legends of the blues. Alligator's releases range from classic blues artists like James Cotton and Carey Bell to contemporary blues-rock performers like Coco Montoya and Tinsley Ellis to the gospel-tinged blues of Mavis Staples. As of early 2006 Alligator's artists have won two Grammy awards, received more than 30 Grammy nominations, and been honored with some 70 W.C. Handy Awards.

Now Alligator is facing new challenges as the face of the blues changes, and the label searches for young blues artists to carry forward the music. "I feel it's my responsibility to be on the cutting edge of bringing new artists to public attention," Iglauer says. "However, the quality of younger artists that I'm hearing isn't as good as I'd ideally hope for. So the only younger artist I've signed in the last few years is Shemekia Copeland, who is terrific. Otherwise, I'm still looking for artists that I need to assure the future of the blues."

Alligator Records takes its name from a nickname of its founder, Bruce Iglauer. He was dubbed Alligator for his habit of clicking his teeth together to play the drum parts while listening to music. He liked the word because it evoked the South, birthplace of the blues, and because it sounds dangerous. "I hoped it would convince my distributors to pay me," he jokes. "Plus, it sounds a little like Iglauer, my unpronounceable last name."

Delmark Records

www.delmark.com

Delmark Records made history in 1965 when Junior Wells stepped into the studio to record *Hoodoo Man Blues*. "It was the first time a working blues band went into the studio to record an album," says Bob Koester, owner of Delmark. "I didn't know I was making a precedent."

The band consisted of Junior Wells on vocals and harp, Buddy Guy on guitar (at first billed as "Friendly Chap" due to contractual conflicts), Jack Meyer on bass, and Billy Warren on drums. Junior had the entire album planned out. "All I did was watch," Koester says. "Junior did the record. It was just wham, bam, thank you ma'am."

Koester founded Delmark in 1953 while he was still a student at St. Louis University. He first started recording Dixieland jazz in 1953 as a college student studying film in St. Louis. Koester's first blues recording was of pianist Speckled Red in 1956, when Koester worked at the Blue Note Record Shop in St. Louis.

In 1958, shortly after moving to Chicago, Koester recorded Big Joe Williams. Big Joe went into the studio and, within an hour or so, cut enough songs for three or four LPs, Koester recalls. "He knew every damn tune ever written."

Delmark released Big Joe's *Piney Woods Blues* in 1961 as part of the "Background of the Blues" series aimed at jazz fans because Koester wasn't sure there was a market for the blues. He would soon find out otherwise.

The next important blues recording for Delmark came a year later, when Koester tracked down Sleepy John Estes in Brownsville, Tennessee. Estes had been away from the music world for a couple of decades and was rumored to be dead, mostly on the basis of Big Bill Broonzy, who claimed Estes was already an old man when he met him in 1912. But one day a film-maker working on a jazz film came into Koester's record store to talk to Joe Segal (future owner of the Jazz Showcase club) and mentioned that he had met Sleepy John in Brownsville. Koester wrote to Estes but got no reply, so he made his first trip to the South. It was in the early days of the civil rights movement, and racial tensions were high. It had to have been a strange sight to see a white man from Chicago walking around African-American neigh-borhoods. Still, Koester kept asking around until he finally found Sleepy John living in very poor conditions.

To entice Sleepy John to come north, Koester had arranged some gigs for him and harp player Hammie Nixon at colleges in Indiana, Illinois, and Missouri. Estes agreed, but when it was time to go, Koester realized he had no money for bus tickets; he had spent all his cash on clothing for Estes and his family. He called home, and Joe Segal wired Koester money that he borrowed from the clothing store next door. One of their stops on the trip north was a gig at the University of Illinois at Urbana-Champaign. There Sleepy John was interviewed by a fledging reporter at the U of I student newspaper, future film critic Roger Ebert.

Once in Chicago, Estes recorded his first LP for Delmark, *The Legend of Sleepy John Estes*. In the album liner notes, Koester revealed a coin-cidence: Sleepy John discovered his brother Sam was working at the cloth-ing store next door to Delmark.

Throughout the 1960s Delmark recorded many blues legends who had been idle or unrecorded for years, such as pianist Roosevelt Sykes and Arthur "Big Boy" Crudup, who, a decade or so earlier, had been a major influence on Elvis Presley. Then there was Yank Rachell's *Mandolin Blues*, which brought together Yank with Sleepy John Estes, Big Joe Williams, Hammie Nixon, and young guitarist Mike Bloomfield. During that time Koester and his friends would make the circuit of the West Side clubs to hear Magic Sam, Jimmy Dawkins, Mighty Joe Young, and Luther Allison. All recorded for Delmark.

As extensive and groundbreaking as Delmark's blues recordings are, the jazz catalog is even more impressive. In recording both blues and jazz, Delmark has played a vital role in documenting the work of musicians whose talent and innovation deserved recognition. Delmark, for example, recorded the first records of most of the musicians in the Association for the Advancement of Creative Musicians (AACM). This group of avant-garde jazz musicians included Joseph Jarman, Muhal Richards Abrams, Roscoe Mitchell, Kalaparusha Maurice McIntyre, and Anthony Braxton. Koester explains, "I felt it was really important to cover the AACM activity because no one else was doing it."

In recent years Delmark has continued to record Chicago-area artists meriting more national acclaim, including Lurrie Bell, Willie Kent, Detroit Junior, Dave Specter, Jimmy Burns, Shirley Johnson, Zora Young, and Big Time Sarah. The label has also given the opportunity for longtime sidemen to record under their own name: James Wheeler, who played for years with Willie Kent; Michael Coleman, one-time guitarist for James Cotton; and bass player Aron Burton, who once played in the Albert Collins band.

Delmark's newest venture is a series of music DVDs called "Where the Music Lives." The concept is to record video and audio of musicians performing in historic places. The project is a labor of love for Koester, whose first ambition was to be a filmmaker. But Koester is serving in an executive producer role; for the actual filming and production he has recruited his younger brother, Tom, whose professional film credits include working on shows like *Cops* and *LAPD*. Artists featured in the "Where the Music Lives" series include percussionist Kahil El Zabar performing in an art gallery, saxophonist Fred Anderson at the Velvet Lounge, Lurrie Bell accompanying blues singer Tail Dragger at a West Side Club, and Mississippi Heat playing at Rosa's Lounge.

Earwig Music
www.earwigmusic.com

Three men from the Mississippi Delta inspired Michael Frank to form Earwig Music in 1978. For several years Frank had been trekking regularly to Mississippi, exploring the roots of the music he had come to love. There he became a fan of guitarist Big Jack Johnson, drummer Sam Carr, and harp player Frank Frost, the trio known as the Jelly Roll Kings.

Frank had been working part-time for Bob Koester at Jazz Record

Mart since 1972, when he moved to Chicago from his native Pittsburgh. Koester, owner of Delmark Records, encouraged Frank to record the Jelly Roll Kings and start up his own label. *Rockin' the Juke Joint Down* was issued in 1979. The album was the first recording in ten years for Frank Frost.

Like many of his generation, Michael Frank was turned on to the blues by British rock bands like the Animals, the Rolling Stones, and the Yardbirds. He read the album liner notes to find other recordings by bluesmen like Willie Dixon, Howlin' Wolf, and Muddy Waters. When he attended a Muddy Waters show at a jazz festival in Pittsburgh in 1965, he was hooked on the blues.

While still in college, Frank started buying every blues record he could get his hands on in order to learn about the music, the musicians, the culture, and the history of the blues. On his first trip to Chicago in 1970, he went to Theresa's Lounge on the South Side, where Junior Wells was playing. He was thrilled to meet bluesmen like Lefty Dizz, James Cotton, and Buddy Guy.

Soon after Frank moved to Chicago, he met and befriended David Honeyboy Edwards, Lester Davenport, and Sunnyland Slim. During this time Frank immersed himself in the blues, took a part-time job at Jazz Record Mart, and taught himself to play harmonica.

Frank was convinced that other people should hear the blues, and he wanted to record history as it was happening. After the Jelly Roll Kings album, Frank brought together another group of veteran blues performers: Honeyboy Edwards, Sunnyland Slim, Big Walter Horton, Floyd Jones, and Kansas City Red. He called the resulting album *Old Friends*.

Over the years Earwig has also recorded Louis Myers, Jimmy Dawkins, Lester Davenport, John Primer, H-Bomb Ferguson, Aron Burton, Lovie Lee, Homesick James, Little Willie Anderson, and Big Leon Brooks. Frank also acquired masters of recordings of Sunnyland Slim and Little Brother Montgomery. In addition, Earwig has given opportunities to contemporary performers whose music was steeped in tradition, such as Li'l Ed and Dave Weld, Johnny "Yard Dog" Jones, Liz Mandville Greeson, and Rob Stone.

Vocalist and keyboardist Johnny Drummer came to Earwig in an unusual way. One night Frank was hanging out at Lee's Unleaded Blues, where Drummer has held down a weekend gig since the 1990s. During a break Johnny invited Frank out to the parking lot, to his car, to listen to a cassette tape of an LP he had recorded in the 1980s on his own label. Frank was impressed with what he heard, and Drummer's debut CD, *It's So Nice*, was issued in 1999. Drummer went on to record a second album, *Unleaded Blues*, in 2001.

Another highlight came in 1997 when Chicago Review Press published Honeyboy Edwards's autobiography, *The World Don't Owe Me Nothing*. Honeyboy had told the stories of his life over several years to Michael Frank and Janis Martinson, who transcribed and edited them into book form. To accompany the book, Honeyboy, backed by Carey Bell on harp, recorded a live CD for Earwig.

These days Frank continues to manage and perform with Honeyboy Edwards.

Chapter 6

Just Wanna Play My Axe:

Blues Jams

The blues is spontaneous and improvisational, and that's what makes the blues jam a time-honored tradition. At any blues show, it's not unusual for famous musicians in the house to be invited onstage to play with the band. At a jam, all musicians, professional and amateur alike, get a chance to perform.

Professionals view jams as an opportunity to try out new licks, songs, and instruments. For example, a harp player may join a jam to practice his guitar skills. A jam is also a great place for pros to network with other musicians with the possibility of landing a spot in a band. Sometimes entire bands show up at jams, hoping to impress a club owner for a future gig.

For amateur musicians, the jam can be a chance to learn from more seasoned musicians and, in some cases, from the pros. Some talented amateurs are content with being "weekend warriors"—they just want to have fun playing the blues with a band. Others hope to gain the skills and experience necessary to turn pro. Many blues players have joined professional bands after honing their musicianship at jam sessions.

For the audience, a jam can be an exciting evening. There's no telling who will show up. Famous musicians often attend jams to support their friends or join in the fun. Out-of-town blues musicians who are playing gigs in Chicago may drop in at a jam on their night off. And at most places, there's a core of capable, regular jammers who make the evening enjoyable for everyone.

Most jams begin with a set by the host band. Then the host calls one or more musicians, even entire bands, onstage. It's necessary to have a rhythm section—drums, bass, and rhythm guitar—onstage at all times to lay down the beat and maintain the structure of the song. Other instruments,

Steve Arvey (singing) takes a turn leading the jam at the Harlem Avenue Lounge in Berwyn.
Photo by Karen Hanson.

such as harp, keyboards, guitars, horns, and voice, can be added in various combinations. The host has a responsibility to balance the band instrumentally and provide a complementary mix of styles and abilities.

Blues jams generally fall into three categories: pro jams, mixed jams, and amateur jams. The larger blues clubs generally hold pro jams; nearly all the musicians are professionals—mostly sidemen but sometimes headliners. Smaller clubs may mix pros and amateurs. The jams at neighborhood bars tend to draw mostly amateurs, although the host is usually a pro, and it's common for other pros to show up.

Jam Tips for Musicians

- Bring your own instrument.
- Match your skill level with the kind of jam you're attending. Some jams encourage beginners; others prefer pros.
- Sign up with your name and the instrument you want to play, even if you know the host.
- If you don't know the host, introduce yourself.

- Wait until you're called up to go onstage. Be patient if you're not called until late.
- Make sure you're tuned up before you go onstage. Bring a tuner.
- Learn to play the standard blues tunes, rhythms, and keys. Blues jammers should know what to do when the bandleader calls out a 12-bar blues in A, for example.
- If it's called a blues jam, stick to the blues. Try out other music styles at other kinds of jams.
- Play rhythm until the bandleader indicates you should solo; then watch for the signal to stop soloing.
- Be supportive of the efforts of other musicians, even if they're not perfect. If you make a mistake, keep playing. If someone else makes a mistake, keep playing.
- Keep an open mind. Listen to what the other musicians are doing. You may learn something.
- Respect the amplifiers and equipment of other musicians. Ask before you use anything that doesn't belong to you. Don't readjust the settings on the amp or crank it up to the highest levels.
- Don't get drunk.
- Be courteous to the audience. They're there to be entertained, and in many cases, they paid to get in.
- If you're a professional or semipro, bring along business cards with a current phone number.

Jam Tips for the Audience

- Be supportive. Applaud and cheer, especially for amateurs. It takes a lot of courage to get up onstage and perform.
- Be patient. Sometimes the musicians will have to huddle between songs to talk about keys and rhythms. Remember, they don't have a set list.
- Be forgiving. Someone may hit a clunker or miss a cue. There may be an amateur musician onstage who has little experience playing with a band.
- Be open to new sounds. Some jammers like to experiment. Go with the flow.
- Be accepting of old sounds. Inexperienced musicians can learn a lot by playing the old standards. Besides, because band personnel changes in a jam, even if you hear "Stormy Monday" twice in one night, the two versions are likely to be very different.

Blues Jams

Here's a list of popular blues jams in the city and suburbs. As always, circumstances may change or vary, so you might want to call before you go. Cover charges may apply.

SUNDAY

Backporch Stage at the House of Blues
329 N. Dearborn Street
312/923-2000
9:30 P.M. until closing

Harp player Matthew Skoller hosts.

Dell Rhea's Chicken Basket
645 Joliet Road (Interstate 55 at Route 83)
Willowbrook
630/325-0780
6 to 10 P.M.

Diners munch on fried chicken and coleslaw while the jam goes on in the corner of the lounge section of Dell Rhea's Chicken Basket. All skill levels are welcome.

Jimmy's Woodlawn Tap
1172 E. 55th Street
773/643-5516
4 to 8 P.M.

The back bar in this Hyde Park pub is deserted on Sunday night except for the musicians who come to jam. The focus is on traditional Chicago-style blues, and the atmosphere is very informal. There's a core of regulars, but newcomers are welcome. Serving as one of the hosts is drummer Steve Cushing, who also hosts the radio show *Blues Before Sunrise*.

MONDAY

Buddy Guy's Legends

754 S. Wabash Avenue
312/427-0333
www.buddyguys.com
9 P.M. until closing

The pro jam at Buddy Guy's Legends draws some of the best musicians in the city and occasional out-of-town guests as well. Expect surprises.

The New Checkerboard Lounge

5201 S. Harper Avenue
773/684-1472
7 P.M. until closing

The Old Checkerboard was famous for impromptu jams. Who knows what will happen on jam night at the New Checkerboard?

TUESDAY

Bill's Blues Bar

1029 Davis Street
Evanston
847/424-9800
www.billsbluesbar.com
8:30 P.M. until closing

The jam at Bill's Blues Bar is a hit with both pros and amateurs. Well-known musicians who have dropped by include Li'l Ed Williams, Chico Banks, Chainsaw Dupont, Tommy McCracken, L.V. Banks, and Byther Smith. Aron Burton often hosts.

Fantasy Lounge

4400 N. Elston Avenue
773/685-8083
9:30 P.M. until closing

This jam is so popular it takes place three days a week: Tuesday, Wednesday, and Thursday. The atmosphere is casual and friendly. All skill levels are welcome.

FitzGerald's, in the Sidebar

6615 Roosevelt Road
Berwyn
708/788-2118
www.fitzgeraldsnightclub.com
9 P.M. until closing

The Sidebar, the smaller lounge across from the main venue, provides a cozy setting for an open mike.

Gallery Cabaret

2020 N. Oakley Avenue
773/489-5471
9 P.M. until closing

Fish & the Bluefins host this open jam.

Underground Wonder Bar

10 E. Walton Street
312/266-7761
www.undergroundwonderbar.com
1:30 to 3:30 A.M.

Night owls will enjoy the pro jam at this eccentric, eclectic, electric club that mixes blues, jazz, R&B, and what have you.

WEDNESDAY

B.L.U.E.S.

2519 N. Halsted Street
773/528-1012
www.chicagobluesbar.com
9:30 P.M. until closing

The pro jam on the tiny stage at B.L.U.E.S. is held on the first and third Wednesday of each month. Big Ray often hosts.

Carter's Place

13 W. 9th Street
Lockport
815/838-7811
8:30 P.M. until closing

This long-standing weekly blues jam begins with a set by the house band, New Orleans Beau. Arrive early to sign up. Everyone is welcome.

Fantasy Lounge

(See Tuesday)

THURSDAY

Fantasy Lounge

(See Tuesday)

Harlem Avenue Lounge

3701 S. Harlem Avenue
Berwyn
708/484-3610
www.harlemavenuelounge.com
8:30 P.M. until closing

The jam at the Harlem Avenue Lounge is one of the longest-running and most popular jams in the Chicago area. Musicians are a nice mix of professionals and amateurs. The host varies from week to week, and surprise guests are common. The atmosphere is informal, friendly, and supportive. No cover.

Lane's Lounge

3500 N. Southport Avenue
773/472-6030
8 P.M. until closing

This blues jam is open to all musicians.

Red Line Tap

7006 N. Glenwood Avenue
773/338-9862
9 P.M.

Sign-up begins at 8 P.M. at the Red Line Tap, which is adjacent to the Heartland Café. No cover.

Rosa's Lounge

3240 W. Armitage Avenue
773/342-0452
9:30 P.M.

The pro jam at Rosa's is often hosted by James Wheeler, Ariyo, and Tony Mangiullo.

Chapter 7

Blues All Around Me:

Blues Radio

Chicago has always been a good town for blues radio. From the 1940s through the '70s and later, blues music could be heard on stations like WVON and WGES in Chicago, WOPA in Oak Park, and WBEE in suburban Harvey.

In the early days, blues DJs did more than just spin records. Al Benson, who worked for WGES from the late 1940s through the '60s, not only was a dominant force on the air but was also actively involved in booking, promoting, and recording blues artists. Among other pursuits, he owned Parrot Records, a label that issued records from John Brim, J.B. Lenoir, Dusty Brown, and other blues greats. Sam Evans, also a WGES personality, owned record shops in Chicago.

In the mid-1950s, Big Bill Hill started broadcasting for WOPA in Oak Park. His live broadcasts from clubs like Silvio's and the Copa Cobana (which he owned) introduced many listeners to the blues. Hill was also a manager and promoter. Through the 1960s and early '70s, it was WVON radio, 1450 AM, where people tuned to hear the blues and other African-American music. The station began in 1963 when Leonard and Phil Chess of Chess Records bought a 1,000-watt radio station, WHFC, 1450 AM. They changed the call letters to WVON—"Voice of the Negro"—and went on the air on April 1, 1963. The original "Good Guys" crew consisted of Franklin McCarthy, E. Rodney Jones, Herb Kent (who once worked for WGES), Wesley South, and Pervis Spann, "The Blues Man." Over the years other radio personalities to join the station included Bill "Butterball" Crane, Don Cornelius, Ric Ricardo, Richard Pegue, Ed Maloney, and McKie Fitzhugh (an alumnus of WOPA and WGES).

Blues DJ Big Bill Hill (center), of WOPA radio in Oak Park, dines with B.B. King (left) and singer Fontella Bass.
Copyright and courtesy of the Chicago Blues Museum. The Chicago Blues Museum is a registered trademark.

"They became giants in the blues world and in the radio world," says singer and comedian Manual Arrington, who worked for WVON for nine years beginning in 1969. He and Herb Kent, now a member of the Radio Hall of Fame, went on in 1974 to host a show on WTTW television called *Our People*, focusing on issues in the African-American community.

After Leonard Chess died in 1969, WVON was sold to Globetrotter Communications and moved to 1390 AM, with a stronger, 5,000-watt signal. In the mid-1970s station management hired new hosts and the Good Guys went their separate ways. Then in 1979 Pervis Spann and Wesley South established Midway Broadcasting and bought the 1450 AM frequency. They opened as WXOL but changed in 1984 to WVON when the call letters became available.

In 1986 the format changed to talk radio, and Voice of the Negro became Voice of the Nation and Talk of Chicago. WVON is now owned and operated by Pervis Spann's daughter, Melody Spann Cooper. Today WVON is Chicago's number one talk radio station in the African-American community.

Today's Blues Radio

Today the blues receives almost no airplay in mainstream radio programs. However, you can find blues specialty programs on both public and commercial radio stations in the Chicago area.

SUNDAY

Blues Before Sunrise
WBEZ, 91.5 FM
Early Sunday morning, midnight to 5 A.M.
www.chicagopublicradio.org
www.bluesbeforesunrise.com

Note
Chicago Public Radio announced in April 2006 that WBEZ will discontinue music programming in early 2007.

Blues Before Sunrise is dedicated to the first 50 years of recorded blues, from 1920 to 1970. "I don't play anything that's new," says host and producer Steve Cushing, who prefers to think of his five-hour show as a program about African-American musical heritage. Although Cushing says the show's overnight time slot, from midnight to 5 A.M, does "wicked things to your sleep schedule," he believes the early morning hours are the perfect time for a show about the roots of the blues.

Songs on *Blues Before Sunrise* range from early blues and jazz to gospel and soul. Some artists may be well known, such as Memphis Minnie or Sonny Boy (John Lee) Williamson I; other names have been all but forgotten over the years. It's been Cushing's mission since 1980 to give voice once again to those sounds and to the people who created them.

The songs are all part of his personal collection of blues and other African-American recordings that he's been amassing since he was a teenager. He owns the entire catalog of the Document label, which has released CDs of nearly every prewar blues recording in chronological order. Cushing estimates that about 85 to 90 percent of the songs he plays are on CD; the rest are on LP. Only rarely does he play one of the 2,500 or so 78 records he owns.

Cushing started playing the blues on the radio in 1972 when he was at Columbia College in Chicago. He produced the *Urban Blues Show* on the college's radio station until 1975. From 1977 to 1980 he hosted the *Blues Segment* on Triton College radio. Later that year *Blues Before Sunrise* debuted on WBEZ (91.5), Chicago Public Radio, where Cushing also worked as an engineer. The show became syndicated in 1990.

In his first few programs, Cushing played down-home blues like Muddy Waters and Jimmy Reed, with a little R&B mixed in. He discovered his show was reaching a demographic that had long been overlooked.

"When I first went on the air in 1980, a lot of the stuff hadn't been heard on the air for 20 years," Cushing recalls. "It was welcomed by black seniors." Many of them contacted Cushing to request songs and artists they wanted to hear. As a result, Cushing learned about music he had never known and his tastes expanded. While he still loves the deep blues, he also appreciates other kinds of African-American music.

Cushing also frequently airs interviews he has conducted. In addition to learning and educating others, Cushing's interviews also serve to document and archive people who have created and contributed to the blues. "I made it my mission to seek out the lesser-known names," Cushing explains.

Some of the artists he has interviewed include John and Grace Brim, Billy Boy Arnold, Fred Below, Odie Payne, Earl Phillips, S.P. Leary, Leonard "Baby Doo" Caston, Little Willie Littlefield, Blind John Davis, Percy Mayfield, Homer Harris, Robert Nighthawk, Mississippi John Hurt, and Jody Williams. He has also interviewed people who have contributed to the history of the blues in other ways, such as researcher and writer Gayle Dean Wardlow and Bob Koester, owner of Delmark Records and Jazz Record Mart.

Cushing's favorite interview was with famed singer Alberta Hunter, whom he describes as having a "sparkplug of a personality." Ms. Hunter had just been released from the hospital, and she was in a good mood, Cushing recalls. Although she had been discouraged from giving interviews, Cushing persuaded her to talk with him by impressing her with his rare knowledge of her music and her contemporaries.

"You're the only person left alive who's familiar with the classic blues singers," he told her, and he rattled off a litany of names. "Every time I mentioned a name, her eyes lit up," he says.

"You are speaking names I haven't heard in 20 years," she told him.

Blues Before Sunrise is still broadcast by WBEZ, but Cushing is no longer with the station. He now produces the show independently in his home studio. Cushing receives no financial support from Chicago Public

Radio but finds all underwriting for production and distribution costs himself. *Blues Before Sunrise* is distributed to more than 75 stations nationwide. The Web site links to station Web sites that offer live audio feed.

Cushing and *Blues Before Sunrise* received the Blues Foundation's Keeping the Blues Alive Award in 1998.

Paul Parello's Blues Power

WRMN, 1410 AM
Elgin
Sunday, 10 P.M. to midnight
www.wrmn1410.com
www.chicagobluesman.com

Paul Parello's weekly *Blues Power* radio show features in-studio performances and phone interviews in addition to the latest blues releases. He also hosts a blues show on cable access available on Comcast (check your local listings), with interviews, CD reviews, information on blues history, and performances. The *Blues Power* Web site offers live streaming audio, photos, playlists, and a discussion forum.

MONDAY

Blue Midnight

WPNA, 1490 AM
Early Monday morning, midnight to 5 A.M.
www.wpna1490am.com
www.bluemidnight.net

John Gorny has been hosting *Blue Midnight* since 1987. In the 1950s, 1490 on the AM dial was the home of WOPA, the station of blues DJ Big Bill Hill. Today the station is owned by the Polish National Alliance and specializes (but not exclusively) in Polish-language broadcasts and Polish-American interests.

Blues Breakers
WXRT, 93.1 FM
Monday, 9 to 10 P.M.
www.wxrt.com

Blues Breakers hit the air in the summer of 1984 with a mix of new songs, recordings by blues legends, and previews of live shows. Host Tom Marker, who holds down a regular 8 P.M. to midnight slot on WXRT, emcees acts at the Petrillo stage during the Chicago Blues Festival. Marker also occasionally emcees other live blues shows sponsored by XRT.

WXRT has hosted and recorded live performances by such artists as Willie Dixon, John Lee Hooker, Buddy Guy, Johnny Winter, and Taj Mahal. These recordings have been donated to the Chicago Blues Archives at the Chicago Public Library.

In 1999 the Blues Foundation honored *Blues Breakers* with a Keeping the Blues Alive Award.

THURSDAY

Hambone's Blues Party
WDCB, 90.9 FM
Thursday, 10 P.M. to midnight
www.wdcb.org

Hambone's Blues Party broadcasts a mix of contemporary blues, classic R&B, jump blues, and soul. The host is Scott Hammer (a.k.a. Hambone).

SATURDAY

Beale Street Caravan
WDCB, 90.9 FM
Saturday, 6 to 7 P.M.
www.wdcb.org
www.bealestreetcaravan.com

Produced in Memphis, *Beale Street Caravan* presents live performances recorded in various venues in Memphis and other sites. Each week focuses on a different blues artist with performances and interviews. The show also presents live performances from blues festivals and special events like the W.C. Handy Awards.

Blues Edition
WDCB, 90.9 FM
Saturday, 7 to 9 P.M.
www.wdcb.org

Host Greg Freerksen plays new releases and classic Chicago blues recordings. On the air since 1977, *Blues Edition* is the only locally produced show in WDCB's Saturday night blues lineup. The show has featured interviews with blues artists ranging from Lonnie Brooks to James Solberg to Henry Butler.

Blues from the Red Rooster Lounge
WDCB, 90.9 FM
Saturday, 9 to 10 P.M.
www.wdcb.org

The Red Rooster Lounge has broadcast from KBCO, 97.3 FM, in Boulder, Colorado, since April 1985. The show is hosted by the Rooster (Cary Wolfson), founder of *Blues Access* magazine, which was published bimonthly until 2002. The Rooster has been twice honored by the Blues Foundation with W.C. Handy Keeping the Blues Alive Awards.

Comin' Home
WBEZ, 91.5 FM
Saturday, 9 P.M. to midnight
www.chicagopublicradio.org

Niles Frantz hosts and produces *Comin' Home*, which has been on the air since 1996. Frantz also writes for numerous blues publications and emcees the annual Poconos Blues Festival in Pennsylvania. He serves on the nominating committee for the W.C. Handy National Blues Awards.

On the Web site, you can listen to the show live, view playlists of past shows, and see lists of Frantz's favorite CDs as well as of books and articles about the blues. You can also listen to archived interviews that originally aired on *Comin' Home* and *Eight Forty-Eight*, Chicago Public Radio's morning show.

Chapter 8

They'll Play the Blues For You:

Blues Artists

Chicago boasts more blues musicians than any other city in the world. Many of the musicians who moved to Chicago from the Mississippi Delta and other Southern regions—those who helped shape the Chicago blues sound—are still performing regularly. Pinetop Perkins, David Honeyboy Edwards, and Homesick James, all in their 90s, are still active on the blues scene. Elder statesmen like Lonnie Brooks, Eddy Clearwater, and Jimmy Johnson play the blues in much the same way as they did 40 or 50 years ago. Moreover, the musicians who played in the bands of legends like Muddy Waters and Jimmy Reed, such as John Primer, Hubert Sumlin, Willie "Big Eyes" Smith, and many more, have stepped up to lead their own bands.

The W.C. Handy (or Handy) Awards are given annually by the Blues Foundation to recognize excellence in blues performances and recordings. The awards are presented during the Blues Music Awards ceremony each May in Memphis. The first Handys were awarded in 1980. For information, see the Blues Foundation Web site (www.blues.org).

It's always been a tradition in the blues to pass the music from one generation to the next, and that's what has happened in Chicago. A long list of musicians learned the blues from their fathers, brothers, and uncles. Still longer is the list of musicians who learned the music and paid their dues in the bands of veteran blues players. Even as a younger generation reaches maturity, new blues bands and performers come onto the scene.

Chicago blues artists are also among the most accomplished in the world. Most tour around the world and have recorded multiple CDs. A great number have received W.C. Handy Awards, Grammy Awards, and other major honors.

But the blues tends to be a specialized musical genre. Oftentimes visitors coming to Chicago or novice blues fans are not familiar with the performers by name. These biographies will acquaint fans with more than 80 major blues musicians who live and work in the Chicago area. Listing every blues musician living and working in Chicago would require a second volume of this book, so this chapter offers a sampling of active and well-known artists who live and work in Chicago today. Each profile contains biographical information and a list of selected recordings. A few longer profiles based on interviews represent a cross section of veteran players, younger players, bandleaders, sidemen, and vocalists.

Linsey Alexander
Guitar
www.linseyalexander.com

Veteran guitarist Linsey Alexander, the "Hoochie Man," plays classic Chicago blues spiced up with the occasional joke or double entendre. Watch him take his guitar for a crowd walk-through, where he'll stop often to flirt with the pretty women. Born in Mississippi, Alexander grew up in Memphis, where he learned to play guitar when he received one from a family friend. In 1959 he pawned the guitar and headed to Chicago. These days Alexander is one of the hardest-working bluesmen in the city, appearing as many as six nights a week at Chicago clubs.

Music
• *Someone's Cookin' in My Kitchen* (2003)

Billy Boy Arnold
Harmonica, vocals

Billy Boy Arnold ranks among the legends of the golden era of Chicago blues. As a teen, he learned harmonica from Sonny Boy (John Lee) Williamson, recorded with Bo Diddley, and performed frequently with guitarist Jody Williams. Yet Arnold's music stands firmly in the present. Within the last decade, he's recorded a succession of critically acclaimed CDs, raising his stature as the elder statesman of Chicago harmonica.

Arnold was born in Chicago on September 16, 1935, to parents originally from Georgia. He grew up listening to the blues and became a big fan of Sonny Boy (John Lee) Williamson I. In 1948, at the age of 12, he tracked down Sonny Boy at his home, and

Photo by Chuck Winans (pipphotography.com).

Sonny Boy gave young Billy several harmonica lessons. The budding friendship was cut short when Sonny Boy was murdered in June of that year.

However, Arnold was already on his way to success. He was only 17 years old when he first went into the studio to record "I Ain't Got No Money" for the Cool label. His name was listed as Billy Boy on the record, and the nickname stuck.

About the same time, Arnold met Elias McDaniel, soon to be known as Bo Diddley. Bo helped Arnold make an amplifier from an orange crate, and the two played regularly on Maxwell Street. It was during this time that the characteristic "Bo Diddley beat" developed.

In 1955 the two had a recording date with Chess Records. Arnold was to accompany Bo Diddley on "Bo Diddley" and "I'm a Man" and then record a song under his own name. But after backing Diddley, Arnold got the impression that Leonard Chess didn't like him, so he left Chess and went down the street to the Vee-Jay label to record "I Wish You Would." Arnold quickly recorded several more sides for Vee-Jay, including "I Ain't Got You," "She's Fine," and "Prisoner's Plea."

Arnold's 1963 debut album, *More Blues on the South Side*, was issued by the British label Prestige. But the 1970s and '80s were a slow period for Chicago blues artists, so Arnold took a job as a Chicago bus driver and a truant/parole officer for the state of Illinois. Meanwhile Arnold's songs were made popular by British rock bands. The Yardbirds (featuring Eric Clapton) covered "I Wish You Would" in 1964, and Eric Burdon and the Animals did a version of "I Ain't Got You."

In 1992 Arnold recorded an aptly titled comeback album, *Back Where I Belong*. The album was well received and was followed by several other critically acclaimed CDs. *El Dorado Cadillac* and *Boogie 'N Shuffle* both received W.C. Handy Award nominations. Arnold was also nominated for Best Instrumentalist—Harmonica in 1996.

Arnold rarely plays Chicago clubs, but he performs at festivals all over the world.

Music

- *Chicago Blues Harp* (P-Vine, 2003)—with Snooky Pryor
- *Boogie 'N Shuffle* (Stony Plain, 2001)
- *Live at the Venue* (Catfish UK, 2000)
- *Blowin' the Blues Away* (Culture Press, 1998)
- *El Dorado Cadillac* (Alligator, 1995)
- *Ten Million Dollars* (Evidence, 1995)
- *Going to Chicago* (Testament, 1995)
- *Back Where I Belong* (Alligator, 1993)
- *More Blues on the South Side* (OBC, 1993)—originally released in 1963

Steve Arvey
Guitar
www.stevearvey.com

Steve Arvey learned guitar while in college in Florida after a friend turned him on to the music of Robert Johnson, Lead Belly, and other country bluesmen. During that time he met Barrelhouse Chuck Goering, now a Chicago pianist, who was then playing with a blind saxophonist named Robert Hunter. Arvey joined Hunter's band, and in 1979 he met Bo Diddley. Bo taught Arvey to play bass and hired him for his backing band. In 1981 Arvey formed his own band called West Side Heat. The band toured for the next ten years. In the 1990s Arvey worked as a street musician and played mostly acoustic blues, rock, and Irish music at clubs throughout Chicago. Arvey has also worked with Blues in the Schools.

Music

- *Soul of a Man* (Mad, 2002)
- *It's a Fine Line* (Mad, 2001)
- *Pass the Hat* (1998)—with Kraig Kenning
- *Best from the Vault* (1999)

Chico Banks
Guitar
www.chicobanks.com

The high-energy blues of Chico Banks is inspired by funk, R&B, and rock. The mixture comes naturally for the young blues guitarist who grew up on Chicago's West Side.

Vernon "Chico" Banks was born in Chicago in 1962. His father, Jesse Banks, played guitar with the gospel group the Mighty Clouds of Joy, as well as with the blues bands of Eddie Shaw and Willie Kent.

When he was eight or nine years old, Chico began playing around with his father's guitar, just out of curiosity. By age 15 he was hanging around with neighborhood kids who would get together and play R&B and Motown songs. They'd play in a garage with the door half-open.

At the time, Chico wanted to be a basketball player. Playing guitar was just for fun. But by age 19 he was backing vocalist Johnny Christian in order to earn extra cash. Soon after he was playing all around the West and South sides, sometimes five days a week. Then a friend gave him a tip that James Cotton was looking for a new guitarist because Michael Coleman was leaving the band. Chico decided to go to the audition in the basement at Cotton's house. When he got there he saw five other guitarists waiting to try out.

"I was scared," Chico says. "I thought, man, I'm never gonna get this job."

Chico was worried because he played mainly R&B, and he knew Cotton was looking for a blues player. But when it was his turn, Chico played a fast shuffle, the kind of music he remembered hearing his father play. Whatever it was he played, it got him the job. "Once I got started playing, James said, 'I'm taking him,'" Chico recalls.

Chico toured Europe with the James Cotton Band in the late 1980s and stayed with the band for about a year and a half. Then he heard Otis Clay was looking for a guitarist. He went down to B.L.U.E.S. on Halsted, where Clay was performing, to talk to him about the gig. Clay wanted to take Chico to New York City the very next day. Chico said yes, although he had never even rehearsed with the band. "I didn't know a thing," Chico says. "I learned everything in the van."

After a time with Clay, Chico toured with Buddy Guy and Junior Wells. In the mid-1990s Chico played with Sugar Blue, Artie "Blues Boy" White, Little Milton, and Mavis Staples and the Staple Singers.

In 1996 Chico was in the studio recording with Willie Kent when producer Larry Hoffman asked him to play some of his own songs. Hoffman was impressed, and Chico went on to record *Candy Lickin' Man* on the Blind Pig label in 1997. His effort garnered him a nomination for a Handy Award in 1998 for Best New Blues Artist.

These days Chico is gigging steadily with his own band while still playing with blues legends like Jimmy Johnson and Artie "Blues Boy" White.

Music
• *Candy Lickin' Man* (Evidence, 1997)

L.V. Banks
Guitar

The music of L.V. Banks ranges from Delta blues to soul to rockabilly. Born in Mississippi on October 28, 1932, Banks served in the Army before moving to Chicago in 1965. For a time he was a regular fixture on Maxwell Street. His son Tré is a blues guitarist.

Music
• *Ruby* (Wolf, 2000)
• *Let Me Be Your Teddy Bear* (Wolf, 1998)

Barrelhouse Chuck
Piano
www.barrelhousechuck.com

The boogie-woogie blues piano of Barrelhouse Chuck carries forward the classic sounds of legendary blues pianists like Sunnyland Slim, Pinetop Perkins, Lafayette Leake, and Little Brother Montgomery. It's not surprising—Chuck knew and learned from all of them.

Born Charles Goering on July 10, 1958, in Columbus, Ohio, Barrelhouse Chuck started playing drums at age five but soon switched to piano. In 1972 his family moved to Florida, where he first heard the music of Muddy Waters and his great piano player, Otis Spann. Chuck became hooked on the blues and learned blues piano by listening to records.

By the late 1970s Chuck had formed his own band. Still fascinated by the sounds of Muddy Waters, he began following Muddy around and became acquainted with Pinetop Perkins, who was Muddy's piano player at that time.

In 1979 Chuck drove to Chicago to see Sunnyland Slim, who was playing a regular gig at B.L.U.E.S. on Halsted. Through his friendship with Sunnyland, Chuck met most of the blues legends in Chicago and later developed a close friendship with Little Brother Montgomery.

Barrelhouse Chuck was a member of Mississippi Heat and has toured with Nick Moss and the Flip Tops.

Music
- *Blues Calling* (Bonetone, 2005)
- *Prescription for the Blues* (Sirens, 2002)—with Erwin Helfer
- *8 Hands on 88 Keys* (Sirens, 2002)—with Detroit Junior, Erwin Helfer, and Pinetop Perkins
- *25 Years of Blues Piano* (2000)
- *Salute to Sunnyland Slim* (Blue Loon, 1999)

Lurrie Bell
Guitar
www.lurrie.com

Lurrie Bell is widely regarded as the best traditional guitarist in Chicago today. The "Mercurial Son" of harp player Carey Bell, Lurrie was born on December 13, 1958, and grew up amid the sounds of his father's blues and in the presence of such family friends as Eddie Taylor, Big Walter Horton, Eddie C. Campbell, Lovie Lee, Sunnyland Slim, and Pinetop Perkins. Eddy Clearwater is his cousin.

Photo by Chuck Winans (pipphotography.com).

At age 17 Lurrie Bell played onstage with legendary bluesman Willie Dixon, and by age 19 he was touring with Koko Taylor. After four years with the Queen of the Blues, he (along with Freddie Dixon, son of Willie Dixon) joined Billy Branch and the Sons of Blues.

Bell's contributions to the blues have been significant, despite the fact that, throughout the late 1980s and '90s, he was plagued by mental illness and substance abuse problems, resulting in erratic behavior. However, in recent years, after marrying photographer Susan Greenberg, he's settled down and emerged as one of the hardest-working bluesmen in Chicago.

In addition to his solo recordings and collaborations with his father, Lurrie has appeared on some 50 albums. He was the subject of the documentary film *Mercurial Son: The Blues of Lurrie Bell*, by Paul Marcus.

Music

- *Second Nature* (Alligator, 2004)—an acoustic album originally recorded live in 1991 with his father, Carey Bell, in Finland
- *Cuttin' Heads* (Isabel, 2004)
- *Chicago's Young Blues Generation* (Evidence, 2001)—with Billy Branch
- *Blues Had a Baby* (Delmark, 1999)
- *Kiss of Sweet Blues* (Delmark, 1998)
- *700 Blues* (Delmark, 1997)
- *Young Man's Blues: The Best of the JSP Sessions (1989–1990)* (JSP, 1997)
- *Dynasty* (JSP, 1996)—with Carey Bell
- *Mercurial Son* (Delmark, 1995)

Big James and the Chicago Playboys
Trombone
www.bigjames.com

The trombone becomes a lead blues instrument in the hands of Big James Montgomery. Heading up the Chicago Playboys, Big James delivers the blues fused with soul and more than a little funk.

Big James grew up in Chicago, and at age 19 he joined the band of Little Milton Campbell. He then toured for a couple of years with Albert King before joining Johnny Christian's band, the Chicago Playboys. When Christian died in 1993, Big James did stints with both Buddy Guy and Otis Rush before re-forming the Chicago Playboys along with Charlie Kimble on saxophone, Mike Wheeler on guitar, Cleo Cole on drums, Joe Blocker on keyboards, and Larry Williams on bass.

Music

- *Now You Know* (Jamot, 2004)

Billy Branch

Harmonica
www.billybranch.com

In 1990 Billy Branch recorded the song "New Kid on the Block" for *Harp Attack!*, a CD by Alligator that brought together Chicago's best harmonica players at the time: James Cotton, Junior Wells, Carey Bell, and, of course, Branch. Back then, in that company, Branch was the "new kid."

Today the moniker no longer applies. Branch has been blowing his harp in Chicago clubs for more than 30 years. He's recorded

Photo by Chuck Winans
(pipphotography.com).

numerous CDs under his own name and with others, appeared in movies and television commercials, and entertained crowds all over the world. He's also won multiple awards, such as the 2004 Blues Entertainer of the Year from the 23rd annual Chicago Music Awards.

Branch has also inspired children and teens with his extensive and groundbreaking work with the Blues in the Schools program in the Chicago Public Schools and around the country.

In many ways Branch and his music represent a bridge from Chicago's glorious blues past into the new century. Branch is one of the "next generation" of bluesmen who did not grow up in the rural South. Born in Chicago in 1951, Billy grew up in Los Angeles.

In 1969, at age 18, Branch moved back to Chicago to attend the University of Illinois at Chicago. On one August afternoon, he attended a free blues festival sponsored by the City of Chicago in Grant Park and saw performances by Muddy Waters, Buddy Guy, Junior Wells, Big Walter Horton, and other legends. "The whole experience just blew me away," Billy recalls.

The concert inspired him to again pick up the harmonica, which he had first learned to play at age ten. At the time, he wasn't familiar with the blues, but one of his college buddies was Lucius Barner, the stepson of Junior Wells. Soon Lucius and Billy began hanging out at Theresa's Lounge and the Queen Bee on the South Side, where Billy heard great harmonica players like Wells, Horton, Carey Bell, and James Cotton.

Billy was majoring in political science with plans to go to law school. But he was drawn to the clubs, and as his harp playing skills increased, he started sitting in with the bands in places like the Elsewhere Club and Wise Fool's Pub in Lincoln Park.

In 1975 his career leaped forward when he won a competition against the late Little Mack Simmons at the Green Bunny Club. Soon afterward he made his first record for Barrelhouse Records.

In 1977 Billy formed the

Billy Branch played the role of a preacher in a 1989 movie called Next of Kin, *starring Patrick Swayze, Liam Neeson, and Helen Hunt. His scene was filmed at the Checkerboard Lounge. He also appeared with Albert Collins in the movie* Adventures in Babysitting *(1987).*

Sons of Blues with sons of two blues legends: Lurrie Bell (son of Carey Bell) and Freddie Dixon (son of bassist and songwriter Willie Dixon), along with Garland Whiteside. The band was touted as the next generation of Chicago bluesmen.

"We were the answer to the question 'Are there any young black guys out there playing the blues?'" Billy says.

At the Berlin Jazz Festival, the S.O.B.s played the song "Tear Down the Berlin Wall," written by Lucius Barner.

Once back home, Branch and the S.O.B.s then recorded for Alligator's *Living Chicago Blues, Vol. III* (1980), which was nominated for a Grammy Award, and *The New Bluebloods* (Alligator, 1987).

In 1979 Billy landed a job with Willie Dixon's Blues All-Stars Band as backup harp player, and by the end of his six-year stint, he replaced Carey Bell in the band.

In 1984 the S.O.B.s included Carlos Johnson on guitar, J.W. Williams on bass, and Moses Rutues on drums. They recorded *Where's My Money?* on the Red Beans label, which featured a guest appearance by piano legend Jimmy Walker. The album was rereleased on CD by Evidence in 1995.

In 1990 Branch recorded *Harp Attack!* with three of his mentors: Carey Bell, Junior Wells, and James Cotton. The CD won a Handy Award in 1991 for Contemporary Blues Album of the Year. His critically acclaimed 1995 release *The Blues Keep Following Me Around* featured guitarist Carl Weathersby, who played with the S.O.B.s from the early 1980s until the mid-1990s. In recent years Branch has teamed up to record with James Cotton, Charlie Musselwhite, Kenny Neal, and Carlos Johnson.

These days Billy Branch appears several nights a week in local clubs and continues to record, tour, and work with the Blues in the Schools. Two nights a week Branch and the S.O.B.s perform in clubs in predominantly African-American communities. Billy says it's his way of keeping the blues alive. With his performances he has converted some people who said they weren't fans of the blues into true believers.

"A lot of people don't know that they like the blues," Billy says. "They're just like I was as a kid. Basically, everybody will like the blues if they hear it performed well."

Music

- *Double Take* (Alligator, 2004)—with Kenny Neal
- *Don't Mess with the Bluesmen* (P-Vine, 2004)—with Carlos Johnson
- *Billy Branch & Lurrie Bell and the Sons of Blues* (Evidence, 2001) —originally issued in 1982 on a German label
- *Superharps* (Telarc, 1999)—with James Cotton and Charlie Musselwhite
- *Satisfy Me* (House of Blues, 1999)
- *Blues Keep Following Me Around* (Verve, 1995)
- *Where's My Money?* (Evidence, 1995)
- *Live '82* (Evidence, 1994)
- *Harp Attack!* (Alligator, 1991)—with James Cotton, Junior Wells, & Carey Bell

---

Lonnie Brooks
Guitar
www.lonniebrooks.com

The blues of Lonnie Brooks combines the swamps of Louisiana, the country roads of Texas, and the city streets of Chicago. Onstage, the tall, ever-smiling bluesman in the ten-gallon cowboy hat is as likely to play the sounds of rock and roll and the rhythms of zydeco as he is to play a 12-bar shuffle.

It seems that Lonnie was destined to be a musician from the moment he was born as Lee Baker Jr. on December 18, 1933. The Baker

Photo by Chuck Winans (pipphotography.com).

household was filled with music. Lonnie's grandfather, who played ragtime and jazz banjo, stayed with the family in Dubuisson, Louisiana, for long periods. Whenever Lonnie heard his grandfather playing the banjo, he would stop to listen.

"He would get up early in the morning, say 4 or 5 o'clock. He'd make a fire and play his banjo for an hour, and then go to work," Lonnie recalls.

When he was about ten years old, Lonnie tried playing banjo, but he found it too difficult. That was all right, however, as he was more fascinated with his uncle's guitar.

"To be a star you have to do your own thing. Everybody wants to be like B.B. King and Muddy Waters, but those guys never really made it by playing other people's music."

—Lonnie Brooks

"The strings would ring a little bit longer, it had more sustain," Lonnie says. "I fell in love with it." At night he'd steal off to listen to his uncle play. "I knew it was something I wanted to do," he says.

So when he grew up, Lonnie bought a guitar and taught himself to play. In 1952 he moved to Port Arthur, Texas. After work he'd play his guitar, hoping to catch the sounds of bluesmen he admired, like Lightnin' Hopkins.

"I used to practice eight hours a day, just like going to a job," Lonnie says. "That's how I got good enough for people to hear me play."

After 18 months of diligent practice, he still felt uneasy about playing in front of people. Then a chance meeting with zydeco king Clifton Chenier propelled him into a career as a professional musician.

Lonnie was living in a second-floor apartment with a porch that faced the street. He spent hours on that porch, practicing his guitar. "I kept my back turned to the street because I didn't want to see anything to grab my attention," he explains. The street in those days was nothing more than blacktop covering the gravel road. "You could hear cars coming, crunching on the gravel," he recalls.

On that fateful day he heard the gravel crunching and turned to see a big Cadillac going by. "I'm gonna get me one of them one day," he mused at the time and then turned his focus back on his guitar playing. He didn't even hear the car stop or the man walk up the wooden stairs to his porch. Suddenly he felt a presence, someone looking at him. He jumped, startled, and looked up to see the imposing figure of Clifton Chenier.

"He introduced himself and asked if I was playing with a band," Lonnie says. Chenier said he liked Lonnie's guitar playing and invited him over to his house to jam. "It took only five minutes for me to learn his song," Lonnie says. "I grew up listening to zydeco and country music. That's all they had on AM radio, all day Saturday and Sunday. All of this was in my head, so it was easy for me to learn his music."

Lonnie toured with Chenier's Red Hot Louisiana Band off and on for about a year and a half. He then formed a trio of his own and performed under the name Guitar Junior. He still felt he had a lot to learn.

"The hardest thing was keeping the guitar tuned," he says. Because he was self-taught and played by ear, his guitar was tuned for his own playing style. "I'd tune it up until it felt right," he says. But playing in a band meant he had to tune his guitar with the piano.

In the mid-1950s Lonnie was touring the South as Guitar Junior. He cut his first record, "I Got It Made," in 1957 for the Goldband label in Lake Charles, Louisiana, and went on to record regional hits such as "Roll, Roll, Roll," "Family Rules," and "The Crawl." His swamp-inspired rock and roll was striking a chord with Southern audiences, and now his popularity was growing. "People wanted to hear me in other places," he says.

In 1959 "Guitar Junior" had performed in cities like Houston and New Orleans, but he had never been north. "I was scared to come to Chicago," he explains. "I had never been to such a big city."

It was R&B legend Sam Cooke who encouraged Lonnie to make his way to Chicago. Already a big star, Cooke was headlining a benefit concert in an Atlanta ballpark. Lonnie, as Guitar Junior, was an opening act.

The two men met quite by accident. Lonnie had made arrangements for a cab driver to wait for him after the concert. Cooke had a stretch limo waiting for him. When the concert ended, Lonnie got into his taxi, and that's when he saw Cooke heading for his limo, followed by a crowd of screaming female fans. To escape the girls, Cooke hopped in one door of the limo, jumped out the other door, and slid into Lonnie's taxi. The two rode back to the hotel and struck up a friendship. Sam invited Lonnie along on his caravan tour.

While Lonnie admired Cooke's smooth, soulful sounds, he knew that type of music wasn't right for his rock-and-roll style of guitar playing. But Cooke had a brother in Chicago, L.C. Cooke, who had his own band and was looking for a guitar player. When the tour arrived in Chicago, Lonnie stayed and hooked up with Sam's brother. Because there was already a Guitar Junior (Luther Johnson) in Chicago, Lee Baker changed his name to Lonnie Brooks and set out to learn Chicago-style blues.

When they weren't playing, L.C. Cooke and Lonnie made the rounds of Chicago's many jazz and blues bars. Lonnie especially liked the West Side bars and became enthralled with the sounds of Otis Rush and

Magic Sam. Lonnie was listening to Magic Sam one night when, suddenly, the Chicago blues all made sense to him.

"The night I got it," he recalls, "Magic Sam had had a fight with his girlfriend, and he'd been drinking. I watched him, and he was squeezing the strings, with so much feeling coming out, and I thought, that's it!"

He rushed back to his apartment and began playing what he had seen Magic Sam do. "I could remember everything I heard," he says.

Throughout the 1960s and '70s, Lonnie worked in Chicago bars, sometimes 10 to 15 hours a day. After working in Jimmy Reed's band for a while, Lonnie released his first album, *Broke and Hungry*, in 1969 under his previous stage name of Guitar Junior. He also continued his disciplined practice schedule. He knew he couldn't be Magic Sam, Muddy Waters, B.B. King, or Howlin' Wolf—he wanted to develop his own style. "I knew from what I did before, if I hadn't been so different, I wouldn't have gotten so far," Lonnie says.

In 1978 Lonnie recorded "Two-Headed Man" and three other songs for *Living Chicago Blues*, an anthology put out by Alligator Records. He signed a contract with Alligator and released *Bayou Lightning* in 1979. Lonnie then recorded a series of albums, creating an impressive body of work with his own signature sound. His album *Live from Chicago: Bayou Lightning Strikes*, released in 1988, received a Grammy nomination.

Through the 1980s and '90s he performed in festivals and concert venues all over the world. He appeared on the *Late Show with David Letterman*, on *Hee Haw*, and in the movie *Blues Brothers 2000*. In 1998 he coauthored *Blues for Dummies* with his son Wayne Baker Brooks and Cub Koda. He's been inducted into the Louisiana Music Hall of Fame and Texas Music Hall of Fame.

Lonnie also mentored his two sons, Wayne and Ronnie Baker Brooks, as they began to play the blues. Both sons have struck out on their own to develop their own unique sounds, but they still play frequently with their father's band.

Lonnie expects that the new generation will change the blues. After all, that's what he has done throughout the span of his 50-plus years in music. "Everything's gonna change—nothing stays the same," he says.

Music

- *Lone Star Shootout* (Alligator, 1999)—with Phillip Walker and Long John Hunter
- *Deluxe Edition* (Alligator, 1997)

- *Road House Rules* (Alligator, 1996)
- *Satisfaction Guaranteed* (Alligator, 1991)
- *Bayou Lightning* (Alligator, 1990)—recorded in 1979
- *Live from Chicago: Bayou Lightning Strikes* (Alligator, 1988)
  —recorded live at the Chicago club B.L.U.E.S. Etcetera (now closed)
- *Wound Up Tight* (Alligator, 1986)
- *Let's Talk It Over* (Delmark, 1977)
- *Live at Pepper's* (Black Top, 1968)

Ronnie Baker Brooks
Guitar
www.ronniebakerbrooks.com

After playing for 12 years in the band of his famous father, Lonnie Brooks, Ronnie Baker Brooks is well schooled in the sounds of traditional blues. But like many of his generation, he has developed a contemporary sound, influenced by hard-edged blues guitarists like Jimi Hendrix, Albert Collins, and Stevie Ray Vaughan.

Ronnie was born in Chicago on January 23, 1967. He began playing guitar as soon as he could hold one and first appeared

Photo by Chuck Winans (pipphotography.com).

onstage at age nine with his dad's band at Pepper's Lounge. Whenever Lonnie was home from the road, Ronnie would ask him to teach him some new guitar licks. Soon Ronnie learned bass, and he and his dad would jam together.

In 1986 Ronnie joined his father's band, and in 1987 he cut his first record with the Lonnie Brooks band for the CD *Live from Chicago: Bayou Lightning Strikes* (Alligator, 1988).

Ronnie gradually took on more responsibilities in the band, often performing before Lonnie took the stage. At the 1992 New Orleans Jazz and Heritage Fest, Ronnie led the band for Lonnie, who had become ill. By the time Ronnie left his dad's band in 1998, he was well prepared for a solo career. His first CD, *Golddigger*, was produced by singer Janet Jackson. In 2000 he was nominated for a Handy Award for Best New Artist.

If Ronnie isn't touring or playing his own gigs, it's not unusual for him to show up at his father's shows and sit in with the band.

Music

- *Ronnie Baker Brooks Live* (Watchdog, 2002)—recorded at Chord on Blues in St. Charles
- *Take Me Witcha* (Watchdog, 2001)
- *Golddigger* (Watchdog, 1998)

Wayne Baker Brooks

Guitar
www.waynebakerbrooks.com

The music of Wayne Baker Brooks may be classified as blues, but it isn't confined to it. This contemporary guitarist incorporates elements of rock, R&B, funk, and hip-hop.

On his debut CD, *Mystery*, Wayne wrote or cowrote all the songs. The CD includes guest appearances by his father, bluesman Lonnie Brooks, and his brother, guitarist Ronnie Baker Brooks.

Wayne Baker Brooks coauthored Blues for Dummies *along with his father, Lonnie Brooks, and Cub Koda. The book, published in 1998, comes with a CD with classic songs by Chicago artists, including Muddy Waters, Little Walter, Howlin' Wolf, and Buddy Guy. The book has been translated into 38 different languages.*

Wayne was born in Chicago in 1970. Although he grew up with the blues, Wayne didn't start playing guitar until he was 20 years old. He made up for lost time, however. Soon he was playing in his father's band, keeping up a schedule of some 200 performances a year. Though he's now busy building his own career, Wayne still occasionally opens the show for his famous father.

In 1999 Wayne performed for First Lady Hillary Rodham Clinton at the historic Chess Studios in Chicago. Bo Diddley, Koko Taylor, and Lonnie Brooks joined him onstage. In 2004 he performed at the Major League Baseball All-Star Game at U.S. Cellular Field.

Wayne is also a budding actor. He appeared in the movies *Blues Brothers 2000*, *Barbershop*, and *Barbershop 2*.

Music

- *Mystery* (Blues Island, 2003)

Nora Jean Bruso
Vocals
www.norajeanblues.com

Photo by Chuck Winans
(pipphotography.com).

One minute Nora Jean Bruso will make you get up and dance. The next she'll make you want to sit down and cry. Nora's soulful vocals contain a raw power and grit that reach deep into the hearts of her audience. "I want them to feel what I feel," says Nora.

Nora dazzled the national blues scene as a fresh new artist in 2002 with her debut CD, *Nora Jean Sings the Blues*, on which she's backed by an all-star band of Willie Kent on bass, James Wheeler and Billy Flynn on guitar, and Eddie Shaw on saxophone. In reality her CD marked a comeback for Nora, who first recorded under the name Nora Jean Wallace with guitarist Jimmy Dawkins in 1984.

Although Nora has spent most of her life in Chicago, she still considers Mississippi her home. "It's there in my heart and in my mind," she explains.

Born in Greenwood, Mississippi, the hometown of Robert Johnson, Nora grew up in a family of 11 brothers and four sisters. Her father, Bobby Lee Wallace, was a blues singer and a sharecropper. Her mother, Ida Wallace, was a gospel singer. Her uncle, Henry "Son" Wallace, was also a blues singer. Her grandmother ran a juke joint, Miss Mae's, and at night Nora would sneak out of bed and go down to listen to the music.

Nora was only six years old when she made her first paid performance by singing Howlin' Wolf's song "Howlin' for My Darlin'" for an older brother's friends. After her family moved to Clarksdale, Nora worked in the cotton fields, but she kept singing. In high school she won a talent contest and was invited to sing at other schools.

Nora first took the stage in 1977, a year after moving to Chicago. She had been staying with her aunt Rose, who one day came home from work to hear Nora singing to herself.

"Damn, girl, you can sing!" her aunt told her, and she immediately took her to meet a friend, Scottie, who fronted a band called Scottie and the Oasis. Scottie asked Nora what she could sing, and she chose "Tonight Is the Night," by soul singer Betty Wright.

"What key?" Scottie asked. Nora, who never had any formal

musical training, had no idea. "You just start singing, and we'll find the key," he told her.

Nora joined the band and played with Scottie in clubs throughout the South and West sides until 1982, when Scottie was shot and killed, and the band broke up. After that Nora sat in with various bands around town. One night she was singing at Mr. T's on Lake Street and St. Louis when Jimmy Dawkins recognized her. He was getting ready to cut a record, and he asked if she had ever written any songs. She hadn't, but she was willing to try. "Write some songs," he told her, "and I'll put you on a record."

"I went right to work on that song!" Nora recalls. The result was "Oh My Love" and "Untrue Lover." She recorded both songs with Dawkins and then hit the road with his band. They toured the United States and Europe and appeared together at the 1989 Chicago Blues Festival. The last show she did with Dawkins was in New York in 1992.

But Nora's two sons were growing up, and they needed their mother around. She decided to quit the road and devote her time to providing her kids with a stable home. While she continued to sing at church and for weddings and funerals, she never thought of returning to a full-time professional career.

That changed in 2001, when out of the blue, guitarist Billy Flynn called her up and asked her to record with him. She cut three tracks on his CD *Blues and Love*.

The experience inspired her to start taking her career seriously. She

Spotlight

Nora Jean Bruso has written more than 700 songs. That's not bad for a woman who is just now learning to play the piano and write musical notation. In the past she's had to sing out the parts for the musicians to imitate on their instruments. Yet she's always had a natural aptitude for music and lyrics.

"Jimmy Dawkins told me once, 'Nora, you're gonna be a good songwriter,'" she recalls. "He'd be looking at me, and he'd say, 'What you thinkin' about? You look so sad.'"

Nora says she has always felt emotions deeply and found she could express herself when she wrote songs. "Now I can't stop," she says. "I've got stuff coming out of me I never knew I had in me."

Nora says every song she writes has a story behind it. For example, the song "Make Me Over," which appears on her third CD, was based on a time her heart was broken by a man. People relate to her music because it's about real life, she says. "I don't make stuff up," she explains.

started gigging in clubs around town. One night when she was singing in the 290 Sport Juice Bar on the West Side, she met her future husband, Mark Bruso. They soon married, and he encouraged her to cut her own CD. She called on her old friends, people like Willie Kent and Eddie Shaw, to record with her. "It was to let people know I'm back, and I've still got it," she says.

People got the message. Her next CD, *Going Back to Mississippi*, shot straight to the top. Now that she's back, Nora is determined to be the next big blues star. "I want to get bigger than B.B. King," she says, with a full, hearty laugh. "I want to get larger than Koko Taylor."

Music
- *Going Back to Mississippi* (Severn, 2004)
- *Nora Jean Bruso Sings the Blues* (Red Hurricane, 2003)

Jimmy Burns
Guitar, harmonica
www.jimmyburnsband.com

Mississippi-born Jimmy Burns plays classic Chicago-style blues with slide, Delta country blues, and even a bit of rock and roll. His vocals are smooth and powerful, and it's no wonder—Burns began his musical career as a singer of gospel and R&B. He made his first recordings at the tender age of 16 with the doo-wop group the Medallionaires.

Born on February 27, 1943, in Dublin, Mississippi, Burns taught himself to play guitar at age ten when a woman loaned a guitar to his mother, who also played a bit. Burns picked it up and learned to play in open tuning. He still often plays that way. "I still like open tuning because it's such a rich sound," he says.

He put the guitar down when he moved to Chicago a few years later. In the 1960s he recorded a couple of singles as a vocalist. In the 1970s and '80s he was focused on raising a family and operating a barbecue restaurant he owned on the West Side, but in his spare time he continued to play the guitar and perfect his musical style. In the 1990s he came back to professional music. "I guess it was just in my blood," he explains. Or maybe it was in his DNA. Burns is the younger brother of guitarist Eddie Burns, who played for years with John Lee Hooker.

Before long Jimmy Burns was playing with the Rockin' Johnny

(Burgin) band at the Smoke Daddy. This gig led to his first CD, *Leaving Here Walking*, recorded on the Delmark label. The album earned two Handy Award nominations in 1998 in the categories of Comeback Album of the Year and Blues Song of the Year (for "Leaving Here Walking").

"If anything, I've gone beyond my expectations," he says. "I'm very happy because of it."

Music
- *Back to the Delta* (Delmark, 2003)
- *Night Time Again* (Delmark, 1999)
- *Leaving Here Walking* (Delmark, 1996)

Aron Burton
Bass

After a lengthy career as a sideman, bass player Aron Burton stepped into the spotlight in the 1990s as a bandleader. In that time he released three CDs and garnered four W.C. Handy nominations in the category of Blues Instrumentalist–Bass.

Born on June 15, 1938, in Senatobia, Mississippi, Burton toured with the R&B groups the Victory Travelers and the Players in the 1950s. In 1955 he moved to Chicago, where he played with Freddie King in the late 1950s. After a stint in the Army in the early '60s, Burton played and recorded with Wild Child Butler and Carey Bell. He toured with Junior Wells from 1969 to 1972.

In 1978 Burton joined his brother, guitarist Larry Burton, in Albert Collins's original Icebreakers band. The brothers backed Collins on his Grammy-nominated 1990 album, *Ice Pickin'* (Alligator).

For two decades Aron Burton worked as a landscaper and horticulturist with the Chicago Park District's Garfield Park Conservatory. He also owned a nightclub called the International, which was located on Madison Street.

Music
- *Good Blues to You* (Delmark, 1999)
- *Aron Burton Live* (Earwig, 1996)
- *Past, Present and Future* (Earwig, 1993)

Eddie C. Campbell
Guitar

Eddie C. Campbell was born in 1939 in Duncan, Mississippi, where his parents were sharecroppers. In 1945 the family moved north to Chicago in search of work.

Don't mess with this kid. In his youth Eddie C. Campbell won 16 knockouts as an amateur boxer. He also learned karate.

When he was eight Eddie's mother bought him his first guitar. Later she took him to the 1125 Club on Madison Street, where he met Muddy Waters. Muddy told the young Eddie that when he learned to play a song, he'd let him up onstage. By age 12 Eddie had learned "Still a Fool," and Muddy allowed him to sit in with the band.

By the mid-1950s Eddie was performing with Luther Allison, Willie James Lyons, Big Monroe, Willie Buckner on drums, and Pee Wee Madison on harp. Later, Campbell and his band backed Percy Mayfield, Lowell Fulson, Tyrone Davis, and Little Johnny Taylor. He also performed with Little Walter, Howlin' Wolf, Otis Rush, and Mighty Joe Young.

In 1963 Eddie became band director for Jimmy Reed. He stayed with the band until 1976, when Reed died. Later, he worked with Koko Taylor briefly, and then he joined Willie Dixon's All-Stars. Campbell lived in Europe from 1984 until 1992.

One of Campbell's most famous songs is a Christmas tune, "Santa's Been Messin' with the Kid," which he wrote and recorded in 1977. Lynyrd Skynyrd covered the song on *Christmas Time Again* (CMC International, 2000).

Music

- *The Baddest Cat on the Block* (JSP, 2000)—originally released in 1985
- *Gonna Be Alright* (Icehouse, 1999)—recorded in the 1980s
- *Hopes and Dreams* (Rooster, 1997)
- *King of the Jungle* (Rooster, 1996)—originally released in 1977
- *That's When I Know* (Blind Pig, 1994)
- *Mind Trouble* (Double Trouble, 1994)
- *Let's Pick It* (Evidence, 1993)—recorded in Amsterdam in 1984

Eddy Clearwater
Guitar
www.eddyclearwater.com

Photo by Chuck Winans
(pipphotography.com).

Eddy Clearwater calls his music "rock-a-blues"—a cross between blues, old-time rock and roll, and R&B. "I like a lot of energy in my music," Eddy says.

He says he makes his live shows "as live as possible." He has often appeared onstage wearing a colorful feathered Indian headdress, a practice that earned him the nickname the Chief. Onstage, the tall, lanky Clearwater energizes the crowd with his easy grin and growling vocals.

"People can stay at home and hear good music on their stereo systems," Eddy says. "I like to give them more."

But it's not all fun and games. Every now and then he'll change gears and play a deep, moaning blues that reveals his West Side soul roots.

Growing up with his grandparents in the South, Eddy was always taught that the blues was the devil's music. "I never saw it that way," he comments. "I always saw it as the music of the people."

Born Eddie Harrington on January 10, 1930, in Macon, Mississippi, Eddy was raised by his grandparents in Mississippi and Birmingham, Alabama. When he was 11 or 12 years old, he picked up his uncle's guitar and taught himself to play. Soon he was proficient enough to play with the gospel band in his church in Birmingham. On occasion he played with the legendary gospel group the Five Blind Boys of Alabama.

But he also listened to the blues, and he didn't see much different between the two musical genres. Both kinds of music, he believes, carry messages about people and life. "The blues is about truth and feeling, and so is gospel," he says.

In 1950, when Eddy was 15, his uncle sent him a $15 Greyhound

A left-hander, Eddy Clearwater learned to play guitar by turning a standard guitar around the other way. To this day he still plays upside down, high strings on the top and bass strings on the bottom. Other left-handed blues guitarists who play or played in this way are Carlos Johnson, Otis Rush, and the late Albert King.

bus ticket to Chicago. In Chicago he continued playing gospel at the Church of God in Christ at 40th and State Street. But on the radio he would hear the music of Muddy Waters, Little Walter, Jimmy Reed, and Howlin' Wolf, and he wanted to play the blues. In the early 1950s Eddy began playing clubs on the South and West sides of Chicago, sometimes working for only $5 or $6 a night.

Eddy rarely wears his famous Indian headdress in the clubs, but he usually puts it on at festivals. He acquired the headdress years ago after he saw it at a friend's house during a house party. His friend said she wouldn't sell it, but she would give it to him as a good luck charm, provided he would never part with it.
Photo by Chuck Winans (pipphotography.com).

Eddie Harrington became Eddy Clearwater at the suggestion of Jump Jackson, a blues drummer and promoter. Jackson told Eddy he'd act as his booking agent, but he wanted him to change his name to something catchier. Jackson decided on Clearwater as a pun on Muddy Waters.

As Eddy's musical style grew he picked up the influences of Chuck Berry's rock and roll and the West Side sounds of Magic Sam Maghett. He first met Magic Sam in the early 1960s. One night Eddy heard on the radio that Magic Sam would be playing at the Blue Flame on 39th and Oakwood, only a couple blocks from Eddy's house.

Eddy arrived early and took a seat close to the stage. Toward the end of the first set, Magic Sam broke a string. At the break Sam went to the microphone and asked if anybody had an E-string he could borrow. Eddy told Sam he had extra guitar strings at home. "I ran home and got two E-strings," Eddy says. That was the beginning of a close friendship between the men.

Eddy's next big influence was the great Willie Dixon. Eddy had been playing mostly covers of other people's songs, but Dixon encouraged Eddy to write his own songs and publish them. Songwriters not only get more recognition, Dixon told him, but they also get more money. Eddy took Dixon's advice, and to this day he emulates Dixon's philosophy of songwriting. "He wrote about the common things in life, things that people can relate to," Eddy comments.

Eddy's career continued to gain steam over the years. He was 50 years old in 1980 when his debut album, *The Chief*, on the Rooster label, was released.

Now in his 70s, Clearwater hasn't slowed down. With a full performance schedule, he is still a prolific

Eddy Clearwater (real name, Eddie Harrington) is a cousin of Carey Bell (whose last name is also Harrington) and Carey's son, Lurrie Bell.

songwriter and regularly finds his way into the recording studio. Within the last few years, his work has gained wide acclaim. His song "Don't Take My Blues," which appeared on *Mean Case of the Blues* (Bullseye), was nominated for a W.C. Handy Award as Blues Song of the Year in 1998. In 2000 his album *Reservation Blues* was nominated for W.C. Handy Awards in three categories. In 2001 he won the Handy for Male Artist of the Year–Contemporary Blues.

In 2003 he was honored by the Chicago Music Awards as Best Blues Entertainer. His 2003 CD, *Rock 'N' Roll City*, was nominated in 2004 for a Grammy for Best Traditional Blues Album. Eddy served on the Board of Governors of the Chicago Chapter of the Recording Academy in 2004–05.

Eddy continues to experiment with his style—on his latest CD he's backed by a masked band called Los Straitjackets—but he never strays too far from his roots. "The basic foundations of the blues are still underneath," he says.

Music
- *Rock 'N' Roll City* (Rounder, 2003)
- *Reservation Blues* (Bullseye, 2000)
- *Cool Blues Walk* (Bullseye, 1998)
- *Mean Case of the Blues* (Bullseye, 1997)
- *Boogie Your Blues Away* (Delmark, 1995)
- *Flimdoozie* (Rooster, 1995)—recorded in 1986 with Otis Rush
- *The Chief* (Rooster Blues, 1994)—a reissue of a 1980 recording
- *Help Yourself* (Blind Pig, 1992)

Sam Cockrell
Vocals, bass
www.samcockrell.com

Sam Cockrell and his band, the Groove, play a fusion of R&B, soul, funk, rock, and blues. Cockrell grew up on the South Side of Chicago. At age nine, inspired by the Jackson Five, he formed his own band, which he named the Brothers of the Ghetto. He became a professional musician before he graduated from high school in the late 1960s.

In the early 1970s he changed the band's name to the Majik and recorded three R&B singles in Memphis. Another single, "Gotta Get Up" (recorded in the early 1980s), ranked in Billboard's Top 100. The song was written by Cockrell and Kevin Bell from Kool & the Gang. Bell also appears on the record.

Music
- *Colorblind* (Boom Boom Records, 2001)
- *I'm in the Business* (Boom Boom Records, 1999)—guests include Carl Weathersby, Jimmy Johnson, Maurice John Vaughn, and Michael Coleman

Michael Coleman
Guitar
www.funkymichaelcoleman.com

Photo by Karen Hanson.

Michael Coleman says the funk in his music comes from his heart. "I grew up in the projects in the 1970s, listening to some of the best music ever made," says Coleman.

Coleman has played the blues guitar in the Chicago area for more than 30 years, most notably for harmonica great James Cotton. *Guitar World* magazine once voted him one of the top 50 bluesmen, along with Stevie Ray Vaughan, Lonnie Brooks, Robert Cray, Buddy Guy, and Son Seals.

Coleman was born on June 24, 1956, in Chicago. His father, Cleo Williams, was a drummer in the 1960s and '70s for Willie Kent, Johnny Christian, Otis Rush, Junior Parker, and Morris Pejoe. Every morning his mother would listen to blues artists like Little Milton and Muddy Waters on the radio. As a child, he also saw the blues played on the street and at local events.

Coleman received his first guitar, a Mickey Mouse guitar, as a gift from his mother. At age eight he joined the family band, playing bass. By age 14 he was playing with Midnight Sun, a top-40 band, and at North Side clubs with Johnny Christian and Aron Burton. In 1977, at age 21, he was on the road with Muddy Waters, and a year later he toured Europe with Eddy Clearwater.

In 1979 he joined the James Cotton Band and stayed there for nearly ten years. He recorded with Cotton on his CDs *High Compression* (Alligator, 1990), *Harp Attack!* (Alligator, 1990) and *Live from Chicago* (Alligator, 1986).

In 1987 Coleman recorded under his own name for Alligator's *The New Bluebloods Collection*, which also featured Li'l Ed Williams, Valerie Wellington, Maurice John Vaughn, Donald Kinsey, Melvin Taylor, Dion Payton, and John Watkins. Coleman formed his own band, the Backbreakers, in 1991.

Music
- *Do Your Thing* (Delmark, 2000)
- *Shake Your Booty* (Wolf, 1994)

Joanna Connor
Guitar

Joanna Connor's fast-fingered fretwork has earned her a solid place among contemporary blues guitarists. On the spectrum of blues, she falls on the rock side, but the blues she's loved since childhood form the basis of her music.

Joanna wasn't the typical teen in Worcester, Massachusetts. Born on August 21, 1962, in Brooklyn, New York, she grew up listening to her mother's eclectic record collection of jazz, reggae, and blues. In high school, while her friends were listening to

Photo by Chuck Winans (pipphotography.com).

pop music, she was grooving on the Rolling Stones and Jimi Hendrix albums and attending Buddy Guy shows.

She took up playing guitar seriously at age 15, when her guitar teacher introduced her to the music of Robert Johnson, Blind Willie McTell, and Big Bill Broonzy, and showed her how to play slide.

Joanna was 22 years old when she arrived in Chicago in 1984. She began hanging around the Checkerboard Lounge, where Dion Payton was playing.

"I used to follow Dion around like a puppy," she says. But at the time, there were no white female guitarists in Chicago. Payton, and nearly everyone else, doubted she could really play. But he changed his mind one night at B.L.U.E.S. on Halsted, when at the invitation of Lonnie Brooks, Joanna sat in with the band. Dion was so impressed with Joanna's performance that he invited her to play in his 43rd Street Blues Band. Joanna began a regular gig with Payton at the Checkerboard Lounge and Kingston Mines until 1988, when the Mines offered her a solo spot, and she formed her own band.

For several years Joanna toured extensively all over the world, playing with a range of blues and rock artists, such as A.C. Reed, Jimmy Page, Buddy Guy, Robert Cray, Otis Rush, Poi Dog Pondering, Luther Allison, Albert Collins, and Los Lobos. Recently she's stayed closer to home to raise her son and young daughter. She now plays nearly every night at Chicago and suburban clubs.

Music

- *Nothing but the Blues* (Inakustic Gmbh, 2001)—recorded live in Germany
- *Slidetime* (Blind Pig, 1998)
- *Big Girl Blues* (Blind Pig, 1996)
- *Rock and Roll Gypsy* (Ruf, 1994)
- *Fight* (Blind Pig, 1992)
- *Believe It!* (Blind Pig, 1989)

Katherine Davis
Vocals
www.katherinedavis.com

Vocalist Katherine Davis has sung it all: gospel, swing, jazz, opera, and, of course, the blues. Trained as an opera singer, Katherine worked in the Second Chance Gospel Opera from 1984 to 1985. Then she landed the parts of Ma Rainey and Bessie Smith in the Kuumba Theatre production of

In the Heart of the Blues.

Davis was raised in the Cabrini Green housing project in Chicago and moved to the South Side in 1967. Her mother's family boasted both jazz and opera singers. Her grandfather, Earl Campbell, performed with Louis Armstrong and Count Basie. Her mother dreamed of becoming a professional singer, and Katherine honored her with her song "Dream Shoes."

Davis has toured the United States, Canada, Japan, and Europe and has recorded with Mississippi Heat, Erwin Helfer, and Louisiana Red. She has also taught through the Blues in the Schools program. An accomplished cook, Katherine wrote *A Blues Woman's Cookbook* and appeared on a panel discussing soul cooking at the 2005 Chicago Blues Festival.

Music
• *Dream Shoes* (Southport/Katy D, 2000)

Willie Davis
Guitar

Willie Davis played for years as the lead guitarist in Willie Kent and the Gents. He's also played and recorded with numerous Chicago blues artists, such as Johnny B. Moore, Larry Taylor, Barrelhouse Chuck, and Detroit Junior. He gigs regularly with the Larry Taylor Soul and Blues Band as well as with his own band, the Willie Davis All-Stars, which often includes young guitar whiz Brian Lupo.

Devil in a Woodpile
Acoustic blues band

The multitalented Rick "Cookin'" Sherry (he plays harmonica, jug, washboard, and kazoo) leads Devil in a Woodpile, an acoustic blues-folk band that plays regularly at Buddy Guy's Legends' weekend acoustic sets and at the Hideout. Devil in a Woodpile has often performed with Delta blues guitarist Honeyboy Edwards. Sherry backed Edwards on his CD *World Don't Owe Me Nothing* (Earwig, 1997). Band members include Joel Paterson on guitar and Tom Ray on bass.

Music

• *In Your Lonesome Town* (Bloodshot, 2005)
• *Division Street* (Bloodshot, 2000)
• *Devil in a Woodpile* (Bloodshot, 1998)

Johnny Drummer
Keyboards, harmonica, drums, bass, vocals
www.johnnydrummermusic.com

When Johnny Drummer was growing up in the Mississippi Delta, he never dreamed he'd one day travel to exotic places like Russia, Latvia, and Holland to play music. "I used to watch the birds fly and wish I could follow them," recalls Drummer, who was born Thessex Johns on March 1, 1938, in Alligator, Mississippi.

His wish came true. Johnny has per-

Photo by Karen Hanson.

formed at festivals and clubs all over the world, and he's been the star performer at Lee's Unleaded Blues on the South Side since 1974, when the club was known as the Queen Bee. Most weekends Johnny and his band, the Starliters, entertain the crowds with his smooth blues and R&B.

Although he started his career as a drummer, these days Johnny is a vocalist and keyboard player, with a little harmonica thrown in the mix. He's also an accomplished songwriter—he wrote 12 of 14 tracks on each of his CDs for Earwig.

Music has always been part of Johnny's life. He grew up hearing his stepfather and two brothers play their guitars. At age seven he sang at the Pleasant Valley Church in Alligator. Later, he would see musicians like Little Milton and Ike Turner come through his town.

In 1954 he visited Chicago to stay with his mother for a few months. He returned again in 1955 but left and went back south. In 1956 he joined the Army, where he learned to play the drums. After his stint was up in 1959, he returned to Chicago for good.

Johnny settled on the South Side. Soon he was sitting in with pianist Lovie Lee and harp player Carey Bell, who needed a drummer in their band. He then spent a year with Eddie King and later formed his own band. In the early 1960s he recorded a couple of songs, but they were never released.

From 1974 until 1994 Johnny held a full-time job with the Chicago

Thessex Johns named himself Johnny Drummer in the early 1960s after watching the movie Johnny Guitar, *starring Sterling Hayden as "Johnny Guitar" Logan.*

Board of Education to support his family, but he kept playing music. After working with Junior Wells he learned the harmonica, and in the 1980s he started playing keyboards, which he had first learned at age 12. Over the years Johnny Drummer and the Starliters have opened for Junior Wells, Willie Mabon, Tyrone Davis, Koko Taylor, Denise LaSalle, and Z.Z. Hill.

Music
- *Unleaded Blues* (Earwig, 2001)
- *It's So Nice* (Earwig, 1999)

Little Arthur Duncan
Harmonica, vocals

Little Arthur Duncan has played harmonica in Chicago off and on since the 1950s. Born in Indianola, Mississippi, in 1934, Duncan grew up on the Woodburn Plantation, where B.B. King spent his childhood. He started as a drummer but switched to harmonica after moving to Chicago in 1950 and meeting Little Walter. He roomed with Walter and Jimmy Reed for a time.

Duncan played with John Brim and Floyd Jones. In the 1960s and '70s he worked a day job as a construction worker and played music in the evenings. He also ran a bar on the West Side. He recorded his first CD, *Bad Reputation,* for Blues King Records in 1989. He's often compared to Jimmy Reed.

Music
- *Harmonica Blues Orgy* (Random Chance, 2002)—with Willie "Big Eyes" Smith, Martin Lang, and Easy Baby
- *Live in Chicago* (Random Chance, 2000)
- *Singin' with the Sun* (Delmark, 1999)

Chainsaw Dupont
Guitar
www.chainsawdupont.com

Photo by Steve Pasek, Big Productions.

The story of David "Chainsaw" Dupont mirrors the stereotype of the bluesman. He was born in the Mississippi Delta, picked cotton as a child, and moved to Chicago as a teen. He dropped out of school, spent years on the road with his guitar, and lived through dangerous situations, including one that put a bullet in his chest.

But Dupont is a relatively young man, and his style of blues is contemporary, as he musically and lyrically blends the sounds of Chicago blues, rock blues, funk, New Orleans, swamp boogie, and more. Then again there's his acoustic alter ego of Whip Jr., whose songs are like poetry accompanied by a melodic 12-string guitar.

Dupont was born in 1956 on August 13—Friday the 13th—in the tiny town of Macomb, Mississippi. His mother, a former piano player who once took lessons from Fats Domino, worked on a plantation. His father, a young boxer known as the Whip, left the family for New Orleans when David was a child.

By age six Dupont was already working in the cotton plantations. The conditions were harsh, and nobody made much money. On weekends his mom's house became a roadhouse as people from near and far would come over and party to the sounds of an old jukebox. Dupont remembers two guitar players, brothers called Son Sausage and Bob Sausage, who were regular visitors. "Sometimes they wouldn't have but two or three strings on their guitars, but we would sit at their feet and be amazed," he recalls. "I knew then I wanted to be a guitar player."

The family didn't have much, but one day his mother bought him a Lone Ranger toy guitar. Dupont taught himself to play simple songs from a book.

At age 14 Dupont ran away from home to New Orleans, determined to find his father. He stayed for a time with relatives, but he never tracked down his father. After learning that his mother had died in a car crash in Mississippi, David went to stay with his brother in Chicago.

Once in Chicago he attended high schools on the West and North sides. One day at a friend's house, he was listening to a record by Sly and the Family Stone and became fascinated by a guitar part in one of the songs. "I couldn't get it out of my head, you know," he says. He made up his mind that he was going to be a guitarist.

For a while he played in a Jimi Hendrix–style band. In 1973, his sophomore year, he dropped out of high school. For the next decade he wandered the country, drifting aimlessly back and forth between New Orleans, Atlanta, and Houston. Life was tough, and for long stretches of time, he found himself homeless.

In Houston he hooked up with a Jamaican reggae band that was heavily into smoking and dealing ganja weed. One day a man came to the apartment to buy some pot. While Dupont was making the transaction, he saw the guy stuff some of the bandleader's weed into his pants and then go into the bathroom. When the guy returned, he had a gun. He ordered Dupont onto the floor and proceeded to take all the ganja and money in the room. Then Dupont heard a shot.

"I didn't even really know I was shot," he says. "Then I felt something warm and wet on my chest." He spent three days in the hospital recovering from his wound.

Through all the bad times, Dupont kept finding encouragement. In 1981 he was playing at Tipitina's in New Orleans with Jimmy Thackery and the Nighthawks. Thackery told him he had to hear a new guy in town, Stevie Ray Vaughan. "He said this guy is the closest thing you're ever going to hear to Jimi Hendrix," Dupont says.

So after the gig Dupont went over to the club where Vaughan was playing. At that time Stevie Ray had not yet hit it big and didn't have security guards, so Dupont went to his dressing room and struck up a conversation. Vaughan invited him to jam at the next set. They played "Voodoo Chile" and "Superstition."

"At that time it gave me a boost to keep going because I didn't know where I was going with my music," Dupont recalls. "I was just drifting."

In the late 1980s Dupont had moved back to Chicago. Still struggling to jump-start his career, he began hanging out at the Checkerboard Lounge. One night he spotted Buddy Guy and approached him with the idea of getting some advice from a blues master. He asked Buddy how to go about getting a manager. Buddy's advice was harsh, but it was what Dupont needed to hear. "He told me, you don't go asking people to manage you," Dupont recalls. "You go out and play your ass off, and a manager will come to you."

Dupont took his words to heart and concentrated on playing. Things starting turning around in 1995, when he landed a job touring with Junior Wells.

Eventually Dupont met Steve Pasek, who became his manager and record producer. Within two years he had recorded two CDs and an EP (extended play) that received play on commercial radio. Today Chainsaw works regularly in blues clubs like Kingston Mines and Bill's Blues Bar in Evanston.

David has turned his life around in other ways. He credits his faith in God and his wife, Norma, who is always there in his corner rooting for him. "She has been fully supportive of me," he says.

Music
- *Bourbon Street Breakdown* (Big Productions, 2005)
- *Hoodoo Ya* (Big Productions, 2004)—EP
- *Lake Street Lullaby* (Big Productions, 2003)

David "Honeyboy" Edwards
Guitar
www.davidhoneyboyedwards.com

The life of David "Honeyboy" Edwards parallels the history of the blues. He was born in the Mississippi Delta in 1915, the same year as Willie Dixon, Muddy Waters, Memphis Slim, Johnny Shines, Eddie Boyd, Floyd McDaniel, Josh White, Brownie McGhee, and Robert Jr. Lockwood. His father was a sharecropper, and he picked cotton as a child. He spent time with Robert Johnson just days before Johnson died. He recorded 15 songs for Alan Lomax and the Library of Congress in 1942 and performed on

Photo by Chuck Winans (pipphotography.com).

the *King Biscuit Time* radio show on KFFA radio in Helena, Arkansas. After moving to Chicago in the early 1950s, Honeyboy performed on Maxwell Street and recorded for Chess Records.

Now in his 90s, Honeyboy continues to perform around the world. His music echoes with the rhythms and sounds of the Mississippi Delta, as he plays much the same way he did more than 70 years ago when he first picked up a guitar.

Honeyboy has lived in Chicago for more than 50 years. Unlike most Chicago bluesmen, whose paths to Chicago were more direct, Honeyboy took a roundabout way. More than any other bluesman, Honeyboy traveled a larger geographic area, according to his manager, Michael Frank. From 1932 through 1956 he spent time in 13 different states. His memories of the past remain vivid, Frank says. "He still comes up with stories about things I've never heard," comments Frank.

In 2002 Honeyboy Edwards received the National Heritage Fellowship from the National Endowment for the Arts. In 2005, at the age of 90, he was honored with a W.C. Handy Award for Best Acoustic Blues Artist. He was inducted into the Blues Foundation's Blues Hall of Fame in 1996.

Frank met Honeyboy in 1972, and by 1976 the two were performing together in North Side clubs—Honeyboy on guitar, Frank on harmonica. After Frank founded Earwig Records in 1979, he recorded Honeyboy with Sunnyland Slim, Floyd Jones, Kansas City Red, and Big Walter Horton. The album was called *Old Friends*. Since then Honeyboy has recorded several other albums, and his previously unreleased recordings have been issued, including the songs he recorded for the Library of Congress in 1942.

Honeyboy still keeps up a schedule of regular performances. He enjoys playing and talking to people, Frank says. "He's very open and sociable," he explains. "He's special in terms of his outlook on life, which has really kept him going."

Spotlight

David "Honeyboy" Edwards tells his story in The World Don't Owe Me Nothing: The Life and Times of Delta Bluesman Honeyboy Edwards, *published in 1997 by Chicago Review Press. He was also the subject of a 2002 documentary called* Honeyboy, *produced and directed by Scott Taradash. The film includes interviews with B.B. King, Sam Carr, Alligator Records' Bruce Iglauer, and Earwig Music's Michael Frank, Honeyboy's longtime manager. For more information visit the film's Web site: www.honeyboyfilm.com.*

Honeyboy Edwards played at the 2005 Chicago Blues Festival accompanied by guitarist Tom Shaka (left) and bassist Aron Burton (standing).
Photo by Karen Hanson.

Music

- *Mississippi Delta Bluesman* (Smithsonian Folkways, 2001)
- *I've Been Around 32* (Jazz Records, 2001)
- *Shake 'Em on Down* (Analogue, 2000)
- *World Don't Owe Me Nothing* (Earwig, 1997)
- *Crawling Kingsnake* (Testament, 1997)
- *Delta Bluesman* (Indigo/Earwig, 1992)—Honeyboy's Library of Congress recordings
- *White Windows* (Evidence, 1988)

Deitra Farr
Vocals
www.deitrafarr.com

When Deitra Farr was seven years old, she went down to a park where her uncle, a trombone player, was performing with a top-40 band. She took a look at the band's female singer and pulled her uncle aside. "When you get tired of her," she told him, "give me a call."

Ten years later the call came. Deitra was 17 years old and a senior in high school. Her uncle told her the band would be auditioning a new singer. No problem for Deitra.

"I had a whole show prepared," she recalls. Though she had no professional experience, Deitra outsang the ten other women who auditioned, and she won the job.

Photo by Andy Ford/Courtesy of Deitra Farr.

Self-assured, determined, and independent: this is Deitra Farr today as she has built an international reputation as a dynamic vocalist and creative songwriter. Deitra breaks all the stereotypes of a blues diva: she's young, city-born, and college educated. In fact, when she first came onto the blues scene in the early 1980s, she had a hard time getting a gig. "A lot of the club owners rejected me right out," she says.

But Deitra didn't give up. She found that her fellow musicians—people like Sunnyland Slim, Eddie Taylor, Lefty Dizz, Johnny Littlejohn, Louis Myers, and Mama Yancy—all liked her singing style. Because they were working blues musicians, she took their opinions seriously. "This is what they do—they're the real deal," Deitra says. "If they could see something in me, could they be wrong?"

Deitra's love of singing began early. As a child, she fell in love with the music of Diana Ross and the Supremes after seeing them on the *Ed Sullivan Show*. "I thought, oh, man, I want to do this!" she recalls. For years she kept a scrapbook of Diana Ross—her first role model, according to Deitra.

She says her first chance at stardom was smacked down. It happened in the early 1970s when she was attending Holy Angels School, a predominantly African-American Catholic school on the South Side. The choir director decided that, for the spring festival, the children should sing gospel songs to reflect their heritage. Deitra was selected to sing the song "Trouble Don't Last Always." When the day came for the performance, Deitra was prepared to sing her big solo. Then right before the show went on, the choir director decided he would sing the song himself. "I've been hurt all these years," she says. "My big break was snatched away from me."

But Deitra could not stay away from music; she seemed fated to be a singer. Twice she had the opportunity to study under teachers with impressive credentials. At Kenwood High School she sang under the direction of renowned musician and composer Lena McLin. After high school she attended Loop College (now Harold Washington College), where her teacher was James Mack, a well-known arranger for Little Milton and Tyrone Davis.

It was fate again that nudged Deitra into cutting her first record, in 1976. She had been singing in class, and one of her classmates asked her to join a group called Mill Street Depot, which was trying to get a record deal. They recorded a demo called "You Won't Support Me," and to Deitra's surprise the record company released it. It made the Billboard and Cash Box record charts.

Deitra's heart was set on music, but she was urged by her parents to choose a more practical goal. She transferred to Chicago State University and began studying health education. That came to end, however, the day she was told she had to work on a cadaver. "That dead body ran me right out of there!" she says.

Still torn between the artistic and the practical, she began working at the University of Chicago at one of the dorms. Again fate seemed to be calling her. Phil Guy came to the school to give a concert. Deitra's friends urged her to go up onstage and sign with Phil. She could never resist a dare. "He was very complimentary," she says.

Phil was playing in those days at the Checkerboard and Theresa's, and Deitra started hanging out there. But a music career still eluded her. In 1981 she graduated from Columbia College with a degree in journalism.

Meanwhile she had hooked up with Erwin Helfer and was practicing her blues singing nearly every day while she was still working a day job. Soon she developed stomach problems and went to a doctor, who told her the pain was caused by stress and referred her to a psychologist. The shrink told her something she never expected to hear: "Quit your day job."

Deitra took his advice. Her coworkers threw her a going-away party, and Deitra departed to devote her time to the blues. When her stomach pains stopped, she took it as a sign. "Life has this way of making you do things you're supposed to do," she remarks.

Since then she has toured with Sam Lay and recorded with Koko Taylor, Dave Specter, and Matthew Skoller. In 1990 she toured Europe, Iceland, Canada, and Israel as a representative of the Chicago Tourism Bureau.

Then in 1993 she became the vocalist for the band Mississippi

Heat. She recorded two CDs with the band: *Learned the Hard Way* (Van der Linden, 1993) and *Thunder in My Heart* (Van der Linden, 1995). Deitra was nominated for a Handy Award in the category of Traditional Female Blues Artist in 1995.

In 1996 Deitra decided to leave the band and focus on her solo work. In 1997 she recorded her first solo CD, *The Search Is Over*, produced by the legendary Johnny Rawls.

Throughout the late '90s and after the turn of the century, she made regular trips to Europe. She had fallen in love with the continent, and the fans there loved her, too. She was particularly attracted to Rome, which she first visited in 1990. "When the plane was landing in Rome, I knew I was home," she says.

A few years later she went back to Rome, to see Pope John Paul II. "I could not get Rome out of my system," she says.

In 2000 she decided to move to Rome. She recalls, "I took my birds, I took my son, I took four suitcases and we left." She had no intentions of coming back.

Everything seemed to be working out. She hooked up with a Roman band and began touring throughout Europe. She found an American school for her son, and he was doing well. But her idyllic existence was cut short with the terrorist attacks of September 11, 2001. At that point, she couldn't get a visa for her son, and she and her son were required to move back to the United States. However, as an artist, she's had several opportunities to visit and perform in Europe since then. She took a trip in 2004 with the Chicago Blues Festival Tour with Jody Williams and Andrew "Jr. Boy" Jones. She still has many good friends and fans in Europe. "I have all these fans all over the world, being who I am," she says.

Spotlight

Deitra Farr graduated from Chicago's Columbia College with a degree in journalism and has written for the Chicago Daily Defender, *the* Chicago Blues Annual, *the Italian blues magazine* Il Blues, *and* Living Blues. *She has also written poems and many of her own songs. On her CD* Let It Go!, *she wrote all 12 songs and even the liner notes.*

"I've been writing songs since I was a child," Deitra says. "I've always been a songwriter."

Music
- *Let It Go* (JSP, 2005)
- *The Search Is Over* (JSP, 1997)

Billy Flynn
Guitar
www.billyflynn.com

Born in Wisconsin on August 11, 1956, Billy Flynn has been a mainstay on the Chicago scene since 1975, when he joined the band of Jimmy Dawkins. He toured frequently with the guitar legend for four years. In the late 1980s Flynn joined the Legendary Blues Band and played with Pinetop Perkins, Willie "Big Eyes" Smith, and Calvin Jones. In addition to his solo work, Flynn has played and/or recorded with many Chicago-area artists, notably Jimmy Dawkins and Mississippi Heat.

Music
- *Chicago Blues Mandolin* (2005)
- *Billy's Blues* (2005)
- *Blues & Love* (Easy Baby)
- *Smoke Daddy Band* (Easy Baby)
- *Big Guitar* (Easy Baby)—guitar instrumentals
- *Blues Today* (Easy Baby)

Diamond Jim Greene
Acoustic guitar

Diamond Jim Greene performs regularly at weekend acoustic sets at Buddy Guy's Legends. Greene learned to play guitar after he met Blind Arvella Gray, a street performer, in Chicago. In the 1980s Greene lived in Virginia, where he was inspired by the acoustic music and Piedmont-style fingerpicking of John Cephas, John Jackson, Archie Edwards, and Saffire: The Uppity Blues Women.

Music
- *Just a Dream* (Black Magic, 1995)—recorded in the Netherlands

Liz Mandville Greeson
Vocals, guitar
www.lizmandvillegreeson.com

The songs of Liz Mandville Greeson cover the full range of blues: slow, sultry burners, blues-rock, shouts and songs tinged with R&B, gospel, or country overtones. Her lyrics take on universal themes about love and relationships that appeal to both

Photo courtesy of Liz Mandville Greeson.

men and women wherever they may be in life's journey.

Liz believes the blues can articulate people's feelings while also creating a little distance from them. People can take their feelings, look at them, laugh at them, and dance to them, she says. "I try to give people space to have this cathartic experience," Liz explains.

Liz says that her songs appeal to people "between the ages of 30 and dead." By then, she says, "you begin to understand what it's like to be an adult." More mature audiences have experienced loss, heartbreak, and financial and relationship troubles, she says. Once a person is past a certain age, popular music is no longer satisfying; blues appeals to more mature adults, she says. Over the years Liz has learned that for women of all ages and all sizes, sexiness is not a look but an attitude. Still, for Liz the visual appeal of her show is also important. "I'm very much into giving people something to look at," she says.

But even that has evolved to be more inclusive. Early in her career she had decided her performance was going to be perfect, right down to her appearance. She fixed her hair perfectly, carefully crafted her makeup, and put on a slinky dress. Once onstage she turned on the steamy sex appeal. She soon realized the approach backfired. "Women would grab their men and go," says Liz, adding that there isn't much point in singing to an empty room.

Liz realized that she had fallen out of touch with women because during the long stretches on the road, she had interacted nearly exclusively with men. She decided to make a conscious effort to see what was going on in the lives of other women. And she learned to look at the faces in the crowd and try to relate individually to each one of them. "These are the people that the blues speak to," she says of her audience.

Liz grew up in Wisconsin, the daughter of parents who loved to travel and were avid fans of all the arts. Her mother, a teacher, was a theater buff and loved music, although she herself couldn't sing. Her father, a fine artist, had trained at the Art Institute of Chicago. He taught her to paint in acrylics and pastels, a hobby she still practices in her basement studio. Liz says she drew upon this artistic influence for her stage presentation.

As a child, Liz heard an eclectic mix of music ranging from Johnny Cash, the Weavers, and Arlo Guthrie to Odetta and Mahalia Jackson to Arthur Fielder and his orchestra. She loved Tina Turner and listened to Etta James, Gladys Knight, Aretha Franklin, and Irma Thomas.

Liz moved to Chicago to study theater in 1979, just when disco was waning and the hair bands were gaining popularity. To Liz pop music was like a vast wasteland. The songs left her flat. "I couldn't relate to any of them," she remarks.

Then she met her ex-husband, Willie Greeson (then known as Willie Phillips), who played with the Legendary Blues Band. He introduced her to Chicago's blues and R&B scene. She got hooked on the music.

"I just mined his record collection, and when I was hungry for more, I'd go to those used record stores in town where you could buy an album for a dollar," she recalls.

She would take the records home and play them over and over. "I'd learn them lick for lick, note for note, in that artist's key," says Liz, whose voice can span four octaves.

Liz was not entirely self-taught, however. She studied eight years with Evanston voice teacher and baritone Doug Susu-Mago, who taught her to think of her voice as an instrument and to regard her performance the same way an athlete thinks of a game. She learned to loosen up and relax. Later, Liz graduated with a degree in music from Columbia College in Chicago.

In the early 1980s Liz started touring professionally with the R&B cover band the Supernaturals. For ten years they played in little towns across the upper Midwest and through Canada. While Canadian fans really supported the blues, the gigs were tough. They'd sometimes have to drive 16 hours across the Canadian plains to reach the next club.

But years on the road allowed Liz to sharpen her skills and learn new songs. She'd become obsessed with an artist—Sam and Dave one week, Otis Redding the next—and she'd learn their music. She also picked up a lot of licks by listening to the instrumental solos of artists like Louis Armstrong and Junior Parker.

In 1994 she met bassist Aron Burton at Rosa's Lounge. "He took a fatherly interest in my career and was a great mentor to me," she says. She recorded two tracks with Burton on his 1996 release, *Aron Burton Live* (Earwig), and appeared with him at the 1994 Chicago Blues Festival.

During her college years, 1994 through 1999, she took on a steady gig at Blue Chicago. She worked with Willie Kent, Michael Coleman, Maurice John Vaughn, and the late George Baze. During this time Liz recorded two tracks for the *Red Hot Mamas* CD (1997), produced by Blue Chicago owner Gino Battaglia.

She developed her own songwriting style and has written all the songs on her (to date) four CDs, along with the song "Back in Love" for Johnny Drummer on his 2001 CD, *Unleaded Blues*. Liz gets ideas for her lyrics from her own experience and from conversations with women. She wrote "Juicehead Man" while driving the tour van and "Walking on Eggshells" after watching a friend go through an experience with an abusive husband. But sometimes, Liz says, song ideas come from out of the blue. "I get a lot of ideas in the shower," she notes.

The songs on her CDs, she says, are examples of a contemporary take on the traditional blues. "I tip my hat to it and carry it forward," she says.

Music
- *Back in Love Again* (Earwig, 2003)
- *Ready to Cheat* (Earwig, 1999)
- *Look at Me* (Earwig, 1996)
- *Tell It Like It Is* (Earwig, 1988)

Buddy Guy
Guitar
www.buddyguy.net

When Buddy Guy isn't touring the world, he can often be found hanging out at his club, Legends, in the South Loop. Often the club patrons—some who came to Chicago expressly to see Buddy—don't even notice him as he sits quietly alone at the dark end of the bar. When asked, he will gladly sign an autograph or pose for a picture with fans, but rarely does he seek the spotlight, even in his own club.

It's a life of paradox for a man who is possibly the most famous blues musician in the world. Early in his career Guy suffered from stage fright, and he still considers himself shy. For years he has lived a peaceful life in the south suburbs, but his face and his music are instantly recognized by blues fans and rock fans alike. The few shows he performs every January at Legends are always sold out, and he draws massive crowds whenever he plays at the Chicago Blues Festival.

Guy's musical career has spanned five decades and has crossed over into the worlds of

Photo by Chuck Winans (pipphotography.com).

rock and pop music. His explosive style has influenced an entire generation of guitar players. Along the way he's garnered every award and honor imaginable. He has received multiple Handy Awards. His 2003 CD *Blues Singer* won a Grammy for the Best Traditional Blues Album. He won Grammys in the category of Best Contemporary Blues Album for *Damn Right, I've Got the Blues* (1991), *Feels like Rain* (1993), and *Slippin' In* (1995).

He also received a Grammy in 1996, in the category of Best Rock Instrumental Performance, for his contribution to *SRV Shuffle*, a tribute to Stevie Ray Vaughan. His cowinners were Jimmie Vaughan, Eric Clapton, Bonnie Raitt, B.B. King, Robert Cray, Dr. John, and Art Neville. In 2005 he was inducted into the Rock and Roll Hall of Fame.

In many ways fame has sought Buddy Guy, not the other way around. Ask him about his success, and he will tell you, "I have been very blessed." He credits the blues musicians who went before him—"the old guys."

George "Buddy" Guy was born on July 30, 1936, in Lettsworth, Louisiana. At age 13 he made his own guitar and taught himself to play. In the early 1950s he began his professional career by playing gigs in the Baton Rouge area.

Guy moved to Chicago in 1957 and was encouraged by Muddy Waters. In 1958 he entered—and won—a headcutting contest at the Blue Flame Club against Magic Sam and Otis Rush. His achievement led to his recording two singles for Artistic Records. He also recorded briefly for the Cobra label.

In the early 1960s Buddy worked as a session guitarist for Chess, where he recorded with Muddy Waters, Little Walter, Willie Dixon, and Sonny Boy Williamson II (Rice Miller). In 1962 he had a hit of his own with

"Stone Crazy." In 1965 he toured England with the American Folk Blues Tour.

His partnership with Junior Wells began about 1965. The two frequently worked together in Chicago clubs, and they recorded together for Delmark on Junior Wells's seminal album, *Hoodoo Man Blues*. In 1967 Guy signed with Vanguard; his two 1968 albums, *A Man and the Blues* and *This Is Buddy Guy*, are today considered blues classics.

In 1972 he bought the Checkerboard Lounge at 43rd and State Street. At a time when the blues appeared to be waning in Chicago, the Checkerboard became an incubator for new talent and a popular venue for established artists like Muddy Waters, Willie Dixon, Jimmy Reed, B.B. King, and Howlin' Wolf.

Buddy sold his interest in the Checkerboard in the early 1980s and opened his new club, Legends, in 1989. Within a few years his fame skyrocketed with the release of the Grammy Award–winning album *Damn Right, I've Got the Blues*. The CD caught the attention of the rock world, and Buddy was proclaimed the best guitarist in the world by rock icon Eric Clapton.

Buddy Guy is still working a full schedule of tour dates and still producing new, original material that pushes the boundaries of contemporary blues.

Music

- *Blues Singer* (Jive, 2003)
- *Sweet Tea* (Silvertone, 2001)
- *Every Day I Have the Blues* (Cleopatra, 2000)
- *Buddy's Baddest: The Best of Buddy Guy* (Silvertone, 1999)
- *Last Time Around: Live at Legends* (Silvertone, 1998)
- As Good as It Gets (Vanguard, 1998)
- *Live—the Real Deal* (Silvertone, 1996)—with G.E. Smith and Johnnie Johnson
- *DJ Play My Blues* (JSP, 1994)—originally issued in 1982
- *Slippin' In* (Silvertone, 1994)
- *Feels like Rain* (Silvertone, 1993)
- *The Very Best of Buddy Guy* (Rhino, 1992)
- *Drinkin' TNT 'n' Smokin' Dynamite* (Blind Pig, 1992)
- *The Complete Chess Studio Recordings* (MCA, 1992)
- *Damn Right, I've Got the Blues* (Silvertone, 1991)
- *Alone & Acoustic* (Alligator, 1991)

* *Stone Crazy!* (Alligator, 1990)
* *A Man and the Blues* (Vanguard, 1990)—originally issued in 1968
* *Live–This Is Buddy Guy* (Vanguard, 1989)—originally issued in 1968

Phil Guy
Guitar

A little younger and funkier than his older brother Buddy, Phil Guy has performed regularly in Chicago for more than four decades. Born on April 28, 1940, in Lettsworth, Louisiana, Phil learned to play the blues on a guitar that once belonged to Buddy. In the late 1950s and early '60s Phil performed around Baton Rouge, notably with blues singer Raful Neal. He recorded with Neal and swamp-blues harp player Slim Harpo.

Phil arrived in Chicago in 1969. He played for a time backing Buddy and Junior Wells. He has also played with Byther Smith and Jimmy Dawkins.

Music
* *Say What You Mean* (JSP, 2000)
* *Chicago's Hottest Guitars: Chicago Blues Session, Vol. 25* (Wolf, 1998)—with Lurrie Bell
* *Breaking Out on Top* (JSP, 1995)
* *Tina Nu* (JSP, 1994)

Erwin Helfer
Piano
www.erwinhelferpiano.com

For more than four decades, Erwin Helfer has entertained crowds in Chicago and around the world with boogie-woogie blues piano. Born in 1936, Helfer grew up on the South Side. He taught himself to play piano, and in the late 1950s he played jazz in New Orleans. In the 1960s and '70s he worked frequently with piano master Jimmy Walker. Helfer also recorded with vocalist Mama Yancy, wife of blues pianist Jimmy Yancy.

Helfer earned a bachelor's degree in music from the American Conservatory and a master's degree in music from Northeastern Illinois University. In addition to performing he gives private piano lessons.

Music

- *St. James Infirmary* (Sirens, 2003)—with saxophonist Skinny Williams
- *I'm Not Hungry but I Like to Eat* (Sirens, 2002)
- *8 Hands on 88 Keys—Blues Piano Masters* (Sirens, 2002)
  —with Barrelhouse Chuck, Detroit Junior, and Pinetop Perkins
- *Heavy Timbre—Chicago Boogie Piano* (Sirens, 2002)
  —with Blind John Davis, Sunnyland Slim, Willie Mabon, and Jimmy Walker; originally recorded in 1976
- *Rough and Ready* (Testament–City Hall, 1994)—with Jimmy Walker

Tom Holland

Guitar

www.shufflekings.com

Left-handed Tom Holland is one of the youngest blues slide guitarists and bandleaders in Chicago today. His band, the Shuffle Kings, plays traditional Chicago blues influenced by legends like Muddy Waters, Little Walter, and Howlin' Wolf.

Born in 1978, Holland grew up on the South Side listening to his father's extensive collection of jazz and blues records. At age 13 he taught himself guitar by playing along

Photo by Karen Hanson.

with the music of Muddy Waters, Magic Sam, and Earl Hooker.

At age 18 Holland was hanging around South Side clubs and soon began sitting in with Phil Guy. When he was 19 he played his first professional gig, at a South Side beauty salon with guitarist L.V. Banks. For the next four years he played regularly with Banks. Then one night at the Checkerboard, John Primer offered him a job. He joined John Primer's Real Deal Band and toured with Primer through the United States and Canada.

In 1999 Holland joined Eddy Clearwater's band. In his three years with "the Chief," Tom made his first trip to Europe. Meanwhile he formed his own band, the Shuffle Kings. He left Clearwarer and joined the James Cotton band in 2003. When not on the road with Cotton, Holland plays with the Shuffle Kings in Chicago area clubs.

Music
* *Tom Holland and the Shuffle Kings* (2003)

Homesick James
Guitar

Homesick James has played the blues longer than most people have been alive. He was performing professionally by the time he was a teenager, and now well into his 90s, the slide guitarist has become a perennial favorite at the Chicago Blues Festival.

Homesick's guitar style has often been compared to bottleneck master Elmore James, who is a distant cousin. Through the 1950s Homesick backed Elmore on several recordings. Elmore was living with Homesick and his family when he died of heart disease in 1963.

Homesick was born John William Henderson on April 30, 1910, in Somerville, Tennessee. At age 12 he ran away from home and spent the next several years playing music as he moved around the South. Once in Chicago in the mid-1930s, Homesick played in clubs with Lonnie Johnson and Big Bill Broonzy. Through the next two decades he was active on the club scene and recorded for several small labels with artists like Snooky Pryor, Johnny Shines, and Elmore James.

He was dubbed "Homesick" after he recorded a song by that title in 1953 for the Chance label. "James" may refer to Elmore James, and "Williamson" to Sonny Boy Williamson II (Rice Miller), with whom Homesick also claims kinship.

Music
* *My Home Ain't Here* (Fedora, 2004)
* *Got to Move* (32 Blues, 2000)
* *Last of the Broomdusters* (Fedora, 1998)
* *Words of Wisdom* (Priority, 1997)
* *Juanita* (Evidence, 1997)
* *Goin' Back in the Times* (Earwig, 1994)
* *Sweet Home Tennessee* (Appaloosa, 1993)
* *Blues on the South Side* (OBC, 1991)—a reissue of a 1964 recording
* *Ain't Sick No More* (Bluesway, 1973)

Howard and the White Boys
Guitar band
www.howardandthewhiteboys.net

"Howard" is Howard McCullum, whose soulful vocals and bass guitar have driven the band since the late 1980s. The "White Boys" are currently Jim Christopulos on drums, Rocco Calipari on guitar, and, the newest member, guitarist Pete Galanis, who replaced founding member Dan Bellini. Steve Asma and Giles Corey were also members at one time.

Howard and the White Boys began in 1988 when a group of Northern Illinois University students got together and started jamming. The band quickly gained a loyal following with their blues-rock sound tinged with funk and R&B.

In the early 1990s the band met Buddy Guy and began performing regularly at Buddy Guy's Legends. He invited them to tour with him through the Midwest in 1995. In the mid-1990s they won the National Blues Talent Search held at the House of Blues in Los Angeles. They have opened for B.B. King and played with Bo Diddley, Junior Wells, Lonnie Brooks, Luther Allison, Albert King, Chuck Berry, and Koko Taylor.

Music
- *Live at Chord on Blues* (Evidence, 2000)
- *Big Score* (Evidence, 1999)
- *Guess Who's Coming to Dinner?* (Mighty Tiger, 1997)
- *Strung Out on the Blues* (Mighty Tiger, 1994)

Fruteland Jackson
Acoustic guitar
www.fruteland.com

Fruteland Jackson believes in the power of acoustic blues. "It's a calling," says the blues musician, oral historian, and educator. Wherever he performs—at blues festivals, cultural centers, or clubs or in the schools—he finds crowds ready to listen to the stories that acoustic blues can tell the best.

While most young men interested in the blues pick up a Stratocaster and turn up the volume, Fruteland was drawn to the quieter stylings of the acoustic guitar because it is "closer to the fountain," nearer to the roots and his own family and African-American heritage. Fruteland plays in all styles of acoustic blues: country-folk blues, Delta, Piedmont, and contemporary.

"I like all roots music," he comments. "I consider it all blues, even though some of it is on the edges. I try to play it all, a little bit of everything."

A few years ago, inspired by the folk, country, and bluegrass music in the movie *O Brother, Where Art Thou?*, Fruteland learned to play kazoo, mandolin, banjo, lap steel guitar, ukulele, spoons, jug, and something he calls a stick—a percussive instrument fashioned from a pogo stick, washboard, bell, and high-hat cymbal.

Photo by Chuck Winans
(pipphotography.com).

Growing up, Fruteland never dreamed he'd become a professional musician. "I didn't pick this. It picked me," he says. "Nobody could have told me I'd end up here."

When he was just a child, his parents moved the family to Chicago from Mississippi, where he had been born on June 9, 1953, the fourth of six children. His father, a World War II veteran, landed a job as an insurance underwriter. His mother worked as a nurse.

But Fruteland spent summer vacations in Mississippi visiting relatives. His maternal grandparents were founders of a church in Doddsville, Mississippi, and his paternal grandfather was a Baptist minister. His uncle Woodrow "Dick" Chandler played guitar and piano at house parties and juke joints. Often he'd drop by the house and play his music. At the time, Fruteland did not fully appreciate what he was hearing. But he and his uncle were close, and when Fruteland was 12 Uncle Woodrow gave him a guitar. Fruteland would be much older before he learned to play the blues, but the "seeds were planted" there in Mississippi when he was a child, he says.

Back in Chicago, Fruteland played bugle and trombone in the school band. Later, he studied music at Columbia College and Roosevelt University in Chicago. But then he left music behind as he married, had children, and found a job as a private investigator and, later, as an investigator with the State of Illinois Department of Human Rights.

In the early 1980s Fruteland moved to Biloxi, Mississippi, and opened a wholesale seafood company. At work he listened to a local radio station that played the blues. Again, although he didn't realize it, he was being drawn toward the blues.

In 1985 disaster struck when Hurricane Elena hit the Gulf Coast and destroyed his business. Finding himself in a transitional period in his life, he turned to the blues. He began listening to his father's collection of old 78 records, and this time the music touched him in a profound way. He learned everything he could about Robert Johnson, Howlin' Wolf, Little Walter, Muddy Waters, and others. He heard a calling, and he wanted to use the blues to help others.

Since then he's been on the road a lot, sometimes working in schools during the day and playing in clubs at night. He plays at blues festivals all over the country, and in 2004 he traveled to Russia. Locally he often performs the weekend acoustic sets at Buddy Guy's Legends and at Porter's Oyster Bar in Crystal Lake.

He loves the opportunity to draw people into the blues. He believes that the music promotes healing and cross-cultural understanding. "It brings people together who otherwise wouldn't meet," he says.

Spotlight

Through the Blues in the Schools program, Fruteland Jackson annually teaches the blues to more than 50,000 kids and adults throughout the United States and Canada. He also trains and assists other blues artists who are interested in doing Blues in the Schools programs. For his work he received the Illinois Arts Council Folk/Ethnic Heritage Award in 1996 and a W.C. Handy Award for Keeping the Blues Alive–Blues in Education in 1997.

The awards came as a surprise to Fruteland. "I never knew they were watching me," he says.

Music
- *Blues 2.0* (Electro-Fi, 2003)
- *I Claim Nothing but the Blues* (Electro-Fi, 2000)

Carlos Johnson
Guitar

Carlos Johnson's guitar sizzles in the style of Albert King or Otis Rush. When he plays he seems possessed by the music. He may start his performance sitting in a chair, but as the song builds he rises to his feet, feeling the song with body and soul.

After 30 years in the business, primarily as a sideman, Johnson stepped out into the spotlight in May 2004, when he accompanied Otis Rush on a Japanese tour. Rush had suffered a stroke a few months earlier and could barely play or sing, but Japanese fans were thrilled just to see the guitar legend. Johnson, who had spent time in Otis's band early in his career, filled in for his ailing mentor and dazzled the Japanese fans with his guitar prowess.

Johnson was born on January 17, 1948, in Chicago and grew up on the South Side. His mother was a nurse, and his father worked in construction. At age six he learned to play on a

Photo by Chuck Winans (pipphotography.com).

toy guitar. By age 12 he had graduated to a real guitar and made $10 for playing rock music at a neighborhood barbecue. He continued playing in bands through high school.

Early in his career Johnson worked with the R&B group Sheila and the Chandeliers (later known as the Emotions). In the late 1960s and early '70s, he played jazz as well as blues; the jazz influence can be heard in his licks.

Music
- *Don't Mess with the Bluesmen* (P-Vine, 2004)—with Billy Branch
- *In and Out* (Mister Kelly's, 2004)
- *My Name Is Carlos Johnson* (Blues Special)

Jimmy Johnson
Guitar

Jimmy Johnson's stinging guitar work is the essence of the West Side sound, and his smooth vocals reveal his background in gospel and R&B. Johnson still plays regularly in Chicago clubs.

Born Jimmy Thompson on November 25, 1928, in Holly Springs, Mississippi, Johnson is the older brother of soul singer Syl Johnson and Mack Thompson, bass player with Magic Sam. As a child, Jimmy sang in the church choir, and he later joined a gospel group called the United Five in Memphis.

After moving to Chicago in 1950, he found a job as guitarist with another gospel group, the Golden Jubilaires. In 1959 he worked briefly with Magic Sam and Freddie King, but he switched to R&B in the 1960s and performed on the South and West sides. In the early 1970s he decided to return to the blues, working with Jimmy Dawkins and Otis Rush.

Photo by Chuck Winans (pipphotography.com).

In 1978 he formed his own band and recorded four tracks for Alligator's *Living Chicago Blues, Vol. 1*. The effort earned him a Grammy nomination. He recorded two albums for Delmark and another for Alligator, and in 1985 he received a Handy Award, along with Eddy Clearwater, for Best Contemporary Blues Album (Foreign) for their album *I Don't Give a Damn if Whites Bought It*, on the Red Lightning label in England.

In 1988 Johnson stopped performing after he was injured in a car accident in which two band members died. He returned to the blues in the mid-1990s. His 1994 album, *I'm a Jockey*, received a Handy Award for Comeback Album of the year. That year his brother Syl Johnson was nominated in the same category for his CD *Syl Johnson: Back in the Game*.

Music

- *Pepper's Hangout* (Delmark, 2000)
- *I'm a Jockey* (Verve, 1994)
- *Bar Room Preacher* (Alligator, 1985)
- *North/South* (Delmark, 1982)
- *Johnson's Whacks* (Delmark, 1979)
- *Living Chicago Blues* (Alligator, 1978)—an anthology of various artists

Shirley Johnson
Vocals

At age six Shirley Johnson was singing gospel at her church in Norfolk, Virginia. Influenced by the sounds of Ruth Brown, Mahalia Jackson, and Koko Taylor, Johnson performed early in her career, opening for Z.Z. Hill, Aretha Franklin, and Jerry Butler. In the 1980s she recorded two singles for a Virginia record label.

After moving to Chicago in 1983, Johnson worked with Artie "Blues Boy" White and Little Johnny Christian and toured with keyboardist Eddie Lusk. In the 1990s she contributed two tracks each to *Women of Blue Chicago* (Delmark, 1996), *Red Hot Mamas* (Blue Chicago, 1997), and *Mojo Mamas* (Blue Chicago, 2000). Johnson performs regularly at Blue Chicago.

Music
- *Killer Diller* (Delmark, 2002)
- *Looking for Love* (Appaloosa, 1996)

Fernando Jones
Guitar, harmonica
www.fernandojones.com

Fernando Jones is a musician, songwriter, producer, author, playwright, actor, and educator, and the blues is at the center of all of it. The Chicago native paid tribute to the people, places, and sounds of the blues in his 1998 book, *I Was There When the Blues Was Red Hot!*

"Writing my book was my way of showing many of the older, unsung heroes of the blues that a young black man, who learned from them, thought enough about them to document

Photo by Karen Hanson.

them," Fernando says. "Too often elder statesmen of the blues say that black folks don't support the blues. I wanted to show them that we do."

Fernando spent years researching, visiting the blues clubs, interviewing musicians, and hanging out wherever the blues was played. Set in the 1950s, the book tells the story of a group of friends who hang out in a basement blues club.

The book served as the basis for a 16mm black-and-white documentary, released in 1996, that included footage of Chicago blues stars like Buddy Guy, Willie Dixon, and Big Daddy Kinsey. Then in 1998 Fernando crafted his book into an interactive comedy-drama. The play opened at

Gerri's Palm Tavern at 446 E. 47th Street and ran for 256 performances. Fernando wrote all the original music and played a small role.

Born on February 7, 1964, Fernando grew up on the South Side surrounded by the blues. His oldest brother, Foree Superstar, was a blues musician who frequently performed in clubs like the Queen Bee and Theresa's Lounge. When Fernando was four his brother took him to Theresa's. He still recalls the experience vividly. "I remember seeing sharp-dressed people inside and Buick 225s and Cadillacs parked outside," Fernando reminisces.

For his sixth birthday Fernando received his first guitar as a gift. "I've been playing ever since, and I've never stopped," he says.

Fernando, like other kids of his generation, listened to rock, R&B, and soul music, but he was also exposed to the roots of the blues. As a child, he vacationed each summer with his mother's relatives in Mississippi.

Spotlight

Gerri's Palm Tavern, the venue for Fernando Jones's play I Was There When the Blues Was Red Hot!, *played an important role in blues history. The neighborhood bar, which opened in 1933, was located at 446 E. 47th Street, across the street from the famous Regal Theater, where jazz, blues, and soul artists, such as Duke Ellington, Muddy Waters, and James Brown, used to perform. After the show band members would hang out at Gerri's. When the Regal closed in 1973, the Palm Tavern remained open, but it had lost much of its former glamour. In 2001 the City of Chicago used eminent domain to close down the historic building. To date no plans have been announced for the property. In 2004 the Landmark Preservation Council of Illinois placed the Palm Tavern on its list of the Ten Most Endangered Historical Places in Illinois.*

As a student at the University of Illinois at Chicago, he organized the campus's first blues festival, on February 11, 1985. Headliners were Buddy Guy, Junior Wells, Koko Taylor, Magic Slim, and his brother, Foree Superstar.

Fernando graduated in 1987. Two years later, as a member of the UIC Black Alumni Association, he organized the first annual Blues and Heritage Festival.

Since writing *I Was There When the Blues Was Red Hot!*, Fernando has also penned the plays *Blue Eyed Blues, The Train Game, Half Soles Have Souls, I Feel with My Hands,* and *My Round Square Block.*

As an educator Fernando uses the blues to teach and inspire the younger generation. With Blues Kids of America, Ltd., he has designed a blues-based curriculum for kindergarten through 12th grade. In the program he teaches kids to play and sing songs he wrote, such as "The Stay in School Blues" and "Chicago Has Everything You Need."

The children respond well to the blues, he believes. "I think the fact that I come in with live instruments really helps," he says. "I first start off with the band playing something 'groovy.' Then I showcase each instrument. Then I have their attention all the way."

Fernando also writes all original songs for his CDs. His poetic lyrics, both serious and humorous, describe modern themes. "We live in different times, so our music is much more intense," he says.

Music
- *Stranded* (Dude/Indigo, 2004)

Lynne Jordan
Vocals
www.lynnejordan.com

Lynne Jordan can belt out the blues like nobody's business. Always colorfully dressed and sometimes topped with flamboyant hats, Jordan interacts with the crowds, urging on their participation. Her rendition of "If I Can't Sell It, I'll Keep Sitting on It" evokes wide grins from even those who don't get the double entendre.

Jordan's musical offerings are wide ranging. She has covered the Rolling Stones' "Sympathy for the Devil," made a Christmas album, and recorded background vocals for singer-songwriter Tom Waits and for the alternative band Urge Overkill.

Originally from Dayton, Ohio, Jordan attended Northwestern University and studied theater in the early 1980s. Jordan recorded two tracks each for the compilations *Women of Blue Chicago* (Delmark, 1996) and *Red Hot Mamas* (Blue Chicago, 1997). She also appears on the 1997 House of Blues CD *Songs of Janis Joplin: Blues Down Deep.*

Music
- *A Bit O' Fun*
- *Holiday Shivers*—a Christmas album

Vance Kelly
Guitar

Vance Kelly's blues are funky, soulful, and laced with the sounds of classic R&B. Though small in stature, Kelly has a big, powerful voice that can belt out a Delta blues tune or melt around a sexy soul blues melody. An entertainer, Kelly interacts with the crowds, getting people up and dancing or at least bopping around on their barstools. He's backed by the solid sounds of the Backstreet Band.

Kelly learned to mix it up early in his career after spending time in bands that played music ranging from jazz to disco to pop. Kelly says his idol was Johnny Dollar. "I like the variety of music that he does," Kelly explains. "You don't hear the same kind of music all night."

Born on January 24, 1954, in Chicago, Kelly was raised near Maxwell Street. His father was from Mississippi; his mother, a minister, hailed from Missouri. His seven brothers and sisters grew up singing gospel in church. He was born with a serious arthritic condition that crippled his legs. Doctors had to break his legs to straighten them, but even after the treatment physicians doubted the boy would ever walk. Vance proved them wrong. One day at the age of two, he astonished his parents when he got out of bed and started walking.

Kelly began playing guitar at age seven. When he was 15 he was playing his guitar outside when blues singer Mary Lane happened to hear him. She invited him to play for her at the 1815 Club on Roosevelt Road.

In 1971 he got a job with the Concept band, which played mostly funk and love ballads. He stayed with Concept for six years before leaving to join the band Central Light. In 1980 he joined the band of Little Johnny Christian, where he played the blues until 1985.

Kelly then joined saxophonist A.C. Reed, who taught him not only about the music but also about the business of the blues. "He helped me out a helluva a lot," Kelly says. When he left Reed in 1990 to form his own band, Kelly had learned about the responsibilities of being a bandleader.

Kelly and his Backstreet Band played mostly on the West Side until 1992, when they landed the gig as the house band at the Checkerboard Lounge. They performed two or three times a week until the club closed in 2003.

Today Vance Kelly and the Backstreet Band play regularly at the Some Place Else Lounge on the South Side, at the Genesis Lounge in Country Club Hills, and at North Side bars like Kingston Mines.

Music

- *Nobody Has the Power* (Wolf, 2005)—with daughter Vivian Vance Kelly
- *Live at Lee's Unleaded Blues* (Wolf, 2003)
- *What Three Old Ladies Can Do* (Wolf, 2000)
- *Hands Off!* (Wolf, 1998)
- *Joyriding in the Subway* (Wolf, 1995)

Shirley King
Vocals

Shirley King is billed as the "Daughter of the Blues," and with good reason: her father is blues legend B.B. King. In live performances she's a saucy diva, peppering her songs with sexy humor and drawing in the audience to sing and dance along.

Born on October 26, 1949, in West Memphis, Arkansas, Shirley was influenced early on by the music of Etta James, Mahalia Jackson, and Ruth Brown. After moving to Chicago as a young woman, she worked as a dancer before deciding, in 1990, to follow in her father's footsteps as a blues singer. She has also worked in the schools with the Urban Gateway Blues organization and Blues in the Schools.

Music

- *Daughter of the Blues* (Diva, 1999)
- *Jump Through My Keyhole* (GBW, 1994)

Sam Lay
Drums, guitar

Legendary drummer Sam Lay, the "Shuffle Master," started his Chicago career in 1959 in the band of Little Walter. In 1960 he joined Howlin' Wolf's band, where he remained until 1966, when he became a member of the Paul Butterfield Blues Band. He also worked with James Cotton and the Siegel-Schwall Band and recorded on numerous Chess releases. Lay was inducted into the Blues Hall of Fame in 1992.

Perhaps Lay's most historic moment occurred in 1965, when he played with Bob Dylan when Dylan performed electric guitar for the first time at the Newport Folk Festival.

These days Lay performs on both drums and guitar.

Music
- *I Get Evil* (Random Chance, 2003)
- *Live on Beale Street* (Blue Moon, 2000)
- *Rush Hour Blues* (Telarc, 2000)
- *Stone Blues* (Evidence, 1996)
- *Shuffle Master* (Appaloosa, 1993)

Bonnie Lee
Vocals

The "Sweetheart of the Blues," Bonnie Lee has been belting out songs in Chicago since the late 1960s.

Bonnie was born on June 11, 1931, in Bunkie, Louisiana, and was raised in Beaumont, Texas. As a child, she took piano lessons and sang gospel in her local church. Her favorite singers were Ella Fitzgerald and Sarah Vaughn. "I used to sit on the front porch swing and sing along," Bonnie recalls. "I thought, that's what I'm going to be when I grow up."

Although she was a good gospel piano player, she never learned blues piano. "I never could play the blues," she says. "My hands would never move. The right one would go, but the left one would just stay there. But when I played gospel, they'd start moving."

As a teenager, Bonnie began singing with Texas bluesman Clarence "Gatemouth" Brown. She also became a big fan of Big Mama Thornton and would travel from Beaumont to Houston just to see Thornton. One night her friends took her up to the stage and told Big Mama, "We've got a girl here who can really sing."

"I was scared," Bonnie says, recalling Big Mama's imposing size and rough demeanor. "She looked at me and she says"—here Bonnie's voice lowers to a bass pitch—"'Bring her up here.' I thought she was a man!"

But Bonnie mustered her courage and sang with Big Mama. It was a thrill she would always remember.

While still singing in Texas, Bonnie recorded two songs, "Sad and Evil Woman" and "I'm Good," for Mayo Williams on Ebony Records. She moved to Chicago in the early 1960s and began singing jazz. She switched to blues when she hooked up with Sunnyland Slim, whom she had first met years ago in Texas. "He took me under his wing," she says.

She toured and recorded with Sunnyland through the 1970s, also working at times with J.B. Hutto and Eddie C. Campbell. In the early 1980s she began performing regularly with Willie Kent and the Gents. After Kent died in March 2006, she continued to sing with the Gents.

Music
- *Women of Blue Chicago* (Delmark, 1996)—with Karen Carroll, Shirley Johnson, Lynne Jordan, Katherine Davis, and Big Time Sarah
- *Sweetheart of the Blues* (Delmark, 1995)
- *Blues with the Girls* (EPM, 1982)—with Big Time Sarah and Zora Young
- *I'm Good: Chicago Blues Session, Vol. 7* (Wolf)
- *Chicago's Finest Blues Ladies* (Wolf)—with Deitra Farr, Zora Young, Karen Carroll, Melvina Allen, and Mary Lane

Sharon Lewis
Vocals
www.sharonlewisblues.com

Sharon Lewis is a high-energy vocalist who mixes blues with R&B, rock, jazz, and country music. She began singing in 1993 after answering a classified ad for a blues singer. Backed variably by the Under the Gun band, the Mojo Kings, the Next Generation Band, Texas Fire, or the Groove, Sharon has performed in nearly every Chicago-area blues club and at clubs and festivals elsewhere in the United States.

Music
- *Everything's Gonna Be Alright* (Sleeping Dog, 2004)—with the band Under the Gun

Lil' Ed
Guitar

Lil' Ed and the Blues Imperials play the blues with rollicking Chicago shuffles, Chuck Berry–style rock and roll, jump blues, and boogies.

Every once in a while, they'll throw in a slow, deep West Side–style blues.

Lil' Ed Williams leads the energetic show with his raw slide guitar that recalls the influences of his uncle, J.B. Hutto, and of the great slide masters Hound Dog Taylor and Elmore James.

Onstage, Lil' Ed's wild antics charge up the audience. He'll walk through the crowd, jump on a table, or slide down the bar on his knees. He's even been known to jump up on the shoulders of rhythm guitarist Mike Garrett. But Lil' Ed also has a softer side and frequently performs acoustic shows at venues like Buddy Guy's Legends and Bill's Blues Bar in Evanston.

Photo by Chuck Winans (pipphotography.com).

Born on April 4, 1955, Lil' Ed grew up on the West Side of Chicago and started playing guitar at age 12 under the tutelage of his uncle J.B. Ed was only 17 when he formed his first band with his half brother James "Pookie" Young. The two brothers still play together in the Blues Imperials.

Early in their careers, Lil' Ed and Pookie were playing frequently on the West Side, but both had to take other jobs to make ends meet. Ed worked at a car wash while Pookie drove a school bus. They got their big break in the late 1980s, when Bruce Iglauer asked them to record for *The New Bluebloods: The Next Generation of Chicago Blues*, an Alligator Records anthology of new young talent. Lil' Ed and his band played the studio session like a live show, and Iglauer was so impressed that he offered them their own album. *Roughhousin'* was released in 1986.

In the 1990s Ed took a break for personal reasons and dissolved the band. During that time he recorded with guitarist Dave Weld and Willie Kent. In 1998 Lil' Ed reunited the Blues Imperials, and in 1999 the band entertained at the Chicago Blues Festival.

Music
- *Heads Up!* (Alligator, 2002)
- *Get Wild*! (Alligator, 1999)
- *Who's Been Talking* (Earwig, 1998)—with Willie Kent
- *Keep On Walkin'* (Earwig, 1996)—with Dave Weld

- *What You See Is What You Get* (Alligator, 1992)
- *Chicken, Gravy and Biscuits* (Alligator, 1990)
- *Roughhousin'* (Alligator, 1986)

Charlie Love
Guitar, harmonica, saxophone, vocals

Multitalented Charlie Love was born in Chicago in 1956. His father played harmonica, and the young Charlie grew up listening to the music of Howlin' Wolf, B.B. King, and Elmore James. He bought his first guitar in a pawnshop and taught himself to play.

In the 1970s Love played with Lefty Dizz and Buddy Scott at the Checkerboard Lounge. Soon he formed his own band, the Hot Links, and played on the South Side. In 1985 he formed the Silky Smooth Band. He also played guitar and sang in the Casey Jones Band. In 1999 Love beat out 12 other bands in the "Best Unsigned Band" contest at Buddy Guy's Legends.

Music
- *So Happy I Could Cry* (LoveMil, 1988)

Mississippi Heat
Chicago-style blues band
www.mississippiheat.net

Harmonica player Pierre Lacocque heads up Mississippi Heat, an ensemble-style blues band with an original approach to the traditional Chicago-style sounds. While many bands trying to emulate the magic of 1950s Chicago blues churn out tired old cover songs, Lacocque and Mississippi Heat have succeeded in developing their own material. Lacocque is a prolific songwriter, having written most of the songs on the six CDs the band has released to date. ·

Other band members are Spurling Banks on bass, Steve Doyle on guitar, Kenny Smith on drums, and Inetta Visor on vocals. Chicago native Visor, who joined Mississippi Heat in 2001, has a powerful voice often compared to Etta James.

Pierre Lacocque was born on October 13, 1952, in Jerusalem and grew up in Europe. He moved to Chicago in 1969, at age 16, and was inspired to learn blues harp after attending a Big Walter Horton concert at the University of Chicago. As a college student, he gigged with blues bands. After earning his doctorate at Northwestern University in 1978, he began working as a clinical psychologist.

In 1988 Pierre returned to the blues scene, and in 1991 he formed Mississippi Heat with Jon McDonald, Robert Covington, and Bob Stroger. Through the years Billy Flynn, James Wheeler, Bob Carter, Allen Kirk, Sam Lay, Kenny Smith, Katherine Davis, and Deitra Farr have all done stints with the band. Lacocque's brother Michel is the band's manager.

Music
- *One Eye Open: Live at Rosa's Lounge* (Delmark, 2006)
- *Glad You're Mine* (CrossCut, 2005)
- *Footprints on the Ceiling* (CrossCut, 2002)
- *Handyman* (CrossCut, 1999)
- *Thunder in My Heart* (Van der Linden, 1995)
- *Learned the Hard Way* (Van der Linden, 1994)
- *Straight from the Heart* (Van der Linden, 1992)

Joe Moss
Guitar
www.joemossband.com

The blues of Joe Moss is spiced with soul, R&B, and funk, tendencies he picked up naturally during his years with the soul-blues band Scotty and the Rib Tips. Joe was only 19 years old when he joined the Rib Tips at the invitation of bandleader Buddy Scott, who had seen the Chicago native jamming one night at Rosa's Lounge. He began playing with the band in clubs like the Checkerboard Lounge and Lee's Unleaded Blues on the South Side. In 1992 Joe toured Spain with the Rib Tips and recorded with the band on *Bad Avenue* (Verve, 1993).

After Buddy Scott died in 1994, Joe played with numerous Chicago artists until forming his own band in 1997. His first self-titled CD was issued the same year. His brother is guitarist Nick Moss, whose band is the Flip Tops.

Music
- *Monster Love* (212 Records, 2003)
- *The Joe Moss Band* (212 Records, 1997)

Nick Moss and the Flip Tops
Chicago-style band featuring guitar
www.nickmoss.com

Nick Moss wants people to hear the Chicago blues the way it was meant to be played. "There are a lot of bands that play the blues, and they're great musicians, but there are very few bands that actually play the Chicago blues style," Nick says.

For Nick and his band, the Flip Tops, that means capturing the rhythms and sounds of the golden age of Chicago blues. But instead of covering versions of older songs, the Flip Tops bring traditional sounds to original music.

Photo by Chuck Winans (pipphotography.com).

This comes naturally for Nick, who learned the music from legends like Jimmy Dawkins, Willie "Big Eyes" Smith, and the late Jimmy Rogers. It was the best schooling any musician could get, in his opinion. "I got my university studies by the professors who actually wrote the book," Nick says.

Born in 1969, Nick grew up much like any boy in the Chicago suburbs. In school he played football and wrestled. He didn't think a lot about music—that is, not until his older brother Joe began to play guitar.

Joe Moss, who today leads an acclaimed blues band of his own, became Nick's first and main musical guide. One Christmas, when Joe was 12 and Nick was eight, the brothers received guitars. Nick soon lost interest, but Joe stuck with it and by the time he entered high school, he was playing in front of crowds.

Nick noticed that his brother's talents got him a lot of attention, especially from the ladies. "I thought, hey man, that's cool. He's got all these girls around him," he recalls.

Still, Nick had other ambitions. After high school he hoped to play collegiate sports. But those dreams were shattered when a serious kidney ailment sidelined him during his senior year. As Nick lay in the hospital bed week after week undergoing treatment, he became deeply depressed. In an attempt to cheer his brother up, Joe brought a bass guitar to the hospital. This time Nick started playing in earnest.

After Nick was finally released from the hospital, Joe snuck him into Wise Fool's Pub, on Lincoln Avenue, where Little Charlie and the Nightcats were playing. It was a weekday and the crowd was light, but Little Charlie and the band put heart and soul into every song. "They played like it was a packed house, even though there were only five or six people in the room," Nick recalls.

At that moment Nick decided his goal was to play the blues. "I thought, if I could do this for the rest of my life, I'd be happy," he says.

Nick attended as many blues jams as he could. Although he was underage, his size and mature appearance permitted him to enter clubs without challenge. His musical skills quickly improved, and he was getting to know other musicians. One day someone recommended him to Jimmy Dawkins, who was looking for a bass player. Dawkins was impressed enough with Nick's ability to offer him a place in the band.

But after about a year, Dawkins told Nick he should get a little more seasoning, and he let him go. Undaunted, Nick soon landed a job with the Legendary Blues Band and fell under the influence of drummer Willie "Big Eyes" Smith. That's when he began making the switch from bass to guitar.

Nick's next stop was with the great Jimmy Rogers. In a conversation with Dave Clark, who had once played with Floyd McDaniel's band, Nick heard that Rogers was looking for a guitar player to go on the road with him.

Early the next morning the phone rang and the voice on the phone identified himself as Jimmy Rogers. Half asleep, Nick thought it was one of his buddies playing a joke, and he hung up the phone. Fortunately Rogers called back, and Nick got the job.

His three years with Rogers in the mid-1990s was the experience of a lifetime. "Jimmy Rogers was one of the greatest bandleaders to work for," he says. "I was just a kid in the band, and he treated me just like anyone else."

In 1997 Nick struck out on his own with his band, the Flip Tops. They quickly gained fans and respect. In 2001 Nick was nominated for a Handy Award for Best New Artist Debut for his CD *Got a New Plan*. Two years later his CD *Count Your Blessings* garnered a Handy nomination for Contemporary Blues Album of the Year.

Music
- *Sadie Mae* (Blue Bella, 2005)
- *First Offense* (Blue Bella, 2003)
- *Count Your Blessings* (Blue Bella, 2003)
- *Got a New Plan* (Blue Bella, 2001)

Eric Noden
Acoustic guitar, harmonica, piano
www.ericnoden.com

Eric Noden performs regularly at the weekend acoustic sets at Buddy Guy's Legends. Born in 1969 in Kent, Ohio, Noden grew up amid roots music of his grandfather, a folk and country singer, and his father, a guitar player who liked the music of Mississippi John Hurt, Lightnin' Hopkins, Mississippi Fred McDowell, and Rev. Gary Davis. At age 19 Eric played rhythm guitar for a gospel group called the Golden Wonders.

In 1995 he moved to Chicago in pursuit of the blues. In addition to his solo performances, he has played with Billy Boy Arnold, Erwin Helfer, and Devil in a Woodpile. Eric also teaches at the Old Town School of Folk Music in Chicago, gives guitar lessons, and conducts historical and musical workshops.

Music
- *Midwest Blues* (Diving Duck, 2004)
- *55 Highway* (Diving Duck, 2002)

Pinetop Perkins
Piano
www.pinetopperkins.com

Whether seated behind a grand piano or a portable keyboard, Pinetop Perkins plays classic Chicago-style blues with a boogie-woogie beat. Always nattily dressed in a suit, hat, and piano-keyboard tie, the nonagenarian may have lost some speed on the ivories, but he hasn't lost his magical touch. His soft vocals are edged with a Mississippi accent as he sings standards like "How Long Blues," "Kansas City," "Ida B," "Chicken Shack," and "Take It Easy, Baby."

Joe Willie "Pinetop" Perkins, born on July 13, 1913, in Belzoni, Mississippi, was a relative latecomer to the Chicago blues scene. While other bluesmen from the Delta arrived in Chicago in the 1950s, Perkins spent much of his long career as a sideman accompanying some of the most well-known names in the blues, such as B.B. King, Robert Nighthawk, and Earl Hooker. In the early 1940s Perkins appeared on the *King Biscuit Time* radio show, on KFFA in Helena, Arkansas, with Sonny Boy Williamson II (Rice Miller).

Photo by Chuck Winans (pipphotography.com).

Perkins started his musical career as a guitar player. But one night, while performing with Sonny Boy in Arkansas, Perkins was stabbed by a woman who had just had a fight with her husband. The injury was so serious that Perkins could no longer play guitar and was forced to switch to piano full time. He wrote a song about the incident, "Stabbed by an Angry Woman," which appears on *Portrait of a Delta Bluesman* (Omega, 1993).

In the mid-1960s Perkins moved to Chicago, and in 1969 he joined Muddy Waters's band after the death of Otis Spann. In the early 1980s Perkins left the band to form the Legendary Blues Band with bass guitarist Calvin Jones, drummer Willie "Big Eyes" Smith, and harp player Jerry Portnoy.

Perkins has emerged as a star performer and recorded numerous albums as a solo artist. In the 1990s he began getting long-deserved recognition from the blues community. For 11 years straight, from 1993 through 2003, he won with W.C. Handy Awards in the category of Blues Instrumentalist of the Year–Piano/Keyboards. He also received Handy wins for Traditional Blues Male Artist of the Year in 1995, 2004, and 2005. Twice he received Handys for albums: in 1994 for *Portrait of a Delta Bluesman* and in 2005 for *Ladies Man*. The Blues Foundation presented him with a Lifetime Achievement Award in 2005.

Perkins received his first Grammy nomination in 1996 in the category of Best Traditional Blues CD for *Born in the Delta* (Telarc), and he was honored by the Recording Academy with a Lifetime Achievement Award in 2005. In 2000 he was featured in the PBS series *The Blues* in the segment "Piano Blues," which was directed by Clint Eastwood. That year Perkins was awarded the National Heritage Fellowship from the National Endowment of the Arts.

After a move to Austin, Texas, in 2004, Pinetop Perkins performs only occasionally in Chicago.

Music

- *Ladies Man* (M.C. Records, 2004)
- *Heritage of the Blues: The Complete Hightone Sessions* (Hightone, 2003)
- *Pinetop Is Just Top* (Black & Blue/Hepcat, 2002)
- *8 Hands on 88 Keys* (Sirens, 2002)
- *Back on Top* (Telarc, 2000)
- *Legends* (Telarc, 1998)
- *Down in Mississippi* (HMG, 1998)
- *Born in the Delta* (Telarc, 1997)
- *Got My Mojo Workin'* (Blues Legends, 1995)
- *Portrait of a Delta Bluesman* (Omega, 1993)
- *Pinetop's Boogie Woogie* (Discovery, 1993)
- *On Top* (Deluge, 1992)
- *Boogie Woogie King* (Evidence, 1992)—originally issued in 1976
- *After Hours* (Blind Pig, 1988)

Piano C. Red
Piano

Piano C. Red began playing regularly at the original Maxwell Street Market in the 1950s, shortly after moving to Chicago. In the 1980s and '90s, Red's band, the Flat Foot Boogie Men, performed on the blues stage next to Johnny Dollar's Thrift Store. He continued to play at the new Maxwell Street Market on Canal Street until 2006.

Piano C. Red was born James Wheeler on September 14, 1933, in Birmingham, Alabama. He

Photo by Karen Hanson.

learned to play piano at age 12. When he was 16 he moved to Georgia, where he earned the nickname Red because he always wore a red suit while performing. Because there was another Piano Red in the area, Wheeler added the "C," his middle initial (for Cecil).

In 1963 he cut a record for Chess, "Slow Down and Cool It," with "Monkey Wobble Groove" on the back side. He worked as a cab driver for more than 40 years.

On March 23, 2006 Piano C. Red was paralyzed from the waist down after a robbery of a gas station on the South Side.

Music
- *Cab Driving Man* (Scream Diva, 1999)
- *Piano C. Red, Live in Germany* (New Rose, 1992)

Pistol Pete
Guitar
www.pistolpete.net

Pistol Pete plays scorching blues-rock guitar influenced by Jimi Hendrix, Steve Vai, Frank Zappa, and Albert King. Born Benjamin Newell on April 26, 1962, in Los Angeles, Pistol Pete was raised in Chicago by his aunt and uncle, a blues guitarist. Pete started playing guitar at age four. In 2001 he was inducted into the Rockford Area Music Industry Hall of Fame. He gives private lessons and operates a recording studio.

Music
- *21st Century Bluesman* (P-Vine Japan, 2004)
- *Man in the Moon* (2002)
- *Loaded* (1995)

John Primer
Guitar
www.johnprimerblues.com

Born in Camden, Mississippi, on March 3, 1946, John Primer never wanted to be anything but a bluesman. His father, a harmonica player, would jam together with a guitar-playing friend. Young John would listen to his aunt's radio and hear songs by Jimmy Reed, Muddy Waters, Little Milton, Elmore James, B.B. King, and Albert King. "It always inspired me to play the blues," he says.

John was only eight years old when he learned to play guitar. As a young teen, he performed at churches, house parties, and fish fries. But he wanted to play the blues, and when he reached the age of 18 in 1963, he decided to move to Chicago.

"All the famous people were here," he says. Soon he began seeing some of the performers whose voices he knew so well on the records, like Muddy Waters, Howlin' Wolf, and Sonny Boy Williamson II (Rice Miller).

Photo courtesy of Lisa Becker/Becker Booking and Promotion.

He formed the band the Maintainers in 1964 and played West Side clubs like the Place, the Bow Tie, and Lover's Lounge. Four years later he joined the Brotherhood, a soul and R&B band. Then in 1974 he landed a job on the South Side in the house band at Theresa's Lounge. There he played with Buddy Guy, Junior Wells, and Lonnie Brooks. Guitarist Sammy Lawhorn was a steady influence on his musical style.

His big break came in 1979, when Willie Dixon invited him to join his Chicago All-Stars band, along with Billy Branch on harmonica, Willie's son Freddie Dixon on bass, and Lafayette Leake on piano.

Primer remembers Willie fondly. "He was a great guy to work with," he says. "He was a real talented musician and songwriter."

At a festival in Mexico City, Muddy Waters first took notice of Primer. When a spot opened up in his band, Muddy sent harmonica player Mojo Buford to ask Primer to join him. Primer didn't hesitate in saying yes to Muddy. "It was the dream of my life," he exclaims.

Primer already knew most of the guys in Muddy's band—Buford, guitarist Luther Johnson, and pianist Pinetop Perkins. "All those guys used to come down to Theresa's," he says.

Primer stayed with Muddy for two and a half years, until Muddy died in 1983. Then he joined Magic Slim and the Teardrops and played with the band for the next 14 years.

In 1995 Primer formed the Real Deal and released his debut solo album, also called *The Real Deal* the following year. His first solo effort was nominated for a Handy Award in the category of Best Traditional Blues Album.

Primer has gone on to record several more CDs and keeps up a busy schedule of appearances in Chicago and on the road. For Primer life is all about the blues. "You can't paint the blues without the Primer," he says.

Music
- *Blue Steel: A Tribute to Elmore James* (Wolf, 2003)
- *Knockin' at Your Door* (Telarc, 2000)
- *It's a Blues Life* (Wolf, 2000)
- *Blues Behind Closed Doors* (Wolf, 1998)
- *Cold Blooded Blues Man* (Wolf, 1997)
- *Keep on Lovin' the Blues* (Code Blue/Atlantic, 1997)
- *The Real Deal* (Code Blue/Atlantic, 1996)

Otis Rush
Guitar

Three months after suffering a stroke in 2004, Otis Rush traveled to Japan, where he gave an emotional performance in the 18th annual Japan Blues Carnival. Although he could barely sing or play guitar, Japanese fans were honored simply by his presence onstage. Carlos Johnson, another left-hander, assisted with the heavy-duty guitar work.

Rush's worldwide fame is well earned. He stands among the prime innovators of the West Side sound, a style of urbanized Chicago blues featuring blazing guitars and passionate

Photo by Chuck Winans (pipphotography.com).

vocals. His contemporaries are Magic Sam, Buddy Guy, Mighty Joe Young, Jimmy Dawkins, and Luther Allison.

Rush's guitar licks have influenced a generation of both blues and rock musicians, such as Peter Green, Eric Clapton, and Stevie Ray Vaughan. His original songs, like "Double Trouble," "Homework," and "All Your Love," have become classics. His 1998 album, *Any Place I'm Going*, won a Grammy Award for Best Traditional Blues Album. His song "Ain't Enough

Comin' In" won a Handy Award in 1995 for Blues Song of the Year. He was also named Contemporary Blues Artist of the Year in 1995

Rush's vocal style echoes his guitar style—full of raw emotion and rich with vibrato. He was honored with a Handy for his singing as Male Blues Vocalist of the Year in 1994.

Rush was born in Philadelphia, Mississippi, on April 29, 1934, and moved to Chicago in 1948 at age 14. Inspired by hearing fellow Mississippians Muddy Waters and Howlin' Wolf, Rush learned to play blues guitar.

When Led Zeppelin hit the charts with "I Can't Quit You Baby" in 1969, it was Otis Rush's 1956 Cobra recording they were covering. John Mayall and Eric Clapton were also inspired by Otis Rush. Their rendition of Rush's hit "All You Love" appeared on the first album by their band, the Blues Breakers *album, in 1966.*

During the 1950s he played the club scene with the Four Aces, a band consisting of brothers Louis and Dave Myers on guitars and Fred Below on drums. In 1956 he released his first record, "I Can't Quit You Baby," produced by Willie Dixon on the Cobra label.

Rush's career hit a latent period in the 1980s, although his album *Live in Europe*, issued on a French label, received a Handy Award for Best Contemporary Blues Album (Foreign). Rush made a stellar comeback in 1994 with his album *Ain't Enough Comin' In* for Mercury/Universal.

Although illness has sidelined him from active performing, Rush remains an influential force on the Chicago blues scene.

Music

- *All Your Love I Miss Loving: Live at the Wise Fool's Pub Chicago* (Delmark, 2006)
- *Essential Collection: The Classic Cobra Recordings* (Varese, 2000) —Cobra singles recorded in 1956–58; songs include "I Can't Quit You Baby," "Double Trouble," "My Love Will Never Die," "All Your Love (I Miss Loving)," and "Keep On Loving Me Baby"
- *Any Place I'm Going* (House of Blues, 1998)
- *Ain't Enough Comin' In* (Mercury/Universal, 1994)
- *Lost in the Blues* (Alligator, 1991)—originally recorded in 1977
- *So Many Roads, Live in Japan* (Delmark, 1978)
- *Cold Day in Hell* (Delmark, 1976)
- *Right Place, Wrong Time* (Hightone Records)—originally issued by Bullfrog in 1976

Howard Scott
Vocals

Howard Scott and the World Band lean toward the soul side of blues. Howard and his brothers, Buddy Scott and Walter Scott, once backed the great Tyrone Davis. Later, Howard performed regularly with Buddy's band, Scotty and the Rib Tips, which played around the South Side from the 1960s through the '80s. His sister-in-law Patricia Scott is a blues vocalist who frequently appears at the Blue Chicago club.

Patricia Scott
Vocals

Patricia Scott regularly appears at Blue Chicago, performing with John Primer and other veteran blues performers, including Willie Kent and the Gents when Kent was still alive. Patricia appears on two compilation CDs of female blues singers produced on the Blue Chicago label. Patricia was married to the late Buddy Scott, who led the band Scotty and the Rib Tips.

Music
- *Mojo Mamas* (Blue Chicago, 2000)
- *Red Hot Mamas* (Blue Chicago, 1997)

Eddie Shaw
Saxophone, harmonica

Eddie Shaw played saxophone in Howlin' Wolf's band through the 1960s and '70s. When Wolf died in 1976 Eddie and the band carried on as the Wolfgang.

Today the band consists of Howlin' Wolf's bassist, Lafayette "Shorty" Gilbert; Shaw's son, guitarist Eddie Vaan Shaw Jr.; and drummer Tim Taylor, son of Eddie Taylor Sr. (Jimmy Reed's main man on guitar). The Wolfgang's repertoire includes Howlin' Wolf tunes like "Little Red Rooster" and "Howlin' for My Darling." Shaw also performs some tunes on harmonica.

An accomplished songwriter and arranger, Shaw has written material for his own band and for Howlin' Wolf, Magic Sam, and Willie Dixon. His original lyrics draw from both his Mississippi country roots and his urban Chicago experience.

Photo by Chuck Winans (pipphotography.com).

Born on March 20, 1937, in Benoit, Mississippi, Shaw learned to play saxophone in his high school band. By the time he was a teenager, he was playing with bands, notably with Ike Turner, around the Greenville area.

In the late 1950s Shaw's saxophone skills caught the attention of Muddy Waters, who invited the young Eddie to join his band in Chicago. Shaw stayed with Muddy only briefly before joining Howlin' Wolf's band.

In 1968 Shaw recorded with Magic Sam on his album *Black Magic* on the Delmark label. For a time Shaw operated the 1815 Club (also known as Eddie's Place) on Roosevelt Road.

Shaw was nominated for Handy Awards from 1999 through 2004. In 1996 the Living Blues Critics honored Shaw as Outstanding Blues Musician (horn). That year he was also presented with the Howlin' Wolf Award at the Chicago Blues Festival.

Music

- *Four Decades of Eddie Shaw* (North Atlantic Blues, 2005)
- *Papa Told Me* (North Atlantic Blues)
- *Live at the Time Out Pub* (North Atlantic Blues)
- *Too Many Highways* (Wolf, 1999)
- *Can't Stop Now* (Delmark, 1997)
- *The Blues Is Nothing but Good News!* (Wolf, 1996)
- *Movin' and Groovin' Man* (Evidence, 1993)—originally released in 1982
- *Home Alone* (Wolf, 1994)—import
- *This Is Good News!* (Wolf, 1994)
- *In the Land of the Crossroads* (Rooster Blues, 1992)

Eddie Vaan Shaw Jr.
Guitar

Eddie Vaan Shaw Jr. is known for his fiery, fleet-fingered stylings on guitar. Son of saxophonist Eddie Shaw, longtime member of the Howlin' Wolf band, Vaan Shaw was born in Greenville, Mississippi, on November 6, 1955, and grew up surrounded by the music of family friends like Magic Sam, Elmore James, and, of course, Howlin' Wolf himself. He learned guitar from the great Hubert Sumlin and honed his chops on Maxwell Street and in the 1815 Club on Roosevelt Road. Vaan Shaw plays lead guitar with his dad's band, the Wolfgang.

Photo by Chuck Winans (pipphotography.com).

Music
- *Give Me Time* (Wolf, 2005)—recorded in 1994
- *Ass Whoopin'* (2001)
- *Trail of Tears* (1999)
- *Morning Rain* (Wolf, 1993)

Matthew Skoller
Harmonica
www.matthewskoller.com

Matthew Skoller's blues harp is deeply rooted in the sounds of past greats like Little Walter and Sonny Boy Williamson II (Rice Miller), but his songs address the blues of contemporary life. Skoller has also earned respect as a creative songwriter.

Born in New York in 1962, Skoller arrived on the Chicago blues scene in 1987, and in 1992 he formed his own band. In 1996 he won the International Blues Talent Competition hosted by the Blues Foundation in Memphis. That year he also served as an Artist in Residency at the Disney Institute in Orlando, Florida.

His band features his brother Larry Skoller on guitar, as well as guitarist Lurrie Bell and drummer Kenny Smith.

Music
- *These Kind of Blues* (Tongue in Groove, 2005)
- *Tap Root* (Tongue in Groove, 2003)
- *Bone to Pick with You* (Tongue N Groove, 2002)
- *Shoulder to the Wind* (Tongue N Groove, 2001)

Byther Smith
Guitar

Byther Smith learned guitar from a stellar lineup of the best guitarists in Chicago in the 1960s: Robert Lockwood, Louis Myers, Hubert Sumlin, and Freddie Robinson.

Born on April 17, 1932, in Monticello, Mississippi, Smith was raised by his aunt and uncle. As a teen, he played upright bass on country-and-western songs at rodeo shows. He was also interested in boxing but gave it up to play music.

In 1956 Smith moved to Chicago, where his cousin J.B. Lenoir was already established as a blues guitarist. He joined a jazz trio, but his interest in the blues grew as he sat in with Lenoir, Muddy Waters, and Otis Rush. In 1962 Smith landed a job playing rhythm guitar for Otis Rush at Pepper's Lounge.

In the 1970s he played a six-year stint with Junior Wells in the house band at Theresa's Lounge. Later, he toured with George "Harmonica" Smith and Big Mama Thornton.

Music
- *Hold That Train* (Delmark, 2004)
- *Away the Book* (Black & Tan, 2004)
- *Smitty's Blues* (Black & Tan, 2001)
- *All Night Long* (Delmark, 1997)
- *Mississippi Kid* (Delmark, 1996)
- *I'm a Mad Man* (Bullseye, 1993)
- *Housefire* (Bullseye, 1991)

Johnnie Mae Dunson Smith
Drums, vocals

Johnnie Mae Dunson Smith sings with the raw power of the deep blues. One of the first and few female drummers, Johnnie Mae was nearly 80 years old before recording her debut CD, despite the fact that she had been a prolific songwriter for years.

Born in 1921 in Alabama, Johnnie Mae moved to Chicago in 1943 from Alabama. She began singing on Maxwell Street, where she met Eddie "Porkchops" Hines, who taught her to play the drums. A regular at the outdoor market, she performed alongside Floyd Jones, J.B. Hutto, and Eddie Taylor.

In the late 1940s, she worked in West Side clubs with her own band, the Globetrotters. Later, she worked with and managed Jimmy Reed, who recorded several songs she wrote. In 1965 she recorded a single, "You're Going Out That Door," for Checker. Her son is Jimi "Prime Time" Smith.

Music
• *Big Boss Lady* (2000)

Willie "Big Eyes" Smith
Drums, harmonica

Along with great blues drummers like Elga Edmonds and Fred Below, Willie "Big Eyes" Smith helped shape the drumbeat that drove the classic Chicago blues sounds of Muddy Waters. These days Willie has returned to his first instrument, the harmonica.

Photo by Chuck Winans (pipphotography.com).

"I still love the drums," he comments, "but it's hard to front a band when playing the drums."

Born in Helena, Arkansas, in 1936, Willie learned to play harmonica at age 17 just after moving to Chicago. One night his mother took him to see Muddy Waters, and the young Willie was blown away by the drumming of

Elga Edmonds (a.k.a. Elgin Evans). He decided he wanted to learn to play the drums, but he bought a harmonica instead. "Harmonica was the cheapest instrument at the time," Willie explains.

The following year, 1954, he formed a trio. He led the band on harp, Bobby Lee Burns played guitar, and Clifton James, who had bought a set of drums, became the drummer.

Willie recorded on harmonica with Arthur "Big Boy" Spires, but the tracks weren't released. A year later, Willie played on Bo Diddley's classic songs "Diddy Wah Diddy" and "Who Do You Love," on the Chess label.

Drummers were in more demand than harp players at the time, so Willie switched to drums and began gigging off and on with the Muddy Waters band. In 1959 Muddy asked Willie to record with him. The tracks appear on the 1960 release *Muddy Waters Sings Big Bill Broonzy*.

In 1961 Willie became a permanent member of Muddy's band, which then consisted of George "Mojo" Buford, Luther Tucker, Pat Hare, and Otis Spann. Willie remained with the band for 18 years.

In the spring of 1980 Willie and other members of Muddy's band—Pinetop Perkins, Louis Myers, Calvin Jones, and Jerry Portnoy—struck out on their own to form the Legendary Blues Band. Later that year, Willie and the Legendary Blues Band appeared backing John Lee Hooker in the movie *The Blues Brothers*. Willie was the only band member, besides Hooker, to appear onscreen in close-up. Willie remembers the movie as hard work. "We had to shoot the same scene over and over again," he says.

With varying personnel over the years, the Legendary Blues Band recorded four albums and backed Buddy Guy, Howlin' Wolf, and Junior Wells. They toured with Bob Dylan, the Rolling Stones, and Eric Clapton.

Spotlight

Willie says he understands why young people often don't relate to the blues. Every generation has its own sound, he says, and today all that young people want to hear is something with a beat. According to Willie, "As long as they can dance, they're happy."

Willie believes that today's popular music speaks to the younger generation the same way the music of Muddy Waters spoke to his generation. Still, Willie says he wants more from music: "I like a little story, instead of just jumping up and down."

Willie says he loves the life of a blues musician, but it has never been easy. As he says in the lyrics of his song "Hard, Hard Way": "It's a hard, hard way to get the money I need to make."

Music
- *Bluesin' It* (Electro-Fi, 2004)—with the Juke Joint Rockers
- *Blues from the Heart* (Juke Joint, 2000)
- *Nothing but the Blues Y'all* (Juke Joint, 1999)
- *Bag Full of Blues* (Blind Pig, 1995)

Dave Specter
Guitar
www.davespecter.org

Dave Specter was born in Chicago on May 21, 1963. In the mid-1980s, he played in the bands of Son Seals, Hubert Sumlin, Sam Lay, Steve Freund, and the Legendary Blues Band. Since forming his own band, the Bluebirds, in 1989, he has worked in Chicago clubs and toured worldwide. His style unites both blues and jazz.

Photo by Chuck Winans (pipphotography.com).

Music
- *Is What It Is* (Delmark, 2004)—with Steve Freund
- *Speculatin'* (Delmark, 2000)—with Rob Waters on Hammond B3 organ
- *Blues Spoken Here* (Delmark, 1997)—with Lenny Lynn and Eric Alexander
- *Left Turn on Blue* (Delmark, 1996)
- *Blueplicity* (Delmark, 1994)

Rob Stone and the C-Notes
Chicago-style band featuring harmonica
www.robstone.com

The music of Rob Stone and the C-Notes evokes the Chicago-style blues tradition of the 1950s. The band consists of Chris James on guitar, Patrick Rynn on bass, and Willie D. Hayes on drums.

Stone, who was born in Boston, was inspired to play the blues after sneaking into a club one night to hear harmonica player Charlie Musselwhite. He taught himself to play harmonica by listening to the records of Jerry Portnoy, one-time harp player for Muddy Waters. At age 17 Stone spent time with rockabilly legend Sleepy LaBeef.

In 1990 Stone moved to Colorado and worked with blues-rock bands in clubs there. Three years later he met drummer Sam Lay, who was playing with Chris James and Patrick Rynn. Stone sat in and in 1994 joined the band. Stone followed Lay's band to Chicago and played frequently with Lay for four years, picking up the influences of classic Chicago harp players like Little Walter, Sonny Boy Williamson II (Rice Miller), and Big Walter Horton.

In 1998 Stone formed the C-Notes. The group released its first CD the following year.

Music
• *Just My Luck* (Earwig, 2003)
• *No Worries* (Marquis, 1999)

Big Time Sarah Streeter
Vocals

In the tradition of Koko Taylor, powerful vocalist Big Time Sarah sings the blues, soul, and a little bit of funk. Sarah appears regularly at Blue Chicago with her band, the BTS Express.

Born on January 31, 1953, in Coldwater, Mississippi, Sarah moved to Chicago at age seven. As a child, she sang with

Photo by Karen Hanson.

church choirs. She made her first stage appearance when she was 14. In 1979 she teamed up with piano great Sunnyland Slim. She performed at the first Chicago Blues Festival, in 1984.

Big Time Sarah was nominated for a Handy Award in 2002 and 2003 in the category of Traditional Blues–Female Artist of the Year.

Music
- *Million of You* (Delmark, 2001)
- *Blues in the Year One-D-One* (Delmark, 1996)
- *Lay It on 'em Girls* (Delmark, 1993)
- *Blues with the Girls* (EPM Musique, 1982)

Bob Stroger
Bass guitar
www.bobstroger.com

Bob Stroger's steady bass line has laid the foundation of the blues for Otis Rush, Jimmy Rogers, Eddie Taylor, Eddy Clearwater, Sunnyland Slim, and Snooky Pryor. He has recorded with more than 25 artists and performed for crowds all over the world.

Unlike many blues musicians, Stroger did not become interested in music at an early age. Instead, a series of fateful coincidences drew him into the blues.

Photo by Chuck Winans (pipphotography.com).

Born on a farm in Haiti, Missouri, Stroger moved to Chicago in 1955 at age 16 with his father, who had taken a railroad job. The family settled on the West Side in an apartment that happened to be in the back of Silvio's nightclub at Lake Street and Oakley. Every night Stroger could hear the music of blues from performers like Muddy Waters and Howlin' Wolf.

"I could look right out of my back door and into the back door of the club," recalls Stroger, who was working at a factory in those days. "They were in there having fun and dressing so nice, and I thought that's what I wanted to do if I ever got the chance."

Stroger's brother-in-law, Johnny Ferguson, played guitar with J.B.

Hutto in a band called the Twisters. Since Stroger had a car, he was often called upon to drive them to their gigs. Once again, the sounds he heard from the clubs fascinated him, and Stroger decided to teach himself to play guitar. Eventually he started a band with his brother, John Stroger, a drummer. They wore black berets with red circles on top and called themselves the Red Tops.

Later, Bob and John hooked up with Willie Hudson and Willie Kent and formed the Joe Russell Blues Band, with John Stroger calling himself Joe Russell.

Bob decided he wanted to travel and make more money, so he joined a jazz band with saxophonist Rufus Foreman and stayed on for about three years.

Next, Stroger joined Eddie King, who had played with Koko Taylor, and they formed the Kingsmen. In 1965 they recorded the singles "I'm a Lonely Man," "Love You Baby," and "Ha, Mr. D.J." Stroger stayed with King for 15 years. The band split up briefly but then reincarnated as Eddie King and Babee May and the Blues Machine.

In the late 1970s Stroger joined Otis Rush and, for the first time, toured Europe, where they recorded *Live in Europe* (released on CD by Evidence in 1993) and *Lost in the Blues* (released on CD by Alligator in 1991).

Spotlight

No bluesman in Chicago dresses better than Bob Stroger. No matter what the gig, Stroger shows up in a neatly tailored, brightly colored suit, a matching hat, and freshly shined shoes. On his jacket lapel, Bob always wears a gold and diamond pin in the shape and exact scale of his Fender bass. He had the pin custom-made in Mexico in the 1980s.

Bob says his manner of dress shows respect to the music he loves. "I'm representing something. I'm representing the blues, and I dress in appreciation of it," he explains.

Words

"As a boy, I had no idea I'd be playing music. Here I've gone from the cotton fields to around the world four times."

—Bob Stroger

Note

In the days before the Fender bass became commonly used, guitarists used to tune their strings down an octave to play bass lines. Bob Stroger learned the trick from Jimmie Lee Robinson, who once played bass with Magic Sam.

In the 1980s he played regularly with Sunnyland Slim and the Big Four with Sam Burckhart, Robert Covington, and Steve Freund. In the 1990s Stroger played with Jimmy Rogers and with Mississippi Heat. These days Stroger plays frequently in Chicago clubs and at festivals around the United States and in Europe.

Music
- *Bob Stroger and His Chicago Blues Legends: Live at Lucerne* (CrossCut Records, 2002)

Hubert Sumlin
Guitar
www.hubertsumlinblues.com

For more than 20 years, Hubert Sumlin provided the unique guitar sound behind the legendary Howlin' Wolf. Sumlin's work has influenced a generation of blues guitarists as well as rock stars like Keith Richards and Eric Clapton. In fact, Sumlin was named to *Rolling Stone* magazine's list of 100 Greatest Guitarists.

Sumlin, the youngest of 13 children, was born on November 16, 1931, in Greenwood, Mississippi, and grew up in Hughes, Arkansas, just west of Memphis. When he was seven his mother spent a week's pay to buy him his first guitar. By the time he was a teenager, Sumlin was playing regularly at juke joints and house parties around Memphis. He and James Cotton formed a band in the early 1950s.

The story of Sumlin's first meeting with Howlin' Wolf has become mythical through many retellings. In one version Hubert was just ten years old when he first met the Wolf, quite by accident. Late one night the young Hubert sneaked out of the house and went to a local juke joint where Howlin' Wolf was playing. He climbed on a stack of wooden crates to peek inside, but the stack collapsed, sending Hubert tumbling in through the window. He landed on the stage. Wolf allowed the boy to stay and listen to the music. At the end of the night, he took Hubert home to his parents and convinced them not to punish him.

In another version, told to writer Peter Guralnick in *Feel Like Going Home*, Hubert was 17 years old, and a bouncer chased him away from his stack of Coca-Cola crates. Hubert tried to sneak in the club by getting lost in the crowd, but he got caught again. Finally, Hubert's older brother talked to Wolf, who let the boy into the club.

However it happened, Sumlin never forgot the encounter, and when the opportunity came in 1954 to join Wolf's band, he jumped at it. Only 19 years old, Sumlin took the Illinois Central from Memphis to Chicago, where Wolf had already arranged and paid for an apartment and a union card for Sumlin.

At times the relationship between Sumlin and Howlin' Wolf was strained. Once Sumlin quit Wolf to play in Muddy Waters's band (Muddy had offered him more money), but that didn't last long. Within months he was back with his mentor. Another time, Howlin' Wolf fired Sumlin, complaining that Hubert's guitar was drowning out his vocals. Howlin' Wolf sent him home and told him not to come back until he could play without a flatpick. When Sumlin returned a time later, now using his fingers to pick the notes, he had developed his signature style.

Sumlin's sound was well known to British rockers in 1970. When Howlin' Wolf went overseas to record the London sessions for Chess, Sumlin wasn't slated to go. But when Eric Clapton heard of the omission, he contacted Chess and insisted on having Sumlin on the record. Bill Wyman and Charlie Watts of the Rolling Stones and Steve Winwood also appeared on the record.

Sumlin remained with Howlin' Wolf until Wolf died in 1976. Afterwards he was so despondent he didn't play for three months. Eventually he joined the rest of Wolf's band, the Wolfgang, led by saxophonist Eddie Shaw. By the 1990s Sumlin was no longer a sideman. He recorded a series of albums for major blues labels under his own name.

Despite health problems Sumlin still performs. He appeared on the main stage at the 2005 Chicago Blues Festival with former Muddy Waters guitarist Bob Margolin. In 2005 he was nominated for a W.C. Handy Award in the category of Traditional Blues Male Artist of the Year.

Music

- *About Them Shoes* (Tone Cool, 2005)—with Keith Richards, Eric Clapton, Levon Helm, James Cotton, Bob Margolin, and others; recorded in 2000
- *Wake up Call* (Blues Planet, 1998)
- *Legends* (Telarc, 1998)
- *I Know You* (Analogue, 1998)
- *Blues Guitar Boss* (JSP, 1994)
- *Blues Anytime!* (Evidence, 1994)

- *My Guitar & Me* (Evidence, 1994)—a reissue of a 1975 album
- *Healing Feeling* (Black Top, 1990)
- *Heart & Soul* (Blind Pig, 1989)
- *Hubert Sumlin's Blues Party* (Black Top, 1987)

Tail Dragger
Vocals

Tail Dragger was born James Yancy Jones in 1940 in Altheimer, Arkansas, and was raised by his grandparents. He grew up listening to blues on the radio and began imitating Howlin' Wolf. In the mid-1960s he moved to Chicago, where he soon met his idol. He started performing under the name of Crawlin' James until the Wolf himself dubbed him Tail Dragger, reportedly because he'd always show up late.

Photo by Chuck Winans (pipphotography.com).

In the early 1990s he spent time in prison for shooting and killing a bandmate, Boston Blackie, after an argument about pay.

Music
- *My Head Is Bald* (Delmark, 2006)
- *American People* (Delmark, 1999)
- *Crawlin' Kingsnake* (St. George, 1996)

Eddie Taylor Jr.
Guitar

In just a few short years, young guitarist Eddie Taylor Jr. has become a rising star in the Chicago blues scene. A son of the late Eddie Taylor Sr., who was lead guitarist for Jimmy Reed, Eddie bears a close resemblance to his famous father, physically and musically. The young Eddie was only 13 when his father died; he learned to play guitar by playing along with his father's records.

Born in 1972, Edward Taylor Jr. was the sixth of eight children of Eddie Taylor Sr. and singer Lee Vera Hill Taylor. Eddie Jr.'s brother Tim Taylor is a drummer who plays frequently with Eddie Shaw and the Wolfgang. His stepbrother, Larry Taylor, is a drummer and soul-blues vocalist.

Starting out, Eddie played frequently with respected blues musicians who were also family friends: Willie Kent, Hubert Sumlin, Johnny B. Moore, and John Primer. He spent some time with Eddie Shaw and the Wolfgang before forming his own band.

He released his first CD, *Lookin' for Trouble*, in 1998, but it would be another seven years before his second CD was released. In 2002 Eddie became seriously ill with kidney failure. He recovered after receiving the transplant of a kidney donated by his brother Milton.

Eddie's first CD, *Lookin' for Trouble*, was a tribute to his father. He also recorded one of his father's songs, "Ride 'em on Down," for *The Best of West and South Side Blues Singers, Vol. 2* (Wolf, 2004).

Music
- *Worried About My Baby* (Silverwolf, 2004)—backed by Johnny B. Moore, Willie Kent, Tim Taylor, Rockin' Johnny Burgin, and Kenny Barker
- *Lookin' for Trouble* (Wolf, 1998)

Koko Taylor
Vocals
www.kokotaylor.com

Since the 1960s Koko Taylor has been singing the blues in her tough, gritty, soulful voice. The Queen of the Blues has been an international star, averaging 200 performances per year all over the world. Although her performance schedule has slowed down a bit due to recent illness, she continues to shine as Chicago's own symbol of a blueswoman.

Singing the blues is what Koko Taylor knows, and it's who she is. The genuine quality of Koko's music and her personality appeal to people as much today as

Photo by Chuck Winans (pipphotography.com).

they did a generation ago.

"My music hasn't changed," Taylor says. "Blues is blues. You take a song like 'Wang Dang Doodle'— that's the blues. What I'm singing today is blues."

The roots of Taylor's blues spring from her childhood near Memphis, where she grew up on a sharecropper's farm. Born Cora Walton on September 28, 1935, Koko was only four when her mother died. Her father raised young Cora and her five siblings in the Baptist church, where they would sing gospel music. They could hear B.B. King and other blues musicians playing on the radio. Although their father forbid it, the children would often sneak away to sing and play the blues on their homemade instruments.

In 1954, at the age of 18, Koko moved to Chicago with her husband, Robert "Pops" Taylor. She found work as a housecleaner, but she knew she wanted to be a singer.

"When I first came to Chicago, getting into the singing business, it was kind of rough back then," Taylor recalls. "I would go around to the clubs on weekends, and that's when I'd have the chance to listen to the live blues."

She spent a lot of time at Silvio's on Chicago's West Side. In those days, the blues was all you could hear.

Words

"The young people today are mostly listening to hip-hop, be-bop, and anything but the blues. They don't play the blues on the radio. They don't give the young people a chance to hear and know about the blues."

—Koko Taylor

Note

Koko Taylor has appeared in the movies Wild at Heart *(1990),* Mercury Rising *(1998), and* Blues Brothers 2000 *(1998). She also was featured in Martin Scorsese's PBS series* The Blues *(2003).*

Spotlight

The Koko Taylor Celebrity Aid Foundation provides social services to people in the arts and entertainment field. The foundation assists artists and their families in times of illness, injury, death, or long-term crisis. The foundation also helps families with burial costs and insurance counseling and educates artists about their rights in the music industry. The foundation is supported by donations, benefits, fundraisers, sponsorships, and volunteers. Koko is chairman of the board, and her daughter Cookie is the executive director. For more information, or to make a donation, visit the Web site (www.kokotaylor.com/foundation.html).

"Music wasn't plentiful and out, like today," Taylor says. "Today music is blues, jazz, rock, pop, rap, hip-hop, everything."

One night in 1962 Willie Dixon heard her sing, and she was on her way to stardom. Dixon produced her first single, "Honky Tonky," on the tiny USA label. When she signed with Chess Records in 1963, Dixon continued to write and produce for her. In 1966 Taylor's recording of the Dixon-penned song "Wang Dang Doodle" shot up to number four on the R&B charts.

In 1967 Taylor performed "Wang Dang Doodle" for European audiences on the American Folk Blues Tour. She was backed by Little Walter on harmonica and Hound Dog Taylor on guitar. The song still remains her favorite. "It's about having a good time on Saturday night," she comments.

Spotlight

Koko Taylor holds the record for winning more W.C. Handy Awards (25 as of this writing) than any other female artist. In 1999 she was inducted into the Blues Foundation Blues Hall of Fame and received a Lifetime Achievement Award. Taylor has also been nominated for several Grammy Awards (eight as of this writing). She won in 1984.

In 1993 Mayor Richard M. Daley proclaimed a "Koko Taylor Day" and the Chicago City Council named her Legend of the Year. Koko was named Chicagoan of the Year by Chicago magazine in 1998. In 2004 she received the National Heritage Fellowship from the National Endowment for the Arts.

Through the 1970s Taylor continued to tour extensively. She signed with Alligator Records in 1975 and went on to record some of her best work. In 1984 she won the Grammy Award for the Best Traditional Blues Album for her contribution to the Atlantic Records compilation *Blues Explosion.*

Four years later, in 1988, Koko was seriously injured when her tour bus went over a cliff in Tennessee. Her husband, Pops, never fully recovered from his injuries and died a few months later.

Despite numerous health problems since about the mid-1990s, Koko Taylor has continued to contribute her talents to the world of the blues. In addition to performing and recording, she ventured twice into the blues club business. In 1995 she briefly operated a club on Rush Street. Her second club, Koko Taylor's Celebrity on South Wabash, operated for several months until it closed in 2003.

Music

- *Deluxe Edition* (Alligator, 2002)—features a collection of Koko's hits on the Alligator label; guests include Buddy Guy, Carey Bell, Pinetop Perkins, Mighty Joe Young, and B.B. King
- *Royal Blue* (Alligator, 2000)—with guests B.B. King, Johnnie Johnson, Keb' Mo', and Kenny Wayne Shepherd
- *Force of Nature* (Alligator, 1993)—Buddy Guy and Carey Bell make guest appearances
- *I Got What It Takes—The Chess Years* (Alligator, 1991)—recorded in 1975, Koko's first album for Alligator earned her a Grammy nomination
- *Jump for Joy* (Alligator, 1990)—features Lonnie Brooks and Billy Branch
- *Queen of the Blues* (Alligator, 1985)—with Son Seals, Lonnie Brooks, James Cotton, and Albert Collins

Larry Taylor
Vocals, drums
www.larrytaylorbluesandsoul.com

Soulful vocalist and drummer Larry Taylor grew up with the blues. Born in 1955 in Chicago, Larry is the son of Lee Vera Hill Taylor and the stepson of Eddie Taylor, guitarist for the great Jimmy Reed. Larry was raised on the West Side. Musicians such as Howlin' Wolf, Jimmy Reed, Elmore James, Muddy Waters, and Sunnyland Slim were frequent visitors to the Taylor household.

Taylor has worked with B.B. King, Albert King, Willie Dixon, Buddy Guy, John Lee Hooker, Jimmy Rogers, Memphis Slim, and Luther Allison. In 1987 he toured Europe with Willie Dixon's "New Generation of Chicago Blues."

Taylor contributed three tracks to *Chicago's Best West and South Side Blues Singers, Vol. 2* (Wolf, 2004). He has also recorded with Syl Johnson, Jimmy Burns, and his brother Eddie Taylor Jr. His brother Tim Taylor is also a drummer.

Music

- *They Were in This House* (A.V., 2004)

Melvin Taylor
Guitar

Melvin Taylor's music is rooted in traditional blues but is also influenced by the West Side sound and overlaid with jazz. This wide range of musical styles has gained the flashy guitar virtuoso a steady and enthusiastic fan base in the United States and across Europe. Taylor was born on March 13, 1959, in Jackson, Mississippi, and moved to Chicago in 1962. His uncle taught him to play guitar, and Melvin learned the blues by playing along with the records of B.B. King, Albert King, and Jimi Hendrix.

Photo by Chuck Winans (pipphotography.com).

In the 1970s, while still a teenager, Taylor played in a band called the Transistors. In the early '80s he joined Pinetop Perkins and the Legendary Blues Band on a trip to Europe. Taylor proved so popular there that he began booking his own European dates. In 1982 he recorded for a French label.

Taylor often plays at Rosa's Lounge and other Chicago-area blues clubs.

Music
- *Rendezvous with the Blues* (Evidence, 2002)
- *Bang That Bell* (Evidence, 2000)
- *Dirty Pool* (Evidence, 1997)
- *Melvin Taylor & the Slack Band* (Evidence, 1995)
- *Melvin Taylor Plays the Blues for You* (Evidence, 1984)
- *Blues on the Run* (Evidence, 1982)

Nellie "Tiger" Travis
Vocals

The soulful vocals of Nellie "Tiger" Travis have roots in Mississippi, where she grew up singing gospel music in church. She performed in Mississippi and Memphis before moving to Chicago in

1992. In 1999 she was selected as New City People's Choice Entertainer of the Year.

Music
- *I Got It Like That* (2001)—with Billy Branch on harp
- *Heart and Soul* (Bluesox, 2000)—with Shun Kikuta on guitar

Maurice John Vaughn
Guitar, keyboards, saxophone

South Side native Maurice John Vaughn was born on November 6, 1952, in Chicago. He started out playing saxophone with soul and R&B bands as a teenager in the late 1960s. In 1976 he recorded on saxophone with an R&B group called the Chosen Few. But sax jobs were hard to find, and in the late '70s he switched to guitar. In 1979 he toured Canada with Phil Guy. Entering the '80s he was playing the blues regularly with artists like A.C. Reed, Luther Allison, and Son Seals.

In 1986 Vaughn produced and recorded his own album and called it the *Generic Blues Album*. The effort landed him a deal with Alligator Records, and he cut a track for Alligator's compilation album *The New Bluebloods*. Alligator picked up distribution for the *Generic Blues Album* in 1988.

Music
- *Dangerous Road* (Blue Suit, 2001)
- *In the Shadow of the City* (Alligator, 1993)
- *Generic Blues Album* (Alligator, 1988)

Carl Weathersby
Guitar

Carl Weathersby's music reveals the soul influences of Tyrone Davis, Little Milton, Sam Cooke, and Johnny Taylor. But his primary mentor was the great Albert King, who was a family friend.

Carl was born in Jackson, Mississippi, on February 24, 1953, and grew up in Meadville, a small town in the southern part of the state. When he was eight he moved with his family to East Chicago, Indiana, where he has lived most of his life.

The blues came naturally to young Carl. Several relatives were professional musicians, notably Leonard "Baby Doo" Caston, who played piano in Willie Dixon's Big Three Trio in the late 1940s and '50s.

As a teen, Carl taught himself to play guitar by copying the licks from Albert King's song "Crosscut Saw." When he thought he had it mastered, he went to show his father, who was hanging out with a friend. The friend turned out to be Albert King himself, who immediately showed Carl the right way to play the song. From that point King remained an encouraging force in Carl's life.

Weathersby served in the Army from 1971 to 1977 and did a tour of duty in Vietnam. Afterwards he worked as an officer with the Louisiana State Police, but he never gave up his music. In 1979 King invited Carl to join his band on tour. Weathersby played off and on with King until 1981.

In 1982 Weathersby joined the Sons of Blues, the band of harp player Billy Branch. Their 14-year-long partnership produced some of the best Chicago blues of the era, including *The Blues Keep Following Me Around*, Billy Branch's 1995 CD on Verve. Weathersby was nominated for a Handy Award for his cowriting credits on the title track.

Weathersby followed his success with a CD of his own. His debut album, *Don't Lay Your Blues on Me*, was released by Evidence in 1996. Weathersby left the S.O.B.s in 1997. No longer a sideman, Carl was nominated for a Handy for Best New Blues Artist. In 1999, with two more CDs under his belt, Weathersby was nominated for a Handy in the category of Artist Most Deserving of Wider Recognition. In 2000 and 2001 he was nominated in the category of Blues Instrumentalist–Guitar, and in 2001 he received a nomination for Contemporary Blues Artist of the Year.

But just as Weathersby's star seemed to be shining brightest, he suffered health problems. A stroke in 2001 slowed him down for a time, but he has made a good recovery. He continues to play selected club dates and festivals, and in 2004 he recorded with Nora Jean Bruso for her CD *Going Back to Mississippi*. His 2003 release, *Best of Carl Weathersby*, is a compilation of his greatest songs. He self-produced his 2004 CD, *Hold On*.

Music

- *Hold On* (self-produced, 2004)
- *In the House: Live at Lucerne* (CrossCut, 2004)
- *Best of Carl Weathersby* (Evidence, 2003)

- *Come to Papa* (Evidence, 2000)
- *Restless Feeling* (Evidence, 1998)
- *Looking Out My Window* (Evidence, 1997)
- *Don't Lay Your Blues on Me* (Evidence, 1996)

James Wheeler
Guitar

Photo by Chuck Winans
(pipphotography.com).

As a sideman, James Wheeler has backed some of the biggest names on the Chicago blues scene, notably Otis Rush, Willie Kent, Magic Slim, and Otis Clay. Although he was 50 years old before he recorded an album under his own name, Wheeler has played steadily since the early 1960s.

Wheeler was born in Albany, Georgia, on August 28, 1937. He grew up listening to swing and big band music and names Louis Jordan as an early favorite. In 1956 he moved to Chicago, where his brother, harp player Golden "Big" Wheeler, was already playing at house parties on the West Side.

Inspired by the music of Howlin' Wolf, Freddie King, Jimmy Reed, and Elmore James, Wheeler began teaching himself to play guitar. Within a few years he was playing with Billy Boy Arnold. In 1963 Wheeler started his own band, the Jaguars. For the next decade the Jaguars backed a number of prominent blues and soul artists such as B.B. King, Bobby Bland, Etta James, Al Green, Johnny Taylor, and Otis Clay.

In 1972 the Jaguars broke up and Wheeler joined the band of Otis Clay, where he stayed until 1975. After short stints with the Impressions and Buddy Scott's Rib Tips band, he joined Otis Rush in 1976 and played with him for the next seven years.

In 1993 his friendship with drummer Robert Covington and bassist Bob Stroger led to an invitation to join Pierre Lacocque and Jon McDonald in the band Mississippi Heat, where he stayed for several years.

Music
- *Can't Take It* (Delmark, 2000)
- *Ready* (Delmark, 1988)—with Golden Wheeler on harp

Artie "Blues Boy" White
Vocals
www.artiewhite.com

Photo courtesy of Artie White.

Artie "Blues Boy" White has the perfect blues voice: sometimes gruff, other times bittersweet and moaning, but always drenched with emotion and soul.

Although White has been an active voice on the blues scene since 1960, he has done some of his best work in recent years. His 2004 CD, *First Thing Tuesday Morning*, was lauded as Best Blues Album of the Year in 2005 by the Chicago Music Awards. The CMA also gave White an Award of Honor in 2002.

Born in Vicksburg, Mississippi, on April 16, 1937, Artie White began singing gospel music at age 11 as the lead singer with a group called the Harps of David. In 1953, at age 16, he visited Chicago and met Johnny Taylor, Lou Rawls, and Sam Cooke. He returned to Mississippi, where he auditioned for the Jackson Southernaires. He lost out to legendary gospel singer Willie Banks.

Hoping to land a record deal, White moved permanently to Chicago in 1956. He soon joined a gospel choir called the Full Gospel Wonders and then sang for a time with the True Lights.

In the 1960s White switched to secular music and early on had a gig singing with Mighty Joe Young. In those days club owners didn't pay much. White recalls getting paid "two shots of whiskey and a bottle of beer"—the equivalent of $4.50. Bandleaders only made $12 a night. White worked as a truck driver while he kept trying for a hit record. In 1965 he recorded "Don't Jerk Me Around" and in 1968, "She's the One." Sales were modest, but in 1969 White decided to devote himself full-time to music. In 1971 Syl Johnson introduced White to Little Milton, who hired him as his road manager.

In 1977 Artie had a breakthrough hit with the love ballad "Leanin' Tree," which made it to number ten on the R&B charts and sold more than 100,000 copies. He followed it up in 1984 with two more hits, "Jimmy" and "I Need Someone," both on the Jewel label. He recorded with Ichiban for several years, and then in the 1990s he cut several albums for Waldoxy (part of the Southern soul label Malaco). Not long after the turn of the century, he formed his own independent label, Achilltown.

Through the 1980s White owned several blues clubs on the South Side, including Bootsy's at 2335 Cottage Grove. All are closed now. White has served as vice president of the Koko Taylor Celebrity Aid Foundation.

Music

- *First Thing Tuesday Morning* (Achilltown, 2004)
- *Blues in the Past* (Achilltown, 2003)
- *Can't Get Enough* (Achilltown, 2002)
- *Can We Get Together* (Waldoxy, 1999)
- *Home Tonight* (Waldoxy, 1997)
- *Different Shades of Blue* (Waldoxy, 1994)
- *Blues Boy* (Ronn, 1994)

Jody Williams
Guitar

When Jody Williams recorded his 2002 CD, *Return of a Legend*, it had been more than 30 years since he had stepped foot in a recording studio. But the CD was an instant hit, earning Williams a W.C. Handy Award for Comeback Artist of the Year.

Williams was born on February 3, 1935, in Alabama. He moved to Chicago at age six. As early as 1951 Williams was playing with Billy Boy Arnold and Bo Diddley. Throughout the 1950s Williams had been well known in Chicago as both an individual artist and a sideman. But

Photo by Chuck Winans (pipphotography.com).

in the early 1960s he quit the music business, took a job as a repair technician for Xerox, and settled down to raising a family. He had no intentions of returning to music until a chance meeting changed his mind.

In 1999 Williams decided to go to a Chicago club to see Robert Lockwood Jr., an old friend he had recorded with years earlier. There he ran into producer Dick Shurman, who recognized him. Through the urging of Shurman and others, Williams was persuaded to try his hand at playing again.

It was, indeed, the "return of a legend." In the early and mid-1950s, Williams released a number of singles, including "Looking for My Baby" on the Blue Lake label and "Groan My Blues Away" and "I Feel So Alone" for Relic. His theme song, "Lucky Lou," an upbeat instrumental, recorded for Argo, served as an inspiration for Otis Rush in the song "All Your Love."

Williams was also a popular session guitarist in the 1950s and early '60s for Chess and other labels. He recorded with Howlin' Wolf on "Evil" and "Forty-four Blues" and with Bo Diddley on several songs, including "Who Do You Love?" Jody backed Billy Boy Arnold on "I Ain't Got You" and "I Wish You Would," both released on Vee-Jay. He also recorded with Willie Dixon, Earl Hooker, Jimmy Rogers, Otis Spann, B.B. King, and Otis Rush.

It was a failed lawsuit that soured Williams on the music business. In 1957 the pop duo Mickey and Sylvia had a hit record with the song "Love Is Strange." When Williams heard it he immediately recognized the tune as a song he had written and played backstage for Sylvia a year earlier. He sued RCA Records over the rights to the songs, but the judge decided against him. Rights were given to Mickey and Sylvia and to Bo Diddley.

At the 2005 Chicago Blues Festival, Jody was awarded the Howlin' Wolf Award by Jay Sieleman, head of the Blues Foundation.

Music
- *You Left Me in the Dark* (Evidence, 2004)—with appearances by Lonnie Brooks and Robert Lockwood Jr.
- *Return of a Legend* (Evidence, 2002)

Zora Young
Vocals
www.zorayoung.com

When Zora Young was a young girl growing up on the South Side of Chicago, she sang in the church choir at the Greater Harvest Baptist Church. On her way to rehearsal she would walk by Theresa's Lounge on 48th and Indiana. At the time, she was too young to get into the club, but from the outside she could hear the sounds of blues bands featuring the likes of Buddy Guy and Junior Wells, and the experience stuck somewhere in her mind.

Zora was just seven years old in 1955, when she moved from Mississippi to the South Side of Chicago. The church had always been an important part of her life. Her stepfather was a preacher, and her mother was a gospel singer. But as a teen she also listened to R&B and Motown, to vocalists like Gladys Knight, Dinah Washington, and Paula Greer. In the 1970s she began singing soul and R&B in clubs on the South and West sides. Soon she was touring the South and Midwest on the "chitlin' circuit," singing at small blues clubs for primarily African-American audiences. She felt she was on her way to success. "They were not big places, but it was big for us," Zora recalls.

By the early 1970s she was opening for Tyrone Davis and Bobby Rush. She was still singing more soul than blues. But in the late '70s she made the move to the North Side clubs—and to the blues—hoping to make money and tour more extensively. "I heard if you sing the blues, you can see the world," she explains. "I knew I hadn't seen it by singing R&B."

The first place she tried out the blues was at a small place in Old Town where John Belushi used to hang out. She faked her way through. "I sang a verse from every blues tune I ever heard, but they liked it," she says.

She soon realized she didn't know much about singing the blues. She went about educating herself, listening to old records and learning about the culture and heritage of the blues. "You'll never really do it well until you respect it," she notes.

She made it to Europe for the first time in 1981, and she's been going back every year since then. "They seem to like me over there," Zora says.

In 1982 she recorded her first album on a Paris label. Sharing the bill on *Blues with the Girls* were two other Chicago blues singers, Bonnie Lee and Big Time Sarah. The backing band included Hubert Sumlin.

Spotlight

Zora Young appeared in a Timex commercial that aired in the mid-1980s. She beat out 160 other women in an open audition to get the part of a blues singer in a New York nightclub.

The audition was grueling. The day was sweltering hot, too hot to wear a wig. Zora wore a "big ol' flowered dress," and her makeup had melted by the time her turn came to sing. But her powerful voice and the experience she'd had onstage convinced the producers she was right for the part.

Timex flew her to New York and drove her around town in a limo. It was her first time to New York City. Hairstylists and makeup artists dolled her up, and they put her in a sexy sequined dress. Surrounded by 170 actors as extras, she was the star of the set. "I was queen for a week!" Zora exclaims.

In 1983 Zora became an actress when she landed a part in *Heart of the Blues*, a stage tribute to Bessie Smith. Along with vocalists Katherine Davis and Valerie Wellington, she performed in the musical until 1985.

"Music has been good to me," she says. "I've seen places I wouldn't have seen otherwise."

Music
- *Tore Up from the Floor Up* (Delmark, 2006)
- *Travelin' Light* (Delmark, 2001)
- *Learned My Lesson* (Deluge, 1994)

Suggestions for Further Reading

Bloomfield, Michael. *Me and Big Joe*. San Francisco: RE/SEARCH Publications, 1980.

Bogdanov, Vladimir, Chris Woodstra, and Stephen Thomas Erlewine, eds. *All Music Guide to the Blues*, 3rd ed. San Francisco: Backbeat Books, 2003.

Brooks, Lonnie, Cub Koda, and Wayne Baker Brooks. *Blues for Dummies*. Foster City, CA: IDG, 1998.

Broonzy, William. *Big Bill Blues: William Broonzy's Story*. New York City: Oak, 1964.

Caston, Leonard. *From Blues to Pop: The Autobiography of Leonard "Baby Doo" Caston*. Los Angeles: John Edwards Memorial Foundation, 1974.

Cohodas, Nadine. *Spinning Blues into Gold: The Chess Brothers and the Legendary Chess Records*. New York City: St. Martin's Griffin, 2001.

Collis, John. *The Story of Chess Records*. New York City: Bloomsbury, 1998.

Danchin, Sebastian. *Earl Hooker: Blues Master*. Jackson: University of Mississippi Press, 2001.

Dixon, Willie. *I Am the Blues*. New York City: Da Capo, 1989.

Eastwood, Carolyn. *Near West Side Stories: Struggles for Community in Chicago's Maxwell Street Neighborhood*. Chicago: Lake Claremont Press, 2002.

Flerlage, Raeburn. *Chicago Blues as Seen from the Inside*. Toronto: ECW Press, 2000.

Glover, Tony, Scott Dirks, and Ward Gaines. *Blues with a Feeling: The Little Walter Story*. New York City: Routledge, 2002.

Gordon, Robert. *Can't Be Satisfied: The Life and Times of Muddy Waters*. New York City: Little, Brown, 2002.

Green, Stephen. *Going to Chicago: A Year on the Chicago Blues Scene*. San Francisco: Woodford, 1990.

Grove, Lori, and Laura Kamedulski. *Chicago's Maxwell Street*. Chicago: Arcadia, 2002.

Guralnick, Peter. *Feel Like Going Home: Portraits in Blues and Rock 'n' Roll*. Boston: Little, Brown, 1999.

Jones, Fernando. *I Was There When the Blues Was Red Hot: A Tribute to a Chicago Blues Family*. Chicago: Fernando Jones, 1989.

PoKempner, Marc. *Down at Theresa's . . . Chicago Blues: The Photographs of Marc PoKempner*. Munich: Prestel, 2000.

Romano, Will. *Incurable Blues: The Troubles and Triumph of Blues Legend Hubert Sumlin*. Backbeat Books, 2005.

Rowe, Mike. *Chicago Blues: The City and the Music*. New York City: Da Capo, 1981.

Segrest, James, and Mark Hoffman. *Moanin' at Midnight: The Life and Times of Howlin' Wolf*. New York City: Pantheon, 2004.

Spann, Pervis. *The 40-Year Spann*. www.pervis-spann.com.

Tooze, Sandra B. *Muddy Waters: The Mojo Man*. Toronto: ECW Press, 1997.

Waterman, Dick. *Between Midnight and Day: The Last Unpublished Blues Archive*. New York City: Thunder's Mouth Press, 2003.

Whiteis, David G. *Chicago Blues: Portraits and Stories*. Chicago: University of Illinois Press, 2006.

Wilcock, Donald E. *Damn Right I've Got the Blues: Buddy Guy and the Blues Roots of Rock-and-Roll*. San Francisco: Woodford, 1993.

Sources

Chapters 1, 2, and 3: Historical facts about former blues clubs were gleaned primarily from *Chicago Blues: The City and the Music* (1981), by Mike Rowe; from *Chicago Blues as Seen from the Inside* (2000), by Raeburn Flerlage; from *Down at Theresa's . . . Chicago Blues* (2000), by Marc PoKempner; from the Blues-L online discussion group; and from numerous discussions with Chicago blues artists as well as with Bob Koester and Michael Frank. Information about the current clubs was gathered through the clubs' Web sites; through conversations with club owners and managers; and by personal visits to the clubs. All descriptions are based on personal observation and experience.

Chapter 4: Historical information was gathered through the City of Chicago Mayor's Office of Special Events and other documents in the files at the Chicago Blues Archives, which contained newspaper accounts from the *Chicago Tribune* and the *Chicago Sun-Times* and Chicago Blues Festival programs dating back to 1983. Information about the stages and tips about navigating the fest are based on personal observation and experience.

Chapter 5: Most information was gathered through personal visits, observation, and experience. The following people provided additional information about specific places: Bob Koester and the Delmark Web site for Jazz Record Mart; Steve Balkin for the Maxwell Street Market; the City of Aurora and the Fox Valley Blues Society Web site for the Leland Hotel; Gregg Parker for the Chicago Blues Museum and Muddy Waters home on Lake Park Avenue (descriptions of the Lake Park Avenue home were based on photos taken by Raeburn Flerlage); the Westmont Park District for Muddy Waters Park; Steve Pasek and Greg and Jenny Campbell for blues tours; and Kevin at the Blues Heaven Foundation for Chess Studios. Additional information about Chess Studios was found in "Strange Voodoo: Inside the Vaults at Chess Studios," published in Blues Access magazine, no. 36, winter 1999; and from *Spinning Blues into Gold: The Chess Brothers and the Legendary Chess Records* (2001), by Nadine Cohodas. Additional information about the Leland Hotel and the City of Aurora was taken from an interview I conducted with Henry Townsend in 2000. Gravesites were located through Find a Grave (www.findagrave.com).

Chapter 6: Information about historical blues record labels was gleaned from *Chicago Blues: The City and the Music* (1981), by Mike Rowe, and from the excellent Web site of the Red Saunders Research Foundation (www.redsaunders.com). Another important source was the official Web site of Vee-Jay Records (www.veejay.mu). The pages about Alligator, Delmark, and Earwig are based on interviews with the owners and on the information from the labels' Web sites (www.alligator.com, www.delmark.com, and www.earwigmusic.com, respectively).

Chapter 7: Credit goes to Liz Mandville Greeson and Tom Holland for the lists of blues jam etiquette. Other sources were John Primer, Jimmy Burns, Chico Banks, Ted Aliotta, and Michael Charles. Some jams were located with assistance of the *Chicago Reader* and the Chicagoland Blues Society.

Chapter 8: Facts about blues radio history were obtained from *Chicago Blues: The City and the Music* (1981), by Mike Rowe, and from the WVON Web site (www.wvon.com). Information on current stations was gathered through interviews with Steve Cushing, Greg Freerksen, Buzz Kilman, and Manual Arrington; through radio station Web sites; and from listening to the stations.

Chapter 9: The majority of biographical facts were gathered from the Web sites of Alligator, Delmark, and Earwig; from artist Web sites, album liner notes, and press kits; and from interviews with the artists. Some facts were confirmed by consulting the *All Music Guide to the Blues*, 3rd ed. Album information was found on the Web sites of Alligator, Delmark, and Earwig, as well as artist Web sites; release dates were confirmed through Amazon.com. Information about W.C. Handy Awards was found through a search of the Blues Foundation's Web site (www.blues.org). All descriptions are based on personal observation and experience.

About the Author

Karen Hanson works as a freelance journalist in the southwest suburbs of Chicago. A longtime blues fan, Hanson has profiled blues artists and reviewed CDs for several blues Web sites and publications. She has also hosted online blues chats and forums. She teaches writing and literature at DeVry University in Tinley Park.

Index

B

H

THE PITY HEART

A NICK DRAKE NOVEL

DWIGHT HOLING

The Pity Heart
A Nick Drake Novel

Print Edition
Copyright 2019 by Dwight Holing
Published by Jackdaw Press
All Rights Reserved

ISBN: 978-0-9991468-7-3

Cover Photo: "Frigid" (Alvord Desert, Oregon) © 2019 Scott Smorra

For More Information, please visit dwightholing.com.

See how you can **Get a Free Book** at the end of this novel.

For the Nurses

Rose Virden Wiley
Patricia Wiley Holing
Emily Virden Holing

What was it like to be a woman in Vietnam? We saw the worst that man could do to man, and we saw the very best of the human heart.

— Jean Youngstrom Diebolt, MSN, RN

(Vietnam Women's Memorial dedication)

The cattails were stiff with rime, and the frozen blades of sedges looked sharp enough to slice. I wore a down vest over my ranger uniform and wool gloves with the trigger finger cut off. A thin covering of snow crunched beneath my boots as I hoisted a canoe from the bed of the pickup and carried it to the edge of the lake. The shallows were slushy and a pair of mud hens squawked as I shoved off. Sunrise was still an hour away.

I hugged the shoreline as I paddled quietly toward a distant marsh. The fall migration was winding down, but ducks and geese by the thousands were still touching down on Malheur Lake each evening to rest before continuing their long journey south. Some were headed to Mexico, others all the way to South America. The government was paying me to give the birds a fighting chance. Only a year ago it had paid me to do the same for the South Vietnamese.

A poacher was treating the lake as his personal slaughter-house. He wasn't the first illegal hunter I'd encountered since moving to Harney County, Oregon, following three tours capped by a six-month stint at Walter Reed Hospital, but he was sizing up to be the most heartless.

The first time I heard blasts coming from across the wildlife refuge, I thought there were a dozen shotguns firing away. It turned out it was only his. He'd made a Gatling gun out of five 12-gauge barrels and mounted it on a swivel in the bow of a boat fitted with a blind made of chicken wire braided with fresh tules. He maneuvered the boat close to a raft of ducks and geese and then fired through an arrow slit, knocking down scores of birds before they could take wing. When he spotted me, he quickly scooped up his kill with a long-handled net and sped into a marsh.

The next time I saw him, I was in my canoe. He disappeared into another marsh. I paddled after him, but he doubled back to where I'd left my truck and slashed an X across the US Fish and Wildlife Service emblem on the door. He stabbed all four tires to boot.

I had spent a lot of time talking with other combat veterans about the need to control our anger and curb our thirst for revenge. To a man, we all said we could handle it on our own. We were lying, the same as we lied about our flashbacks, guilt, and drug abuse. I told myself it was only a truck and I wasn't angry nor desired retribution. But I wasn't about to shirk my duty. Good people who believed I deserved a second chance had put their reputations on the line by recommending me for the job, and I learned on the battlefield that trust was more important than courage. You never squandered it, you never betrayed it.

After my second encounter with the poacher, I made a blind of my own on a rise overlooking the refuge, set up a spotting scope, and waited for him to return. He came back two days later, and I studied his movements for three more to learn his habits. He stuck to a pattern, moving from marsh to marsh in a clockwise direction. The marshes provided him cover and access to the open water where the big flocks of waterfowl rested in the middle. The poacher mimicked a beaver, always leaving himself at least two back doors for escape. Since I was the only ranger in a district as big as some states, he no doubt assumed I could only choose one at a time.

That was his mistake. I had no intention of chasing him again.

The top of Steens Mountain turned golden with alpenglow as I continued paddling. The birds took the changing light from the rising sun as their cue and started to stir. I could make out flocks of blue-winged teal, harlequin ducks with heads as masked and colorful as a court jester, and the spoon-like bills of northern shovelers. Tundra swans mixed with snow geese. Canada geese outnumbered both species four to one.

The muffled drone of an outboard motor supplied baritone to their quacks and honks. The poacher was making his way along a channel in the marsh right ahead of me. He was sticking to his pattern and would enter the open water, cut the engine, and let the current push his blind silently toward the biggest rafts. When he drew as close as the broadside of a barn door, he would launch his murderous fusillade.

I eased my canoe into a thick stand of cattails, crouched low, and waited. The outboard stopped put-putting. The boat coasted into view. The camouflage only went around the bow and sides, leaving the stern open. The poacher tilted the outboard to raise the propeller from the water. Then he slipped an oar over the stern and used it as a rudder to steer his blind toward the unsuspecting waterfowl.

I judged his speed at two miles per hour, did the math, and came up with a yard per second. A 12-gauge shotgun firing bird-shot had an effective kill range of fifty yards. I counted to sixty before exiting the cattails and swapping the paddle for my Winchester.

"Fish and Wildlife," I called out. "You're under arrest."

His head jerked around. He wore a greasy billed cap with sheepskin-lined earflaps that were blackened from chewing tobacco dribbling from the corners of his mouth. He bared horselike teeth that were equally stained.

"Wrong, neighbor," he brayed. "You ain't got nothing."

I snugged the butt of the rifle against my shoulder. "I got something, all right."

He eyed the .30-30. "I'm only out for a Sunday cruise. You ain't gonna shoot nobody."

"It's not Sunday."

"What's your name, neighbor?"

"Nick Drake. What's yours?"

"You got a badge you can show me, Nick Drake?"

"It's pinned to my chest."

"I can't see it."

"You will when I cuff you," I said.

His lips curled back. His gums were also the color of tobacco. "I'm gonna lower my prop and be on my way."

"Touch that tiller and I'll start drilling holes below your waterline. You better hope I don't miss high."

The poacher stopped talking. He was stalling, thinking that the longer he could keep the paddle out of my hands, the sooner my canoe would broach and cause me to lose my line of fire. That would give him the chance to rush for his 12-gauge machine gun and swivel it toward me. I leaned to starboard and pressed my right knee against the gunwale to counter the drift while holding the Winchester steady.

"Looks like we got us a Mexican standoff," he said. "You can't board me while holding onto that long gun, and I ain't about to offer you a hand up."

"I'm going to board you, but first you're going to get off."

"What?"

"You heard me. Go on, jump in the lake. Once I'm on your boat, I'll throw you a line and tow you to shore."

"You're crazy. I'll drown if I don't freeze first."

"Am I?" I levered a fresh cartridge.

The clank of the brass entering the chamber was followed by thunder booming in the distance. The poacher looked up, but I kept my eyes locked on him. The thunder boomed again. It struck me that I hadn't seen a cloud since paddling away from shore.

A shadow that was neither duck nor goose darkened the water, and then came a familiar whine that turned into a shriek, followed by two more sonic booms. Four fighter jets flying in close formation screamed low overhead, their afterburners turning the glassy surface of the lake into froth. I ducked instinctively and then grew angry at myself. I hadn't had a flashback for a while and thought I was over them.

I started to raise my head when the explosions came in quick succession, metal pinged on metal, and shrapnel flew all around me. I ducked lower.

"Kiss the grass and cover your ass," I shouted and waited for the men's usual call back of "Don't worry mom, it's only napalm."

I couldn't recall having ordered my squad's DJ to radio for air support. No matter, the fighter jets were here, and their pilots were making the cold, split-second calculations that risking scouts' lives might save an entire company marching behind.

"Here it comes again," I yelled to the men, but couldn't hear their replies over a renewed round of rapid-fire explosions.

Bomb fragments whistled around me. More explosions came, one after another, beat upon beat upon beat, until they all rolled into one continuous drumming that seemed to rise up and pass directly overhead. Rain began to splatter.

Only it wasn't rain.

Droplets of water fell from the webbed feet and downy bellies of thousands of spooked birds taking off from the lake as one. Daylight streamed through dozens of BB-sized holes in the bow of the canoe. Birdshot rolled around in the bottom like it was in a pinball machine. I watched as the motorized duck blind disappeared into the marsh, the poacher holding the outboard's tiller with one hand, the other raised high in the air with the middle finger extended.

I looked up at the sky. Four jet trails snaked lazily overhead as I worked to keep the perforated bow above the water. The fighters had come from the west. The closest base was Kingsley Field in Klamath Falls, home to an Air Force interceptor squadron that also served as a training base for pilots readying for the war.

I was sure the trainees who'd roared by were eager to get into the action overseas. Fighter pilots were cocky by nature, but experience told me when the cherries got in-country, they'd quickly discover being in the real deal was nothing like buzzing birds on a lonesome lake in the high desert. North Vietnam's air force consisted of little more than a handful of cast-off MiGs, but its mobile batteries of surface-to-air missiles were scoring plenty of direct hits, four hundred in one year alone. I knew that for a fact because my squad of 1st Cavalry Army scouts had been tasked with searching for downed pilots along with our usual job of tracking the enemy.

The air was warming as the sun climbed higher, and I was closing in on the spot where I'd left my truck. I started paddling faster at the thought of the poacher doubling back to work over the Ford with his blade again.

A distant whine caused me to look over my shoulder and

slow my strokes. Three black dots appeared on the horizon. The fighter jets were back and closing in fast. They were returning to their home base after the training exercise and were on a path to pass right overhead again. I was wondering where the fourth went when I spotted it trailing behind.

The three zoomed by. When the fourth reached the lake, I couldn't hear its turbine. A loud bang punctuated the silence. The bubble canopy snapped off and tumbled away. Red flashed and the copilot shot straight up from the rear of the cockpit. The jet kept going. I recognized it as a F-101 Voodoo. I turned back to the skyrocketing copilot still strapped in his ejection seat and waited for it to release and fall away and for the parachute to deploy. Neither did. Up he went until gravity took over and then down he plunged. The water erupted where he hit.

I didn't wait to see if the pilot ejected too or if the fighter crashed and went up in a fireball. I was busy paddling my crippled canoe to the splashdown. Bubbles marked the spot. I kicked off my boots and scrambled over the side. The cold punched me hard in the chest. I treaded water for a moment as I filled my lungs before jackknifing down. Malheur Lake was fed by snowmelt. The lake spread for miles and was the drain for a 1,500-square-mile basin, swelling in spring and shrinking in summer. It never got very deep. The seat had landed right side up in a thick bed of mud. The copilot was still sitting. I grabbed his flight harness and tried to pull him. He wouldn't budge.

My eyes stung as I struggled to keep them open in the murky gloom. He was belted to the seat by five straps that all connected to a round buckle above his crotch. As I worked to rotate the buckle to spring the release, I searched for signs of life. He still wore his oxygen mask, but its hose had ripped free from the air tank and now floated above his head. I peered into the helmet's visor, trying to make eye contact, but the tinted plastic was too dark. "Lt. Ramirez" was embroidered on the chest of his flight suit. The word "Toro" and a pair of bull's horns were painted in red on the top of his helmet.

My lungs burned. I gritted my teeth, clamped my lips to keep from taking a breath, and finally twisted the buckle open. The belts released and I grabbed the copilot's flight harness again, wrenched him loose, and kicked for the surface as white lights strobed.

The cold air tasted sweet as I sucked it in. The canoe had drifted away. I hooked my arm across his chest and swam for shore. The distance wasn't far and the water was shallow. I scrambled the last ten yards, half carrying, half dragging him.

Once I hit solid ground, I unfastened his helmet. His pupils were fixed. He wasn't breathing. I rolled him on his side and slapped his back. Water drained from his mouth. I started resuscitation. I covered his mouth with mine and blew in air. I pounded on his chest. I pumped his arms. I rolled him on his side and slapped his back again and repeated the process over and over.

I finally gave up and sat next to him. I hugged my knees to my chest and admitted to myself what I'd known all along. Hitting the water without a parachute was the same as hitting pavement. Air Force Lt. "Toro" Ramirez was dead before he'd settled on the bottom.

A white pickup truck with emergency lights on the roof and a gold star emblazoned on the door rolled to a stop. Harney County Deputy Sheriff Pudge Warbler took his time getting out before ambling over to my rig. He rapped on the fogged driver's side window with the back of his knuckles.

"Looks like you made yourself a Paiute sweat lodge in there," he said.

I turned the heater's blower down. "I hadn't planned on going swimming this morning."

The old deputy wore a small brim Stetson and a holstered .45. He glanced at the dead man still lying beside the lake. "Oh Lord, what's with you and bodies anyway, son? If you're not tripping over them in a gully, you got them falling on you from an airplane."

"He didn't fall, he ejected. And it wasn't a plane. It was a F-101 fighter jet. A Voodoo."

"I know that already. I called it in after you radioed me and dispatch filled me in on the particulars." Pudge's ranch house doubled as a sheriff's department substation. It was closer to the

Malheur National Wildlife Refuge than the main office up in Burns. "An alert went out from Kingsley Field. The base commander is sending over a team."

"And the jet he bailed out of, did it go down too?"

"No, it made it back okay."

"Lucky for the pilot. That took some flying without a canopy and whatever else was going on with the aircraft. I didn't hear its engine." I pointed at the body. "Wonder why he punched out and the pilot didn't?"

"I'm sure the Air Force will be asking that themselves."

"They're taking charge?"

The deputy pushed the brim of his hat up. "Harney County may be my jurisdiction, but the Air Force takes the lead when there's an accident involving one of their planes. You know the military."

Pudge was a veteran too. His build matched the bulldog he had tattooed on his forearm when he joined the Marines at the onset of World War II.

"Is that your canoe down by the willows?" he said. "Looks half sunk. That happen when you rescued him?"

"You mean recovered."

"What were you doing on the lake?"

"Trying to catch a poacher."

"You and me both," he said.

"How's that?"

"I got some rustlers on the loose. They're taking steers like it's the help yourself buffet at the Fourth of July county picnic. I got to catch them or I'll have an even bigger problem on my hands. If the ranchers get ahold of them first, it'll be shoot, shovel, and shut up. You want some help dragging your canoe over and putting it in the truck? We got time. It's gonna take the flyboys a while to get here from K Falls."

I left the warmth of the pickup. My jeans were still damp. So was my shirt. We walked past the copilot. Pudge stopped and leaned over to take a look. His eyes stayed on the helmet I'd placed over the dead man's face.

"Toro. Like in bullfighting, huh?"

"It's his call sign. All fighter pilots have them. They get them at a naming ritual during flight school or in combat."

"Us leathernecks got ours by doing something particularly brave or especially stupid," Pudge said. "What was yours?"

"My rank."

"Sarge, huh?"

I nodded. Most of the men in my squad never knew my real name.

The canoe's bow rested onshore where I'd left it after retrieving my boots and rifle. Pudge crouched and ran his fingers over the birdshot holes.

"Feels like a cheese grater. You didn't mention your poacher was shooting at you. I hope you shot back."

I didn't reply, not wanting to admit to being frozen by a flashback again.

"Well, this goes a little beyond killing ducks out of season. The moment he pulled the trigger on you put him square into my camp too."

"Don't you have your hands full tracking down rustlers?"

Pudge stuck out his chin. "The day I can't handle two varmints at once is the day I'm gonna stop being half-retired and hang it up for good. Until then, I'll help you catch him before he shoots something bigger than a Christmas goose."

We turned the canoe over to drain it and then carried it to my truck and slid it into the bed. I jumped in and used the tie-downs I carried for securing my motorcycle to make it fast.

The deputy returned to the body. "It doesn't sit right leaving him out in the field like this, but we can't move him any farther than what you already did. It's their investigation now."

"I can understand why the pilot didn't circle back to get a visual," I said. "He had his hands full trying to keep his plane in the air. But it doesn't say much about the other pilots. They must've known something was going sideways. A squadron always maintains constant radio contact, but no one turned around."

"And I bet that's another question the blue yonder brass will be asking," Pudge said.

~

THE AIR FORCE arrived in cars, not planes. A sedan followed by a Chevy Suburban and a paneled van all painted the same leaden gray pulled in behind our pickup trucks. They had blue and white license plates bearing the words Official Use Only.

The passenger in the sedan was in charge. He wore a pilot's jumpsuit and blue flight cap.

"Capt. Vincent Dominic, US Air Force, 59th Squadron," he announced with a salute. He had a hint of a Texas drawl. "And you are?"

"Deputy Pudge Warbler, Harney County Sheriff's and he's Nick Drake, US Fish and Wildlife. You boys made pretty good time. I'm guessing the state police let you slide on the speed limit."

The captain didn't acknowledge that, nor did he introduce his driver who stood beside him. The man was beady eyed and wore a sidearm hanging from a webbed belt cinched low on the waist of his uniform like a gunslinger. Dominic didn't introduce the rest of his team either. Two men jumped from the van and began unloading and setting up equipment. Another pair exited the Suburban. They wore dark blue berets with "Air Police" flashes on them—the Air Force's version of MPs—and bore rifles at port arms. They marched straight to the body and took up guard positions at the head and foot.

"Are you the one who pulled him from the water?" Dominic asked me.

"That's right."

"Where exactly?"

"Ninety-eight yards straight out." I pointed to the spot.

"You seem pretty certain about that."

"I had to swim him in. I counted every stroke to mark the distance from where he landed. His ejection seat never separated. I had to unbuckle him from it."

"And it's still there?"

I nodded.

The captain barked an order. "Smith, Rawlings. We have equipment in the water. Hundred yards shy two. Straight out from my mark. Double time. Go!"

The pair from the van had finished inflating a gray raft piled with coiled ropes, swim fins, and dive masks. They raced it down to the shoreline, splashed into the water, and started paddling as if under enemy fire.

"What about the canopy?" Dominic said.

"It came off right after the jet passed the opposite shore."

"Is it in the lake too?"

"Not at the speed it was hurtling backwards."

"Did you see where it came down?" I shook my head. "How come?"

"I was busy keeping an eye on Lieutenant Ramirez. His chute never opened."

"Parachute failure hasn't been determined yet," the captain said.

"I saw him go up and I saw him come down. No silk. It never deployed. The ejection seat didn't release either."

"The Air Force is in charge of investigating this incident. Is that clear?"

"As rain. All I'm telling you is what I saw and what I did."

"And I'll tell you again. This is our investigation. It's vital all this remains classified. The nation is at war. We can't have information or equipment that could fall into enemy hands. We need to find that canopy."

"It won't be easy. It could be anywhere in the refuge. That's three hundred square miles of lakes, marshes, channels, and open desert."

"We're the US Air Force. We take on a mission, we always complete it. We'll find that canopy. Count on it."

"Because you need it to determine if the lieutenant panicked and pulled the ejector handle or if the Voodoo's equipment malfunctioned," I said. "I didn't hear the jet's engine."

Dominic took a step toward me. "Are you Air Force?"

"No."

"Ever flown a jet?"

Again, I said, "No."

"Then what would you know about a sophisticated supersonic weapon system?"

I could've told him I'd received training on a variety of fighter jets and their ejection seats when tasked with looking for downed pilots, that I knew some versions of the F-101 Voodoo had a dual handle ejector system and others a single, but it would have been a waste of breath. Dominic struck me as the type of officer who couldn't see past his prejudice that his branch of the military was superior to all the rest.

When I didn't reply, he confirmed it. He looked me up and down, taking in my nonregulation haircut, a week's worth of stubble, and muddy jeans. "How about you keep your opinions to yourself and let men who wear real uniforms do their job."

Pudge groaned. "Son, I think you flew without oxygen once

too often not to recognize a couple of real soldiers when they're standing right in front of you. Maybe that's because the only action pilots ever see is from the safety of five miles up, not down on the ground where the fighting is so close you don't know if it's your blood or the enemy's you're wearing."

Dominic shifted his glower to Pudge and worked his jaw before saying, "My apologies, Deputy. No disrespect intended. I'm sure you can understand that losing a man has put us on edge. Now, if you'll excuse me, I'm going to oversee the retrieval of our equipment."

"One more thing," I said before he turned away.

"Now what?"

"You should advise the base commander to halt training flights over this area."

"And why would I want to do that?"

"We're right in the middle of the Pacific Flyway here. It's like an aerial interstate for migrating birds. Millions pass through every spring and fall."

"So?"

"Flyovers are dangerous this time of year."

"Training fighter pilots is in the national interest. We have a higher priority than worrying about ruffling a few feathers."

"I'm talking about dangerous for pilots. Those four jets were flying pretty low. When you get back to base, ask the pilot who was flying the one Ramirez punched out of if he had a bird strike. A fifteen-pound Canada goose hitting a canopy could cause it to blow off. Imagine what it would do to the fan blades if it got sucked into the turbine. Maybe one did. Maybe a bunch did. Maybe that's why the jet was flying a lot slower than the others."

"There could be a lot of reasons for that," Dominic said quickly.

"I'm sure the pilot will know why."

"And I'm sure you know why it's important to keep this matter under wraps." Dominic snapped a curt salute and marched over to the two APs guarding the body. The beady-eyed driver shot us a warning look before following at his captain's heels.

I 'd seen the sun go horizon to horizon by the time I pulled into the old railroad lineman's shack I called home on the outskirts of No Mountain. I offloaded the canoe and placed it next to my Triumph motorcycle. Both looked the worse for wear. I'd been slowly rebuilding the two-wheeler after a rough and ready pursuit across Hart Mountain National Antelope Refuge had left the front fork bent and the piston rings fried. The gas tank looked as if it had been worked over by a ball-peen hammer.

The long day was catching up to me but falling asleep was never easy. I put on a pot of water to boil, made a mug of tea from herbs I'd picked in the summer, and sat down to drink it at the rickety table in the tiny kitchen that was steps from my narrow bunk.

Pudge Warbler and I had stayed long enough at Malheur Lake to watch the divers bring up the ejection seat and place it into the back of the van along with the dead copilot. Captain Dominic's only goodbye to us was a final salute. We watched the convoy speed off.

"Talk about stiff upper lips," Pudge said. "The captain told us everyone was on edge because they'd lost a man, but not a single tear was shed. No one said words over Ramirez's body or even looked at him until it was time to load him on the litter and haul him away. It's been twenty-five years since I was on Iwo Jima, and I still get a lump in my throat whenever I think of my buddies who fell."

I hoped that someday my remembrances would be limited to that.

"Well, it's their show now," Pudge said, "but I still need to file a report, national defense secrets or not. Come by the house in the morning and I'll take your formal statement." He patted his paunch. "I'll ask November to bake us some Indian fry bread for breakfast."

As I sat next to the stove drinking tea, Toro Ramirez led a parade of ghosts of pilots and crew members downed in Vietnam. My squad had made some successful rescues—cutting flyers down from trees they'd parachuted into, arriving in the nick of time to halt black-clad guerrillas who'd cornered a bomber crew in a rice paddy—but the memories of arriving too late outnumbered them. I inhaled the steam curling from my mug, but instead of tasting sage and peppermint, my nostrils filled with the acrid smoke from burning rubber and blazing jet fuel.

I knew the smell would soon be joined by the cries for help from men trapped by flames. I jumped up and reached for one of the cans I kept on the kitchen shelf. Each can was filled with pebbles. I added a new pebble every morning and another every night to mark how long I'd gone without shooting heroin. There was a year's worth of pebbles now. I gripped the can and began to rattle it next to my ear to drown out the echoes of dying men along with the voice inside my head, begging me to give in and have a fix. *Only one*, the voice promised. *I swear, only one.*

THE NEXT MORNING I drove through No Mountain. The one-blink town boasted a post office, combination tavern and dry goods store, and a smattering of buildings with false fronts that appeared to lean against each other for support against the prevailing winds that blew regardless of the season. The two-lane highway that doubled as Main Street didn't have a traffic light, not even a stop sign.

All that slowed me down was a cattle guard that marked the entrance to Pudge Warbler's ranch. I clattered over it and pulled in behind a red Jeep Wagoneer hitched to an empty two-stall horse trailer. The rig belonged to Pudge's daughter and served as her mobile large animal veterinarian hospital.

The front door to the ranch house was left unlocked as was the custom throughout Harney County. Gemma Warbler was sitting across the dining table from her father. Her face was tan from spending days in the field tending to sick and injured livestock. She wore a denim shirt with pearl snap buttons and her hair in a ponytail.

"Well, hello stranger," she said over a coffee cup she gripped with both hands and held halfway to her lips. "Pudge was telling me why we haven't seen much of you lately."

"You know how it is. Goes with the territory when your district covers ten thousand square miles."

"Tell me about it," she said.

Spending a lot of time behind the wheel was something the deputy's daughter and I had in common. Gemma's patients lived on the far-and-few-between sheep and cattle ranches spread across the largest county in Oregon and tenth biggest in the country. My district stretched from the Malheur down to the Sheldon National Wildlife Refuge on the Oregon-Nevada line and west to the Upper Klamath Lake Refuge.

"I understand you had yourself a busy time yesterday dodging buckshot and falling fighter pilots," she said.

I sat down at the table. "The poacher got lucky and caught a break."

"And next time you run into him?"

"He'll be the one getting caught."

"What about the man who fell from his plane?"

"He wasn't so lucky."

Gemma hid a grimace by sipping coffee. Pudge noticed me looking at their empty plates.

"That's right. November's been waiting on you to get here before she takes anything off the stove. You know how she is when it comes to mealtimes. You better prepare yourself for an earful being late."

I didn't have to wait long to receive it. The door between the dining room and kitchen swung open as a woman with skin the color of tanned buckskin and coal-black eyes bumped it with her hip. She carried a skillet of eggs and bacon and a basket of Indian fry bread. It was dusted with powdered sugar that matched the cobweb-like strands that streaked her long, black braid.

"*Amamu'a, Tsua'a Numudooa Nubabe,*" I said in halting Paiute, using her birth name, Girl Born in Snow, and not the one given to her at a Bureau of Indian Affairs boarding school sixty years ago.

She acknowledged my good morning and mispronunciations by issuing a string of sounds that rose and fell like water bubbling in a brook. The glottal stops were similar to Vietnamese. This time her meaning was lost on me. I turned to Gemma for translation. November had taught her Paiute after moving to the ranch to help raise her following her mother's death.

"Are you sure you want to know before you eat?" she said.

"That bad?"

"She said you speak *numu* like a bighorn sheep who has gas in all four stomachs after eating too much brittlebush in winter."

"A *hoonu*," I said, showing off my growing vocabulary.

November tsked. "That is only one kind of fart. There are many types. It depends on which story you are telling, which people you are, and the dialect of *numu* you speak." The old woman was a *Wadadökadö*, a Wada Root and Grass-Seed Eater. "Our language is simple. Why are you taking so long to learn it?"

"Because *numu* is like music. I have to get all the chords and notes right to make it sing."

She wrinkled her nose. "Now your words smell like what a white man's bull leaves behind after it has emptied all of its stomachs. *Madukanna kutsu kwedapu.*"

Pudge groaned. "Oh Lord. Are we gonna talk our breakfast or eat it?"

November set the skillet and basket of fry bread down and sat opposite me. The food was passed family style. I realized how long it had been since I had last eaten and dug in.

Pudge splashed hot sauce on everything but the sweetened fry bread. "I see you got the horse trailer hitched up," he said to Gemma. "You picking up a patient somewhere?"

"No patients this time. These horses are strong and healthy."

"Whose are they?"

"Mine."

The old deputy's mouth fell open. "What?"

"I bought them from Lyle Rides Alone. I'm going to pick them up after breakfast. Lyle's been selling off a lot of his herd in preparation for winter, especially now that he's getting up there in age. He decided he didn't need the expense of stabling so many cutting horses."

"You didn't pay for nags that are one trot away from the glue factory, did you?"

Gemma's ponytail swished. "This pair is special. The filly is the fastest I've ever seen cut and head. You should see her when she gets the drop on a cow. She never blows up."

"And the other one?"

"A three-year-old colt."

"He gelded yet?"

"No."

"I hope you know what you're getting into with the likes of him."

She smiled. "I do."

"Tell me you didn't spend your hard-earned money on some wild-eyed stallion for me." Pudge patted his hip where he still nursed an old gunshot wound. The injury right before an election had cost him his longtime job as sheriff. Most people in Harney County still called him "Sheriff" as a sign of respect. "You know I haven't been in the saddle since I got plugged, and I'm not about to get up on some young buck who'll always be trying to prove his worth."

"Lyle Rides Alone offered the pair as a package deal. It was too good to pass up. Maybe Nick would enjoy riding him." Gemma turned to me. "How about it? You do know how to ride, don't you?"

I waved a piece of bacon. "Sure, I have my Triumph."

"Riding a horse is not the same as a motorcycle."

"It can't be that much different."

Father and daughter cawed like a pair of crows sitting on a wire.

"Tell you what, hotshot. When I bring them home, I'll give you a call and you can show me what you got."

"I don't have a saddle," I said.

"I got one you can use," Pudge said a little too quickly.

November stared across the table. "You told us you were in the cavalry. How could you not know how to ride a *pooggoo*?"

"The Army swapped horses for helicopters a long time ago," I said.

"When I was taken to the white man's school, they forbid us from riding *pooggoos*. If we said *pooggoo* or spoke any *numu*, the teachers would take a leather strap to our backsides. Do you know why?"

I shook my head.

"They wanted to beat what they called the Indianness out of us. They were following orders. If white men couldn't kill us with their guns, they would kill us with their words by taking away ours."

"I'm trying to learn your words." As soon as I said it, I could hear how hollow it sounded.

"You need to try harder," the old woman said. "Our words and our stories are what keep all Paiute people from being forgotten forever."

Pudge mopped up the last of his eggs with a pinch of fry bread and then pushed away from the table.

"That's enough history lesson for now. Drake and I got to tend to the present. Come on, son. Let's get that report out of the way so I can get back to catching my rustlers and you your poacher."

Deputy Warbler's home office was crowded with bookshelves holding classics and histories, a glass-fronted gun cabinet, and a well-worn leather couch. Drifts of papers covered his desk. A shortwave radio blinked and hummed on a table. Next to it was a facsimile machine. Pudge called the apparatus newfangled but admired it grudgingly. He once confided that the first time it rang and began churning out a transmission, he shouted for Gemma and November to come watch as the document magically appeared. "I thought they'd rolled up a sheet of paper on their end, stuck it in the telephone wire somehow, and whoosh, out it came on my end," he chuckled.

Pudge pointed at the leather couch as he eased into a wooden swivel desk chair. "Make yourself comfortable. It's only a formal statement, not a tooth that needs pulling."

He asked routine questions and jotted down my answers. What time did I arrive, what was I doing there, what did I see, and what did I do before and after the copilot ejected.

"That's it," he said. "Painless, huh?"

"For me, yes, for Toro Ramirez, not so much."

The old deputy dipped his head. "May he rest in peace."

"What will become of your report?"

"I'll send it in, but it'll either wind up in a drawer or the circular file. Bust'em won't want to spend any more of his budget looking into something the feds have called their own." Bust'em was Sheriff Buster Burton, the victor in Pudge's reelection campaign. "You know how the little go-getter is, guided more by politics than police work. The last thing he'd want to do is rankle someone with more stars on his uniform than him. Especially now with this."

Pudge held up a sheet of shiny facsimile paper with the US Air Force seal in the upper left-hand corner and two typewritten paragraphs below it.

"What is it?"

"It came in the middle of the night. It's a memo from the base commander at Kingsley Field canceling the downed pilot alert. He goes on to thank the sheriff's department for calling it in. The second part isn't so chatty. It spells out what will happen if we talk to anybody about it. It cites a bunch of secrets acts and classified information laws."

"That's pretty unusual," I said.

"That the Air Force doesn't want to broadcast to the world that one of its trainees screwed up or there's a SNAFU with a very expensive piece of taxpayer hardware? Can't say I blame them."

"I meant the speed you got the memo. You remember how slow orders move up and down the chain of command. Yet this got signed, sealed, and delivered faster than the jets that flew over me. Mind if I take a look?"

Pudge thought about it before handing it over. "I suppose it can't hurt seeing that your district supervisor up in Portland probably got one like it. If you had a facsimile machine, you would've known about it already."

The language was typical military bureaucratese. The signature had a lot of flourishes and was smudged from being faxed, but the name and title typed beneath it was as loud and clear as a drill instructor hurling insults at boot camp. Maj. Peter Hardiman, Base Commander.

"What do you know. Whistling Pete," I said.

"What's fireworks got to do with anything?" Pudge said.

"The base commander. It's his call sign. I know him."

"You do?"

"It was during my last tour. He was a captain then, a flight squadron leader. He got shot down in the North during a raid on Hanoi. Lucky for him, his ejection seat worked. Even luckier, my squad was able to get to him before NVA regulars found him."

"Small world, you and a foxhole buddy ending up within spitting distance stateside."

"We weren't exactly buddies. It was a mission and he was the objective. I was with him for three days though. That's how long it took us to get him to a place where a Huey could land safely for an EVAC. Pilots had bounties on their heads. It was a foot race and coming in second wasn't an option."

Hardiman was pretty banged up when we reached him, but at least he could walk. His copilot couldn't. Both his legs were broken. The squad took turns carrying him on their backs. We used up all our morphine syrettes on the injured man by the end of the second day. His cries of pain grew so loud that Hardiman ordered us to leave him behind lest the enemy heard him. Hardiman had rank on me, but it was my squad, my mission. I gagged the copilot to stifle his screams and we kept on going.

I handed the letter back. "Thanks for breakfast. I got to get to work."

"Going back to Malheur?"

"Eventually. The poacher will probably lay low for a couple of days. I'll use the time to check up on the other refuges."

Pudge raised an eyebrow. "Including the one near Klamath Falls?"

"It's on my list."

"Why do I think it got moved to the top?"

"Upper Klamath Lake is a major stopover during the fall migration, the same as Malheur."

"And why am I thinking birds aren't the only things that fly you're gonna be looking into?"

"As long as I'm over there... What is it people around here say? It wouldn't be neighborly if I didn't stop by and say howdy."

"You're gonna use seeing an old buddy as an excuse to poke your nose into where it doesn't belong, aren't you?"

Even though I didn't know Toro Ramirez and hadn't served with him, I felt a duty toward him. Though I'd been trying to get as far away from the military as I could, I knew I'd never be able to shake the feeling of being responsible for another soldier's life.

The old deputy was watching my face. He sighed. "Son, do me a favor."

"What is it?"

"You find something about that flyboy who died in my juris-diction that even sniffs wrong, I better be the first person you call."

GEMMA WAS CROUCHING between her Jeep and the horse trailer as I walked out to my truck. She wielded a pair of needle-nose pliers while holding strands of rubber coated electrical wire. I asked her if there was a problem with the trailer's brake lights.

"The main lead to the connector was failing, so I dissected a length of speaker wire from the 8-track and used it to create a bypass," she said.

"Spoken like a true surgeon."

Gemma finished matching the colors of the wires, twisted reds to reds and greens to greens, and started wrapping the splices with electrical tape.

"You'd be surprised how similar working on cars and cows is. I had a professor whose favorite tool in the surgery was an engine hoist. It worked great for extracting calves stuck in utero." She wiped her forehead with the back of her palm. "Stand behind the trailer for me, would you, and let me know if the lights flash when I tap the brakes and try the turn signals."

I gave her the high sign when the taillights lit up. Gemma slid out from behind the wheel. "Thanks."

I asked her if she was on her way to pick up her new horses.

"Yes, and I'm pretty excited. I haven't owned one since I left for college."

"Where are they?"

"Lyle's spread is in Harney Valley just north of Malheur Lake."

That put it under the stricken F-101 Voodoo's flight path. "When you're out there, ask him to keep an eye out for a bubble canopy from that fighter jet. The Air Force wants their property back."

"How big is it?"

"About six feet long and made of acrylic and has some metal banding. It would be hard to miss if it's laying in his fields."

"Okay, I'll tell Lyle, but I wouldn't hold your breath waiting for him to look for it. He's pretty busy keeping an eye out for rustlers."

"Have they hit his place too?"

Gemma nodded. "A lot of the ranches in the valley have lost stock. The Harney County Cattlemen's Association held a meeting about it the other night. Pudge went and told them not to try to apprehend anybody on their own."

"I can imagine how that went over."

"They all but put him on a spit and roasted him. What about it? Are you going to take me up on my invitation to go riding?"

"It'll have to wait a couple of days or so."

Strands of hair had loosened from her ponytail and were brushing her cheek. She blew at them. "I'm getting the impression it's more than horses you're trying to avoid."

"I don't know what you're talking about."

"Sure you do." Gemma blew at the loose strands again. "Harney County is plenty big, I grant you, and we both have our jobs, but you have a way of being gone when you're just down the road. What gives? I've hardly seen you since summer, and the only time I have is when Pudge and you are working on something together."

"It's my first fall migration. There are all those birds to keep an eye on, and now I got this poacher to deal with. I got new fences to keep cattle out of the antelope refuge at Hart Mountain that need regular checking, and..."

She cut me off with a wave. "Yeah, yeah, yeah. I get it. We'll see how busy you are when the snow starts falling in earnest. Perhaps then you can start to work on mending some fences around here."

"Look, I have to go to Klamath Falls for a bit. Maybe when I get back we can go for that ride."

"Klamath, as in where Kingsley Field is?"

"That's right."

"You and the pilots there have something in common."

"What would that be?"

Gemma's ponytail had fallen in front of her shoulder. She flicked it back. "You both like to keep everything up in the air."

5

Two bald eagles were hunting golden-eyed ducks on Upper Klamath Lake rather than their usual prey of fish. Eagles mate for life and this pair had perfected hunting as a team. The male made a noisy entrance from the west by screaming and flapping his huge wings as he hurtled toward a raft of ducks while the female glided in silently from the east, using the glare of the sun to mask her arrival and give her precious, lethal seconds undetected. I watched them from a pullout on the highway that ran alongside the shoreline. Theirs was the same strategy used by packs of lions, wolves, and humans since the dawn of time.

The lake was fed by rivers whose ice-cold headwaters flowed from the bottom of 2,000-foot-deep Crater Lake, the caldera of a volcano that blew its top more than 7,500 years ago. The subterranean waters emerged into sunlight and carved their way through forests and pastureland for fifty miles, washing rich nutrients into the Upper Klamath. Large redband rainbow trout swam in the lake's food-plentiful depths while shorebirds stalked tadpoles and invertebrates in its shallows. Migratory waterfowl stopped off in spring and fall in the same numbers as touched down on Malheur Lake.

The air flowing through my truck's open window was crisp, and I'd welcomed the chance to pull over. The drive from No Mountain had proven tricky. Fishtailing on patches of black ice had turned my knuckles white more than once. I lowered my binoculars to drink the last of the coffee from a thermos and wished I had brought some of November's sweetened fry bread instead of a stale store-bought sandwich.

I still had a few miles to go to reach Kingsley Field. I hadn't called ahead to arrange a visit with Maj. Peter "Whistling Pete" Hardiman. Surprise had always served me well in-country and old habits were hard to shake. Maybe I was wasting my time. Maybe Hardiman wouldn't be there or even remember me. Maybe I would learn that the lieutenant's death was one of those unfortunate costs of putting men, machines, and weapons together in high stress situations. Casualties were as inevitable in peacetime as in war, and whether the cause was accidental, intentional or collateral, the outcome remained the same. Dead was dead.

I watched the stealthy female eagle stretch out her legs and uncurl her powerful talons as she zeroed in on her target. She plucked a two-pound duck off the water without causing a splash. Her mate switched from playing the distractor to assailant and swept back his wings. He dive-bombed at the front-line of goldeneyes that had managed to scramble from the water and nailed his target midair. Hunter and huntress cheered each other's success with piercing shrieks as they turned for shore and flew wing tip to wing tip to a treetop aerie to devour their lunch unharried by ravens. I finished my sandwich, screwed the top back on the thermos and drove on, equally resolute to learn the truth of why Toro Ramirez had paid the ultimate price.

THE GUARDHOUSE at Kingsley Field was made of pink pumice blocks, testament to the region's violent volcanic past. A thick metal pole painted with black and white stripes blocked the entrance to the base. Two uniformed guards were on duty. They wore sidearms and dark blue berets with AP flashes, but they weren't the pair who'd been at Malheur Lake. One of the guards took my ID and placed a phone call. He spoke, listened, and then hung up. He told the other guard to conduct a visual while he wrote down my information in a logbook.

The other guard walked around my pickup, writing down the license plate number and looking into the bed. He eyed the gun rack in the rear window that cradled the government issue Winchester and 12-gauge pump shotgun.

"We don't allow civilians to bring personal weapons on base," he said.

I showed him my badge. "I'm a law enforcement officer with US Fish and Wildlife."

"That's not the same as being a cop."

He held out his hand for the guns. My debate whether to tell him about the holstered .357 magnum Smith & Wesson in the glove box was short-lived. I left it where it was while I slid the two long guns from the rack. He carried them inside. The guard who'd been logging my name leaned out of the doorway and handed me back my driver's license.

"You know where the base commander's office is?"

"Never been here," I said.

"Straight ahead. Right at the first intersection. Follow it to the two-story building that's made out of the same bricks as these. You'll see a sign. The tarmac is off-limits. We don't want anyone having a fender bender with the aircraft that are parked on it, day and night, and ready to take off within ninety seconds of an alert. And whatever you do, don't drive onto the runway. You're likely to get a F-101 up your ass."

"Duly noted," I said.

The top floor of the base headquarters was bisected by a hallway lined with narrow cubicles. It led to a large anteroom. Beyond it was a closed door. The top half had a frosted pane with the words "Maj. Peter Hardiman, Base Commander" lettered in black.

A twenty-year-old with a boot camp haircut and blue uniform jumped up from the desk parked out front of Hardiman's office. He gave a textbook salute.

"Sir, good afternoon, sir. Airman First Class Edwins. I have the privilege and honor of serving as Major Hardiman's adjutant, sir. The major ordered that I inform you he is presently on the telephone. He also ordered that I inform you to please make yourself comfortable while he completes the call. May I retrieve a cup of coffee for you, sir?"

Edwins had yet to drop his salute. "At ease, Airman," I said.

His arm went down, but his posture remained ramrod stiff. He kept his eyes locked straight ahead.

"Did the major tell you how long he'll be?"

"Sir, no, sir. May I get you that cup of coffee now, sir?"

"No thanks. Okay if I sit over here?" I pointed to an empty chair close to the young airman's desk.

"Sir, yes, sir."

Edwins waited until I sat down before taking his own seat behind the desk. A telephone book would've fitted easily between his spine and the back of the chair. He folded his hands on his lap and continued to stare straight ahead.

I looked around the room. The squadron's emblem hung on the wall. It depicted a red-eyed black bat with outstretched wings on a yellow moon with the number 59 stitched at the top and the words *Freiceadan Dubh* at the bottom. It was Gaelic for black watch and underscored the pride of the 59th in flying interceptors through storms in the dead of night. Other wall art included photographs of aircraft, a group shot of pilots and ground crew gathered in front of a row of fighter jets, a map of Oregon, and another of North and South Vietnam.

"Where are you from originally?" I asked the young airman.

"Kansas, sir."

"Which part?"

"Wichita, sir. Home of McConnell Air Force Base. I grew up watching the pilots do touch-and-gos. It is why I joined the United States Air Force, sir." Airman First Class Edwins hesitated. "Sir, may I ask you a question?"

"Sure, but you can lay off the sirs. I'm not military."

"Sir, that is not my understanding. Major Hardiman informed me you are a sergeant in the United States Army, 1st Calvary."

"Was."

"Sir, Major Hardiman informed me you and he served together in Vietnam."

"It was a while ago."

"He also informed me that you were decorated for your bravery and service to our country. Sir, I salute you." The young airman jumped up and did so.

The hardness of the chair started to dig into my backside. I hadn't been on a military base or around active service personnel since my discharge from Walter Reed. I was beginning to think I'd made a mistake coming here.

"Sir, may I ask you what it was like?"

"What was what like?" I said, knowing full well what he meant.

"Combat, sir. Facing the enemy. All of it. Is it true the Vietcong use blowpipes and poisoned darts, that the women fight right alongside the men, that they ride water buffaloes into battle?"

"A lot of stuff goes down there, but don't believe everything you hear."

"I want to be there," he said, his voice rising. "It is why I enlisted. I do not want to be stuck behind a desk stateside while the war passes me by. It could be over any day now."

I turned away from the wall art and studied him. Red spots had formed on his cheeks and the whitewall haircut made his ears look oversized. The war in Vietnam had been waged continuously since before he was born, first by the French and now by Americans and Australians. The way it was going, no end was in sight. Before I could tell him that, the door to Hardiman's office opened and Whistling Pete strode toward me.

"Nick Drake, you old son of a gun. I did a double take when the front gate called. I figured you were still in-country. What are you doing way out here?"

"Working." I wondered if he'd read his team's report from yesterday.

Hardiman ushered me into his office and closed the door. US and Air Force flags drooped from standing flagpoles. The windows provided views of the runway, jets parked on the tarmac, and a large hangar next to it. Hardiman gestured at a visitor's chair.

"What's with the uniform?" he asked as he sat behind his desk. "I thought you were a lifer like me."

"I took the Freedom Bird home a year ago. Now I'm with Fish and Wildlife. When did you make major?"

Hardiman opened a humidor between a bronze statue of a screaming eagle and a model fighter jet on his desk. He plucked out two cigars and held one up. I waved him off.

"Are you sure? They're Cubans. The real thing. I got a buddy who picks them up when he's dropping off supplies at Guantanamo."

"I quit."

"Good for you." He put one back, cut the tip off the other, and lit it with a Zippo that bore a miniature red-eyed bat on a yellow moon emblem.

"Getting shot down did two things to my career," he said between draws. "The sad thing is it knocked me right out of combat duty. No way the brass wanted to risk having an ace get shot down twice. Bad for recruitment PR. I tried to fight them on it, but what could I do? As a consolation prize, they swapped my silver bars for this gold oak leaf." He blew smoke at the major insignia on his shoulder.

"I wasn't too happy about it at first. Flying combat, well, it was all I knew how to do, all I'd ever been trained for and wanted to do. But then a brigadier general sat me down and gave me the Air Force facts of life. Pete, he told me, you can do more good for your country and kill more of the enemy by training other pilots to drop the bombs for you." A cloud of smoke billowed around him. "And you know what? He was right."

Hardiman tapped the cigar's ash into a shallow silver bowl that looked like a golf trophy of some sort. "This place, Kingsley Field? It's a stepping stone. The general laid it all out for me. Spend a couple of years here, do a good job, and the gold oak leaf will become a silver one, and I'll make lieutenant colonel and get a bigger base to go with it. Two years after that I'll become a full bird. Each step along the way I'll be commanding bigger and more important bases. Who knows what will happen after a few years as a full colonel. You know what us Air Force pilots always say. The sky's the limit." He grinned and leaned back in his chair.

"Sounds like you won the grand prize after all you went through."

"You know, I'm forever in your debt. Don't think I'll ever forget what you and your men did for Clancy and me."

I never saw Hardiman and his copilot again after we loaded them onto the Huey, nor heard from them. My squad boarded another chopper that was diverted mid flight. We were dropped off at a hot LZ to help reinforce another squad taking fire. Just another day as a grunt on the ground.

"How did Clancy make out?" I asked.

"They took off his right leg in Da Nang before flying him to the naval hospital in Yokosuka. They kept him in Japan for a month to stabilize him before shipping him home. We lost touch after that. You know how it is. You're either in the war or you're not." Hardiman said the last part while staring at me through a cloud of cigar smoke.

"You're probably wondering how I knew you were here," I said.

"Now that you mention it. Did you read about me in *Stars and Stripes*?"

"I live in Harney County now. I saw your name on the letter you sent to the sheriff there. I'm the one who pulled Lieutenant Ramirez from the lake."

"Well, I'll be. My men's report didn't list you by name. They mentioned a game warden being there, is all. They did name the sheriff's deputy. Pudge Warbler. Can't forget a moniker like that. They said he's a real character too. I'll have a word with my men and make sure they correct the report."

"Captain Dominic's report," I said. "He's the one Deputy Warbler and I spoke with."

"That's right. The captain is the senior squadron leader here. I didn't fly with him in 'Nam, but he earned himself a commendable service record. Almost as good as mine." He grinned again. "That earned him a ticket out here to train the next crop of pilots. Sounds like I should be thanking you and not the deputy for finding one of ours."

"I wish I could've pulled him out alive, but he went down without his chute opening."

"A sad day, indeed. I was on the phone telling his parents. Goes with the job."

"I feel responsible for him. I made it and he didn't." I tried blinking away the image of the dead copilot's face, but couldn't. "It would help me to know what happened that caused him to die. Like, why did he bail, but not the pilot? Why didn't his chute deploy? And how come none of the other pilots circled back around to get a visual?"

Hardiman jabbed his cigar at me and his tone changed. "You say you read my letter? Then you know the entire matter is classified. I don't need to tell a soldier like you what secret means."

"No, you don't, but you know how it is when a team member falls. You want to make things right even when you can't."

Hardiman's face remained hardened. "To repeat, I am not at liberty to discuss the incident."

"Understood. Look, besides stopping by to say hello once I learned you were here and wondering about the accident, I did want to talk to you about something related to it. Did Dominic pass on my advice about halting training flights over the Malheur Wildlife Refuge while the bird migration is on?"

"No, he did not. We had a man down and more important matters to address. What's this all about anyway?"

I gave him a quick rundown on the waves of birds filling the skies. "They go north in spring to nest and bear their young and then head south in fall before the heavy snows cover their feeding areas. I'm talking about birds by the millions."

Hardiman stubbed out his cigar even though it was only half smoked. "You raise a good point. No reason for our pilots and aircraft to take unnecessary risks. I'll talk to Captain Dominic about shifting our training exercises. Fair enough?"

"Sounds good."

"Look, I hate to give you the bum's rush but I have a call with PACAF. They're running the air show from Honolulu and want to pick my brain about the things I saw while flying over the North. I can't afford to disappoint the top brass. That'd be a bad career move. Are you going to be in Klamath Falls long?"

"Today and tomorrow. I have some work I need to do at the Upper Klamath Lake Refuge."

"Perfect. Why don't you come over to my place for dinner tonight? Did I tell you I'm getting married? Wait until you meet her. She'll knock your socks off. And cook? Well, you be the judge. Say around 1900? I have a bottle of sour mash I've been saving for a special occasion."

He scrawled an address and phone number on a piece of paper and slid it across the desk. "See you then, soldier."

Edwins offered to escort me to my truck, but I told him not to bother since it was parked in the lot right out front. When I reached the bottom of the stairs, I went to the back door instead, skirted the rear of the building, and walked toward the hangar I'd seen from Hardiman's office window.

A side door was unlocked. The hangar was void of people, but three planes were parked inside. One was a small, two-seater prop. I recognized it as a Cessna O-1 Bird Dog. Like my squad of scouts on the ground, the Air Force used Bird Dogs to track enemy movements from the air. The second aircraft was a Korean War vintage F-86 Sabre. The old fighter jet's cowl was open and engine parts were strewn across a tarp on the ground. The third plane was a F-101 Voodoo. It was missing its bubble canopy. The rim around the cockpit was scarred. I circled the aircraft, examining its nose and the front of its wings. The bottom of the fuselage aft of the turbine was blackened.

"Help you?" a voice called from behind me.

I turned around and faced a short man dressed in grease-stained coveralls and wearing a black knit watch cap. He was gripping a spanner like it was baseball bat.

"Nick Drake," I said. "Fish and Wildlife. And you are?"

"Name's Sallis."

"Nice to meet you, Sallis." I hooked a thumb at the F-101. "Is this the jet that ran into problems yesterday?" He nodded. "That's what I thought. I was checking it for bird strikes."

"Don't know nothing about that," he said. "I've been working on the Sabre mostly."

His coveralls didn't have any military patches on them. "Are you a civilian contractor?"

"Yep. I ground crew next door for the commercial flights that use the field. Been doing it for twenty years. Started when United was still flying in and out of here and then in '59 when West Coast Airlines took over the route. Wait, it's not called that anymore. Merged this year. Now it's Air West, though most call it Air Worst." He laughed, and the snort sounded like a car with a faulty ignition.

"And that leaves you time to moonlight for the Air Force?"

"We only get four commercial flights a day here. One going north and the other going south in the morning. And then they switch around and go the other way in the early evening."

"What do you do for the Air Force?"

"Whatever they ask. If it drinks gas, I can fix it."

"The base doesn't use enlisted men for ground crew?"

"They do, but they often come up short on manpower. Most of the boys who come through here want to fly, not keep 'em flying. And the ones who can work on planes want to get to the overseas bases as quick as they can to earn the extra sixty-five bucks a month combat pay."

"Have you started working on the F-101 yet?"

"I've been ordered not to touch it. I've been trying to get this ol' gal up in the air for the past week." Sallis pointed the spanner at the Sabre like Babe Ruth pointing to the spot in the outfield where he was going to hit a home run. "They use it as a trainer for the still-wet-behind-the-ears pilots. You say that one got hit by a bird? Must've been a helluva big bird. Like a swan or something."

I looked back at the jet. The word "Voodoo" was painted in script beneath the cockpit. "That's the first time I've ever seen that."

"What?" the grease monkey said.

"The name of the plane's model written on it. You never see Skyhawk painted on an A-4 or Bird Dog on a Cessna O-1 like that one over there."

"You got it all wrong. That ain't for the plane, it's for the pilot who flies it. Voodoo is his call sign."

"Because he only flies Voodoos?"

"No, because of his name. Well, his initials. It's a play on them. V. D."

"As in Vincent Dominic?"

"That's right," Sallis said. "Captain Voodoo."

"Was he flying that yesterday?"

"Yep. I was here when he touched down."

"He must've used a lot of black magic behind the stick to be able to fly that home without a canopy. Looks like he had a flameout too." I pointed at the black streaks beneath the tail.

"Captain Voodoo's got the touch, all right."

"Did you know his copilot, Lieutenant Ramirez?"

"I talked to him once or twice. From Arizona, originally." Sallis frowned. "Poor guy."

"It was over quick for him, I'm sure," I said.

"Yep, that too. Helluva way to go."

"What do you mean, that too?"

"Ah, the usual crap. He had a pretty rough go of it while he was here. He was a cherry like a lot of them but took more ribbing than most over his call sign. Couple of the guys would wave a red flag in front of him and pretend to be matadors. Stuff like that. Some of it got racial. You know, him being a Latin and all."

"Anybody in particular?"

The mechanic shifted the spanner and glanced around. "Pitzer mostly."

"Who's he?"

"TSgt. Jimmy Pitzer. You know, a technical sergeant. His call sign is Doberman, not because his last name sounds like the dog, but because of the way he is."

"He's someone's attack dog."

He snorted. "You got it."

"Dominic's?"

Sallis nodded. "Right again. Doberman never leaves Voodoo's side."

The air over Klamath Falls hung heavy with the sweet and sickly smell of pulp and fresh-cut timber. Dozens of lumber mills used the river that flowed from the lake to power their saw blades. They operated day and night. The town's schools, churches, and taverns catered to the needs of millhands, lumberjacks, ranchers, and farmers. The Klamath Indians, who lent the lake, town, and county its name, lived on the north side. Military personnel stationed at Kingsley Field lived on the south. Hardiman's house occupied the top of a rise in the Klamath Hills across a valley bridled by creeks and meadows.

"Beautiful place," I said as he greeted me at the front door.

Hardiman led me around to a deck. It was a clear night and the full moon afforded a panoramic view of the twinkling lights of the town and the shimmering lake and jagged silhouettes of the snowcapped peaks of the Cascade Mountains beyond.

"Not bad, if I do say so myself," he said. "One of the perks of being base commander. All right, so much for the nickel tour. It's freezing out here. I have a fire going in the den. How about a cocktail?"

"Sure," I said. "But leave the booze out of mine."

"Really?"

"Really," I said.

"Okay. One virgin Manhattan it is."

I followed him inside. The den was paneled in dark wood. Short lengths of pine and madrone crackled in a stone fireplace. A seating arrangement of two arm chairs and a couch were positioned to take full advantage of the glow and warmth from the blaze.

"Park yourself anywhere. I'll be right back," he said.

I took in the room. The books on the shelves were all best sellers at one time or another, and the paintings on the wall looked as if they'd previously hung in a hotel room. There were no personal photographs, no trophies, no souvenirs brought home from vacation. It was typical officer quarters for those who confined their worldly possessions to a couple of suitcases and were ready to pick up and move within an hour of being reassigned.

As soon as Hardiman came back I planned to ask him why Dominic led the team to Malheur Lake to retrieve Ramirez's body. That was highly irregular. A leader and his squadron always underwent a debriefing following any flight—combat or training—and surely one involving a fatality would have confined them all to base while the cause was investigated. Yet Dominic had hopped from his crippled F-101 right into the gray sedan and sped from Kingsley Field to Malheur Lake in record time. He never let on to Pudge and me that he was the pilot. Nor did Hardiman when I mentioned Dominic's name earlier.

I didn't get a chance to ask any questions. Hardiman returned with a glass in each hand. His face was beaming as he gave me one.

"Let me introduce you to my fiancée," he said.

He stepped aside. A woman with short brown hair and eyes

to match and wearing a gold cross hanging from a thin chain trailed behind him.

I nearly dropped my glass. "Carla," I said.

"What?" Hardiman said.

"Hello, Nick," she said. "I'm glad to see you looking so well."

"Does someone want to fill me in here?" Hardiman said.

"We know each other," I said. "Carla saved my life."

He turned to her. "How? When you were a nurse in Vietnam?"

"At Walter Reed after I transferred from the Tay Ninh MASH following Tet." Carla kept her eyes on mine as she said it.

"You never told me you were in-country," I said.

"You were the patient. We were treating you, not me."

Hardiman turned back to me. "Wait a second, you were a shell shocker at the nuthouse where she works?"

"We don't call it that," Carla said. "Not every wound sustained in combat is physical."

Hardiman's eyes went to the alcohol-free drink in my hand. "I didn't know and I didn't mean it the way it sounded. Just caught me off guard is all. You were so gung ho and balls-out when we were in 'Nam together, the way you took on the enemy while leading Clancy and me out."

"Do you still listen to The Beatles?" I asked Carla.

"When I have the time. And you?"

"Blackbird singing in the dead of night." I all but sang the line. "But I find I don't need to as much as I used to."

"That's progress," she said.

"I feel like I'm at some kind of secret society here." Hardiman gulped his Manhattan.

"It was Carla's idea. She had this 8-track player and got me to sing along with this new tune by The Beatles whenever I was going through a rough patch." I didn't add that she specifically chose the song because I was haunted by the image of a black bird that appeared when my squad was ambushed, leaving me the only survivor. The hallucination kept following me wherever I went. "I got hooked on H in Saigon. Carla and her music helped me kick it."

He flinched. "You were a hype, not a boozer?"

"Are and always will be, though I haven't used in a year."

"I knew you could do it," Carla said.

"What happened?" Hardiman said. "They give you morphine in the field after you took a bullet and got addicted? I hear that happened to a lot of GIs."

"That may have been the start, but I was already primed and ready." I raised my glass. "I'm sorry. Where are my manners? Congratulations are in order. To both of you."

That got Hardiman beaming again. Carla smiled, but not before she glanced at her shoes. I knew that if she was getting married, it meant that her first fiancé had finally been listed as KIA. He was also a pilot who'd been shot down on a bombing run over Hanoi. Carla had told me about him during the long hours we'd spent together in the ward. She said she would never lose hope that one day he'd walk through the door and back into her life.

Hardiman drained the rest of his Manhattan and smacked his lips. "All right. How about that dinner? Is it ready, honey?"

"Why don't you go on into the dining room and I'll bring it out."

We sat down at a mahogany table. "Where did you two meet?" I asked.

"Washington DC. I was there getting my commission and there was a party afterward. Some folks from Walter Reed were invited. Carla came with a fellow nurse. Her friend knew another pilot who was getting his commission too and, well... I consider myself the luckiest guy in the whole world."

"When is the big day?"

"That's a story in itself. I wanted our wedding to be in Washington or at the Air Force Academy in Colorado Springs—I graduated there." He opened a bottle of red wine and started to pour me a glass, but then stopped halfway and took it for himself. "And Carla wanted a small affair. Her only family is a sister. We were going back and forth when, in typical Air Force fashion, the slot at Kingsley opened up and I was on the first plane out."

He tried the wine and gave an approving look. "God knows what my long-distance phone bill amounted to over the past few months. Carla and I were missing each other so much that she flew out for a visit a few days ago. And now that she's here, well, we're talking about doing two weddings. A quick visit to the justice of the peace here to make it legal and then as soon as I can get leave, head back East for a real showstopper complete with a raised saber arch and a flyover. It's important careerwise I invite all the right people."

Hardiman sampled more wine. "What about you? You married?" I shook my head. "Got a girlfriend? Surely where you are isn't all cowboys and sheep." He laughed, his face flushing.

Carla came in bearing a large platter. "Hope you like prime rib and Yorkshire pudding."

It was a far cry from the Jell-O she used to spoon feed me when I was going cold turkey.

"I told you she could cook," Hardiman said.

Over dinner, Carla asked me about my work and life.

"I'm getting used to it. I've been studying up on wildlife and nature. It's part of the job to know it. Harney County is beautiful in its own way. Turns out, wide-open spaces appeal to me."

"It must feel liberating not to be in a jungle," she said wistfully. "They're so confining. I felt that the year and a half I was stationed over there."

I was still surprised that I hadn't known she'd been a combat nurse. "Harney County is certainly a lot drier than 'Nam. It's a high desert basin. That means the rivers and creeks, the few that there are, don't flow to the sea like everywhere else."

"Where do they go?"

"To the lowest spot and then disappear."

"That sounds, I don't know, otherworldly."

"The countryside can seem like that. Salt lakes that come and go. A pure white desert as flat as this table. And lots of geysers and hot springs."

"Are they like mineral baths?"

"Yes. The Paiute have used them for healing purposes for thousands of years. They're great for easing muscle pain after a hard day's physical labor. At night, soaking in hot water beneath all the stars while listening to the music of great horned owls and coyotes, well, it's pretty magical."

"You make it sound poetic."

I shrugged and tried some more of the prime rib.

"What about the town you live in and the people?"

"No Mountain? It's not much more than a wide spot in the road with a population of less than two hundred, and most of them are living on distant ranches. There's only seven thousand people in the whole county. But the folks are good people. Hard working, no-nonsense types."

"Straight shooters, goldarn it," Hardiman said, mimicking a cowboy's drawl. "I want to meet that deputy I heard about." He winked at Carla. "His name is Pudge Warbler. Wears a star on his chest and a six-shooter on his hip."

Carla gave a little frown. "You mentioned Paiutes. Is that the Indian tribe living there?"

"The Paiute live throughout the Great Basin, from Washington down to Arizona, and from here over to Utah. There are many different bands and two main groups, the Northern and Southern Paiutes. Where I live, the people are *Wadadökadö*."

"You pronounced that as if you speak the language. Do you?"

"I've been trying to learn it. It makes my job easier. My life too, for that matter."

"No one has much good to say about the Klamath Indians around here," Hardiman said. "The government revoked their reservation and was paying them off when the redskins took all the money and spent it on firewater." He helped himself to another glass of wine.

"What I've learned from the Paiute is there are two sides to every story, especially when it comes to the way Native people have been treated," I said.

Hardiman opened his mouth, but Carla spoke before he could. "And what about your job? What exactly do you do?"

"Mostly keep an eye on the refuges to make sure cattle aren't grazing where they're not supposed to and keep people from hunting out of season. I spend a lot of time hiking, canoeing, and watching birds."

"It all sounds lovely. I'd love to see that." Carla turned to Hardiman. "We should pay Nick a visit."

"Sure, honey," he said. "Right after the wedding. We'll make it our honeymoon."

I never got the opportunity to speak with Hardiman alone and ask him why Dominic was in charge of investigating his own accident. I said my goodbyes after dessert and drove to a strip of motels that lined the highway on the north side of Klamath Falls. I checked into a room with a swaybacked bed and a heater whose blower ticked louder than an old windup clock. I couldn't stop thinking about how two very different people I had met under very different circumstances during the war had wound up meeting each other and then the three of us reconnected because a pilot had dropped from the sky into a lake in the middle of nowhere. The thought of how random life could be made sleep seem even more elusive than ever.

I scrunched the limp pillow behind my head and began reading a paperback I'd borrowed from Pudge Warbler. It was a collection of Paiute legends, one of several books about the Native people the old deputy kept on his office bookshelf. Pudge professed they belonged to November—she'd learned to read and speak English while enrolled in the Bureau of Indian Affairs school—but I suspected he read them as avidly as she did.

The legends had been told around campfires, handed down from generation to generation as a way to keep cultural traditions alive and pass on knowledge about surviving in a harsh and unforgiving land. Some of the stories were reverent, others lively and ribald.

I had started the book while camping at Malheur Lake during my weeklong stakeout of the poacher. The location was especially fitting given the first legend. Wolf, called *Mu naa'a* in the Paiute language, *numu*, was the father of creation. His little brother Coyote convinced him to create a world out of darkness. The other animal people—the first people, or *nuwuddu*, as the Paiute called them—were still living in darkness when Wolf created the world. They learned what he had done and wanted to live there too.

The *nuwuddu* began walking in search of it, each holding onto the animal's tail in front so as not to get lost in the dark. They walked for five days. Eventually they saw a tiny sliver of light at the end of a long, dark passageway. They moved toward it. Leading the line was Bald Eagle. When he reached the end of the darkness, he poked his head out and the light turned it white. When he turned around to tell the animals following behind what he had seen, his tail stuck out of the opening and its feathers turned white too.

They emerged into the world at a place the Paiute called Malheur Cave. From there, the *nuwuddu* spread to the ends of the world that *Mu naa'a* had created, each choosing where they wanted to live and what they wanted to be, from Bighorn Sheep who liked living high up in the mountains to Ground Squirrel who made his home beneath the rocks. The Paiute, who Wolf created afterward, referred to themselves as the second people and considered the animals their brothers and sisters.

The legend I read in the motel was about four friends. Rock, Obsidian, Coyote, and Deer traveled the land together, though

Rock and Obsidian moved slowly and had to stay in the basins while Coyote and Deer ran very fast and could go into the mountains. One night, the four friends were sitting around the campfire talking about when they would receive their power, or *puha*. The Paiute believed that *puha* could reside in any natural object, and some were supernatural. Rock explained that they would all have to have a good dream in order to receive their *puha*, and then they would become powerful friends and help one another.

They went to sleep around the campfire and dreamed their dreams. In Rock's dream, he saw what he was going to become. So did Obsidian. But Deer had a bad dream as did Coyote. When the four friends awoke in the morning, they told each other their dreams. Obsidian said he dreamed he'd become very powerful and could fly through the air, but when Deer saw him coming, Deer ran away in fear. Obsidian hit Deer and knocked him down. Rock said his dream was similar. He was flying through the air too, and Coyote saw him coming, but Rock was flying so fast he struck Coyote.

Coyote didn't like Rock's dream at all. He said in his dream, he picked up a stick and started hitting Rock and broke him apart. And then he leaped up and did exactly that and smashed Rock into pieces. Deer said his dream was the same, and he jumped up too and started hitting Obsidian with his hooves and busted him into tiny pieces. Then Coyote and Deer ran off in different directions and were never friends again. Rock and Obsidian remained friends forever, and their dreams of receiving the power to fly came true. From that day on, the Paiute used obsidian to make arrowheads to hunt the deer, and whenever coyotes approached their wickiups, the Paiute picked up rocks and threw them at the coyotes to make them run away.

I closed the book, set it on the nightstand, and turned off the light. The ticking from the blower grew louder and set me tossing and turning as if strapped to a metronome. Finally, I drifted off to sleep.

Faces began to appear, some recognizable, others as if standing behind a curtain of gauze. The poacher wearing his earflap hat leered at me, his rotten teeth dripping with tobacco juice. Four faceless riders on horseback herding stolen cattle turned their wild-eyed steeds toward me. Toro Ramirez cried for help as he plunged to earth, but I was powerless to save him. Voodoo Dominic watched his copilot's plunge through lifeless eyes. Whistling Pete and Carla came running arm in arm from a big white church and ducked under an arch made of crossed sabers held aloft by two columns of pilots dressed in blue. When the couple was halfway through, the sabers began slicing downward. Carla called for help, but I was as powerless to save her as I was the copilot.

I could hear Pudge's drawl and Gemma's laugh in the darkness. November was speaking too, but in Paiute words I could not understand. The four of us were walking hand in hand through a long dark tunnel, searching for a pinpoint of light that would lead us from the pitch-black night. Then I heard more voices barking commands and the roars of jets and the whoosh of missiles. A coyote howled so shrilly, it shattered rock as easily as a soprano breaking glass and a herd of unseen deer with saber-sharp hooves clattered straight at me. All the voices and sounds began to swirl as everyone pushed and shoved in a rush to reach the light. I stumbled and lost my grip on Gemma's and November's hands as four galloping horses with hooded riders thundered toward us.

I awoke in a pool of sweat on the swaybacked bed in an overheated room as fingers of dawn reached through the slats of the blinds in the motel room. I tried to hold onto the dream to find its meaning, but it kept slipping away. Finally, it faded altogether.

Upper Klamath Lake was connected to a smaller lake by a mile-long channel that bisected a freshwater marsh. Birdcall punctuated the silence. Hardstem cattails rising from their watery beds waved in the breeze. Pond turtles rested on half-submerged logs while muskrats slinked from their dens to feed on water lilies and snails. A broad bench of pastureland bordered the wildlife refuge to the north. Alfalfa farmers operated a network of ditches and sluices on it. They diverted water from the Wood River to irrigate their hayfields and then redirected the runoff back into the refuge.

While the farmers were in charge of controlling the headgates on their end, I was responsible for maintaining the outfalls. Screens had been attached to them to prevent migratory fish from mistakenly swimming up the narrow sluices and ditches from the lake. I needed to inspect them and fix any that were broken or clogged before the snows covered them up.

The outfalls of a half dozen sluices were positioned along the western edge of the mile-long channel. I wore a pair of chest waders and trudged the channel's length checking the screens. The first couple were intact and doing their job, but the third had been knocked loose by a wooden fence post that had fallen into a narrow ditch upstream and tobogganed down the chute. It was jammed into the mouth of the outfall. Pulling it loose was wet, muddy work, and fixing the broken screen and refastening it took tin snips and a pair of pliers.

Twisting the wires in the screen made me think of Gemma repairing the taillights on her horse trailer and her invitation to go riding. She was right that I had made myself scarce since summer. It wasn't only because of work and the distances between the refuges. I had felt myself growing close to her, but the locked ward at Walter Reed was too fresh in my memory and so was the battlefield where I'd lost my squad. Staying clean was day to day and relapsing was only a fix away. The last thing I needed was to let someone I cared about down again.

The next outfall was in good shape, but the last two were also blocked and their screens broken. It took me until late afternoon to complete the job. By then, my fingers were numb, and my legs ached from standing in icy water. The thought of trying to warm up all my moving parts in a tepid shower in the cheap motel room left me even colder, and remembering the sway-backed bed sealed the deal.

"Screw it. I'm going back to No Mountain," I announced to a yellow-crowned night-heron who was observing my efforts from his perch in a willow. And I knew the perfect hot springs on the road home.

THE SKY WAS DUSKING as I crossed over the Harney County line, turned off the highway, and bounced along a rutted dirt road that wound through a scrubby landscape whiskered with sagebrush, withered juniper trees, and dried out wooly sunflowers, their golden springtime blossoms but a distant memory. The road ran along the top of an escarpment that rose from an otherwise endlessly flat desert. It ended at a turnaround. I parked and followed a trail that led to an outcropping of rocks encircling an aquamarine pool. The surface of the water bubbled, and wisps of steam carried a slight odor of overcooked eggs.

I kicked off my boots, stripped out of my clothes, and eased into the hundred degree natural bathtub. It was a welcome relief from the cold. I felt for and found a submerged slab of basalt that formed the equivalent of a lounge chair. I settled onto it and leaned my head back onto the pool's edge that had been smoothed by other heads resting on it for thousands of years. The rock faces surrounding the hot springs bore evidence of its longtime use by the Paiute. A pair of big shouldered human figures painted in red danced on one. A spiral and a rattlesnake were etched into another. Carved outlines of pronghorn and deer raced across still another.

The soothing water covered my chest and rose over my shoulders, leaving only my head exposed. Dusk turned into night and other stars joined the North Star as the Milky Way—or, as the Paiute called it, the Dusty Trail—stretched on forever. My thoughts turned to Carla. When I was locked in the ward, she threw out the standard medical guide for dealing with veterans like me. She always called us by our first names, not by our rank and last name. She asked about our lives before Vietnam. Carla came up with using music as medicine. She convinced even the most cynical soldiers to try yoga and meditation. I don't know if she did it for others, but when I was really going through it, having nightmares or begging and threatening for a fix, she'd crawl into my bed and hold me tight or rub my shoulders and back and whisper song lyrics until I calmed and fell asleep.

Her admission that she'd been at Tay Ninh during some of the bloodiest fighting of the war made me wonder how she'd been able to escape the trauma. MASH units often took fire, and working to save the lives of the wounded was a nonstop horror show. Thousands of combat nurses served in 'Nam when I was in-country, yet none were ever admitted to the ward at Walter Reed while I was a patient. What made them immune from battle fatigue? Or were they?

A shooting star streaked across the night sky, its tail red and sparkling like a noisy, showy firework. As it faded, I wondered what a caring and courageous woman like Carla saw in a self-promoter like Whistling Pete Hardiman? I shouldn't have been surprised that he refused to share the circumstances surrounding Ramirez's death. All branches of the military operated on a need-to-know basis. Though I could've written off his reaction as embarrassment that a fatal accident had occurred on his watch or that he was trying to sweep it under the rug to preserve his chances for advancement, it sure felt like a stiff-arm to me. So did Dominic's behavior, for that matter. Rather than deter me as intended, it only piqued my desire to learn the truth.

My fingertips were as wrinkled as prunes and the heat was sapping my strength. I climbed out of the water and got dressed in the light of the moon. The turnaround was on a pitch atop the escarpment, and I could see into the basin below. Tiny pinpoints of lights shining in the vast desert expanse marked remote ranches connected to the highway by unpaved roads. They were hardly used.

Even the two-lane highway that crossed Harney County had little traffic any time of day or night. Yet now, four pairs of headlights were traveling in convoy fashion south from No Mountain. They slowed, turned onto a ranch road, and stopped. Headlights from another, larger vehicle that had been waiting in the dark blinked on.

I reached into my truck and pulled out my binoculars. The moon was bright and the air clear, allowing me to bring the vehicles into focus. There were four pickup trucks towing trailers. The larger vehicle was a semi hauling a shiny silver livestock trailer perforated with ventilation holes.

Dust began to rise as the pickups backed up to the semi. Men got out and started shooing cows from the smaller trailers into the big one. The entire exchange was over in fifteen minutes. The pickups began to leave, one after another. They drove back north. The tractor trailer was the last to depart. It headed south.

I climbed into my truck and made the bumpy drive back along the dirt road and down the backside of the escarpment. I turned north on the highway. When I reached where I thought the trucks had met, I slowed and looked for a turnoff or fresh dirt on the blacktop left by their tires.

Finally, I found it. The road was unmarked and ungated. I turned and drove slowly before reaching a *T* in the road. The top of the *T* was too wide to be a regular ranch road. I turned right and hit the high beams. The lights illuminated a straight, empty stretch. It was a dirt airstrip.

I drove until my headlights showed fresh scarring made from multiple sets of tires. I got out to look at the tracks. The first thing I noticed were piles of cow pies. *Madukanna kutsu kwedapu*, November had called it at breakfast, or at least the bull's version. The second thing I saw was a coyote. A big one. He was standing at the edge of the airstrip looking at me, his ears perked slightly forward, his hackles raised, his bright white canines gleaming. He started to advance. I didn't have time to rush back to my truck and grab the Winchester. I searched for a rock and picked it up.

By the time I looked up, the coyote had disappeared.

9

Gemma Warbler knocked on my door at eight in the morning. She was wearing a tan cowgirl hat with a beaded Indian hatband and held a pair of buckskin riding gloves.

"How was Klamath Falls?" she asked.

I looked over her shoulder. The red Wagoneer and horse trailer were parked out front.

"Cold. Do you need help with your taillights again?"

"They're working just fine, thank you very much. I'm here to pick you up to go riding. The trail starts on the other side of the river and it's easier if we drive there."

"Sorry, I'm busy today."

"You don't look it. You haven't even put on your boots yet."

I resisted glancing down at my socks. "I got in late. I need to talk to your father."

"How come?"

"I saw some pickups off-loading cattle to a tractor trailer in the middle of the night. They could be his rustlers."

"Where?"

"Alongside the highway from Klamath. They rendezvoused on a dirt airstrip."

Gemma smiled. "Ranchers move their herds all over the place this time of year. They're either taking them to pastures at lower elevations in advance of blizzards or to slaughterhouses. They use a spoke-and-hub system for transferring. Airstrips are favorite hubs because they're flat, wide, and plentiful. Harney County is dotted with them. A lot of ranchers fly because everything is so remote. I've been taking lessons myself. As soon as I get my pilot's license, I'm going to buy a plane and take my mobile surgery airborne."

"I still need to tell your father what I saw."

"Sure, but it'll have to wait. Pudge left for Burns early this morning. Sheriff Burton called an all-hands-on-deck meeting. The Harney County Cattlemen's Association is pressuring him to do more to stop the rustling and Bust'em knows who has the most muscle around these parts come election time."

"All right, I'll swing by the house this evening and talk to him then."

"Perfect. That leaves us all day to go for a ride."

I put up my hands. "I need to get back to the Malheur. I still have a poacher I need to stop."

"You're in luck. Where we're going is on the north shore of the lake. You can look for him there. Come on, put on your boots. Giddyap, hotshot."

GEMMA DROVE with a heavy foot and only one hand on the wheel even though she was pulling a loaded trailer on a single-lane gravel road. She used the other to point out landmarks to test me as we cut across Harney Valley.

"Okay, what's the name of this river?" she said as we bumped over a wooden bridge.

"The West Fork of the Silvies," I said.

"And how did it get its name?"

"There was a French fur trapper with the Hudson Bay Company who explored here back in the 1820s. It's a misspelling of his last name."

"Very good. You've been studying up."

Knowing the lay of the land had saved me plenty of times in 'Nam. I wasn't about to give up all of my old habits.

Gemma aimed her index finger at the Jeep's windshield. "And the East Fork is only a couple of miles up ahead. What's on the other side of it?"

"The Steens Highway. I've driven it a few times. Farther east are the Stinkingwater Mountains, and east of them is the Malheur River. The name is also of French origin. It means misfortune. And, yes, I know it doesn't drain into Malheur Lake. It's a tributary of the Snake."

"*A* plus. Did you know Malheur is also the name of the Indian reservation that once occupied Harney Valley?"

"No. When did it change to the Burns Paiute Reservation?"

"Oh, so I got you on one. The Malheur Reservation was created by Ulysses S. Grant, but it was short-lived. It only lasted a few years."

"How come?"

"Because of the Bannock War of 1878."

"I'm guessing that was a fight over land."

"And you'd be correct," she said.

"Who were the Bannock?"

"They were originally Northern Paiute people but associated with the Shoshone. They lived across the Idaho border on the Snake River Plain. White settlers moved into their homeland and called in the cavalry after some starving members of the tribe raided a homestead or two. Their chief, Buffalo Horn, gathered a war party to defend his people. A group of Paiute warriors from here went to join their brothers. The chief was killed and the Bannock lost the war."

"But if all that happened in Idaho, why did the reservation here get taken away?"

"The cavalry captured the survivors, Paiute and Bannock alike, and brought them back here for internment. After a while, the government transferred them to the Yakima Indian Reservation in Washington. That gave white settlers a green light to move onto reservation land. The government was unwilling to kick them off, and so the Malheur Indian Reservation's borders were officially erased and the legal protection that went with them."

We passed a wooden signpost on the side of the gravel road. An oval surrounding a cross with a small diamond in the middle was carved in it.

"That's a shaman's symbol," Gemma said. "We crossed into a section of the new reservation. It's taken all this time to give the Paiute back some of their land." She pointed her finger again. "We're almost there."

A cluster of squat buildings lay ahead. "What is that place?" I asked.

"It's the Will family's camp. The grandfather is a tribal elder. He lives there with his sons and daughters and grandchildren."

Gemma slowed as we turned onto a rough dirt road that ran between single-wide trailers and wooden shanties. Most of the cars and trucks parked around them were junkers. A pair of yapping yellow dogs chased us. A flock of skinny brown hens scratching for food clucked and then lifted their feathery skirts and hightailed it. Gemma parked in front of a faded white trailer and turned off the engine.

"Come on. I'll introduce you."

The front door opened. A boy who looked about twelve and wore a wool-lined brown corduroy jacket two sizes too big came outside. He was followed by an old man who wore a red bandanna headband tied around his shoulder-length white hair. His skin was furrowed like a freshly tilled field.

"Good morning, Dr. Gemma," the boy said.

"Hello, Nagah. I'd like to introduce you to Nick Drake. Nick, meet Nagah Will and his grandfather, Tuhudda Will." And then she switched to Paiute. "*Amamua, togo'o.*"

I recognized the words for 'morning' and 'grandfather.' *Tuhudda*, I knew, meant deer.

Gemma spoke some more. She said the Paiute words quickly. The boy laughed and the old man nodded.

"I told them you were a greenhorn, and Nagah and I will need to teach you how to ride," she said.

"Is there a reason we didn't do that at your place first?"

"Oh, didn't I tell you?" Her eyes twinkled. "Nagah saw the canopy fly off that fighter jet."

I turned to him. "Did you see it come down?"

"It's somewhere near the double snakehead," the boy said.

"Where's that?"

Gemma answered for him. "It's where the East and West Forks of the Silvies intertwine and then empty into the lake. When we get there, you'll see why the Paiute refer to the mouth as two snakeheads."

"Then what are we waiting for?"

"Whoa, cowboy. First things first. I'll get the horses unloaded and then introduce you to the one you're going to ride." She paused. "Devil's Thunder."

"I thought you said he was a colt?"

Gemma laughed. "If only I had a camera. The look on your face..."

The colt's real name was Wovoka. Gemma explained that

Lyle Rides Alone named him after a famous Paiute shaman whose name meant cutter in English. Both horses were cutting horses bred for their ability to separate cattle from the herd. The Paiute rancher named the filly Sarah in honor of Sarah Winnemucca who was the daughter of a legendary war chief. After the Pyramid Lake and Bannock Wars, Sarah Winnemucca traveled the country telling people about the Paiute's plight.

Gemma led the filly and colt from the trailer and tied them to a split rail fence that doubled as a hitching post. Sarah was a sorrel with a white blaze. Wovoka was a light buckskin with knee-high black socks and a black tail and mane to match.

"Aren't they beautiful?" she said. "Come here and hold your hand out so Wovoka can smell you. He needs to get to know you before he'll let you ride him. If he wants, stroke his muzzle. I'll saddle him while you do."

Nagah had already brought the saddles over. He had to stand on his tiptoes to put the blanket on Sarah. Gemma stroked Wovoka's neck and rubbed his shoulder and then put a blanket and saddle on him. He remained calm except for a slight twitch of his tail.

"Okay, untie him and lead him up and down the road a little bit," Gemma said. "Don't try to sit him. You're not ready."

"I'm not or he's not?"

She laughed again.

I took the lead rope and started walking slowly. Wovoka followed. By now, several people were standing in the doorways of the trailers and shanties watching me. No one said anything. The rock faces with the pictographs surrounding the hot springs showed more expression.

I walked to the end of the rutted dirt road and back. "What now?" I said.

"He seems okay with you. Let me swap his halter for a bridle," Gemma said.

When she was finished, she handed me the reins. "Okay, hold onto the saddle horn with the reins in your hands, put your left boot in the stirrup, swing your right leg up and over, and sit him. Whatever you do, don't yank on the saddle horn or the reins. Keep everything nice and smooth."

I was right about mounting a horse being the same as straddling my Triumph; that is, if my motorcycle had been twice as tall and the colt had a kickstand. Wovoka started moving forward as soon as I put the toe of my boot in the stirrup.

"Hold up," I said. "Hold up."

Wovoka whinnied. Someone snickered.

"Keep going," Gemma said. "You're committed now."

I swung my leg over and plopped onto the saddle. Wovoka started to rear.

"You're yanking his reins," she said. "He's got a bit in his mouth. Loosen your grip."

I didn't even know I'd pulled the reins close to my chest. I eased up and they slackened. Wovoka settled right down.

"That's it," Gemma said. "Now lean forward, pat him on the neck and tell him he's a handsome boy."

"Really?" I said.

"Really," she said.

"Good horse. Attaboy."

"Now ride him up and back. Keep it at a walk. When you're ready to turn around, gently pull back on the left rein while applying gentle pressure to his girth with your inside leg. Nice and smooth."

Everything went without a hitch. Wovoka made the turn with only the slightest of prompts from me.

"Attaboy," I said again.

I rode Wovoka toward Gemma who was adjusting the cinch on Sarah. "I think I got the hang of it."

The yellow dogs thought otherwise. The pair came rushing

back from wherever they had slunk. One started yapping right in front of the colt. The other circled around and nipped at his hocks. Wovoka threw his head down and tried to bite the dog in front, nearly yanking the reins from my grip. At the same time he kicked and bucked. Then he shot forward. The yellow dogs howled in pursuit.

Cutting horses were bred for their fast starts and stops, but there was no stopping Wovoka. The colt reached a gallop in seconds. I didn't even try to rein him in. Instead, I leaned forward until the saddle horn was pressed against my chest. I kept my hands on either side of his neck as if holding onto the handle bars of my Triumph. It was the same position I'd get into when letting the bike rip down the lonely blacktops or speed across the empty salt flats of Harney County at full throttle.

The dirt track coming from the Will camp was short and the gravel road we'd driven in on was coming up fast. Wovoka would need to either come to an abrupt halt or turn. Stopping would pitch me right over his head. Since a left turn led to the unknown, I leaned right as we neared the intersection and gave a gentle push with my knee. Wovoka didn't break stride, and we took the sharp turn at a gallop.

The straightaway ran all the way back to the wooden bridge. I leaned even lower until my chin was pressed against his neck and my hands were on either side of his mane just behind his head. His lungs sounded like mighty bellows, and his heartbeat kept time with the steady pounding of his hooves along the road. The rush of wind blew thorough my hair, and I wished I had on my motorcycle goggles. It was a much better view sitting higher up than when I rode my Triumph. As Wovoka kept galloping, I felt something I hadn't felt since leaving Vietnam.

I felt alive.

10

Gemma and the Wills were standing right where I'd left them. No one seemed anxious or surprised when I rode Wovoka back into camp at a brisk walk. The old man glanced at me and then said something to Gemma in a long, unbroken string of Paiute. I asked her what he said, but he answered in English before she could translate.

"I told her the horse honors the name Lyle Rides Alone gave him. He made you like a Ghost Dancer." Tuhudda Will spoke slowly, pausing occasionally, and saying some words louder than others. "You sat so low, we could not see you as he galloped. We thought you fell off and broke your neck." He stuck his finger toward my heart but did not touch me. "Maybe you did. Maybe you are a spirit now."

"Maybe," I said.

Tuhudda Will said, "You have heard of the Ghost Dance?"

"A little. Native people believed the dance would reunite them with the spirits of their ancestors and the spirits would help them drive off the settlers."

"Only some people believed this to be so. It started with

Wovoka who now lives in the spirit world. He was *Tövusidökadö*. A Pine Nut Eater. I am *Wadadökadö*."

"Like November," I said.

"Yes, Girl Born in Snow." His voice turned wistful. "Long ago, I asked her to take me as her husband, but she would not have me."

Tuhudda Will grew silent and seemed to be drifting far away. And then he said, "Wovoka had powerful medicine. This is so. He had a vision during an eclipse. All the white people were swallowed by the earth and all the dead Native people emerged and lived in a world free of invaders. Wovoka believed for this to happen, the Paiute must live in peace and dance a sacred version of the round dance. He called it the Ghost Dance and it spread across the land."

"I thought it started on the Great Plains," I said.

His red bandana shook back and forth. "No, the people of the plains learned of it from the Paiute, but they made it their own. Some believed peace would not rid the land of white men as Wovoka had dreamed, and they used the Ghost Dance as a call for war. The Lakota made Ghost Shirts to protect themselves from the soldiers' bullets, but they did not. When the cavalry massacred Lakota men, women, and children along the creek known as Wounded Knee, the dream of whites being swallowed by the earth died with them."

The old man grew silent again. His eyes searched me as I sat on the buckskin named for the Paiute spiritual leader. They stopped at my holstered revolver. "You were a soldier. I can see it in the way you hold yourself."

"I was," I said. "But no longer."

"A warrior is always a warrior, even in death. You do not fear the horse, but you fear something." His gaze remained fixed on me. "It is yourself."

I did not dispute him, nor turn away.

As we were talking, Nagah Will disappeared. He came back astride a small chestnut pony. He was riding bareback.

"Grandfather, we should go now to find the piece of the airplane," he said.

Tuhudda Will put his hand on Wovoka's neck and spoke into the colt's ear. "Nagah will show you the way. Be watchful. The land between the double snakehead is dangerous and even a horse as powerful as you can step into trouble quickly."

GEMMA and I followed Nagah on his pony down the main road for about a mile before turning off and cutting across a field that had never felt the blade of a harrow. Sarah was frisky. The sorrel filly bobbed her head while high stepping. Wovoka showed no signs of being tired after his run.

"Have you known the Wills long?" I asked Gemma.

"Yes, but I've seen more of them lately because of work. They raise sheep and have had a problem with CL, caseous lymphadenitis. It's a bacteria that causes wasting disease."

"I didn't see any sheep around their place."

"That's because they're grazing down in Catlow Valley now. The family takes turns being the shepherd and living in a wickiup there for a month at a time."

"All alone?"

Gemma nodded. "Some might think it a lonely life, but the Wills have been doing it for a long time. Nagah started when he was seven or eight. The family drops him off with a bag of food and a slingshot."

"That's a lot of responsibility for such a young boy," I said.

"He takes it very seriously. It's how he got his name."

"He wasn't always called Nagah?"

"No, it wasn't until after a pack of coyotes attacked the herd one night. It was his first season shepherding. He grabbed his slingshot and went out to scare them off, but the herd had already panicked. He chased after them. The Catlow Valley lays between Hart Mountain and Steens Mountain. The sheep ran up the side of Steens and got themselves stuck on top of a very high ridge. He tracked them there, but it was so steep and they were so frightened, he couldn't drive them down. He stayed with them and waited. A few days later Tuhudda Will came to bring him more food and saw that his grandson and the herd were missing. He finally found the boy and, together, they were able to bring the sheep down."

"So, what is the meaning of Nagah's name?"

"Tuhudda Will was proud of how brave he'd been and gave him the name of a Paiute legend. It goes like this. Long ago, when the world was young, the people of the sky were restless and walked everywhere and made trails throughout the heavens. Nagah was a mountain sheep. He liked to climb as high as he could to get a closer look at the stars. One time, he climbed to the top of the very highest peak, but the trail below him fell away and he had no way to get down. He was stuck on top and so he stayed there. Shinoh, his father, was traveling across the sky and saw him. He realized how brave his son was, and he did not want him to die. Shinoh turned him into a star so that other living things on Earth could always see him shining brightly. And though he is a star, Nagah cannot leave his perch on top of the mountain. He does not move like other stars but serves as a guide for travelers."

"He's the North Star," I said.

Nagah Will had ridden ahead of us. He stopped his chestnut pony atop a rise and looked over his shoulder. "We are almost there."

Gemma urged Sarah into a trot to catch up to the boy. I clicked the inside of my cheeks and Wovoka broke into a trot too. The top of the rise provided a view of the two forks of the Silvies as they wound sinuously toward Malheur Lake. I half-expected to see the poacher motoring across the water in his duck blind boat. The rivers narrowed and bulged in spots like a rattlesnake swallowing a field mouse. The waters of the lake shimmered in the sunlight. The two forks intertwined in the marshes and then separated, forming two spade-shaped mouths.

"I see what you mean," I said. "Two snakeheads."

"Let's hope they don't bite," Gemma said.

"It looks pretty boggy down there. The jet's canopy could be underwater or sunk in the mud."

I pulled my binoculars from the saddle bag and started searching. I asked Nagah where he was when he saw the canopy blow off.

"In the meadow." He pointed right below us. "It is a good place to gather wild onions."

"And did the canopy come down fast or slow?"

"As slow as mist that forms over the river when the sun comes up."

"That's good." I lowered the binoculars.

"Why?" Gemma said.

"It means when the canopy stopped hurtling backward and started to fall, it was right side up. An air pocket was trapped in the bubble and slowed its descent like a parachute."

"So?"

"There's a good chance that prevented it from nosediving into the marsh and burying itself. It could still be on top some-where." I clicked the inside of my cheeks again. "Let's ride down to the meadow."

This time Wovoka and I led the way. When we reached the

meadow, I reined in until Nagah caught up. "Show me where you were."

The boy slid off his pony and searched the ground. "Here. See the holes where I pulled out the onions?"

"Can you point to where you saw the canopy falling?"

The boy got on his knees and then looked toward the lake. He aimed his finger. "I watched it until the shrub willows blocked it."

"How far past the thicket, do you think it was?"

"I could've hit it with my slingshot if I had been standing in front of them."

"Okay, say fifteen or twenty yards on the other side. Let's go take a look."

Nagah jumped back on his pony and we rode over. The shrub willows were a foot or so taller than me and bunched on the banks of an oxbow. The water was dirty brown. Water striders left ripples as they skated across the surface in search of smaller insects to devour. More thickets of shrub willows crowded the other side.

"Fifteen or twenty yards would put it on the other side of the oxbow. I'm going to make my way around it and take a closer look."

I dismounted and held the reins out to Gemma. "Wait here. That poacher could be hiding in there. He's already shot at me once."

"Hold your own reins," she said and slid off Sarah. "I'm going with you."

Nagah didn't try to hide his grin. He agreed to stay with the horses.

A deer trail led through the willows. We followed it, pushing branches out of the way and ducking under others. The ground was soggy. Muddy water oozed above our ankles. It made a sucking sound as we stepped. The thicket thinned on the other side of the oxbow. It bordered another meadow, this one smaller than the one where Nagah had picked wild onions.

"I don't see anything," Gemma said.

"Maybe it fell farther out."

We crossed the second meadow. Desiccated grasshoppers killed in autumn's first freeze littered the ground. A pair of cottontails quit nibbling grass and darted into the brushy understory. The sound of burbling grew louder as we neared another line of thickets. I started to push through the shrubs.

"Careful. The river's close," Gemma said.

I walked a few steps and then the ground beneath me started to sink. I tried to scuttle backwards, but my feet were anchored in the mire. Gemma snatched the back of my jacket and yanked hard. I flung out my hands and made a grab for branches. The ground I'd been standing on turned to water without making a splash. Gemma and I quickly retreated.

"The snake almost got you," she said with a nervous laugh.

"It's alive, all right. Always moving, always changing shape and direction."

"Maybe it already gobbled up the canopy and spit it into the lake."

"If it did, we'll never find it."

Our progress blocked, we turned and headed back to the oxbow. Gemma started to retrace our steps on the deer trail. I thought of the poacher and his clockwise pattern when emerging from the marshes that ringed the adjacent lake.

"Let's make a complete circle," I said.

There wasn't so much as a cottontail trail to follow on the midnight to six side of the oxbow. The willows seemed thicker and the going much slower. The branches were tugging at our clothes and whipping our faces. Gemma's hat was knocked off so many times, she wound up carrying it.

"I think we're almost to the meadow," I said. "I can see daylight up ahead."

Only it wasn't sun shining on the clearing where Nagah waited. It was sunlight reflecting off acrylic. The canopy had come to a rest on a clump of willows shorter than the others. It fit over the top branches as snugly as if the woody shrub were the cockpit of a F-101 Voodoo.

11

I t was Nagah Will's idea how to haul it back. The three of us lifted the canopy and carried it to the meadow. The boy found two fallen lodgepole pines trapped in the oxbow. He stripped the dead branches from their trunks and made a travois, a traditional Paiute drag sled for hauling goods behind dogs and horses. We lashed the jet's canopy on top. Wovoka grew skittish as we tied the tips of the travois poles to either side of his saddle. Once I sat him and clicked the inside of my cheeks, he quickly adapted to his new role as a draught horse and maintained a steady gait as we rode back to the Will camp.

"Can you tell if there's anything wrong with the canopy that might explain why it blew off?" Gemma asked as she rode alongside me.

"No, but I'm no expert. The way it's supposed to work is the pilot gives the command to bail out. Then he triggers the charges that blow the canopy off. The pilot and copilot both have rockets under their seats that launch them from the cockpit, but in a two-seater like the Voodoo where the copilot is sitting right behind the pilot, he has to punch out first, otherwise his feet and legs would be burned by the rockets beneath the pilot's seat."

"But the pilot didn't eject," Gemma said.

"Exactly."

"Then why did the copilot bail out if the plane was still able to fly?"

"I've been asking myself that ever since I saw him plunge into Malheur Lake."

We crossed the meadow filled with wild onions, rode up and over the rise, and started across the field that had never been plowed. As we neared its middle, the buzz of an airplane filled the silence.

"Sounds like one of your flying cowboys is heading home," I said.

Nagah looked up. "That plane was flying around here yesterday. It circled over the double snakehead a few times and flew very low."

A single-engine plane was closing in on us. It sounded familiar. I had heard ones like it plenty of times in-country. It was a Cessna O-1 Bird Dog.

"That's the spotter plane from Kingsley Field. They're searching for the canopy," I said.

"Maybe there's a reward for finding it," Gemma said. "Nagah could use the money to pay for college when he's older."

"Maybe," I said.

The plane flew over us. It banked and circled back around. This time it came in at a much lower elevation. Bird Dogs were equipped with cameras. I could all but hear the shutters click as the plane passed overhead. It banked again and circled around before flying away to the west.

No doubt the pilot was radioing the base about our find. I wondered how long it would take Voodoo Dominic and

Doberman Pitzer to show up at the front door of the lineman's shack to retrieve the canopy.

I didn't have to wonder long. They were waiting for us on the straightaway that Wovoka and I had galloped down earlier. Dominic had been behind the stick of the Bird Dog. He'd landed it on the gravel road and was standing in front of it with Pitzer at his side as Gemma and I drove away from the Will camp with the canopy strapped to the roof of her Jeep.

"That's government property you have there," the captain said by way of greeting as I stepped out of the Wagoneer.

"I told you it landed somewhere on the refuge," I said.

"And I told you we would find it and for you to butt out."

"Looks like I completed your mission for you."

Gemma got out from behind the wheel and walked over. "Are you going to introduce me to your friends, Nick?"

Dominic gave a salute. "Capt. Vincent Dominic, US Air Force, at your service, ma'am."

"And you are?" she said to the beady-eyed technical sergeant who was wearing his web belt with the sidearm hanging from it.

"He's TSgt. Jimmy Pitzer," Dominic said. "We're based at Kingsley Field. It appears you've recovered a valuable piece of Air Force equipment."

"Indeed," she said. "It there a reward?"

"Excuse me, ma'am?"

"For finding it. The reward money would go a long way toward helping out the people whose land it wound up on."

"I don't know about any reward."

While Dominic spoke, Pitzer walked over to the Jeep. He glanced at the canopy tied to the roof before circling the trailer. He banged the side with his fist. Wovoka and Sarah whinnied inside.

"Don't do that," I said.

"Why not?" he said.

"The horses don't like it."

"What are they going to do about it?"

"Open the back door and find out."

He started toward the rear of the trailer and then held up. "You'd like me to do that, wouldn't you?"

I turned back to Dominic. "The canopy is too big for you to fit in the Bird Dog. Since you can't take it with you, I'll bring it to Kingsley for you. Now that I know Major Hardiman is commander there, I'll be coming by regularly."

"The major told me he knew you. He also told me you know his fiancée, that she was your nurse when you were locked up at Walter Reed." He sized me up and down like he had at the lake. "What happened, did you turn tail when the bullets started flying?"

"I'll tell you if you tell me what happened when you were flying the jet that lost this canopy. You forgot to mention you were the pilot when you came to retrieve Ramirez's body. Was it because you didn't want to admit you screwed the pooch by telling him to bail?"

The captain's expression hardened. "I don't make mistakes. Just because you know Major Hardiman, doesn't give you a free pass. I told you before, whatever happened is classified. Step out of line again and you'll find yourself in the brig with another charge to add to the list. I could turn you over already for having violated the AP's direct order to stay away from the tarmac and runway. That's right, I know about your visit to the hangar. A ground crewman told me."

"We can talk about those violations with the major when I return the canopy to him."

"You're not returning it anywhere." Dominic motioned to Pitzer. "Sergeant, secure the equipment."

Pitzer pulled out a folding knife and quickly cut the ropes binding the canopy to the Wagoneer. He gripped the edge of the plastic bubble and gave it a yank. It clattered when it hit the gravel.

"Hey," Gemma said. "That's my car."

"Oops," he said.

"He needs a leash," I said to Dominic.

Gemma ran her fingertips along the Jeep's roof rails and gutter. "It's scratched. You're going to have to pay to get that fixed."

"I don't see nothing," Pitzer said.

"Oh yeah? Well, I'm going to file an insurance claim and a police report."

"With who, that fat old deputy?"

Gemma closed in on him and jabbed her finger into his chest. "That fat old deputy happens to be my father. You don't want to underestimate him. It's never worked out too good for those who did."

Pitzer was still holding the folding knife with the blade out. His eyes narrowed and his mouth tightened. My Smith & Wesson came out of the holster without making a sound.

"Stand your man down!" I barked at Dominic. "Now!"

The captain's eyes widened at the sight of my gun pointed at his chest. I didn't blink. He did.

"Sergeant, secure the canopy and drag it out of the way so these people can pass."

"But, but..." Pitzer said.

"On the double," Dominic ordered.

Pitzer did as he was commanded.

Dominic pushed my gun barrel away. "I've already radioed the base and ordered a detail to come retrieve our property. I'll be sure to mention you in my report. And don't think I'll ever forget you pulled a gun on me."

"Neither will I."

GEMMA DROPPED me off at the lineman's shack. The only thing we'd spoken about after we got in the Jeep and drove back to No Mountain was Carla.

"What is her name?" Gemma had asked.

"Who?"

"The nurse. Your friend's fiancée that the captain mentioned."

"He's not a friend. It's Carla. Her name is Carla."

"How long was she your nurse?"

"The entire time I was at Walter Reed, but she wasn't the only nurse working there, and I wasn't the only patient she was treating."

"Is she pretty?"

"I hadn't really thought about it."

"Yes, you have."

We made the rest of the trip in silence.

As I got out of the Jeep, Gemma said, "Don't do that again."

"What?"

"Think that I can't handle myself against a jerk like that sergeant."

"He was holding a knife," I said.

"I know that."

"But what you didn't know is whether or not he'd use it."

"Well, neither did you," she said.

"I knew he would." I sighed. "In war, it's the only thing you can think. You have to."

Her expression softened. "You're not in Vietnam anymore, Nick. You're back home. The sooner you embrace that, the better. For you, for all of us."

As she drove away, I thought I heard Wovoka whinny as the

trailer bounced when its wheels hit the blacktop. Suddenly, I wanted another chance to ride him.

It was still early afternoon and I was keyed up. Dominic's insistence on taking possession of the canopy did little to snuff out my suspicions about his copilot's death. I decided to go back to Malheur Lake and search for the poacher. I threw some gear in the back of my pickup and set off. I didn't get very far.

The radio crackled. Static and Pudge Warbler's voice filled the cab. "Where are you?"

I picked up the microphone. "On my way to Malheur."

"You haven't been already? Gemma told me at breakfast she was going to pick you up and go look for the jet canopy on the other side of the lake."

"We've already been and gone. We found it."

"There anything not jake about it?"

"Only that Dominic was pretty anxious to get it back." I gave him a quick rundown.

The deputy let me listen to static while he mulled it over. "I suppose I should be surprised that he didn't mention he was piloting the jet, but I'm not. It's why I radioed you. I'm here in Burns and came across something you ought to take a gander at."

"What is it?"

"It's better shown than spoken. I'll be in the office until late tonight. Bust'em has me working overtime on this rustling business."

"Maybe when I get a free moment, I'll make my way up there."

"You do that," he said and signed off.

I put the mike back in its cradle, cranked a U-turn, and floored it.

12

My first day in Vietnam was in 1965. I stepped off a troop plane at Bien Hoa Air Base to join another 2,500 GIs that were already assembled and awaiting orders. It was about the same number of people who lived in Harney County's biggest city, Burns. The sheriff's office occupied a blocky two-story building painted a sickly pink color. The jail cells were on the second floor and a covered walkway connected them to the statelier brick courthouse next door.

Before Pudge Warbler took a bullet trying to break up a domestic dispute that cost him his reelection for sheriff against Buster "Bust'em" Burton, he commanded the department from the front office. Now he took whatever empty desk he could find. I found him in the coffee room. He had set up shop at a Formica table an arm's length from the refrigerator. He'd pushed aside a collection of Styrofoam cups holding various levels of cold coffee and a stack of back issues of *Field & Stream* to make room for his short brim Stetson and a pile of papers.

"You made good time getting here," he said.

"You made it sound important."

"No, I made it sound interesting." His grin was sly.

"What do you have?"

"Let me get our college boy in here. He's the one who thinks he spotted something." Pudge tilted back in his chair and yelled through the open door. "Hey, Orville. Drake's here."

Orville Nelson was technically an intern in the sheriff's department. He'd volunteered earlier in the year to acquire law enforcement experience while waiting until he turned twenty-three, the earliest age that the FBI academy at Quantico would consider applicants. Sheriff Burton had him filing papers and fetching coffee, but Orville soon proved himself invaluable when it came to operating any sort of electronics, from the reel-to-reel tape recording equipment in the interview room to the facsimile and Xerox machines. He was a whiz at research, able to ferret out all sorts of information using nothing more than the telephone, his determination, and the department's newest acquisition, a microform reader. His help on a recent murder investigation had earned him a steady, if modest, paycheck.

The baby-faced FBI hopeful hurried into the coffee room. He was dressed in a pressed white shirt and tightly knotted black tie as if he'd already been sworn in by J. Edgar Hoover.

"Hello, Ranger Drake. It's good to see you again." He was clutching a manila folder and began waving it at the same speed as his words. "I've discovered a statistical anomaly I think you'll find of interest. The odds of it having occurred are very low. If I had time and the proper calculating equipment like the kind they use at Quantico, I could tell you them precisely."

"You sound like you haven't reduced your intake of Shasta Cola since I saw you last," I said.

"Actually, I've switched over to the diet version they introduced this year to cut down on sugar. I need to maintain my weight. The FBI has strict physical requirements for applicants. Did you know artificial sweetener was discovered by accident in the late 1800s? A Russian chemist working with coal tar forgot to wash his hands. When he went home for supper, he took a bite of bread and found it unusually sweet. He licked his fingers and found they were sweet too. Eureka! He named it saccharin."

"That's a sweet story, son," Pudge said, "but why don't you go on with telling what it is you found."

"Of course. Sorry. I understand you were present when the copilot ejected from the F-101. I know because Deputy Warbler asked me to file his report. As is his custom, he faxed me hand-written notes. I typed them up before presenting them to Sheriff Burton for sign off." He stopped to take a breath.

"It was the mention of Kingsley Field that caught my attention. I remembered reading about another fatality involving an airman stationed there. It happened in the summer. I read every report involving unusual deaths or crimes I can get my hands on. I'm working on developing an encyclopedic knowledge base." He took another breath. "Right now, I'm keeping it all in a logbook. Once I get to the academy, I'll input the information into the new computing system the FBI installed so any agent can access it."

"What's so interesting about this other accident?" I said.

"Right. Sorry. Two fatalities at a base the size of Kingsley in a few months' time is unusual. Three is an aberration."

"Slow down. What third? Wait, tell me about the second first."

"A ground crewman was killed."

"How?"

"He was run over by a Lockheed C-141 Starlifter. That's a cargo jet the military is using for supplying the war. It was on a refueling stop coming home from the Pacific."

"What happen, did he get drunk and wander onto the runway?"

"No. According to the newspaper story, he was an exemplary airman. He finished among the top of his class in ground crewing and maintenance. Before enlisting, he was an Eagle Scout. He'd only been at Kingsley Field a short while and was awaiting his orders to go overseas."

"For goodness sakes, Orville, tell him what the report said about how he got hit by the plane," Pudge said.

"Right. Sorry. As far as they can tell, he hit his head while inspecting the landing gear while the plane was parked on the tarmac and it knocked him out. He fell in between the double set of rear wheels on the starboard side. Each tire is five feet high. No one could see him. They didn't find his body until after the plane taxied and took off."

"The pilot wouldn't have even felt a bump," I said. "The Starlifter is a freight train with wings. It can carry trucks and tanks and two hundred soldiers."

"After hearing about your copilot and remembering the fatality on the tarmac, I went back and looked up Kingsley Field on the microform reader. We have most of Oregon's newspapers going back a few years on microfiche now. Of course, the FBI is using a computer for storing and searching. I can't wait to get there."

"Until you do, tell him what you found here," Pudge said with a sigh.

"Right. Sorry about that, again. It happened in late spring. A pilot was reported missing."

I asked him if the pilot had been in a plane crash.

"No, he wasn't flying at the time. He lived off base and didn't come to work after a weekend. No one has seen him since."

"Maybe he went AWOL. That's been happening a lot lately," I said.

"For new recruits and draftees who oppose the war, maybe, but this pilot was a veteran. He'd been highly decorated during the Korean War. He was a trainer, not a trainee."

"How does that connect with your statistics?"

"Here, you can read it for yourself." Orville handed me the folder.

The microfiche printout was white type on a black background that made reading difficult. The pilot's name was Capt. Macon "Elvis" Kane. He got his call sign because he was from Mississippi like Elvis Presley and styled himself after the singer. Kane played his music, wore his hair in a pompadour, and mimicked Presley's curled lip smile. He even waggled the wings of his fighter jet when he flew.

Kane's candy apple red Corvette Stingray was spotted parked near a popular fishing spot where the Williamson River flowed into Upper Klamath Lake. His tackle box, shoes, and a jacket were found on the shore. The Klamath County Sheriff's Department surmised he'd gone fishing alone and either fell or stepped into a hole deeper than the top of his chest waders. They filled, he drowned, and the current from the river carried him into the lake. They dragged a grappling hook behind a boat for a few days, but never snagged his body.

I looked up from the printout. "All right. You got my attention. What do you think it means other than a six-month string of bad luck?"

Orville brightened at being asked his opinion. "There is always a cause for statistical aberrations. The trick is finding it. I brought this up to Sheriff Burton when I gave him Deputy Warbler's report because, as you know, he grew up in Klamath Falls and was a deputy there before he transferred to Harney County."

Pudge grunted. "To run against me and take my job, you mean."

"I asked the sheriff about Kingsley Field," Orville continued. "He said it was always a source of headaches when he was a deputy. The airmen are there a short time. They're young, they drive fast, and they like to party when they're granted leave. The sheriff told me that whenever he pulled one over for speeding or got called into a tavern to break up a fight, the Air Police would show up and tell him they'd handle it."

Pudge winked at me. "Sounds like any town near any base. You should've seen San Diego when I was a boot at Camp Pendleton. We'd get leave and there wouldn't be a bottle of beer left in the whole town or a bar without a stool or two broken over someone's head come Sunday morning. The Shore Patrol carried a lot more weight than the city cops ever did."

I asked if Sheriff Burton was going to do anything about it.

"No. He said all three deaths were clearly accidental, but even if they weren't, there was nothing he could do because first, it's a military matter, and second, Klamath County isn't his jurisdiction anymore." Orville frowned. "But, darn it, statistical aberrations don't happen every day."

If my radar hadn't already been triggered by Hardiman and Dominic stonewalling me, I may have been inclined to agree with Sheriff Burton that the three deaths were unfortunate, yet unrelated. But I'd learned the hard way that not trusting my gut could cost lives.

I thumbed through the rest of the contents of the folder. I checked the dates. The report about the dead ground crewman and missing Korean War ace occurred right before Hardiman had become base commander. I wondered how long Dominic and Pitzer had been stationed at Kingsley. I asked Orville if he could get his hands on the service records of those two plus Ramirez's.

"Yes, sir. I'll get right on it."

Orville spun on his heel and marched from the coffee room, his earnestness reminding me of Hardiman's adjutant who rode the desk outside his office. The next time I was at Kingsley—and I was sure there would be a next time—I'd see what Airman First Class Edwins knew.

I WAITED in the coffee room while Pudge went to fetch something else he wanted to show me. He returned carrying a cylinder of paper. He unrolled it and tacked it over the old rodeo posters and snapshots of deputies dressed in camouflage, showing off trophy deer that crowded the cork bulletin board. It was a map of Harney County. Red dots speckled it. He explained that each dot marked a ranch that had reported a rustling.

"I know," he said. "Looks like the entire county has broken out with a case of chicken pox. Show me where you saw those pickups off-loading cows."

I ran my finger down the highway that led back to Klamath Falls. "Here," I said. "The map even shows the airstrip."

Pudge took a closer look. "That's the Double J Ranch. I doubt that strip gets much use anymore. The owner passed some time back. His wife is leasing the grazing rights to other ranchers."

"Gemma told me ranchers do a lot of cattle transfers this time of year to get ready for winter."

"She did, did she? Well, she ought to know since she knows more than most about ranching. I'd like to take credit for all her smarts, but everyone knows it's November who raised her proper, me being too busy sheriffing up here."

"Do you think that's what I saw, a legal transfer?"

"Probably, but I got to tell you the Cattlemen's Association has a burr under its saddle right now, and Bust'em is feeling its prickles. That means so are all us deputies. He made me lead on busting this gang since I'm the one who lives on a ranch and not in a ticky-tacky apartment here in Burns like the rest. As soon as I can, I'll drive down to that airstrip and take a looksee."

"How will you know if they were rustlers or not?"

"Probably won't be able to tell anything, but who knows,

maybe something got left behind that says something. A matchbook from somewhere else or a license plate got knocked off one of the stock trailers when it was backing up. You never know. It's not like the old days, that's for sure."

"When rustlers would cause a stampede?"

"You sound like you went to the picture show when you were a kid. But, yeah, that's what they did. They'd raid a cattle drive on horseback. While the honest cowboys were trying to sort everything out, the rustlers would peel off a bunch of cows, drive them into a canyon and switch their brands by burning a new one on top. Then they would ride out and act like the cows were theirs all along. The old-time Harney County deputies would have to catch them red-handed."

"And now?"

"Some rustling is still done on horseback and brand switching, but your modern cattle thief drives an air-conditioned four-by-four. He steals a small bunch of cows from a holding pen or a fenced pasture near a road, loads them into a stock trailer, and then drives to a slaughterhouse that doesn't ask a whole lot of questions."

"All those red dots make it look like a big, organized gang."

"You're right, and they've been mighty busy. They're still taking cows a few at a time, but they're hitting a lot more places a lot more often."

"Could a rancher be buying them, switching the brand, and mixing them in with his own herd?"

"Harney County may be big, but all the ranchers know each other and exactly how many head their neighbor is running. If someone's herd was suddenly to swell, well, he'd have some serious explaining to do."

"Then they must be taking them out of the county."

"We've put the word out to all the cattlemen's associations in the neighboring counties to be on the lookout. They're worried about getting rustled themselves."

"What about taking cattle out of state?"

"Nevada and Idaho maybe because of all the back roads in an out, but not California. They got agricultural inspection stations on every route leading in. They'll stop you for bringing in so much as an apple. Same with Washington State."

The old deputy stabbed the map with his finger. "Something tells me this bunch has got a new trick up their sleeve. I got to figure out what it is and fast. If I know where they're gonna hit next, I can stake it out and catch them in the act."

"And if they run?"

"Shoot their tires out."

"What's to stop them from shooting back?"

"Not a thing," he said. "Not a blessed thing."

13

The *Burns Yellow Pages* listed five gun shops. I took them in alphabetical order. The first was a hardware store that displayed rifles and shotguns along the back wall between shelves of paint cans and upright ladders.

"Can I help you?" a portly man wearing bib overalls asked.

"Shotgun shells. Twelve-gauge duck and goose loads," I said.

"How many boxes you need?"

"None. I'm looking for a man who has been buying them in unusual amounts."

"Describe unusual?"

"By the hundreds."

"Piss poor shot, he needs that many."

"Does anyone come to mind?"

The hardware store clerk hadn't shaved for a couple of days, and it made a sandpapery sound when he rubbed his jaw. "Can't say that it does. Most people, they buy a couple of boxes start of duck season and maybe a couple more when it's dove time. Most of our ammo sales are for deer rifles and .22s. The deers are for hunting deer and the .22s for popping varmints."

I thanked him and went to the next address. I knew trying to get a bead on the poacher's identity and where he lived by tracking down shotgun shell sales wasn't much of a strategy, but I'd always been the kind who needed to do rather than wait. It was because of my hyperadrenalism. My body had always produced too much of it, especially in times of stress. It had helped in combat, but the aftereffects and coming down from it had never been easy. The shrinks at Walter Reed said it was one of the reasons why I craved heroin. It was the only thing I knew strong enough to stanch the flow.

The next listing for guns for sale was a corner in the boy's department of a clothing store. The saleswoman informed me that they stocked a few BB guns and pellet rifles, primarily around Christmastime.

The third was a pawn shop. A couple of ancient shotguns were on display, but most of the weapons were cheap handguns kept under glass. The owner told me he didn't stock any ammunition at all. He pointed to a sign on the front door: No Loaded Weapons Allowed.

"I call that my life insurance policy," he explained. "People hawking guns either stole 'em or are in desperate need of money. Those looking to get their hands on a pawned gun are also short of money, otherwise they'd buy a new one. Both types are as likely to turn it around on me and say stick 'em up."

The fourth was a sporting goods store. It carried everything from bikes to boats. The hunting section was well-stocked. The rows of shotguns came in a range of sizes from .410 to 10 gauge. There were pumps, double-barreled side by sides, and over-and-unders with fine engraving on the metal parts. Boxes of shells were stacked on tables according to gauge and pellet size, from number 8 quail loads to double-aught buckshot.

I asked for the store manager. He wore a white polyester shirt under a tan vest that had a row of ballpoint pens clipped to the breast pocket. I told him who I was and what I was after.

"We're the largest store of our kind in Harney County and sell more shotguns and shells than any competitor by far, but I doubt you'll find your man looking through past store receipts," he said.

I asked him why.

"Because he won't be buying store loads. That'd be too expensive for the amount of shooting you say he's doing, even if he were to buy them all at our annual sale at the end of duck hunting season."

"He'd load his own."

"You got it. Most shooters who are serious about shooting do. They save money reusing shells and can control their loads. You know, add heavier pellets or more powder depending on whether it's duck or goose they're going after or what the wind and rain are doing."

"You sound like you have some experience."

"My grandpa showed me how to load shot. He was what was called a commercial hunter back in the day. He told me he always loaded his own rounds because he wanted to trust when he pulled the trigger the barrel wouldn't blow up in his face."

"What did he hunt?"

"Whatever flew or walked. He sold ducks and geese to the meat markets and the feathers of cranes and swans to women's hat makers in New York City."

"Did he live in Burns?"

"Still does. He's nearly ninety. He did a lot of shooting down where you say your poacher is operating."

"When was that?"

"Before it became a refuge sixty years ago. Teddy Roosevelt did that. He said it was to protect all the birdlife from the commercial meat and feather hunters. Grandpa said the president was aiming his pen at him when he signed it into law. It put him straight out of business. Well, that and changing fashions. Women's hats got smaller and big feathers went out of style."

My poacher was killing more birds than he could eat. He must be selling the meat somewhere. Maybe he was selling the feathers too. My own vest was filled with goose down. Those were new leads I could follow.

I glanced around the store. "Do you sell handloading equipment here?"

"Not to speak of. We stock some starter kits that include a loader, a handful of BBs, some wadding, and gunpowder, but your weekend hunter doesn't stick with loading by hand for long. They'd rather spend their time watching TV or going out in the marsh with their buddies rather than sitting in their garages cleaning the mud off used shells."

"Where would a serious shooter get what he needs?"

"There's places in Lakeview and Klamath Falls that sell it in bulk."

"Mind if I ask you one other thing?"

"If I can answer it, sure, go right ahead."

"Does your store take government purchase orders?"

"As long as Uncle Sam is still good for it, I don't see why not." He cocked his head. "What did you have in mind?"

"When I parked in the lot, I saw you were having a clearance sale on boats and trailers."

"That's right. Not much call for them this time of year with the weather about to turn even nastier. Was there one that caught your eye?"

"There's a sixteen-foot skiff on a trailer. It has a fifty horse-power outboard on it."

"How about if I ask you something?"

"Sure, go ahead."

"This boat you're after, is it something you're going to be using to go after hunters?"

"If they're shooting out of season, using an illegal gun, or going over their limit, then yes. It's my job to stop them. Do you have a problem with that?"

"Not at all. My grandpa may have shot more than his share, but he always used a regular gun. The man you're talking about?" He shook his head in disgust. "Here's my advice. Swap out the fifty for a hundred. The transom on that skiff can handle an outboard of that size just fine. As my grandpa said when he switched from shooting birds to driving whiskey down from Canada during Prohibition, you never want to be outgunned or outrunned."

The fifth and final gun shop was tucked behind a feed and grain store on the road between Burns and Hines. I parked my truck towing the new boat and trailer around the corner. Gunsmithing was advertised in small letters on the front door. I tried the knob, but it was locked. I could see a light glowing through the glass panel in the door. I pressed my nose against it and looked in. A man sat at a workbench. He wore gold-rimmed glasses with clip-on magnifying lenses and was concentrating on something held in a small vise. I rapped the glass to get his attention. He looked over, squinted, and then flipped up the clip-on magnifying lenses. Shaking his head, he came to the door and opened it a crack.

"It's five o'clock," he said. "I'm closed for the day. Come back tomorrow." He started to shut the door.

"Wait," I said. "I live out of town. I only need a minute of your time."

"What is it?"

"I'm looking for a special shotgun. It's one of a kind, multiple barrels, and takes handloads."

"I don't sell guns. I repair guns."

I could see past him. There was a glass-fronted gun cabinet similar to the one in Pudge Warbler's home office.

The gunsmith acknowledged my stare. "Those are collectibles. I do sell a gun now and then when a customer chooses not to pick up an item they've left for repair. I have a ninety-day pay or stay rule."

"I'm not looking to buy. I'm looking for information." I flashed my badge. "I'm after a poacher. He's using a 12-gauge Gatling gun."

"I've never heard of such a thing," he said a little too quickly, a little too loudly.

"There's a reward for information. Does that help your memory at all?"

He tried to close the door without answering, but I had my boot stuck in the gap like I was a Fuller Brush salesman.

"I'll find out if you know him one way or the other," I said.

"I've done nothing wrong."

"Then stop acting like you did. All I want is information. This man is dangerous. He's already shot at me with the gun you made for him and you're going to have to answer for it."

"That's preposterous. I made no such gun. I have no connection to this person."

Sometimes during interrogation when I was in-country, I could get more information by not saying much at all and letting them rush to fill the void. Other times, I'd hit them with the presumption of guilt. I could learn a lot by how they professed their innocence.

"I'm not sure what the penalty is for aiding and abetting attempted murder, or maybe it's accessory, but we can ask Sheriff Burton." I started pushing on the door. "Come on, let's go talk to him."

"Wait, wait. I've only met him twice." The lenses of the gunsmith's glasses were thick and made his eyeballs look the size of a cow's. "I don't even know his name. He paid in cash."

"Describe him."

The gunsmith's face soured. "He's big and brutish and wears a filthy hat. His face is pockmarked. He's very unsanitary. He does not take care of his personage. He chews tobacco and spit on my workshop floor."

"Did you make the gun for him?"

"Of course not. All he wanted from me was a special firing pin. He didn't tell me what it was for. I swear. I don't know anything about poaching."

"But you did know it was to fire a 12-gauge shell. He had to have given you the specs."

"Of course, but I wasn't thinking about that. I was only thinking about the challenge. He said it needed to be able to fire and retract and fire and retract very quickly without overheating or jamming. I've never made anything like that before. I like solving problems. I do crosswords." He looked at me expectantly.

"Turning a shotgun into a machine gun is hardly the same thing."

"I was intrigued, that's all. Intrigued." His voice went up an octave.

My anger swelled and I could see myself kicking the door wide-open, grabbing him by the front of his green apron, and shoving him against the wall while I demanded how could he turn a blind eye to something so deadly, something that was used to try to blow me out of the water. I could see my expression reflected in his thick glasses, and I could see his reaction in the widening of his already bulbous eyes.

He started stuttering. "I, I, I'm sorry. I didn't mean to—"

"You said two times. You met him twice. When was the first and when was the last?"

"It was the beginning of September. He showed up here with a crude sketch of a shotgun he was adapting. He said he was running into problems with a stock firing pin."

"So, you custom made him a new one and it worked."

"I suppose it did, but I don't know for sure. I never live fired it to test it. I had it ready for him the first of October. When he picked it up, he said if it didn't work, he'd come back. He said I'd better hope it worked because the last thing I'd want is for him to be dissatisfied. That was a threat. He threatened me. That should count for something," he whined.

"Do you know where he lives?"

"No. I told you he didn't give me his name, address, or phone number. He paid in cash. But I don't think he lives in Burns."

"What makes you say that?"

"He told me he was going to try the firing pin at home to make sure it worked. When I asked if he was concerned all the noise would alarm his neighbors, he said he didn't need to worry about that."

"Meaning he lives somewhere out of town."

"Yes, about an hour or so, I believe."

I pushed the door open wide. "You said you didn't know where he lived."

The gunsmith flinched. "I don't. I swear. But when he picked up the firing pin, it was an hour until sunset. Because of his threat, I wanted to know if he was going to try it out right away since I didn't want to have to worry all night that it might not. He laughed at me and said he didn't care if I lost any sleep, that I'd have to wait until tomorrow to find out because it would be getting dark when he got home, and he wanted to shoot it when it was light out. Don't you see? That means it must take him an hour to drive home."

"What kind of truck was he driving?"

"I didn't see it. He must've parked around the corner. Everyone does."

I handed him my card. "If he comes back or gets in touch

with you, call me. There's my telephone number as well as my radio channel."

"You mentioned a reward. I told you everything I know."

"The only one who knows if you did is the poacher. When I catch him, I'll ask him."

14

I spread out my own map of Harney County on the rickety kitchen table. A pot of chili was warming on the stove and a pie pan of cornbread was baking in the oven. The radio was tuned to the college station in Eugene. The DJ was playing Buffalo Springfield's latest album, *Last Time Around*. The group's LPs were late night favorites when I was in-country because the mellow guitar riffs, easygoing lyrics, and lilting harmonies helped soldiers come down after a firefight.

I cut a length of string matching the map's scale for sixty miles, tied one end to a pencil, pressed the other end down on Burns with my thumb, and drew a circle. If the gunsmith was telling the truth and the poacher had driven straight home at a reasonable speed, he was holed up somewhere inside that radius.

The lineman's shack fell within it. So did all of No Mountain, from the leaning storefronts on Main Street to the ranch down the road where Pudge, Gemma, and November lived. So did the Will's camp, the double snakehead, Malheur Lake, the Burns Paiute Reservation, and dozens of ranches scattered north, east, west, and south of Burns. It was a lot of territory to search for the no-name poacher and his Gatling shotgun, but I'd hunted dangerous men before. Some had been lying in wait in tunnels, others waiting to leap out from behind green curtains. All had been more determined than him to kill me. All had much more to lose if they didn't. I'd hunted for GIs too, soldiers who failed to come back after a patrol or downed airmen like Whistling Pete Hardiman. The hardest to find were POWs taken far behind enemy lines, stripped of their uniforms and hope, and stuffed into cages made of bamboo.

The trick to finding men, be they enemy or fellow countrymen, captor or captive, was to think like them. I'd put myself in their position. Where would I hide if staging an ambush? What signs would I leave behind if lost or seized for those who might come looking for me?

I took another look at the map and decided to go back to where I'd last seen the poacher. Pudge had told me he was going to look for something that may have been left behind at the dirt airstrip as he searched for the rustlers. Maybe I could find something the poacher had dropped that would lead me to his lair.

The cornbread was done, and I pulled it from the oven as the last track of the Buffalo Springfield album faded away. The DJ took to the mike and reported news about an upcoming protest march on the nation's capital. It was shaping up to be the largest rally ever against the Vietnam War. He directed his listeners in the university town to check the bulletin boards for ride shares to DC. Then he dedicated the next set to peace and started it off with "The Times They Are A-Changin'."

I sat at the table eating chili and mopping up the bowl with a hunk of cornbread as Bob Dylan gave way to Joan Baez and she gave way to Country Joe and the Fish. I knew the words to most of the songs, and though I could understand the singers' anger and passionate calls to end the war, I doubted music would ever be enough. Too much was at stake: politics, power and pride, not to mention money, both the cost of waging war and the profits being made from it.

Despite the lingering heat from the oven and the warmth cast from the wood stove, the shack turned cold. I cleared the table and looked out the kitchen window. It was as if the DJ was seeing what I saw because he'd put on "A Hard Rain's A-Gonna Fall." I watched sleet slanting sideways as Dylan sang about being ten thousand miles in the mouth of a graveyard and traveling through black forests where homes in valleys met damp prisons and the executioner awaits. The silhouette of a coyote slunk in front of the window as the sagebrush started to droop from the weight of slush.

So did any hope I had for peace from the war raging both inside and out.

IN THE MORNING, I scraped ice off the windshield and drove to the Malheur Refuge. Dawn and daylight showed little difference. The sky was leaden and the passing scenery dulled from dampness. The patches of snow around the lake were thicker than when I had launched the canoe. It seemed like weeks ago but was only days. I backed the new trailer into the water up to the tops of the tires and slid off the skiff. The new outboard started right up, and I set a course straight down the middle of the lake. It put me more than sixty yards from either shore and would keep me out of range should the poacher be lying in wait in the tules. Out of range, that is, as long as he was armed only with a shotgun.

I wore a wool knit cap pulled down low and an oiled canvas barn jacket over my down vest to guard against the cold. The .357

magnum revolver rode in its holster at my hip. Some people traveling on open water in wet weather might choose a slicker or waterproof poncho, but I'd learned in the jungle where it was always either raining or humid never to wear clothes that rustled or got in the way of drawing a gun.

The ducks and geese rafting in the middle of the lake shook off their torpor as the skiff approached. Some paddled away. Others took wing. I followed a tongue of top water browned by runoff that led to the double snakehead. The mouths looked even more dangerous from the water. I kept them to port and followed the shoreline until I came to the entrance of a channel where the outermost cattail appeared to be leaning into the wind while all the rest bent with it.

I slowed the skiff and approached it. There was a bend in the plant's stalk level to my shoulders. Someone had reached out from a similar position, grabbed the cattail, and gave it a tweak. Someone had made himself a guidepost. Before nosing the skiff into the channel, I made sure the butt of my revolver was clear of my jacket's hem and I could grab the Winchester without looking down. I twisted the throttle to give it a little gas and eased forward.

Fog hung low over the channel. The skiff's bow separated the flat water into a *V* and the churning prop left a foamy wake. The cattails on either side thrummed as the surge plucked at their stalks. The wavering tremolo of a hidden loon's call came from somewhere to my right. Another loon answered the ghostly call from my left.

I checked both guns and leaned forward as if a few more inches would allow me to see farther into the mist, hear more over the whirr of the outboard. The channel ran straight for a while and then started making lazy *S* turns. It was hard to tell how much marsh lay between me and the lake. It could be yards. It could be miles.

I'd been keeping time by counting silently as I steered. It was another trick learned when stalking foes at night where even a quick glance at the radium dial of a field watch could draw enemy fire. I was coming up on two hours and I had enough gas for five. I'd give it another thirty minutes before turning around and heading back.

The channel narrowed to where the cattails brushed both sides of the skiff. If the poacher was hiding in them, I was already dead. I steered through another series of S turns. The sky lightened. The fog lifted. The channel ended in a pond the size of a swimming pool. At the far end, where a diving board would be if I were in a backyard, the shore was scarred by a pair of ruts carved by a truck pulling a trailer. I let off on the throttle and nosed the skiff onto the makeshift boat ramp, pulled up the prop, scrambled toward the bow, and stepped onto land.

With the skiff secured, I followed the ruts, carrying the Winchester at port arms. The track led through a thicket of shrub willow. A stand of stunted junipers grew on the other side of a small clearing. The tire tracks widened, made by a truck and trailer pulling to the side and stopping. It was a camp site. A stump had been pulled in front of a fire ring, the stones blackened not only by flames and smoke, but by tobacco juice. I crouched and poked the cold ashes. Shards of bones poked out like needles sticking from a pin cushion. I couldn't tell if they'd come from a duck or a goose that had been impaled on a stick and roasted over coals.

A pile of curled wood shavings lay at the base of the stump. While the poacher sat waiting for his meal to cook, he'd whittled with the knife he'd used to slash the X across the door of my truck and puncture the tires. I started making widening circles looking for more clues. The outer circle took me right up to the juniper trees. When I reached them, I pinched my nose. Despite the sleet that had wetted the site, the stink of human piss and shit was thick.

The stand of trees was a makeshift outhouse. As the poacher had squatted, he'd done what others did when seated on a public toilet. In the nearest trunk that served the same as the wall of a stall, he'd carved his initials.

A. J. was here.

15

M y phone rang the next morning. It didn't ring often, and when it did, it was either a wrong number or my district supervisor in Portland calling to check up on me. Most times I didn't bother to answer, but I thought it might be the gunsmith with news about the poacher.

"Drake," I said.

"Hello, Nick. It's Carla."

"How did you get this number?"

"That's a funny way to say hello," she said.

"Sorry, you surprised me is all." I fumbled some more. "I don't remember giving it to you and I'm not sure it's even listed."

"Not in your name. I tried that first when I called directory assistance. Did you know it's still 113 in Oregon? It's 411 everywhere else. Anyway, I asked the operator to try US Fish and Wildlife Service in No Mountain. Is this your office?"

"Sort of." I tried to think of a way to ask her why she was calling. "How's Pete?"

Carla paused. "Okay, I guess. I mean, he's not here. He was called down to California for a meeting. It was unexpected, but that's the military for you."

"Travis," I said, naming the Air Force base near San Francisco.

"Yes, that's the one." She paused again. "Listen, the reason I'm calling is, I woke up this morning and had an idea. I know it's spur of the moment, but I find myself at loose ends. I don't know a soul in Klamath Falls outside of Pete. You made where you live sound so lovely that I thought I'd come over and see it for myself."

"It's a long drive and it's been sleeting here."

"I grew up on the East Coast. I know all about driving in winter weather," she said quickly.

"What I meant is, it makes for a long trip back and forth even in good weather."

"Then I'll take two days."

"No Mountain is barely a town, much less a city. There aren't any motels here. The only place that serves food is a tavern."

Carla sighed. "Are you going to make me ask you?"

"Ask me what?"

"For you to invite me to stay in your guest room. Come on, Nick, you do have a guest room, don't you?"

I heard a slight quaver in her voice. I thought of how she'd looked down at her feet when I toasted her and Hardiman, and the little frown she tried to cover with a smile whenever he spoke. The buildings on No Mountain's Main Street weren't the only things with false fronts.

"No, as a matter of fact I don't, but that's okay. I know people who have a ranch nearby that do. Look, come on over. Even with the weather turning, it's beautiful here and I can show you around."

"That would be great. Tell me how to find your house and I'll be on my way."

I gave Carla directions and then drove over to Pudge's to ask if he knew anybody with the initials A. J. and if he could put Carla up for the night.

November was sitting in a rocker on the front porch when I pulled up. She had a Pendleton blanket draped over her shoulders and was shucking dried corn, dropping the crinkly brown husks into a woven basket clenched between her moccasins.

"You met Tuhudda Will and his grandson," she said. "How did he seem?"

"Very wise," I said.

"You can see that already in a twelve-year-old?"

"I thought you were talking about Tuhudda."

"I do not need to ask about him. He has not changed since we were children."

"He told me he wanted to marry you, but you wouldn't have him."

"Our marriage would have been cold and stormy. We were born in the same moon during the same winter. His people named him Tuhudda because a deer ran through the snow outside their wickiup the moment he came into this world."

"And you came into it when your mother was caught outside in a blizzard," I said, having heard the story from Gemma about how Girl Born in Snow received her Paiute birth name.

November shucked another ear of corn. The dried kernels were a mix of purples, reds, and oranges. When the husk was stripped, she placed the ear on a woven plate that had the same diamond design as the basket at her feet. The kernels would later be ground into flour.

"Do you still see the black bird?" she asked.

When I was new to No Mountain and first met her, November pronounced that I was visited by a spirit in the form of a black bird. How she knew about the hallucination that had plagued me since the day everyone in my squad but me was annihilated was a mystery, but I did not question her then and I did not now.

"Not as often as I used to."

"Perhaps it has finally decided to become either Raven or Eagle and is no longer in between."

"Perhaps," I said.

She shucked another ear. "You are visited by another first people spirit now. Which *nuwuddu* is it?"

"None."

"Not Coyote?"

I swallowed my surprise. "I have seen some coyotes here and there, but unlike the black bird, they were real."

"How can you be sure? Coyote is a trickster. His *puha* is powerful, but he uses it only for his own benefit. Coyote makes you see what you want to see, but you cannot always trust your eyes."

"That's why when I see a coyote, I throw a rock to make it run away."

November's head bobbed. "You have been reading my book. Rock and Obsidian also have powerful *puha*, but there are many stories about how Coyote tries to trick them too."

"Tuhudda Will is named for a deer and Deer shattered Obsidian," I said. "What does that make Tuhudda?"

"Deer is not Coyote. Deer has always been a friend of *neme*." She used the local dialect for the word the Paiute called oneself with *numu* being plural and the name of their language. "Like Deer, Tuhudda Will has always provided food for his family. He has done this even when his land was stolen."

"Is that how the Wills got into shepherding? Gemma told me how Nagah got his name."

She'd shucked the last ear, stood, and picked up the plate of corn. "The book you have been reading, have you finished it?"

"Not yet." I reached for the basket of husks to carry it inside for her.

"Pity. You still have much to learn."

"Pudge told me it's unusual for someone like you to trust someone like me and share such knowledge."

"And who is someone like you?"

I shifted the basket of husks. "You know, an outsider."

"Is that how you see yourself?"

"Why, do you see me some other way?"

She grunted. "You have much to learn. I don't know if you can. I don't know if I can teach you anything."

"Then, why do you try?"

November tsked and raised the plate of shucked corn toward the house. "For them. I gave Gemma's mother my word as she passed into the spirit world that I would teach her daughter about this life and the next. You have been visited by *nuwuddu*, not once, but twice. Maybe you have *puha*. Who am I to question if this is so? But as long as you have come into Gemma and her father's life, I must do what I can to help you see more clearly for their sake. Now, bring those husks inside. They are not to waste."

PUDGE WAS in his office cleaning rifles. The room smelled of Hoppe's gun oil. He sat on his swivel chair and ran a steel rod with a swab on the end through the bore of a lever-action Marlin. Though it looked similar to my Winchester, it took a bigger round, the .45-70 Government, so named because it had originally been used in US Army Springfield rifles during the Indian Wars. A bolt-action .30-06 with a mounted scope lay on his desk and was next in line for cleaning.

"Are you going or coming?" I said.

"I've been, but I'm going back. That airstrip? I think you may be onto something," he said.

"The rustlers are using it?"

"If not rustlers, then it's the most unusual group of cowboys I've ever come across."

"What did you find?

"It's what I didn't find. I searched high and low and didn't come up with so much as a cigarette butt. The whole place was neat and tidy except for some cow pies and tire tracks. Now, you put a bunch of cowpunchers together and when the work's all done, one of them is going to break out a six-pack, probably two. They'll stand in a circle drinking beer and jawing. But there wasn't a crushed can chucked in a bush anywhere. Not an empty tin of dip nor an empty pouch of chaw. Either they were the cleanest cut, hardest working cowpokes in a big hurry to finish the job and get onto the next one or they were rushing to get those cows loaded and moved out before anybody drove by and saw them."

"The ones I saw were in and out in fifteen minutes," I said.

"That's a world record for loading steers," Pudge said. "Your forty-eight-foot stock trailer holds about sixty head."

I asked him if he planned on staking out the airstrip.

"I may. First, I'm gonna check out some other strips in the area. I had Orville take a look at the map and put dates to all the red dots when the ranchers said they'd been rustled. He could see the pattern quicker than me. They hit three or four ranches in a night. They started near Burns and are moving southeast like a river that's busted through a dam. If I take a look at some of those airstrips in the direction they're going, maybe I can hopscotch ahead and be at the right one when they show up."

The deputy finished cleaning the Marlin. He shouldered it and adjusted the sights. Then he picked up the .30-06. He pulled the bolt back, made sure it wasn't loaded, stood it on its butt, and ran the steel rod down the bore.

"Do you know a man whose first name starts with an *A* and last name with a *J*?" I asked.

"As a matter of fact, I do."

"Really? Who is he? Where does he live?"

"On the front of a twenty-dollar bill." Pudge chuckled.

"You got me." I told him about the initials carved in the tree.

"Nobody springs to mind, but sounds like he could be your poacher, all right. You check the phone book? It covers the entire county."

"Yes, but the only listings starting with *J* are in Burns. For a small town it has a surprising number of Joneses and Johnsons. I believe he lives about an hour or so from Burns. He may not even have a phone."

"Then you'll have to go to the county courthouse and look at the census records, property tax files, and so on. You could ask the college boy to do it once he's done collecting the service records of your flyboys."

"Has he made any progress?"

"I believe some, but not all. Orville is good at letting you know when he's got what he's been asked to fetch or when he's hit a brick wall. In the meantime, I'll ask around and see if anyone knows your A. J."

I told him I needed another favor. "I have someone from out of town visiting today. There's no room at my place to put her up for the night, and I was hoping she could sleep here. It'll only be the one night. She'll drive back to Klamath Falls tomorrow."

Pudge was pulling the cleaning rod from the .30-06. He stopped halfway. "She? Klamath Falls? Something you want to fill me in on, son?"

"You remember how you said it was a small world that Hardiman and I knew each other from 'Nam and ended up in

Oregon? It gets even smaller. His fiancée is a nurse who worked at Walter Reed when I was there."

"And now she's coming over to No Mountain for a visit. I noticed you didn't mention her boyfriend. Will the major be needing a place to stay too?"

"No, he's down in California."

"Her boyfriend being the same base commander who wrote an official letter ordering the county sheriff to keep out of Air Force business."

"I hadn't thought about that. I see how it could put you in an awkward position. Forget it. I'll come up with something else."

"It isn't me I'm worried about." Pudge gave me a stern look to say who was.

"I suppose she can get a motel room up in Burns," I said.

Pudge resumed cleaning the rifle. "That wouldn't be neighborly. There's no law saying I can't have a guest in my own house. Your nurse friend can stay in Gemma's room. She's working all the way out by Whitehorse Ranch. Some sort of epidemic. Won't be back until tomorrow. What's this nurse's name?"

"Carla."

"Got a last name to go with that?"

I hesitated. "I don't know it."

"What do you mean you don't know it?"

"I never asked her."

"She was nursing you for six months and now is on her way over to spend the night while her fiancé is out of town." Pudge shook his head. "Oh Lord, what have you gotten yourself into now?"

16

Carla arrived in a rental car. The subcompact looked like it wouldn't hold up in any sort of Harney County wind. She explained that Hardiman's vehicle was government property.

"Do you need to rent every time you go somewhere?" I asked as I invited her in.

"I usually call the base and Pete sends a driver. He's a nice boy. Well, young man, I should say."

"Would that be his adjutant, Airman First Class Edwins?"

"Yes. I like him. He's very earnest and about the only person I've met at the base that seems nice. Some are down-right rude."

"Captain Dominic and Technical Sergeant Pitzer," I said.

"Oh, so you've met them." Carla made a face. "The first time I went to visit Pete at his office, those two were there meeting with him. The captain saw me coming and slammed the door in my face, leaving me standing out in the hall."

"What did Pete say about it?"

"He blew it off. He said the captain didn't know who I was and they were going over something and he didn't want to be interrupted in whatever he was telling Pete. If you ask me, they acted like they had something to hide."

"Now that you're living in Oregon, you can get your own car."

Carla shrugged. She was wearing a puffy white down jacket and kept it zipped, even though the temperature inside the lineman's shack hadn't dropped much since I'd let the fire die out after breakfast.

"Home sweet home. What was it originally?" she asked.

"A house for a lineman. There used to be an old railroad running by here. It was only fifty miles long and used for hauling timber. They needed someone living in the middle to keep cattle and snow off the tracks."

"It's rustic. It suits you."

"You can see why I didn't offer up a guest room. I have something lined up for you though. It's over at Deputy Warbler's."

"You're making me sleep in a jail cell?"

"No, at his ranch. He lives there with his daughter. I'll take you over later to meet him. Since the weather has cleared up a bit, I thought we'd drive down to Frenchglen. That will take us by the Malheur Refuge. It's one of the ones I work on. There are some historical sites along the way. Then we can loop back on a road that follows the shoulder of Steens Mountain. As long as we're not blocked by snow, we should be able to get a pretty good view of the entire basin."

"Sounds like you could become a travel guide."

"I'll stick with rangering. I wouldn't be good around tourists."

We loaded into my truck and set off. "I have to ask you something," I said. "It's a little awkward."

"I'm a nurse. I've heard it all and seen it all. I doubt you can shock me," she said.

"All right. I don't know your last name."

"That's it? I was expecting something else. It's Donovan."

"Like the folk singer? 'Mellow Yellow' and 'Hurdy Gurdy Man.' "

"That's his first name. Donovan Leitch."

"I don't remember you playing him back at the ward."

"I didn't for you. Another patient needed Donovan."

"Did you have a special song for everyone?"

"Music couldn't help some of the men," she said softly.

We drove for a while taking in the scenery. It was all new for her. The sagebrush and tumbleweeds. The emptiness of the high desert. The big sky. The narrow black stripe of the two-lane highway sandwiched between.

"What about you?" I said. "What song did you play for yourself?"

"What makes you think I did?"

"You said you were there during Tet. You worked at the Tay Ninh MASH. I was in a field hospital after being wounded. The nurses and doctors were seeing the worst of it."

"We train for that," she said. "When the choppers are landing and the litters are being rushed in and every surgical bay is filling fast, something clicks and you fall back on your training. It's not boys and men, it's a GSW to the head, a pneumothorax that needs tubing, a leg with a tourniquet the corpsman tied too tight. You can't hear the bombs dropping or the guns firing, no matter how close they're getting."

I regretted bringing it up. I could see all those things. I had seen them. Time and time again. But I could always see the men behind the wounds because they were my men. Their wounds were my wounds. Their deaths too.

We drove in silence some more.

"Joni Mitchell," Carla said abruptly. " 'Both Sides Now.' The first six months I was at Tay Ninh we had forty-five mortar attacks. Forty-five. A pre-op tent took a direct hit. Everyone inside was KIA. I played Joni Mitchell to fall asleep. Sometimes I still do. Hear her, at least. You know it? 'Rows and flows of angel hair and ice cream castles in the air.' She's singing about seeing both sides of clouds and love and life. Before that it was Peter, Paul and Mary."

" 'Leaving On a Jet Plane.' The Freedom Bird pilot played it over the PA during takeoff from Saigon."

We didn't break out singing the lyrics together, but I knew she was singing them in her head the same as I was as we tooled down the highway.

I didn't turn off to the refuge's main entrance at Malheur Lake. Instead, I kept on the highway for a few more miles until it crested a rise. I pulled over.

"There's a footpath here we can take. It's only a few hundred yards but it leads to an overlook." I got out and slid the shotgun from the rear window gun rack.

"What's that for?" she asked.

"Rattlesnakes. It's cold enough so they should be inside their burrows, but you can't trust that. One might be out on a rock basking in the sun."

"Lead the way," she said without a shudder.

Carla was wearing knee-high boots better suited for city sidewalks than rocky trails but didn't stumble. I kept my eye out for snakes and poachers alike.

At the overlook, we could see across the Blitzen River and the grassy fields and marshes on the other side that ran all the way to the lake.

"Blitzen, like the Christmas song?" Carla said.

"Its official name is Donner ünd Blitzen, but everyone calls it the Blitzen. It drains that mountain over there." I pointed to Steens. "It wasn't named for reindeer. Some cavalry soldiers of German origin were chasing the Paiute back in the 1860s and got caught in a thunder and lightning storm out in the open down there. They named it."

"*Donner* means thunder, *blitzen* lightning," she said.

"The weather around here can change in a heartbeat."

I handed her my binoculars. "Look, down there in the nearest field. Those gray birds."

She focused on them. "What are they?"

"Sandhill cranes."

"They're so big."

"They're flying down from Alaska, maybe even as far away as Siberia. Listen. You can hear them call."

Carla cocked her head. "It sounds like the Spanish *r* that rolls. *Arriba, arriba.*"

We returned to the pickup and continued south for a few more miles before turning off onto a gravel road. The fields on either side were table flat and the native bunchgrasses that grew on them were still laying down from last night's sleet storm.

"It's so beautiful," she said. "Raw and stark, yes, but desolate, no."

We arrived at a huge, round, wooden building. Carla viewed the conical roof the same way I did. "The hats," she said, reaching over and squeezing my arm. "The ones the rice farmers wore."

"I know," I said.

"What is this place?"

"It's called the Round Barn. Come on, we can take a look inside."

The outside was sheathed in vertical planks, but the inside was a circular wall made of rock. Juniper posts supported the roof.

"It wasn't used as a barn, but as a covered corral," I said. "They built it to train horses how to pull wagons during the winter. The high desert gets powerful winds and the snow can pile up in drifts while leaving other patches icy and bare."

"Is it from the 1800s too?"

"Yes," I answered.

"Who built it?"

"All the land around here was once part of a big ranch owned by Peter French and Hugh Glenn. It was the largest in Harney County for a while."

"Was?"

"The pair died and the land got sold off in bits and pieces."

"Did they die of old age?"

I hesitated. "They were both gunned down but under different circumstances. The times were pretty rough back then."

"They still are in many parts of the world," Carla said in a soft voice again. "Well, it's a beautiful building and a fitting monument to them. Where to next?"

"Frenchglen. You can guess how it got its name."

The town was even smaller than No Mountain. The two-lane was fronted by a handful of structures, the largest being a white clapboard two-story house with a wraparound porch. Its windows were shuttered.

"It's an old wayfarers inn," I said, "but it closes in fall and doesn't reopen until spring. Not much call for it in wintertime. I brought a thermos of coffee. Let's sit on the porch. No one is going to mind."

The only piece of furniture that hadn't been stored inside was the porch swing, and so we sat side by side. I poured the coffee and handed Carla a cup. I had wrapped leftover pieces of cornbread in a dish towel. I balanced the parcel on my lap and untied the corners.

Carla tried a piece. "Did you bake this?"

"Made, more like it. You mix it, turn on the oven, and try not to forget it's in there."

"I'm impressed," she said.

"It tastes that good?"

"I mean, with everything. Where you're living, your job, how you know all about the animals and the area's history. You've done it. You've turned it around for yourself."

I sipped some coffee. It was warm, not hot. "I'm still a junkie, Carla. The same as I was the day they hauled me into Walter Reed and locked the door. What did the head doctor tell me? Ten years. If I can go ten years without using, I can start to think of myself as cured."

"You're further along than most." Her tone was tinged with sadness. "Some will never be free, never be able to live on their own again."

"There's not a day that goes by that I don't think of the mistakes I made and the men I lost. And if a nickel bag was plopped in front of me, it wouldn't take much for me to go looking for a spoon and spike."

She squeezed my arm again. "As long as you keep saying that aloud and believing it, you'll make it. I know you will."

We finished the cornbread and coffee. "The loop road starts right across the highway. The weather looks like it's holding. The worse thing that can happen is we drive up a few miles and run into snow and have to turn around and go back to No Mountain the way we came."

"I'm game," she said.

The road was graveled, but not too much like a washboard. We crossed over the Blitzen River and then climbed quickly before reaching a plateau.

Carla pointed ahead. "Look, horses. Is this a ranch up here or are they wild?"

"Those are mustangs." I braked to a stop. "You can tell from their rough coats and markings. No clanging of horseshoes either. One of the refuges I work at is down on the Nevada line. The Sheldon. Several herds live there."

We watched them graze. The stallion noticed us. He made

me think of Wovoka. He whinnied and the herd began to move away.

"Do you ride?" Carla asked.

"I did for the first time the other day."

"Did you like it?"

"Yes. I've always ridden motorcycles—I have a Triumph—but a horse, well, there's something different about it."

"Because it's a living being," she said. "Horse and rider, two living things moving as one. You both have to trust each other."

I heard the echo of the types of things Carla used to say when I was going through the worst part of withdrawal, encouraging me to trust her and the doctors and, most importantly, trust myself.

"I suppose you're right," I said.

"I've never ridden before," she said.

"You should give it a try now that you're living in Oregon. The person who owns the horse I rode has two. I could ask her if she'd take you on a ride."

"Her? Who is she?"

"You'll meet her tonight. Wait, no you won't. She's working on the other side of the county. She's Pudge's daughter. A veterinarian. Her name is Gemma."

"Is she your girlfriend?"

"No, no," I said quickly. "We're acquaintances is all. Her father and I worked together last summer."

"Acquaintances? That sounds pretty formal. I say if you go horseback riding with someone, that makes you at least friends. You are working on making friends, aren't you Nick? Remember, what we talked about in group, letting people into your life again."

"Still the nurse, I see."

We were in luck. The road wasn't blocked by snow, and we followed it along the shoulder of the hulking fault-block mountain until we reached the highest point of the route. I aimed the truck at the overlook and turned off the engine. Instead of getting out, we sat there and viewed the great basin below. A brownish trio of shallow lakes—the Mud, Harney, and Malheur —resembled birthmarks while the dark ridgelines of exposed lava were the arteries and the blue-green Silvies and Blitzen Rivers the veins. The flatlands were an artist's palette. Silver dollops of sagebrush shimmered alongside splotches of yellow fields and white salt flats.

"What you said about me living in Oregon, I'm not going to," Carla said abruptly.

"Is Pete getting transferred already? Is that why he went to California?"

"No, I mean I'm not. I'm not going to marry him. I'm going back to Washington."

I let the news wash over me as if I were standing in the middle of the basin below when the wind was blowing gently, not hard. I was surprised, but not shocked.

"Have you told him?" I said.

"I'm waiting until he gets home." I didn't say anything. "Don't you want to know why?"

"Only if you want to tell me."

"I need to tell you because I need to hear myself say it out loud."

"Like me saying I'm a junkie. It makes it more real."

"Exactly." Carla took a deep breath. "I made a mistake. I don't love Pete. I can't."

"Is it because of the pilot you told me about, your first fiancé who was MIA?"

"Partly," she said. "His name was Sean Fitzpatrick. When we got engaged, we knew he'd be sent to Vietnam. He wanted to go. I was finishing nursing school. I enlisted in the Army Nurse

Corps and asked to be assigned there too, so Sean and I could be in the same part of the world together. Crazy, right?"

"No crazier than everything else going on these days."

"When Sean was shot down, I never gave up hope."

"I remember you saying that."

"I met Pete two weeks after Sean was declared KIA. I can't even remember what I did. Where I was. All I knew was I needed the hurt to stop. A girl on the rebound. It's like some kind of joke. A bad joke." Her laugh was one of pain.

I didn't know what to say.

"It wasn't until I got here after having not seen Pete for a while that I realized I'd made a mistake. He was, I don't know, different somehow. I saw a side of him that, well, I don't like very much. And I don't like his friends either. I realized I didn't love him. I couldn't love him." Carla exhaled loudly. "I guess I thought Pete was like Sean. I wanted him to be Sean. I was fooling myself."

All I could think of saying was don't blame yourself, and so I said it. "You didn't do anything wrong. It's no one's fault."

As I said the words, I could hear others telling me the same thing. The shrinks, the nurses, the other combat veterans in group. It was something I was never able to say to myself.

The sun started to drop behind the Cascades to the west and the light softened. "We should head back. It'll be dark within the hour."

"I didn't mean to put such a downer on the day," Carla said. "I've had a good time. Really. But I had to tell someone. It's been eating me up having to put on a face that isn't my own."

"You listened to me plenty back in the ward," I said. "I wish I could be more help."

We didn't say much on the drive back to No Mountain. I'd point out a hawk perched on a fence post, a family of deer grazing in a meadow alongside the road, the North Star—

Nagah—fixed and shining overhead at first twilight. It was nighttime when I pulled behind her rental car at the lineman's shack. I left the engine idling.

"You can follow me over to Pudge's and I'll introduce you," I said. "I'll bet November put some supper aside. She runs the place. Come on, it's not very far."

Carla reached for the door handle. "I'm sorry, but I don't want to go there. I don't know them, and I don't feel like talking with strangers right now. I'm going back to Klamath Falls. Okay?"

"I've made that drive at night. It's long and winding with black ice. Look, Burns is only a half hour away. It's got some motels. Come on, I'll show you the way."

Her shoulders slumped. "A motel sounds even more depressing."

It was unsettling to hear her so down. She'd always been the upbeat voice in the ward, cajoling, cheering, and sometimes scolding to keep us from sinking into the abyss of anger, self-pity, and blame. She could be tender when needed, strong enough to restrain a battle-hardened soldier bent on destruction, and always unflappable, even when finding a patient hanging from a noose made from a bedsheet. When Carla had told me how she would never give up on her missing pilot, it wasn't said in false hope or despair. She said it to let me and the other walking wounded know that our loved ones would never abandon us either.

I couldn't abandon her now. "Tell you what. You can have the bunk and I'll take the floor by the stove. Are you hungry? There's some leftover chili. Maybe some cornbread too."

Carla hesitated and then opened the truck's door. "It sounds like just what the doctor ordered."

17

I stoked the fire in the wood stove, reheated the leftover chili, and warmed the remaining pieces of cornbread. Carla kept her white down jacket on while we ate.

"Sorry, I don't have any wine to warm you up," I said. "Would you like some tea?"

"If it's all the same, I think I'll go straight to bed. I'm exhausted. I guess admitting that I'm really going to break it off with Pete has worn me out."

"The bathroom is behind that door in the corner. It's small, but there's enough room to change in there."

She took some things out of her suitcase and disappeared. I cleared the table and did the dishes. By the time I got my sleeping bag and rolled it out by the wood stove, Carla came out of the bathroom. She was wearing one of my flannel shirts.

"I hope you don't mind," she said. "It was hanging on the back of the door. The nightgown I brought is... Well, this is much warmer."

She got into the narrow bunk and pulled the blankets up to her neck. I turned off the light and slid into the sleeping bag. The fire in the wood stove hissed and crackled. It wasn't the first time I'd slept on the floor. Sometimes I'd wake from a nightmare and find myself under the bunk as if it were a tropical plant with leaves the size of elephant ears that I could hunker beneath while an enemy patrol marched past so close I could see their sandals.

"I haven't been honest with you," Carla said in the darkness.

"How's that?"

"When you asked about what song I played for myself, what I didn't tell you is I did see the men and not just their wounds. It got to me. The whole thing. It got to all of us, nurses and doctors alike, even if we wouldn't admit it to each other or ourselves."

Carla took a deep breath. "I found I was shutting down my feelings one by one. I couldn't smile or laugh, I couldn't even cry. It got to the point where I felt like I was watching myself play someone in a movie. I wasn't even there."

"I know what you mean," I said.

"I know you do," she said. "After Tet, the colonel in charge of the MASH recognized the signs of depression. He ordered me to take a break and rotate home. I could always come back, he said. I can still hear him telling me not to worry, that the war wasn't going anywhere any time soon."

"It'll have to end someday. Americans will never agree to fight a war that goes on without an end in sight. Even World War II only lasted six years."

Carla was quiet after that. I thought she'd fallen asleep. And then she said, "I volunteered to work in the ward at Walter Reed when I got stateside. I thought it could help me as much as I could help men like you who were suffering from combat fatigue."

"Did it?"

"I think so. What I learned most was how to help myself."

"You helped a lot of others too," I said.

"I'd like to think so."

She grew quiet again and this time I was sure she'd fallen asleep. My eyelids were growing heavy too, and I thought maybe I'd be able to drift off without playing the slide carousel of memories that usually started clicking whenever I laid down.

"I'm going back," Carla said.

"To the ward?"

"Not back to Walter Reed. Back to Vietnam."

I sat up. "You're joking."

I couldn't see her in the darkness, but I could tell she was laying on her side, her elbow cocked, her head propped on her fist as she faced me. "I can do more good there. One of the doctors at Walter Reed I worked with? You may remember him. Bald head. Wore reading glasses perched on his forehead. He's going back. He's setting up a special ward at a field hospital close to the front. He thinks if we can get to soldiers showing signs of fatigue more quickly we'll have a better chance of helping them."

Carla took another deep breath. "He told me they're seeing more combat fatigue than any other war. Of course, before Vietnam it was called shell shock and then battle fatigue. Who knows what they'll call it next. One out of ten, he says. One out of ten soldiers over there exhibit the signs. And that doesn't even count combat nurses and doctors. He says there are some studies going on that show it can come on weeks, even months, after soldiers come home."

"There are other nurses who can go. You've done your part."

"I'm going," she said, her voice growing firm. "I have to. It's the only place I can go now. Don't you understand?"

I did. There were plenty of times when I thought the only place I could function was back in-country, that being stateside was too discombobulating, that I couldn't relate to what ordinary people were saying and doing. It's why Harney County appealed to me. There was plenty of room to get lost and few people around that I had to worry about.

"When will you go?" I said.

"I already put in the papers. I'll ship out as soon as I get back. Well, after I see my sister first. She lives in Philadelphia. I'll go straight there. She's a nurse too, but not in the military."

"And after you tell Pete," I said.

"Yes, after I tell Pete."

We were quiet for a while. I lay back down.

"I'm scared," she finally said.

"Then don't go," I said to the ceiling.

"Scared about that, yes, I suppose I am, but scared about telling Pete. Scared of him and how he'll react."

"He'll get over it," I said.

"I don't know if he will. I suppose I think that way because I know what it's like for someone to leave you. Sean left me. I mean, I know he was killed, but I still feel I was abandoned. I've never really gotten over it."

"It's okay to be scared. Everyone gets scared one time or another."

"You don't seem like you scare easily."

"That's because I've faced the scariest thing there is."

"Death?"

"Myself."

Carla didn't say anything, and so I said, "Do me a favor. After you tell Pete and get to your sister's, call me and tell me how you are. Call me before you ship out for 'Nam, okay?"

"I promise," she said. "Thanks. You're a good friend."

I listened to her breathing grow heavy. The sound of it was lulling and I found myself drifting off. That night, for the first time in a long time, I didn't have any dreams.

~

MORNING LIGHT HAD ALREADY FOUND the kitchen window. I stood at the sink and poured a little cold water into a coffee pot that was filled with boiling water and a handful of grounds. It sunk the grounds. I poured a cup and drank it while looking out the window. It hadn't rained during the night and the sky was clear. Someone knocked on the front door. It opened by the time I turned around.

"Good, you're here. I was afraid I was going to miss you," Gemma said.

"Pudge told me you were out by Whitehorse Ranch," I said.

She cocked her head. "Why are you whispering?"

That's when Carla yawned from the narrow bunk and rubbed her eyes. "What time is it?"

Gemma looked at her, looked back at me, and then took a step back with her palms pushed out in front of her.

"The little car out front. I wondered whose it was. I should've knocked before opening the door. Wait a minute, I did knock." She took another step back.

"Hold on," I said. "Let me introduce you. Gemma, Carla. Carla, Gemma."

"The veterinarian with the horses," Carla said. "The deputy's daughter."

"The nurse," Gemma said. "The major's fiancée."

"Ex-fiancée," Carla said. "Or soon to be ex. See, Nick. I'm saying it aloud now."

Gemma dropped her hands. "Well, good for you." She turned to me. "And good for you too."

Carla cocked her head at me. "Just an acquaintance, huh?"

I was still standing with my back to the sink. "Who wants a cup of coffee?"

"I'd love one." Carla flipped back the blankets and swung her legs from the bunk.

Gemma took one look at my flannel shirt and rolled her eyes.

"So, did you want coffee too?" I asked her.

"Make it black," she said.

I poured two cups, handed her one, and placed the other on the rickety table while Carla got dressed.

"Why the rush back from Whitehorse? Your father told me you had some kind of epidemic on your hands."

"It was a false alarm. Feedlot bloat. Pudge called the ranch where I was working and told me he'd been trying to reach you, but you never picked up. Now I see why."

"We went for a drive down to Frenchglen and up the Steens Loop Road. Radio reception up there is always spotty."

Gemma muttered "Sure it is" into her coffee cup.

"What did Pudge want?"

"To give you a message when I got back." She sipped some coffee and made a face. "You didn't let the cold water sit long enough. I can taste grounds."

"What's the message?"

"Orville has what you were asking for." And then she all but mouthed the words so Carla couldn't hear. "The Air Force service records."

"I'll go to Burns and pick them up. Where's Pudge?"

"He left yesterday late afternoon to check out a tip about the rustlers. He isn't back yet, or he'd be the one standing here drinking your bad coffee and pretending not to notice the girl in your bunk."

"Pudge is probably staking out another airstrip."

Carla finished getting dressed and joined us. She added some milk and sugar to her coffee.

"Why aren't you going to marry the major?" Gemma asked.

"I don't love him," Carla said.

"That's a pretty good reason. I wish I'd known that before I got married. It would have saved everyone a whole lot of trouble."

"You were married?"

"For six months. His family owns the largest ranch in the county. We grew up together. We were childhood friends, got married, and then realized it was better when we were just friends. At least I realized it. Now we're friends again, or trying to be. I treat his livestock."

Carla tried the coffee. "I don't think Pete and I will ever be friends. He's not going to like what I'm about to tell him. He'll say it will hurt his career."

Gemma laughed. "My ex? He couldn't understand why I'd want to treat anybody else's cattle. He thought everything I'd ever need in life was right there at the Rocking H."

"I know what you mean," Carla said. "Kingsley Field is Pete's ranch and the fighter planes are his cows. It's like, how could I want anything else?"

Gemma turned to me. "She's all right. I like her."

18

Orville Nelson's office at the Harney County Sheriff's Department in Burns was the file room, his desk a folding table with a pyramid of Shasta Cola cans stacked on it. He'd placed the printouts of the service records of Dominic, Ramirez, and Pitzer in a single folder.

"I'm afraid there isn't much here," the FBI hopeful said as he handed it to me. "The captain's is the most extensive because of his flying record. Vincent Dominic trained in his home state, the Randolph Air Force Base near San Antonio, Texas. It's where he got his call sign. He served two tours in Vietnam. He was based at Tan Son Nhut Air Base. It's near Saigon."

"I know it," I said.

"Dominic racked up a very meritorious record. He shot down two MiGs and led a squadron on several missions, including air cover for bombers and ground troops. Following his second tour, he was reassigned to Elmendorf in Anchorage, and then McChord Field—that's near Tacoma—and now Kingsley Field."

"He sure doesn't stick in one place for very long. When did he arrive at Kingsley?"

"This summer."

"Was that before or after Hardiman became base commander?"

"After. And right after the member of the ground crew was run over."

"What about Pitzer?"

"He was also at Tan Son Nhut, same time as Dominic. He was ground crew. He started off as an airman, worked his way up to master sergeant, was demoted to airman first class, and then worked his way back up to technical sergeant. That's a pay grade above a regular sergeant but one beneath his original rank of master sergeant."

"Does it say what he did to get busted down?"

"Insubordination, striking an enlisted man, and unauthorized use of government property."

"That should've been enough to get him dishonorably discharged, not promoted. He must have friends in high places."

"He earned his promotion to technical sergeant at Kingsley," Orville said.

"From Hardiman?"

"Yes."

"Did he get here before or after the ground crewman's death?"

"Shortly before it."

"Was Pitzer with Dominic at any stateside bases before Kingsley?"

"Elmendorf. Then Pitzer came to Kingsley about the same time as Dominic went to McChord."

"And now they're back together. Okay, that leaves Ramirez. What do you have on him?"

Orville frowned. "He's the only one of the three who was married. Plus, he had a little boy. A one-year-old."

"Does his wife live in Klamath Falls?"

"No. Ramirez trained at Luke Air Force Base. That's near Phoenix. Lots of pilots from there went to Vietnam. The lieutenant was temporarily assigned to Kingsley to pick up some additional training hours in the F-101 Voodoo before heading overseas. His wife and son stayed home in Arizona."

"And his service record?"

"He earned high marks in the classroom and positive comments from his trainers about his judgement, reflexes, and skills behind the stick. He hadn't flown combat yet, so his record doesn't have any of those kinds of commendations."

"When I was in the hangar at Kingsley, I spoke to a civilian contractor name of Sallis. He said Ramirez got picked on by some of the other squad members because of his call sign. They did the matador thing on him. Sallis said it was because he was Latin."

"He's of Mexican descent, but his family has lived in Arizona a long time," Orville said.

"That's in his service record?"

"There's a mention about him being third generation military. His grandfather served in the First World War and his father in the Second."

"Anything about Ramirez being hazed when he was at Luke?" Orville shook his head. "What about while at Kingsley?"

"There's nothing in the report that mentions it."

"Has Pudge seen these?"

"I gave Deputy Warbler the highlights when I radioed him," Orville said. "He was on his way to Harney Valley. It has something to do with the rustlers. Does anything stand out?"

"Outside of Dominic and Pitzer knowing each other since 'Nam and Pitzer being a troublemaker, not really."

I thumbed through the folder hoping something Orville might have missed would jump out. Carla had mentioned how she didn't like the men in Hardiman's command. It wasn't as if she was unused to being around soldiers of all types under all conditions, whether it was in the pressure cooker of a MASH unit in-country or in a heartbreak hotel like a veterans hospital stateside. She'd seen all types, all personalities, and every emotional display possible.

I handed the folder back to Orville. "I need you to run down another serviceman's record."

He opened a can of Shasta Diet Cola and took a swig. "Of course, whose?"

"Major Hardiman's."

"That's going to take a lot more doing than the other men, given he is a senior officer and a base commander," Orville said.

"How did you obtain the others?"

He downed some more soda. "Part of my preparation for becoming an FBI agent is studying various information gathering techniques and putting them into practice. That includes developing relationships with confidential informants." He studied the can. "It's actually better if I don't tell you."

"I wouldn't want to jeopardize your shot at Quantico."

"What I'm doing will increase my chances of being accepted, but I need to protect my CIs. I wouldn't want them to lose their jobs."

"Then you'll do it?"

Orville finished the soft drink and set the can atop the rising pyramid of empties. "Of course. I have a question."

"Fire away."

"Do you know the origin of the major's call sign, Whistling Pete? Knowing where he received it could help start the ball rolling."

"He earned it in Vietnam. That's what he told me when we were over there. On bombing runs, he would dive straight down from behind the clouds and let his payload loose at the very last second before he had to pull up. His squadron mates could hear him whistling all the way down and keep on whistling as the bombs exploded and the flames licked the tail of his fighter jet."

"What song was it?"

"What else, the official US Air Force song. Off we go into the wild blue yonder. One other thing. When you get done with that, I'm trying to find someone who lives in Harney County with the initials A. J. He's not listed in the phone book."

"That should be easy. I can go next door and check the official records."

"Thanks. The next six-pack is on me."

"Make sure it's diet," Orville said. "One day they'll make a cola without caffeine. I wish it would be soon. I don't want to have the jitters when I take my FBI physical."

BLACKPOWDER SMITH'S was the most frequented establishment in No Mountain outside of the post office. The building was on Main Street, had a false front, and housed both a dry goods store and tavern. Its namesake and proprietor sported a billy-goat beard whose tip reached his sternum and a black cowboy hat with a rattlesnake band. He was manning the bar when I came in.

"The usual?" He sounded as if he'd gargled with lye.

"Make it a double," I said.

Blackpowder pushed across a tall glass of water, no ice. "You been keeping yourself scare these days. Working or playing?"

"The fall migration is a busy time of year on the refuges. I'm dealing with a poaching problem at Malheur."

"You're not the first. Everyone who had the job before you did too. They all said the same thing. The beat's too big for one game warden alone."

"Maybe someday that will change."

"Not unless Uncle Sam gets serious about protecting critters and puts more boots on the ground. Rules that look good on paper ain't enough if there's no one to enforce them. You can't put an invisible fence around a place and expect people who see dollar signs flying by instead of birds not to trespass."

"The man I'm after has taken butchery to a new level," I said. "He's built himself a weapon that can fire boxes of shells at a time. I don't have a name, only his initials. I figured if anybody knew or heard of him, it'd be you."

"And that'd be a fact. There's not a soul living in southern Harney County that hasn't been in here to buy groceries, a pair of jeans, or a beer at one time or another. What are they?"

"*A* is in Alpha, *J* is in Juliette."

"I hear you Lima Charlie," Blackpowder said, using slang for loud and clear from his navy days. "I'll see what I can find out. I take it you already asked my favorite chess opponent about this."

"I did, but Pudge didn't know who it might be either."

"Well then, that certainly puts a road apple in the pie. Between us, the only folks in Harney County Pudge and me don't know either died before our time or ain't been born yet. You sure this A. J. fella lives around here?"

"Yes, but maybe he's new to the county."

"It's possible, but then someone would've had to sell or rent him a place and they'd know about him."

"I'm trying to chase that down through public records."

"Of course, he could be living in his vehicle or a tent pitched somewhere or built himself a wickiup."

"I hope not. That leaves a lot of open country to search."

"You wait long enough the weather will flush him out. Once the wind really starts blowing and the mercury refuses to get up off the floor of the thermometer, he's likely to go looking for a warmer place to bunk. Like I said, I'll ask around if anybody's seen him."

"One other thing. He's killing birds by the hundreds. Any thoughts of where he might be selling them?"

"That's a lot of duck and goose dinners." Blackpowder stroked his beard. "There's a couple of butcher shops and restaurants in Burns that might take a few birds without asking too many questions, but not that many. He must be selling them to a wholesaler."

"He'd need a big freezer for storing them for that. It would rule out him living in a tent."

"Not necessarily. Game birds are hung after they're shot. Aging improves the flavor. He'd only need to meet up with his buyer every three days or so. No need for a freezer and no need for electricity either."

"He could also be selling the down feathers to a clothing manufacturer," I said.

"Or a pillow and quilt maker," he mused. "If he's killing as many as you say he is, that's a lot of plucking. Even the fastest pluckers take three minutes or so to clean a duck by hand, ten or more for a goose. Your poacher is keeping himself mighty busy."

"He's keeping me pretty busy too."

"When I ask around about your A. J., I'll see if anybody knows anything about a lot of duck dinners and feathers flying around. How's that sound?"

"That would be a help, thanks." I slid the empty glass toward him. "I'll see you, Blackpowder."

"Count on it," he said. "Hang on a second. Look what the cat dragged in."

Pudge Warbler was striding straight to the bar. He placed his Marlin rifle on top of it. "I need a whiskey," he said.

"Are you joshing me?" Blackpowder said.

"No, I am not."

"Aren't you still on the clock?"

"I'm half retired is what I am and that half is always off the clock and it wants a drink."

Blackpowder obliged. Pudge downed the shot in a single gulp. He wiped his lips with the back of his hand. He turned toward me. It was as if he hadn't seen me until now.

"Did Gemma give you the message to get ahold of Orville?"

"She did. I'm back from talking to him. They both told me you were chasing down a lead in Harney Valley."

"I was chasing more than a lead. I was chasing cattle thieves." He wiped his lips again.

"What happened?" Blackpowder and I said it at the same time.

"Got shot at is what. But I shot back. And I got one too."

"Shot dead?" Blackpowder said.

"Don't know for sure. The truck he was in got away."

"You want another whiskey?"

"No. I'm good now. I needed that one though. It's been a long day cleaning up the mess the rustlers left behind from last night." His face was awash with disgust.

"What else can I get you to wet your whistle, so you'll tell us what the hell happened?"

"I was doing what I get paid to do. What I don't get paid to do is let 'em get away. And that's what happened."

Blackpowder knew better than to push his old friend, and though I'd only known the deputy a little while, I knew better too. Sure enough, the old lawman told us when he was good and ready.

19

Pudge had gotten a call from a rancher on the other side of Tuhudda Will's camp. The rancher had seen a circle of headlights off in the distance the night before. In the morning he went out to take a look and found tire tracks and cow pies on an old dirt airstrip. He came to the same conclusion as Pudge and me and called it in.

Pudge added a new red dot to his map and drove out to investigate. On the way, he stopped by the Will camp to ask if anyone had seen anything unusual. Tuhudda Will told him that he'd had a vision during the night. The buffalo had come back to Harney County in the same numbers as when his father and his father's father used to hunt them. Pudge knew that Oregon's buffalo had all been killed off except for a small herd still holding on in the state's northeastern corner at the base of the Wallowa Mountains, but still he listened.

"I could hear their thunder as they ran across the valley," Tuhudda said in his slow but deliberate manner.

"It was probably a cattle stampede," Pudge said. "The rustlers I'm after could've been chasing them in their pickup trucks."

"No, it was *bagootsoo*," Tuhudda insisted. "I could smell their breath, feel their heat."

Pudge turned to Nagah. "Did you hear any buffalo?"

The young boy shook his head. "I sleep too hard, but I believe Grandfather. If he saw it in his dream, then it must have happened, if not here, then somewhere."

Against Pudge's better judgement, he agreed to Tuhudda's request to let him show him where the buffalo ran. The elder Paiute and his grandson joined him in the front seat and they drove away from the camp toward the eastern side of Harney Valley. They stopped off at the dirt airstrip where the rancher had seen the circle of lights. There were fresh tire tracks and cow droppings, but like the other strip, it was clean of any evidence dropped by rustlers.

"See," Pudge said to Tuhudda. "Cows, not buffalo. Come on, I'll run you back home."

Tuhudda folded his arms across his chest. "This is not where *bagootsoo* ran. That place is farther."

Pudge sighed and they got back in his truck and kept heading east. It was late in the afternoon when they crossed the Steens Highway and entered another section of the Burns Paiute Reservation. They crossed a narrow wooden bridge over Nine-mile Slough and drove until dark.

"We're gonna have to call it quits," Pudge told the Wills as he turned the truck around. "I'll take you back to your camp and maybe we can pick it up tomorrow or the next day."

It was a two-hour drive back. Halfway there, the front right tire went flat. It took some time to change it.

Finally, they were back on the road. Pudge was getting hungry. It was way past his suppertime and he knew November wouldn't spare her opinion about his lack of manners for not calling and telling her he'd be late.

Tuhudda hadn't spoken since they'd turned around. Pudge

figured he'd fallen asleep, but then the tribal elder sat up and said, "I hear them."

Pudge stifled a groan. "The buffalo?"

"No, not *bagootsoo*. A pickup truck pulling a stock trailer. It turned onto the road ahead of us. It is crossing Ninemile right now."

Pudge stepped on the brakes and rolled down his window. He could hear the beat of heavy wheels drumming on the wooden bridge over the slough.

"Son of a bitch," he muttered. If he'd been alone, he would've stepped on the gas already. "You two are gonna have to get out right here. I'm gonna go have a looksee. I'll come back and fetch you when I'm done. Here, I'll give you a flashlight and canteen."

Tuhudda Will crossed his arms again. "The boy and I go with you. They are stealing Paiute cattle also. Your fight is our fight. This is so."

Once again, Pudge ignored his better judgment. "Don't say I didn't give you the chance." He gunned the truck. From the corner of his eye, he was sure he saw the old Paiute smiling.

Taillights flashed on the other side of the wooden bridge. The pickup ahead was towing a livestock trailer and closing in on the Steens Highway intersection. Pudge wanted to stop it before it reached pavement.

He caught up to it and hit the lights and siren, but the rustlers sped up, the rear wheels of the trailer shooting up gravel that pinged off the front grill of the deputy's pickup.

"Son of a bitch," Pudge muttered again. "Hold on."

He steered off the gravel road and punched it. They tore through tumbleweeds and sagebrush as they gained ground on the rustlers. In seconds he and the Wills were right alongside the cab of the other truck. He barely glanced over, concentrating instead on the open field illuminated by both sets of headlights and looking out for gulches. He kept his foot on the gas. The truck pulling the stock trailer couldn't keep up. The old lawman passed it. When he was clear, he steered back onto the gravel road, raced ahead a few hundred feet, and then slammed on the brakes and spun the wheel. The deputy's pickup skidded sideways and came to a stop pointing back the way it had come.

"Now get the hell out before they ram us!" he shouted.

Tuhudda and Nagah jumped out. Pudge did too. He pulled the Marlin from the gun rack and used the door as a shield. The rustler's truck kept coming, its headlights aimed straight at them. Tuhudda and his grandson stood off to the side of the road. Neither appeared frightened.

The old lawman shouldered the Marlin and aimed at the front tires. Before he could fire, flame flashed from the passenger window of the oncoming truck. The echoes of shots fired from a semi-automatic followed. The rounds whistled overhead. Pudge pulled the trigger, levered the Marlin, and fired again. Glass exploded.

The rustler's pickup veered off the gravel road. As it roared past, Pudge saw a hole in the passenger side of the windshield and the stricken face of a man slumping next to the driver. Truck and trailer bounded over the rough terrain and then swerved back onto the gravel road and kept on going.

"Get in!" Pudge shouted.

The trio jumped back in the pickup. Pudge spun the wheel and chased after the rustlers. The truck and trailer had a few minutes head start. The lawman tried to close the gap when taillights flashed again.

"They're stopping," he said. "You better duck." Tuhudda and Nagah ignored him.

The horizon erupted in a ball of fire. Flames licked the night sky.

"What the Sam Hill?" Pudge said.

He slowed when the heat from the inferno warmed the cab of the pickup.

"Oh, Lord," he said as he breathed in the smell of gasoline and the stench of burning flesh. "They unhooked the trailer, tossed in a gas can, and lit the cows on fire."

The engulfed trailer rocked from side to side as the frantic beasts tried to escape. Their bellows and bleats went on and on. The flames were so intense they melted the aluminum sides of the trailer and its wheels. A couple of the burning cows finally busted loose. They ran across the darkened desert, their flaming hides resembling comets streaking across the sky.

As the sounds of the dying cattle started to fade, Tuhudda Will got out of the pickup and gathered a handful of sage. He walked toward the blaze and waved the sage in a circle and began to sing. Nagah joined him. Pudge radioed the sheriff's office in Burns to alert the hospital and clinics to be on the lookout for a gunshot victim as the plaintive sound of the Paiutes' death song mixed with the smoke and drifted across the sad, lonesome desert and into the night.

20

The icicles that had formed during the night began to drip from the eaves of the lineman's shack as the sun started its climb across a cloudless sky. It had been a couple of days since Carla had returned to Klamath Falls to tell Hardiman it was over. I assumed she had by now. I also assumed she had left immediately after doing so.

I was surprised she hadn't called to let me know she'd arrived in Philadelphia before shipping out like she had promised. I couldn't call her because I didn't have her sister's phone number. I didn't even know her name. All I had was the scrap of paper Hardiman had given me with his address when he invited me to dinner. I called the phone number on it, but no one answered.

I debated calling the main number at Kingsley Field and asking to be patched through to him. Carla had surely told Hardiman she'd visited me while he was in California. Chances were he wouldn't agree to speak with me, but I was willing to give it a shot.

I didn't get a chance. A horn started honking out front. I went outside to look. It was Pudge Warbler.

"Hop in," he said. "I got a line on your poacher's whereabouts."

"Is he there now?"

"Only one way to find out. Come on, grab your gun. Let's go."

We sped down the highway toward the Malheur Refuge but passed it and continued south.

"Did Orville come up with an address?" I asked.

"Blackpowder did," Pudge said. "He put the word out on his grapevine. News travels on it as fast as a facsimile machine. A sheep rancher down in Catlow Valley gave me a call early this morning. He didn't have your number."

"That's where the Wills graze their sheep."

Pudge nodded. "He said back around the first of October he was driving a trailer full of sheep up to Burns. It was morning and the coffee kicked in so he stopped on the side of the road to talk to a man about a horse. He was doing his business when all holy hell broke loose on the other side of the hill. He said it sounded like Vietnam had come to Harney Country."

"The timing is right. It must have been the poacher trying out his homemade Gatling gun with the new firing pin the gunsmith made him. Did the rancher see where he was living?"

"No, he decided to take a pass on getting any closer to all that flying lead. He zipped up and continued on his way. He'd all but forgotten about it until the grapevine reached him. Here we are."

Here was familiar. Pudge turned off the highway onto a gravel road that soon became dirt. I'd driven it plenty of times because it led to Hart Mountain National Antelope Refuge. The terrain was much dryer than the Malheur Refuge. Instead of a huge lake, marshes and rivers, there were miles and miles of sagebrush and old playas ringed by corrugated hills etched with gullies. The only water came in the form of seasonal alkali lakes or from thunderstorms that sent flash floods roaring down the gullies at the speed of lightning.

We reached a fork in the road marked by a rusty piece of sheet metal hanging from two posts. The sheet metal had a crescent moon cut out of the middle. It marked the entrance to a ranch.

"He's living at the Moon's old place?" I said.

"Got to be," Pudge said as he turned onto the lesser-used fork. "It's the only house out here within earshot of the road."

We proceeded slowly. Pudge readjusted his holstered .45 in case he needed to draw quickly. I hadn't put my Winchester in his gun rack, and now raised it from where I'd been holding it pointed at the floor.

"Looks quiet enough," Pudge said as he slowed to a stop a couple of hundred yards short of a ramshackle house no bigger than a single wide.

"There's an outbuilding around back. The poacher could have parked his truck and boat in it."

"Could have," Pudge said.

"I'll get out here and circle around. Maybe we can catch him in the middle."

"If he's poaching birds, he's probably poaching antelope and deer too. That takes something that shoots a helluva lot farther than a scattergun."

"I'll keep it in mind."

"Me too. I'll give you a few minutes to make your way around, and then I'll drive to the front. If your poacher is here, we'll find out if he's neighborly or a good shot."

I stayed low and moved fast. The fields surrounding the house were bone dry and long overgrazed. The only ground cover was a tumbleweed or two and scraggly patches of dried brittlebush. If shooting started, I'd be hiding behind grains of dirt.

I reached a broken-down corral behind the house without drawing fire. The outbuildings were in even worse shape, their wooden walls the color of ash from having baked in the hot sun over many summers and battered by cold winds during many winters. A rusty metal windmill atop an equally rusty water well derrick scratched like a record needle stuck in a groove. I moved toward the largest building. It had double barn doors that swung outward. The left one was slightly ajar.

Loud buzzing came from somewhere inside. It sounded as if the building was a giant beehive. I kept both hands on the rifle and toed the big door toward me. It creaked open and a fluttering whirlwind soon followed as a flock of barn swallows fifty or sixty strong poured out like smoke. When the last of the steel-blue-backed birds had passed, I looked inside.

Sunbeams shined through holes in the roof like spotlights illuminating a theater stage. Black mounds undulated on the floor. The buzzing and movement came from millions of flies swarming over piles of stinking duck and goose entrails. The barn swallows had been gorging on the insects. I stifled a gag, backed out, and closed the door.

Patience had never been Pudge's long suit. He'd gotten out of his truck and kicked in the front door to the house by the time I reached the back door. He was examining the top of a beat-up table with wobbly legs in the front room. It was the only stick of furniture in the place.

"Someone's been squatting in here, all right," the deputy said. "There's a trace of gunpowder on the table. I figure it was used for reloading shells. There's a stink of grease in the fireplace too. It was used for cooking."

"It's worse out back," I said. "He was using a building for butchering birds. It's a charnel house."

Pudge glanced at the stains on the floor made by chewing tobacco spit. "He's not housebroke, is he?"

"He won't be back here anytime soon." I explained how the poacher always left himself two escape routes at the Malheur.

"He's a beaver in the marsh, and on land he's a bobcat, always moving from den to den, never staying in one more than a night or two."

"That could be worth looking into, identifying other abandoned ranch houses and the like, especially now that it's getting pretty darn cold at night." Pudge hitched his belt. "I'll put it on the college boy's to-do list."

"Orville's map of dirt airstrips seems to have paid off. Any word on the rustler you shot?"

The old lawman scowled. "Not yet. His buddy doing the driving didn't drop him off at the Burns hospital, nor have any clinics or doctors in Harney County reported a man with a hole in his chest asking for help. I suppose they could've gone down to Lakeview or over to Klamath Falls, but we put the word out there too."

He paused. "Thing of it is, I hit him square with a .45-70. That slug packs a powerful wallop. He may have bled out by the time they hit the Steens Highway and his good buddy could've dumped him in a ditch somewhere."

"So much for honor among thieves," I said.

"Come on, I'll give you a ride back to your place. I got things to do before I go stake out another airstrip tonight."

We climbed into his truck and headed home to No Mountain.

"I asked Orville to do another search regarding the downed copilot," I said.

"He told me," Pudge said. "I'm not gonna say that you digging into the base commander's service record won't cause some heartburn when it comes back on us, and it will as certain as snow falls in Harney County every November."

We drove in silence for a few miles. The deputy finally said, "I'm sure you got your reason why you added the man whose life you saved in Vietnam to the list."

"I do."

"And I'm also sure you're gonna tell me why since it's the sheriff's department doing the searching and me in the Air Force's sights with that cease and desist letter. Now's as good a time as any, son."

I told him about Carla Donovan, our trip to Frenchglen, our conversation about how there was something about Hardiman, Dominic, and Pitzer that didn't sit well with her. I told Pudge she was breaking it off with him and going back to Vietnam.

"I got to ask if your suspicions about Hardiman don't stem from the fact that you want him to be a bad guy." He puffed his cheeks and then exhaled. "November told me your nurse friend didn't spend the night at our place like you said she was gonna. Where she spent it is your business, but looking to pin the blame on the major for the three dead airmen gets into mine."

"I'm not looking to pin anything on anybody," I said. "I'm only looking for the truth. There's something going on that doesn't sit right. You're right about one thing. Where Carla slept is none of your damn business."

"Now, now. Don't get all riled up."

"I'm not riled anything."

"Then the day when you are ought to be some show. I only hope I'm not on the receiving end." He chuckled.

We passed Malheur Lake. No Mountain came into view.

"Just so we're straight," Pudge said, "I agree that something doesn't seem jake at Kingsley Field. That copilot with the bull-horns painted on his helmet bought the farm after the other two did, and the major seems more interested in keeping us out of it than helping him. But any warm feelings he had for you went out the window once he learned his girlfriend spent the night at your place and then came straight home to deliver a Dear John to his face. No matter how many times you saved his life, he's gonna think the same thing as any man would."

Pudge pulled up to the lineman's shack. As I got out, he said, "One other thing before you go. It's real important to keep in mind."

"And what would that be?"

"Don't go and do something dumb to make the major and his boys even more pissed off. The Air Force has you outgunned six ways to Sunday."

21

I tried calling Carla at Hardiman's house again. There was still no answer. I called Orville Nelson next, but the young FBI hopeful didn't have anything new to report. Getting hold of the major's service record was proving to be as difficult as he had predicted.

The same feeling I used to get when a scouting team was late returning from patrol surged through me. I picked up the phone and dialed 113. When the directory assistance operator answered, I told her I needed a listing for a Donovan, no first name or initial, in Philadelphia.

"I'll need to connect you to the long-distance operator who will connect you to directory assistance in Pennsylvania," the operator said. "Hold, please."

There were a few clicks and then the line hissed as the Pennsylvania operator came on. She said she had listings for over seven hundred Donovans in Philadelphia.

I didn't even know if Carla's sister's last name was Donovan; maybe she was married. "How about hospitals? How many listings are there in Philadelphia?"

"Ten," she said.

"I'll take them all."

I jotted down the names and numbers. I pictured Carla Donovan. I could see the gold cross hanging on the thin gold chain around her neck. I circled the obvious Catholic hospitals and took them in alphabetical order.

I dialed zero and asked for the long-distance operator who placed the call for me. Holy Cross Hospital didn't have a Nurse Donovan. I repeated the long-distance call process again. Mercy Health said it couldn't divulge that sort of information. The third hospital was St. John's. The switchboard operator at the main number redirected my call to the nurse's station on the third floor. A voice with a faint Irish lilt answered.

"I'm trying to reach Nurse Donovan," I said. "It's important I speak to her. It's about her sister."

"Genevieve is with a patient right now. I can leave her a message."

I gave her my name and number, hung up, jotted down Genevieve Donovan next to the St. John's Hospital number and waited. Afternoon turned into evening. I stoked the fire, made tea, and brought out the book of Paiute legends to help pass the time. There were two stories left.

The second to last was a tale about Coyote. One time Coyote was thrown in jail. His cell overlooked a corral. A group of white men were trying to saddle a horse, but the horse wouldn't let them get near. Coyote called to them and said he could saddle the horse right away. They ignored him at first, but eventually let him out and escorted him to the corral.

Coyote had *puha* over horses. He got on and started riding it around, but then made the horse stop and not move no matter how hard he kicked. He told the men the horse wanted a fine saddle with saddle bags if it was going to move again. The men brought him one and Coyote put it on the horse, got back on, and rode around. But then he made it stop again.

The men asked what the horse wanted now. Coyote said a fine bridle and reins covered with silver, a pair of silver spurs, a new white hat, clothes, and a pair of pistols too. They got them and handed the fine goods to Coyote, who filled the saddle bags. He got back on the horse and started to ride. A group of soldiers were there blocking the gate. Coyote kicked the horse to make it look like it was running away with him and tore through the soldiers, out the gate, and galloped away.

Coyote knew the soldiers would come after him. He found a tree and strung all of his money from its branches, sat down, and waited. Pretty soon the soldiers came along. Coyote told them that the tree grew money every day. He said it took a full day for the money to ripen and the current crop was his, but he would trade them the tree for their pack mules, and then they would have tomorrow's crop and the next day's and every day thereafter. Coyote took a rock and knocked the tree and all the money fell down. The soldiers helped him put it in sacks, handed him their pack mules, and Coyote rode away.

A couple of nights later, the pack mules grew hungry and began to bray. Coyote hated the noise. He killed the mules to silence them. Afterward, he realized he had nothing to carry his money and goods. He went to the nearest house and bought a burro and went home.

Still greedy, he came up with another way to swindle people. He shoved his money up the burro's *kwedatse* and then rode to town. He found the richest white man there and told him every day when the burro would take a *kwedapu*, money would come out instead. Watch, he told the rich man. He kicked the burro in the stomach and out plopped the money. Coyote gathered it up. He told the man he would sell him the burro and all the money that came out the next day and the day after and everyday thereafter would be his. The rich man agreed and paid Coyote a lot of money for the burro.

Coyote went on his way, richer than ever, and ready to play another trick on someone who was even more greedy than him.

I AWOKE in the morning still sitting at the rickety kitchen table. The book was closed and shoved to the side. I never got to the last legend. I couldn't recall any dreams. I checked my field watch. It was already nine o'clock in Philadelphia. I called St. John's Hospital. The switchboard operator connected me to the third floor and the nurse with the Irish accent answered.

When I asked for Genevieve Donovan, she said, "Sure, love, she's right here."

"This is Genevieve," the next voice said.

I gave her my name and explained I was trying to reach Carla. "She told me she was going to see you before shipping out to Saigon."

"That's right, but she's not here. I went to pick her up at the airport, but she must have missed her flight or received new orders. It wouldn't be the first time she had a last-minute change of travel plans. She's an Army Corps nurse."

"What flight was she supposed to be on?"

"I don't have the flight number in front of me, but it was TWA to Philadelphia via Seattle. Wait a minute. Who are you, anyway?"

"A friend. I was at Walter Reed. Now I live in Oregon. It's a long story, but we ran into each other out here."

"Are you the reason why she broke it off with the major?"

"She told you about that?"

"Of course. We're sisters. Are you the reason?"

"No, I'm not. I wanted to tell her to stay safe while she's in 'Nam."

Genevieve sighed. "We all want that."

"Could Carla have gone to her apartment in DC instead of coming to see you?"

"I suppose, but she would've let me know. We have plans to go visit the cemetery here and put flowers on our parents' graves. We do it every year on the anniversary of their death. They died in a car wreck."

"I'd appreciate it if you had her give me a call as soon as you hear from her."

"I'll do that. And I have to say, you sure sound a lot nicer than the major. I bet you're better looking too."

I hung up and looked around the lineman's shack. The dishes were all clean. So was my laundry. The kindling box next to the stove was full. There was a cord of wood outside, but it was already split and neatly stacked. I could work on my Triumph. I could patch the canoe. But what I couldn't do was sit by the phone and wait. It was the same when I was in-country. The orders from the top were clear. Our mission was not to wait out the enemy in hope they'd give up. It was to go out and engage them, to search and destroy. The problem was, that's exactly what Ho Chi Minh wanted us to do.

I packed some gear, threw it into the truck, hooked up the boat trailer, and took off.

The fastest route to Klamath Falls was down through Wagontire and then west from Lakeview on Highway 140 past the ranching towns of Bly, Beatty, and Dairy. It took me through the Fremont National Forest, another legacy of Teddy Roosevelt's conservation-mindedness and named in honor of John C. Frémont, better known as "The Pathfinder." He'd led five expeditions to explore the far west, struck it rich in the California Gold Rush, and died penniless in New York City.

The only slowdowns on the two-lane were logging trucks hauling freshly felled ponderosa and lodgepole pines, but even though I was pulling a boat on a trailer, I lead footed around them every chance I could. I got into Klamath Falls by early afternoon and stopped at a gas station. While a pimply teenager handled the pump and windshield squeegee, I dropped a dime in the pay phone and tried Carla at Hardiman's again. After the eighth ring, I hung up.

No one answered the doorbell at the base commander's house atop the Klamath Hills either. I peered in the windows, but the spartanly decorated rooms looked no different than when I had dinner there. I drove back down the hill to the pink pumice guardhouse at the entrance to Kingsley Field.

The same two AP guards as last time were on duty. If they recognized my truck with the US Fish and Wildlife emblem on the door, they didn't acknowledge it.

"I'm here to see Major Hardiman," I said. "Tell him it's Nick Drake."

"Is the major expecting you?" the guard who'd handled the telephone duties before asked.

"No, but he'll see me."

"The major is a busy man."

"Tell him I'm here about Carla Donovan. Tell him I'm here about Lieutenant Ramirez. Or Captain Dominic, for that matter. Take your pick. What you don't want to do is not call him."

He picked up the phone and dialed. After a couple of minutes of talking and waiting and talking some more, he hung up.

"Leave your weapons here."

He nodded to the other guard who circled my truck and then stuck out his hand for the Winchester and shotgun. "It's not like you're a real cop," he smirked. I didn't mention the .357 in the glovebox again.

I left the boat trailer sticking out of the parking stall in front of the base's headquarters. Airman First Class Edwins jumped to attention when he heard my boots on the shiny waxed linoleum in the hallway.

"Sergeant Drake, sir," he said, saluting so hard it left a red mark on his forehead. "If I may, it is good to see you again, sir."

"At ease, Airman."

Before the young clerk could say another word, Hardiman yanked open his office door. "Get in here," he ordered. So much for you old son of a gun.

He slammed the door behind us and we stood jaw to jaw.

"You got some nerve showing up here," he said. "I ought to knock your block off. What the hell do you think you're doing?"

"Making good on a promise."

"And what would that be?"

"To look out for people who looked out for me."

"Is that what you call it? You and Carla were looking out for each other." He blew air out the sides of his mouth.

"Whatever you think happened, didn't. And whatever Carla told you about why she's breaking it off has nothing to do with me. Got that? Nothing. She came over to No Mountain because she needed someone to hear her say it. It could've been anybody, but it was me. And you know what? I'm honored she trusted me."

"I've heard enough bullshit to last a lifetime," Hardiman fumed. "Get out of here before I call the AP and have you dragged out."

"Not until you tell me where Carla is. I called your house. No answer. I dropped by. No one is there. That promise I made? It included making sure she got back home."

Hardiman made the blowing sound again. "She's probably already in her apartment by now. And as far as I'm concerned, good riddance."

"Back in Washington, not Philadelphia?"

"Philadelphia? Why would she go there?"

"To see her sister. She told me that's where she was going. I called her sister. Carla never showed."

"I don't know anything about that. She flew out the night before last. I got in from Travis and was expecting a welcome home cocktail and a I-sure-missed-you-honey kiss when I opened the front door. Instead, I get a thanks but no thanks, here's your ring back, and the equivalent of a swift kick in the nuts."

"She caught the evening northbound flight?"

"What?"

"Her sister told me she was connecting via Seattle."

"Carla didn't go to Seattle. She took a C-141 bound for Dover Air Force Base. If she's going to Philly, she can take a bus or the train from there. It's no more than a two-hour ride. See, that's the kind of man I am. Girl kicks me one and I still say, yes, ma'am, can I have another one, ma'am, here's a free seat on a plane I arranged for you." He blew out both sides of his mouth again.

"What time did the Starlifter take off?"

"Sometime after midnight, I guess."

"You guess?"

"That's when it was due in. It's not like I stayed around the hangar waiting to see Carla off. There wasn't going to be any tears or goodbye kiss. I gave her a lift down to the field, she said adios and told me not to wait. You know what? I didn't. If that makes me not a gentleman, then so be it. I'm still an officer."

"Did Carla tell you she's going back to Vietnam?"

"She did. Why the hell would she want to do that? I could've given her the brass ring. A major's wife, someday a colonel's, maybe even a general's. The world was her oyster. She could've had it all. The big house on the hill at any air base, postings in foreign countries, and all the Georgetown society she'd ever want when I took a job at the Pentagon." Hardiman shook his head.

I turned to go and then stopped. "Why didn't you tell me Dominic was flying the jet Ramirez punched out of? And why did you authorize him to investigate his own accident? No way that's Air Force SOP."

"What do you know about our standard operating procedures?"

"I was in the US Army. There's a manual for everything and demerits if you don't follow the rules to the letter."

Hardiman slapped his chest. "This is my base. I'm the commanding officer. I get to make the rules. I'm not going to tell you anything about what orders I give or why. You got that, civilian?"

"Ramirez wound up in my lake. The canopy off that fighter your men were so anxious to retrieve landed in my refuge. I'm going to do whatever it takes to find out what happened and why. Those are my rules. You got that, Major?"

22

I checked into a different motel this time. It was close to downtown and the neon sign advertised refurbished rooms. The man working the check-in counter wore a red headband like Tuhudda Will, only his hair was black, not white.

"How long do you need the room?" he asked as he pushed the register toward me.

"It depends. Is that going to be a problem?"

"Not if your money's good and you keep your TV turned down after ten and use an ashtray when you smoke in bed."

"I'm pulling a boat. Is there room to park it?"

"We got space around back." He glanced at my rig out front and noted the door emblem. "You work for Fish and Wildlife?"

"I do."

"You going to try to pay with a government voucher?"

"Cash. I'm here on personal business."

"Good. I don't take government vouchers."

"Why not?"

"It's not my government. I belong to the Klamath Nation."

"I'd heard the Klamath sold their reservation."

"We didn't sell nothing. They stole it. Congress passed a law fifteen years ago to wipe us out. You don't believe me? Look at the name of the law. The Klamath Termination Act." He all but spit out the words. "They wanted our land because of the timber on it. Now we have a motel where once we had two million acres."

"I am sorry," I said in Paiute.

"You speak *numu*?"

"A little."

"The Klamath tongue is different. Only the Modoc, Yahooskin, and us speak it. Where do you live?"

"No Mountain. It's over in Harney County."

"I've heard of it."

"By the way, my name is Nick Drake."

"Gordon Loq." He spelled it. "And, no, it's not Chinese. *Loq* is Klamath for what you white people call grizzly bear."

"And Gordon?"

He shrugged. "My parents named me Elijah, but I gave Gordon to myself on account I like this singer, Gordon Lightfoot. I don't know what tribe he belongs to, he's from Canada, but he's got a good, strong voice. He wrote this song, 'Early Morning Rain.' You know it?"

I told him I did. It was a favorite in 'Nam, another after battle come down tune. Peter, Paul and Mary sang it, and that made me think of Carla. "Both Sides Now," her favorite Joni Mitchell song, started playing in my head.

"Here's your key. Room twelve is on the end. You look like the type who comes and goes."

"Thanks. Can I dial long distance on the in-room phone?"

"You got to go through the operator. You can either call collect or charge it to some other number. If you make one up, make sure it's not mine." His stare remained steady and then he cracked a smile.

I backed the boat trailer into a stall, unhitched it, and went to look at the room. It was an improvement over the last motel. The heater fan didn't click and the mattress was firm. I didn't stay long enough to give it a try. I dropped my duffle bag next to the dresser and got back in the truck.

It was closing in on five thirty when I parked on the side of the road leading to the guardhouse at Kingsley Field. The sun set. Several wavering Vs of ducks and geese were silhouetted against the purpling sky. The flocks had passed on overnighting on Upper Klamath Lake and were pressing on to reach the smaller Lower Klamath Lake twenty miles south and just over the state line.

At straight up six o'clock, cars and pickups started streaming toward me. There were no barracks on base. Everyone lived in town. Finally, the car I'd been waiting for passed by the guardhouse and headed my direction. It was an older Chevy with Kansas plates that had been parked in front of the headquarters both times I'd visited.

I made a U-turn and followed. Rust from road salt had eaten holes into the bottom edges of the Chevy's doors and fenders. The driver obeyed the speed limit and traffic signals. He turned onto a side street and parked in front of a modest fourplex. I pulled alongside as he was getting out of the car.

"Is that you, Edwins?" I said.

Astonishment crossed the young airman's face, and then he snapped a salute. "Sir, yes, sir. What a pleasant surprise, Sergeant Drake."

"It is. Do you live here?"

"Yes, sir. In apartment D."

"Do you have a view?"

"Not to speak of, sir. It is a studio."

"Good man, watching your pennies on an airman's salary."

"Are you on your way home, sir?"

"No. The refuge on the upper lake is part of my district. I'll be here a couple of days. I'm heading to dinner. I know a place that serves the best steak in town. Care to join me? My treat."

"Really, sir?"

"Really."

"If you are sure it is not an imposition, sir."

"Other way around, Edwins. I'd enjoy the company."

"Thank you, sir. It would be my pleasure to dine with you."

THE WAITRESS TOOK OUR ORDERS. We both got steaks, his well-done, mine rare. Edwins asked for a Bubble Up and I an iced tea.

"I remember you telling me you grew up next to McConnell Air Force Base," I said. "Do you miss Kansas? And, drop the sirs."

"Yes, sir, if you insist. My folks still live in Wichita and I think of them often, but they tell me they are proud of me."

"Did you want to be based at McConnell after basic?"

"No, I wanted to see the world and am willing to go wherever the Air Force needs me, though I am hoping for Vietnam. I want to be at the base closest to the action."

"They all are. South Vietnam is a small country. About the size of Florida."

"Really? I thought it was bigger."

"Not big enough when the shooting starts." I asked him how long he'd been serving as Hardiman's adjutant.

"Since the major got here. He promoted me to be his assistant. Before that I clerked for the previous commander."

"Most adjutants are of higher rank. You must be very good at your job."

"That is very kind of you, sir."

The waitress brought our meals. His eyes widened at the sight of the steak. "This sure beats SpaghettiOs."

"Stick with being an adjutant and there'll probably be a lot of steaks in your future. Higher rank, higher pay, right?"

"Yes, but while I am grateful for the opportunity, what I really want to do is logistics. It is what I trained for. I know it is not as glamorous as a fighter pilot, but an army is only as good as its supply chain. Did you know Grant was a supply clerk before he became a general? His skill at managing logistics is credited for winning the Civil War."

" 'The line between disorder and order lies in logistics,' " I said.

"That is well put, sir."

"It's a quote from Sun Tzu."

"Who is he?"

"A Chinese general who lived around 500 BC. He wrote a book called the *Art of War*."

"I wonder if I can get it at the base's library?"

"I have a copy I'd be happy to lend you."

"Really? I mean, if it is no imposition, of course."

"None at all. So, logistics. Does that mean you keep track of all the military aircraft that come and go at Kingsley?"

"Yes. I prepare the major's weekly sitreps."

"That must keep you pretty busy. Is there a lot of air traffic?"

The young airman nodded as he chewed his steak and washed it down with Bubble Up. "Most of it is from the training flights. Cargo traffic is less frequent because Kingsley is an alternative West Coast refueling site. Flights from Vietnam take the great circle route, refueling at Elmendorf in Alaska and then continue on to McChord in Washington or Travis in California. We are used when inbound aircraft get rerouted because of weather or if the runways at the other bases are over capacity."

"I imagine all of those have to file manifests. That's a lot of paperwork to keep track of. Is that part of your job too?"

He finished swallowing a forkful of potato. "Operations gives them to me and I file them and then transmit a copy to Military Airlift Command at Scott Air Force Base. That is in Illinois. MAJCOM oversees all airlift activities for the war. If I do not get transferred to Vietnam, I hope to go to Scott."

I leaned forward. "Speaking of manifests, I wonder if you could help me with something. It's of a personal nature."

"What is it?"

"It has to do with Miss Donovan."

"You know her?"

"It's a long story, but yes. I knew her from when I was a patient at Walter Reed."

"She is very nice and very kind."

"She is. Imagine my surprise when Major Hardiman had me over to his place for dinner and there she was. Did you know she flew home?"

"The major informed me when I arrived at work and asked if he needed me to drive her on errands. He said she took a C-141."

"And she would've been added to the manifest, right?"

"Of course. The pilots have to log any changes in weight when they refuel. Why do you ask?"

"That's where I need your help. The night I had dinner at the major's, Carla and I got to talking about old times. She mentioned another nurse who worked at Walter Reed. Carla said I should call her. She was going to get me her phone number when she got home. I haven't heard from her. Would the manifest show if the Starlifter was direct to Dover or made a stop at another base and Carla had to catch a connecting flight?"

"Well, it would show if the flight was direct or not."

"Could you check and see?"

"Check the manifest for you?" Edwin's face reddened. "That is most irregular, sir."

"I know, but I thought I'd ask. If you can't, you can't." I let it sit and then said, "It's just that Carla made this other nurse sound pretty special."

The young airman mulled it over. "She must be for you to be in such a hurry to talk to her. I suppose I could take a look in the morning and let you know."

"That would be a great help. Thanks." I gave him the phone number to the motel.

Edwins looked down at his plate and lowered his voice. "You know, that flight she took was probably carrying fallen soldiers. Most of the planes traveling from Vietnam to Dover are."

"They're coming from Tan Son Nhut?"

"You know of it?"

"Every soldier serving in Vietnam does."

It was the base near Saigon tasked with preparing and shipping home the dead. The fallen who hailed from states west of the Mississippi were taken to Travis Air Force Base where they were offloaded and transported to their home towns. KIAs from states east of the Mississippi went to Dover Air Force Base.

"I'd never known anyone killed until I joined the Air Force," Edwins said. "I mean, my grandpa died, but that was from old age." He studied his plate again. "Now, I know three people. I suppose once my orders come through for Vietnam, I will know even more."

"You knew the ground crewman who was killed in the Starlifter accident?"

"You heard about that?"

"I read it in the newspaper. It said he hit his head."

Edwins frowned. "I feel sorry for his family. He did not even get to Vietnam. It is one thing to die in a war zone, but here?" His frowned deepened.

"The same thing with Lieutenant Ramirez," I said. "His poor wife and little boy. Did you know him too?"

"Not as well. He was only here a short time and admin staff and pilots do not mix very often."

"Does that include the trainers?"

"They are usually stationed here longer and consider themselves staff. There are more opportunities to get to know them because of all-staff meetings and helping them file their reports."

"Does that include Captain Kane?"

"Yes. Everyone knew him. He was one of those larger-than-life types. Every morning rain or shine, he would be out on the tarmac leading calisthenics. He was always challenging the younger pilots to a foot race up and down the length of the runway. They would bet money on it and he beat them every time. On New Year's, the captain held a Polar Bear Swim in the lake. He bet them on that too. The men would jump in and swim out a hundred yards and back. He always came in first."

"Did he really look and act like Elvis Presley?"

"In certain ways. He drove a really sharp car. A red convertible Corvette Stingray. On weekends he would drive down to Reno. When he showed back up for work on Monday, he would have the top down and a blonde sitting next to him. Vroom, Vroom, Va-va-voom. It was what he always said."

We finished eating and pushed our plates away. Edwins said, "The captain had a real sharp plane too."

"The Sabre. I saw it in the hangar."

"I mean his personal plane. It is a P-51 Mustang that was flown in World War II. He restored it. Have you ever seen one? It is the Corvette Stingray of single propeller fighter planes. He would buzz the field at full speed and waggle the wings. It was his Elvis Presley hip shaking move."

"Did he keep it at the base?"

"No, that goes against regulations. He kept it at one of the private hangars on the other side of the commercial terminal."

The waitress asked if we wanted anything else. Edwins passed on dessert and so did I. "Just the check," I said and fished some bills from my wallet.

"Thank you for dinner," the young airman said.

"Anytime. I enjoyed the company and conversation. Come on, I'll drop you off."

We drove to his apartment building. As he was getting out, Edwins said, "I will check that manifest in the morning and call you. But, well, sir, it would be a whole lot better if we kept this between ourselves."

"Roger that," I said. I snapped him a crisp salute. "Good night, Airman."

23

I spent a fitful night worrying about Carla. I wished I'd brought the book of Paiute legends to help pass the time. There was still one left to read. As soon as it was light, I called Genevieve Donovan at work, but she hadn't heard from her sister. I no sooner hung up when the phone rang. It was Edwins.

"I am looking at a copy of the manifest," the young airman said. "It does not list Miss Donovan or any outbound passenger, for that matter."

"That doesn't make sense," I said.

"While it is certainly unusual, it does happen, especially when a flight is running behind schedule. The C-141 did not touch down until 0200. The pilots either forgot to list her or figured her weight would not matter and it was not worth the extra paperwork. They are always in a hurry during turnaround."

"Was it direct to Dover?"

"Yes, the original flight plan says it was nonstop."

"Thanks," I said. "I'm sure I'll hear from her soon."

I wasn't sure at all. Far from it. My radar was pinging Lima

Charlie.

I didn't bother with breakfast but drove straight to the commercial terminal at Kingsley Field. Its size reflected the four flights a day it handled. There was only one check-in counter in the cramped lobby. The adjacent waiting area had no more than two dozen plastic seats.

The Air West reservation agent wore a bright yellow uniform and matching hat pinned to her beehive hairdo. I told her my sister had been booked on the evening northbound flight with a connection to Philadelphia. I gave her the date.

"Our sister who lives in Philadelphia said she never arrived. Could you check the ticketing?"

"What is the passenger's name?" I spelled it for her. Her lacquered fingernails clicked as she typed it into her SABRE terminal. "Hold on, it's processing." Nearly a minute passed. "Here she is. Hmm. It says the ticket was never used, changed, or refunded. Oh well, at least your sister hasn't lost anything. The ticket is as good as money. She has a year to use it or exchange it without a penalty."

"Can you tell me when she bought it?"

"Let me see. Yes, here it is. She purchased it that morning."

By the time she looked up, I was already halfway to the door.

Maybe Carla planned to exchange the ticket after Hardiman offered her free passage, but that still didn't explain why she hadn't called Genevieve to tell her of the change in plans or where she was. I left the passenger terminal, intent on skirting the tarmac and marching straight to Hardiman's office and demand he call someone at Dover to confirm she'd arrived there. I walked past an open bay. A small tractor hooked to a luggage cart was parked inside a hangar-like building. The grease monkey, Sallis, was loading suitcases onto the cart.

"Got a second?" I said.

He didn't look over. "If your bag didn't get off the plane,

check with the girl inside."

"It's not about luggage."

"What then?" He straightened and looked at me. He was holding a red Samsonite by its handle.

"Nick Drake," I said. "We talked a few days ago about the F-101 with the missing canopy."

Recognition crossed his face. "Right. You're the fish and duck guy. Is that what happened, a big bird hit it?"

"Still to be determined. I wanted to ask you about something else. When you're ground crewing next door, does that include helping turn around the C-141s when they stop to refuel."

Sallis swung the Samsonite onto the luggage cart. "As often as I can. They pay me time and a half because those planes land during graveyard shift. I'm happy to give up some shut-eye for the extra dough."

I told him about the one that came in at two a.m. "Did you work that one?"

Sallis picked up another suitcase and threw it onto the cart. "Let me think. Yeah, I did. It was the usual gas it and pass it." He snorted.

"A friend of Major Hardiman's was getting a ride on it. Did you see her board?"

He stopped picking up luggage. "Why ask me?"

"Because I am."

"Well, if she's the major's girlfriend, and I'm guessing that's what she is, how is that your concern?"

"Did you or didn't you?"

"Look, pal. I don't want to get between anything here. Especially something going on between you and the major and the nurse. You understand? I don't want to lose my job, much less get shot at by a jealous boyfriend."

I took a couple of steps toward him. "I didn't say she was a nurse."

Sallis glanced over both shoulders. "Okay, I saw her. She was sitting in a little room they got in the hangar for people in transit who want to get off and use a real john and sit in a real chair while the plane's being refueled."

"Did you talk to her?"

"No. I saw her sitting there is all."

"Then how did you know she was a nurse?"

"The uniform. It's got that winged double snake emblem on it."

"Did you see her get on board before the Starlifter took off?"

"No. I was busy with refueling and conducting a visual on the landing gear. She could've gotten on and off two or three times and I wouldn't've noticed. I got to get back to work. Somebody's bag doesn't get on board, I'm the one they blame."

"Want me to give you a hand?"

"That's okay. I'm good."

"You sure?"

"I'm sure." He glanced around again. "I wouldn't want to give anybody any reason to fire me, but you want to know if she got on that plane? Ask Captain Voodoo or Doberman. They were there. And you didn't hear that from me."

"Understood. Are those the private hangars over there?" I pointed to a row of buildings with small planes parked on either side.

He nodded. "Yeah, why?"

"No reason."

I walked over to them. The hangars had roller doors. Most were pulled shut and padlocked. One in the middle was open. I stuck my head in. The engine cowl was up on a yellow Piper Cub and a gray-haired man was applying a torque wrench to the motor.

"What year is she?" I asked.

"Thirty-seven. First year they made the J-3." He pointed the torque wrench at me. "You a fellow Cubbie?"

"Just appreciate vintage airplanes.

"She's a sweetheart. I been flying her since day one. Why I pay to keep her in a house better than my own." He chuckled.

"I heard there are a few vintage planes here. Is there a club or something?"

"Where you from?"

"Harney County."

"Lot of pilots over there too. No, we don't got a club, unless you count a few of us old-timers getting together on Saturday nights and hoisting a few while swapping tall tales."

"I heard there is a P-51 Mustang here. I'd love to see that."

"That's a spitfire of a plane, all right, but you're going to be heartbroken because it's no longer here."

"What happened to it?"

"It got stolen is what happened. That Mustang was the most valuable old plane here. Why you see all those fancy new padlocks on all the hangar doors. Was a time no one locked anything here, not even the cockpit doors to the planes parked outside."

"When did it go missing?"

"It was a while back. I'd say a month or two after the owner died."

"They never found it?"

"No, and it's a shame too. I used to love watching it buzz the field. That pilot had style."

I HAD A NEED FOR SPEED. To take it full throttle and let it rip. That's what I did when my head was aching with too much information, too few answers, and my adrenaline was working overtime.

If I were back home, I'd take my Triumph out and push the 650cc engine right up to the redline. I'd crouch down low and watch the horizon race straight at me. I wouldn't let off until it ran out of gas. But I wasn't there and my bike was still in need of repair. I thought of the three-year-old colt Wovoka and how fast he could take me flying across the desert. But he was in No Mountain too.

I retrieved my boat trailer from the motel parking lot and towed it down to the launch at the south end of Upper Klamath Lake. I pointed the skiff north and twisted the throttle as far around as it could go. One hundred horses under the lid of the outboard started galloping and I thanked the clerk in Burns who'd talked me into the bigger motor. The lake was smooth as glass and the skiff got up on plane and I flew across the water for thirty miles.

I reached the north end and finally eased back on the throttle. My face felt raw from the wind and cold late autumn air. Frogs croaked from the marshes and a lone wood thrush was calling from somewhere unseen, its two-note trill a continuous *help meee, help meee, help meee*.

I had survived skirmishes, firefights, and full-out battles in Vietnam because I trusted two things: my gut and the men who bore arms beside me. My squad was dead, but I still had my gut and it was telling me danger lay ahead, something was wrong, somebody needed help, somebody I cared for. I had tracked too many lost soldiers and pilots, bands of guerrillas, and platoons of NVA regulars not to recognize the signs. Something had happened to Carla and someone was lying to me about it. I needed to find out who so I could find her.

I made a slow, sweeping turn until the skiff was pointed south and then twisted the throttle wide-open and sped back to Klamath Falls as day turned to dusk and dusk to evening.

24

Town seemed unusually quiet as I drove to the motel. The streets were nearly empty and the storefronts locked for the night. I slowed to make the right-hand turn into the alley that led around to the parking lot. As I tapped the brakes and hit the turn signal, the flashing red that filled my rearview mirror wasn't coming from my taillights. I told myself it wasn't me the cop was pulling over. I made the turn and drove into the lot. The patrol car followed right behind and stopped alongside the boat trailer. I got out to see what was up.

It was neither a city cop car nor a county sheriff's vehicle. Both doors of a gray Air Force Police sedan swung open and two men got out. They were wearing dark blue berets with AP flashes and black leather holsters on their hips. The driver aimed a powerful flashlight at my face.

"Hands where we can see them," he said.

"Those would be the ones shielding my eyes from your light. Do you mind?" I said.

"Keep your hands up." The driver lowered the beam to my chest.

"Do you want to tell me what this is about, or should I guess?" I lowered my hands. He didn't shoot me for disobeying.

"Are you Nick Drake?"

"You know I am. I don't know your names because Captain Dominic didn't introduce you when you came to retrieve Lieutenant Ramirez's body."

The pair exchanged glances. The driver said, "You need to come with us."

"What for?"

"You'll find out."

"I don't think so. It's late. I'm tired. I'm going to bed."

"It's not a request," he said. "It's an order."

"Whose?"

"That doesn't concern you."

"Sure it does. Whose order, Major Hardiman's?"

"I'm not at liberty to say. Now, get in the car."

"I'm not in the military and this isn't a military base. That makes your orders worth less than zero. If someone wants to talk to me, it can wait until morning. I'll be right here."

"You can either get in the vehicle voluntarily or we'll assist you." He stressed the word assist.

"Tell Whistling Pete to try a different tune. Good night."

The driver kept the flashlight pointed at my chest while he moved his right hand toward his holster. He unsnapped the trigger guard strap. His partner yanked his pistol out at the sound of the snap and pointed it at me.

"I'm not going to ask you again," the driver said. "Get in the vehicle."

"Is there a problem here?" Gordon Loq stepped out of the shadows. He was holding a flat, carved piece of wood the size of a rifle stock, only it had no barrel. He gripped it at the narrow end. Embedded in the wider end was a sharpened piece of obsidian set between a row of bear's teeth.

"This is an Air Force matter," the driver said. "Move along."

"Whose air force?" the Klamath asked.

"Whose do you think, Chief?" the driver's partner spat. "Now move it or we'll arrest you too."

"This is Klamath Nation land. You got a passport?"

"A what?"

Gordon started walking toward us. The driver's partner swung his pistol from me to him. "Stop where you are. If you lift that war club, I'll shoot."

"You better have a lot of bullets because I'm not alone." The Klamath whooped. If Ghost Dancer spirits were with him, I could not see them. If his red and black checked wool jacket was a Ghost Shirt, I did not want to see if it stopped bullets.

"Stand down," I said to the AP cops. I turned to Gordon. "It's okay. They're only following orders. It's a personal matter. I'll explain when I get back."

"You sure?" the Klamath said.

"I am." I nodded at the AP driver. "Shall we?"

They didn't handcuff me, but they did pat me down. The .357 was still in my pickup. I got in the back seat. Gordon Loq watched as we drove out of the lot. The driver steered south from downtown. I figured we were going to Kingsley Field or Hardiman's house in the Klamath Hills, but we didn't go to either. The driver cut across town on an unlit street that dead-ended beside a darkened millpond. Another car with its lights off was already parked there.

"Get out," the driver said.

As soon as I closed the door, the driver backed up, executed a one-eighty, and sped off. The dome light in the parked car turned on as the driver opened his door.

"Hello, Voodoo," I said. "Where's your pet Doberman?"

Dominic walked up to me, leaving no more than an arm's length between us. "You don't listen so good," he said, his slight

Texan drawl twanging. "Is there something wrong with your hearing or did you really scramble your brains in Vietnam?"

"I hear fine. And that's a wonder after being in the field for three years alongside artillery firing off night and day and B-52s dropping five hundred pounders."

"I don't get your attitude. We're at war."

"How could I forget? I was there."

Dominic jabbed his finger at me. "You've been told to stop prying into Air Force affairs, yet here you are back again asking questions, making assumptions, and generally being a major pain in the ass."

"You mean a pain in the major's ass."

"That's right, and mine too. Major Hardiman has shown you every courtesy. He has good cause to have you arrested and brought up on charges. The only reason he hasn't is because he's trying to give you a break. No doubt he feels he owes you because of what you did for him in Vietnam, or maybe he's doing it out of respect for Miss Donovan."

He made a face that looked like he'd drunk something sour. "Me? I don't owe you shit. I could strap you in a F-101 and have you at the front gate of Leavenworth Prison within three hours. I'll walk you to your cell and make sure they throw away the key."

"You could try."

"You are interfering with something you have absolutely no comprehension of."

"You're right. Elvis Kane? The ground crewman? Toro Ramirez? I don't understand why they were murdered."

Dominic's mouth grew tighter with each name, but when I said murdered, it fell open. "You don't know what you're talking about," he hissed.

"Tell me I'm wrong."

"Why are you persisting with this?"

"I already told Hardiman. It's because Ramirez fell in my lake. That makes him my responsibility."

"No, it does not!" he shouted. "He is my responsibility and mine alone. I'm the squadron leader. I was flying that plane."

"Finally," I said. "Some truth."

I looked at the millpond. The whine of giant saw blades operating in the mill on the other side echoed. Half-submerged logs stripped of branches floated silently in the dark water waiting their doom. Their shapes reminded me of the bodies of black-clad villagers I'd once seen floating down the Mekong River. The Vietcong had accused them of being anti-communists and sympathizers of the Van Thieu regime. Men, women, and children were shot and hurled into the river as a lesson to other villagers. I wondered if they floated all the way through the twisting, swampy Mekong Delta, or as locals called it the Nine Dragon Delta, and out into the South China Sea.

I thought about the Freedom Bird I had flown home on. It followed the great circle route with a refueling stop at Elmendorf before dropping me off at McChord to catch a commercial flight back to the real world, a world that I was unprepared for and could only handle by increasing my daily use of heroin that was so easily scored in the back alleys of Saigon.

As I stared at the dark and gloomy millpond, things began to come into focus. I wondered how fast I could reach it and dive in and hide among the logs should Dominic pull out his sidearm and start shooting.

"The Golden Triangle," I said.

"What?" he said.

"The Golden Triangle. It's the region at the confluence of the Mekong and Ruak Rivers. I walked patrols along the Mekong more times than I can count. The Golden Triangle is where most of the world's opium poppies grow, where nearly all the heroin comes from. When I was in-country, it was more plentiful than a can of Budweiser at the PX."

I glanced at the millpond and then back at Dominic. "When I got home and needed to score, the pushers would always say their product was the real deal. Some of them even labeled it. Golden Triangle. Nine Dragons. They weren't against the war in Vietnam. No way. It was making them rich."

Dominic continued to glare, but I didn't stop talking.

"There were always stories in-country about GIs sending stuff home. Most of it was the usual war souvenirs. A bayonet taken off a dead VC. A brown uniform stripped from the corpse of an NVA regular. A red flag with a yellow star taken down from the inside of an enemy tunnel."

I scowled. "But there was also scuttlebutt about other stuff being shipped home. Small packets of marijuana and heroin smuggled home in duffle bags and larger amounts hidden in the landing gear of cargo planes. The most vile rumors were about kilos of scag being hidden in coffins shipped home from Tan Son Nhut."

Dominic's glare grew fiercer.

"That's it, isn't? What you and Pitzer have been doing. You were both based at Tan Son Nhut. You got yourself transferred to the bases along the great circle. You've been establishing an inbound supply chain and Kane, the ground crewman, and Ramirez found you out and had to be silenced."

As I was saying it, I knew there would be no sprinting for the millpond should Dominic draw his pistol. I was going to lunge at him instead. I'd never backed down from a gun pointed at me yet and I wasn't about to start.

The captain surprised me. He didn't make a move for his holster. He shook his head and spoke in a low voice. "You have no idea what you're doing. No idea at all. You need to drop this and drop it now. If you don't, you'll screw up everything and more people could die."

Now, he looked over at the millpond. I wondered what he was seeing when he saw the logs. Were they bombs he'd dropped on enemy installations and cities and villages alike? Did they haunt him as much as the floating villagers haunted me?

Dominic turned away from the dark water. "If I tell you, you have to promise to drop this and go home to Harney County and let us do our job."

"Who's us and what job?"

"Promise? On your honor. On the memory of the men you served with and who died."

"I'll always honor their memory. Forever."

Dominic breathed in and breathed out. "Pitzer and I discovered the smuggling while we were stationed at Tan Son Nhut. Well, Pitzer learned of it first and then told me. He was chief of my squadron's ground crew. He overhead some guys talking about easy money to be made handling, quote unquote, special shipments. He told them he wanted in. Given his record of being busted down, they believed him."

He turned his palms up. "Pitzer told me and I informed the commanding AP officer who I knew from when we were both at Randolph in San Antonio. He sent it up the chain. It got kicked up all the way to the Air Force Office of Special Investigations. The order came back down. Instead of the AP at Tan Son Nhut busting the operation right then and there, they'd launch a more comprehensive investigation to see how widespread the smuggling was. The AFOSI decided the best way to do that was by using men who weren't AP."

"You and Pitzer," I said.

The captain nodded. "I was due for rotation and could use my new role as a trainer to look at other bases. The commander ginned up a reason to send Pitzer packing. We both went to Elmendorf, didn't find anything there, and so we split up, me to McChord and him to here."

"But then Kane and the ground crewman got killed. Did they hear something or stumble onto it?"

"That's what we think, but it's nothing anyone can prove. Accidents do happen. Their deaths were enough reason to transfer me here so Pitzer and I could watch each other's backs."

"And Ramirez?"

Dominic exhaled. "They were trying to kill me. Toro was collateral damage. Either somebody told them I was part of an investigation or they suspected it. My F-101 was rigged. The turbine flamed out on that training flight. That set off the ejection protocol. The canopy blew and Toro bailed."

"Why didn't you punch out?"

"Because I'm Texan stubborn, that's why!" he shouted. "I rode broncos as a kid. I was flying a crop duster over my old man's fields by the time I was thirteen. Nothing bucks me off. Nothing. I was determined to land that plane and find the men who tried to kill me. I got the Voodoo's engine restarted and flew her home with the wind in my teeth. When I landed, Hardiman was there with the news that Toro was dead. They must've rigged his chute too. The major said I should be first on the scene to secure any evidence. He ordered the F-101 quarantined."

"So Hardiman knows."

"Of course, he does. He's the base commander."

"And the radio? Why didn't you flash a Mayday? No one else in your squad turned around. I saw that."

"It was rigged too. I suppose they did that in case I radioed in and named names on my way down."

"Who is they? You keep saying they?"

Dominic shook his head. "I can't tell you that. The investigation is a long way from over. We don't want to tip anybody off until we identify them all."

I was watching him closely, trying to get a read on him as he spoke. It was hard in the darkness with the only light coming from the sawmill across the blackened pond.

"Why should I believe you?" I said.

"Because I'm telling the truth. If I weren't, do you think you'd still be standing here?"

We stared at one another. "The thought of people desecrating the fallen makes me burn," I said. "They need to be stopped."

"They will. We're the Air Force. Can I trust you to keep your promise and go home and let us complete our investigation without any more interference?"

"You can, but when it's over, I need to know you caught them."

"That decision is above my rank, but if I can, I'll tell you myself."

"Then I'll head back to Harney County in the morning."

"Good. Come on, I'll give you a ride back to your motel."

"Okay, but one more thing."

"What is it?"

"Hardiman's fiancée, Carla Donovan. He told me he arranged for her to take the Starlifter to Dover. He dropped her off to catch it. Do you happen to know if she got on?"

"I'm sure she did. Why?"

"She's re-upping for duty in Vietnam. I wanted to say goodbye before she deploys. I'd heard the plane got into Kingsley late."

"You hear a lot for a civilian."

"Hardiman told me. He didn't stick around to see her off."

"I could check for you."

"You didn't see it land or take off?"

"No, I was home asleep. That it?"

"Yes, that's it."

Before following him to his car, I took a last look at the half-drowned logs floating in the dark waters of the millpond. Above the whine of the saw blades, a coyote howled. I wasn't sure from where.

G ordon Loq was behind the reception counter when I returned to the motel.

"I owe you an explanation as well as thanks," I said.

"You don't owe me nothing," he said.

"I'm ex-military. I knew the base commander at Kingsley Field from before. He was engaged, but his fiancée broke it off. He got the wrong idea I had something to do with it."

"All those guys over there think they own the town, but they don't. We've been here longer. A lot longer. You don't look like they worked you over."

"They didn't. Only talked."

"You served in Vietnam?"

"I did."

"I had a cousin went over there."

"You told me the Klamath Nation didn't recognize the US government?"

"They got us surrounded, don't they?"

I couldn't tell if he was grinning or not.

Gordon said, "Truth is, a lot of our people go into the military. It's not like there's a lot of jobs around here for us. And school? The history they teach is all messed up. Custer?" His expression showed what he thought about that.

"Which branch did your cousin serve in?"

"Marines. He's as tough as they come. A real warrior. He came back without a scratch on the outside, but he was a lot different inside than when he left. He couldn't stay in my aunt's house no more, so he moved deep into the forest. He lives the old ways. Some say he became a grizzly bear." Gordon Loq paused. "For his sake, I hope he did. That way he can have peace for a few months out of the year when he hibernates. It's better than falling through the ice like others."

"What do you mean by that?"

"It's a Klamath saying for people who get hooked on the white man's alcohol. They drink so much they think they can walk across the lake when it's frozen." He glanced toward the window that was frosting on the outside. "They can't."

Gordon shrugged. "Yeah, first smallpox then whiskey and now heroin. Who knows what they'll think of next to use to try to wipe us out."

"Heroin?"

"That's right. I got another cousin who works in a clinic in town. She says they're seeing all sorts coming in who got hooked and are messed up. Some are Klamath, but most are white folks."

"Heroin in a little town like Klamath Falls?"

"A lot of it, she says. And town's not so little it doesn't got big problems like anywhere else. Though this heroin deal is pretty new, I got to say."

"Where are they getting it?"

"She says they buy it on the street. Probably off Sixth Street in the old part of town. It's always been rough there. Flop houses and drunks and hookers." Gordon reached behind the counter and hoisted the carved stick with the obsidian blade and bear teeth. "It's the kind of place you don't go at night without carrying something like this."

I said good night and went to my room. Dominic's admission that the Air Force was trying to bust a drug trafficking ring cleared up a lot of things. But Gordon's news that the home of Kingsley Field was newly awash in heroin couldn't be a coincidence. The stuff sold on the street had to come from the shipments being smuggled from Vietnam.

Though I'd given my word to leave the job of rounding up the traffickers to the Air Force, they were looking at it from the top down. It was the same way generals planned a battle, but every grunt on the ground knew it took fighting from the bottom up to win. Hardiman, Dominic, and Pitzer had no idea of the evil they were up against. They didn't know what heroin did to people and what they'd do to get it. I did. I'd seen it destroy others. It had nearly destroyed me, and it would if I ever let it take hold again. I'd also seen what heroin did to pushers, how the money turned them into killers, knowingly selling death one fix at a time.

When I was in-country, I never asked the men in my squad to do something I wouldn't do myself. I always walked point even though plenty of others with my rank gave the dangerous job to their subordinates. I did it because I was good at it. What I wasn't good at was sitting by and letting others do the hard work. I opened the door to my room again and walked into the night.

The oldest and seediest part of town wasn't that far from the motel. Most of the buildings were made of scarred, dirty brick. Some were boarded up. What streetlights there were shone dimly. A few of the parked cars looked like they were being lived in. I kept one eye on the ground to avoid tripping over the potholes in the sidewalk and the other on the lookout for pushers.

The halo from a distant traffic light slowly changed from green to yellow to red. I crossed the street and walked toward it. I was halfway to the next curb when something scooted from an unlit doorway. I whirled to face it.

"Help a veteran out?" a voice called.

A gaunt face stared from the shadows. The man was sitting in a wheelchair. He had straggly hair and wore a dirty army field jacket. The footrests of the chair were pushed to the side, and he propelled himself with his right foot. His left leg ended above the knee.

I searched his green jacket for divisional patches but saw none. "What's your name, soldier?"

"Deeds, Charles. Corporal, 101st Airborne," he responded automatically.

"Drake, Nick. Sergeant. First Cav. Where did you see action?"

His scowl revealed missing teeth. "Where didn't I?" He smacked his thigh that ended in a stump. "Got this in Operation Junction City."

I recalled it was the largest airborne assault in the war. The battle lasted nearly three months.

"I got hit the second week we were into it. Help me out, would you? Any spare change will do. Bills even better. You know what I mean?"

He sniffed. His eyes were rheumy and his lips chapped from licking them in the cold, dry air. I recognized all the signs.

"I give you anything, you're going to use it to fix," I said.

His scowl grew. "I'm in pain, Sarge. Real pain. See this?" He smacked his thigh again. It made the stump jump. "My unit got hit with mortars. Shrapnel sliced it off like it was butter. I'm in pain, real pain. Help me out, come on."

"You can score around here?"

His hack brought up phlegm. Deeds raised his arms like they

were wings. "I got my own Freedom Bird that comes and takes me wherever I need to go. How about it?"

"What about me? I need some too."

Deeds lowered his arms and pushed the sidewalk with his only shoe to back up his chair. He peered at me suspiciously. "You use?"

I nodded and pulled out a couple of dollar bills. I held them up and out of his reach. "Where?"

He looked side to side. "How do I know you're not a narc?"

"We were both in-country. We saw what we saw and we did what we did."

"Roger that," he said, the words nearly a moan.

I moved the handful of bills closer. He grabbed for them, but I didn't let go and closed my hand over his and squeezed. "Where?"

Deeds winced. "It's way too cold for anyone to be out here selling on the street. They're holed up where it's nice and warm. There's a bar down Sixth. Smitty's. Dude there named James. He's got a red beard. He'll hook you up."

I let go. He snatched the bills and pushed backward until the recess of the doorway swallowed him up.

Smitty's was a dingy spot on a corner of an alley. The second *t* in the neon sign in the blackened window was burned out. The front door swung inward. The clack of pool balls was louder than the conversation of the patrons hunched on stools and staring deep into their glasses. I found an empty toward the end of the bar and climbed aboard.

The bartender took his time. He didn't bother wiping the grimy surface. "What'll it be?"

"Whatever is on tap."

"Show me you can pay."

I put a dollar on the bar. He picked it up, filled a schooner, and slid it. I had to give up alcohol the same time I did junk. I raised the schooner and pretended to drink.

The faces of my fellow barflies reflected in the grimy mirror behind the bar. They were a mix of millhands, truck drivers, and a couple of old-timers who were long past having punched a clock. None had a red beard. I glanced toward the top of the mirror and viewed the room behind me.

One of the men playing pool was unshaven. His whiskers were red. Two stripes and the eight ball were all that were left on the table. The man with the beard was lining up the cue ball on the eight. Two could play Coyote, I thought. I waited until he hit it before walking over. As the black ball sunk in the far corner pocket, I put a quarter on the rail.

Red beard stared at it. "What's that for?"

"Next game," I said.

"This table's private."

I took out a five-dollar bill and put it under the quarter. "Where I come from, a challenge is only good if there's a little money behind it. You win, you keep my five bucks and I go back to my beer. I win, I get your five and take on the next guy with a quarter."

He finally shook his head. "Five bucks, huh? Okay, big spender." He matched my bill. "Slot your quarter and rack 'em."

The skinny guy he'd beat smirked and leaned against the wall.

"Name's Nick," I said.

"James. Prepare to lose."

He was a fair shot, but like a lot of hustlers, he tried to impress people by trying fancy shots instead of sticking to the basics of knocking balls in holes. He dropped two solids with his break, banked in a third, but the cue ball rolling back edged a stripe into the side pocket. I'd played plenty of pool in PXs and bars while on leave, including most of the boom-boom rooms on Tu Do Street in Saigon. I ran the table.

"That was lucky," James said. "I set it up for you."

"Slot another quarter and we'll see."

"Make it twenty and you got a game."

We took back our fives. I put a twenty on the rail. Andrew Jackson's face stared back at me. I thought of the poacher. I asked myself what was I doing there. I should be home in Harney County doing my real job instead of chasing half-baked ideas.

James matched it, slotted another quarter, and racked. I broke. Nothing sunk. He knocked in a couple but scratched. I finished him off. No trick shots, nothing fancy, only straight-ahead pool.

He fumed. "Okay, double or nothing."

"No, I'm up for something else," I said.

"What?"

"Deeds said you're the guy."

"Who's Deeds?"

"You know who. How about it?"

"How about what?"

"What I want."

I rolled up my sleeve and turned the inside of my arm toward him. The tracks were old and purpled, but the scars still visible.

"Out back," he said.

James held onto his pool cue and walked down a hall. I followed him past a filthy bathroom and out a door. It led to the alley. The skinny guy followed behind me. He was carrying a cue too.

James faced me. He slapped his palm with the butt of his cue. "We beat the shit out of narcs."

"Good. They deserve it," I said.

"Why do you think I can hook you up?"

"Deeds told me."

"He's a junkie. Junkies will say anything. Did you give him money?"

"A couple of bucks. I'm prepared to give you a lot more. Or should I say, the man you work for."

"How much more?"

"Depends on how much he can sell me."

"You got the money on you?"

"Do I look like a first timer?"

"No one wants any competition around here," James said. "Now, beat it."

"No competing. I plan on opening up a new market for your boss."

"I don't got a boss."

"Everyone has a boss. I want to talk to him."

"What's this new market?"

"Burns."

"Over in Harney?" He laughed. "Burns is a hick town."

"What do you call this? Everybody has needs, but no one is there to fill them. I plan on being that person. Go tell your boss. He'll want to hear what I have to say. I'm talking about a lot of weight. Maybe he'll even give you a bonus. If he finds out you didn't tell him, well, I don't want to think about what he'll give you."

My eyes never left him as he thought about it.

"Maybe I'll mention it to someone. Maybe if someone's interested, then we'll see. Where are you staying?"

"Pick a place and time to meet tonight. This is a onetime offer."

"You saw Deeds poke his head out of his little rat hole? There. Midnight. No guarantees anybody will show."

"I'll be there."

I WENT BACK to my room and laid on the bed and stared at the clock and counted down the minutes until midnight. I felt nothing. I was in the same gray zone I'd enter before boarding a chopper bound for a hot LZ. Time would slow until it seemed as if it had stopped and then it would suddenly speed forward to catch up the minutes that had been lost as the engine roared and the blades whirled and the .50 calibers spat.

The temperature had dropped considerably when I left the motel room and started walking back to where I'd encountered Deeds. Black ice had formed in the gutters and I had to hop over it when crossing the streets. If the town had seemed unusually quiet before, now it was downright mute. The stoplights had been switched to flashing yellow. The streetlights appeared even dimmer.

I reached the block where Deeds had rolled out of his doorway. No one was standing out front. No lights were on in the building. A couple of cars were parked on the block, but their windshields had already sprouted frost. I approached the recessed doorway. Deeds had rolled himself all the way in with his back wheels up against the closed door.

"Pretty cold to be outside," I said.

He didn't answer.

"Deeds?" Still no answer. He must have fixed and was on the nod. He'd freeze if he stayed outside. I tried another tactic. "Corporal. Attention!"

Nothing. I stepped into the gloomy cavern of the doorway. Deeds stared back, but his eyes were unseeing, his face blue. The drool hanging from his lips had turned to ice. I sensed someone rushing in from behind me. As I turned to meet him, something swished. I ducked but caught a hard blow at the top of my forehead. Blood immediately streamed into my eyes. I stumbled backward and sat down on Deeds' frozen lap. I felt the wind as whatever hard had hit me came swinging again. I threw my forearm up to block the blow. Bone cracked.

Two pairs of hands grabbed me, yanked me forward, and slammed me face down onto the sidewalk. One of the assailants landed on top of me and jammed his knees between my shoulder blades while the other grabbed my right arm and shoved the sleeve up. Fingers squeezed above the bend in my elbow. My veins bulged.

A hot spike jabbed me. "No!" I yelled. "Not that."

But it was. Warmth flooded my body. An old friend was back.

"Look what we got here," a voice said. "Two junkie soldiers went and OD'd themselves."

Somewhere a car with a bad starter cranked over and over. The hands let go, and I fell from the sky and plunged into the black waters of the millpond.

26

I sunk down and down. I bumped into limbless logs and tried to push them out of my way. Their bark was as soft as flesh and the logs weren't logs, but bodies. I wasn't in the millpond, but the Mekong, and I was floating along with the dead.

Someone was shouting, *Breathe! Breathe!* But I was underwater and didn't dare open my mouth. I kept floating along. The river ran straight and then took a series of sweeping turns that swung me left, then right, and then left again. It hit rapids and whitewater slapped my face.

Stay with me, they said. *Stay with me.*

I closed my ears to the slapping and listened for the lapping of the sea instead. Its gentle waters were calling beyond the river, beyond the delta, to come feel their loving embrace, to bathe in their forgiveness, and float without pain forever. I could feel the pull of the warm current and taste the first hint of salt. I was almost there. I was almost home.

But then something blared and blared again. Loud voices took its place, the words all jumbled in a tongue I didn't know.

Hands yanked me away from the sea's outstretched fingers. I tried to bat the hands away, but they clasped me tight and then I was traveling down a river again, bumping over shallows, the scrub of gravel beneath me, and the sea slipped farther and farther away.

The river stopped and I was lifted up again. They carried me through cold air. Dogs yapped. Chickens clucked. The scent of sage replaced the smell of the sea. They laid me down. I was naked and cold. I sunk into darkness again until lights flickered. I opened my eyes. From the mist marched the squad I'd led into ambush.

Sarge, what are you doing here? they said.

Looking for you, I said.

What for? they asked.

To say I'm sorry, I said.

What for? they asked.

For getting you all killed, I said.

The VC did that, they said. And they marched away.

More men trooped from the mist. So many I couldn't remember all of their names, only the names of the battles in which we'd fought together. Hue. Van Tuong. Ia Drang. Tet. Vietcong and NVA regulars marched out of the mist too. I didn't know their names, nor did I want to. Two more men marched behind. Toro Ramirez carried his helmet with red bull horns painted on top.

I'm sorry, I said.

I was already dead, he said.

So was I, said the ground crewman walking beside him.

And Elvis Kane? I asked.

MIA, they said. They marched on. Corporal Deeds marched out of the mist behind them.

I'm sorry, I shouldn't have given them your name, I said.

I've been dead since the day I traded my knee for the needle, he said, *but look at me now*. And he ran to keep up with the others.

Two more figures brought up the rear of the parade, but they were still cloaked in mist. I called to them to come all of the way out. But I got no answer.

Drumming started. Chanting too. Hands grabbed me by the arms and legs again and pinned me down. Loops were cinched around my wrists and ankles and the ropes pulled tight. Another needle jabbed my vein, and I waited for the old friend to take me back down to the razor's edge between death and pleasure, but it was not to be this time. Smoke blew up my nose as another needle pricked my scalp over and over again.

Stop! I shouted. *Stop!* I screamed. But I got no answer.

My words were lost to the drumming and chanting. Shadows danced all around. Some were humans, most were not. A dancing shadow started to sing, but the words were beyond my ken and beyond my care. My head split and I asked for relief from the pain. But I got no answer.

I COUGHED. I sneezed. I licked my lips. I opened my eyes and saw a small circle of light directly overhead. I tried to sit up, but my wrists and ankles were tethered. I looked from side to side. I was surrounded by a thicket of braided wood. A tongue of smoke curled from a small fire and lapped at the hole in the sky. I coughed and sneezed again.

"Water," I gasped. "Water."

A shadow moved and then a face loomed over mine. A man's voice spoke slowly, each word deliberate. "He still babbles. Is he in this world now or still in the spirit world?"

I tried to focus. I concentrated on a slash of red. It was a bandana tied around white hair.

Another shadow moved beside his. Threads from a spider's web streaked a long black braid. Dry fingers touched my cheek. "He is in between," a woman's voice answered. "The poison is still within him. I can feel its burn."

"Water," I gasped. "Water."

"His noises are the croaks of frogs," she said. "I will give him a little water."

"He will drown," the man said. "And we cannot untie him yet so he can sit up to drink."

"It is why I have wetted this rag," she said.

I closed my eyes and started to sink again. Cloth dabbed my lips and a few drops of water found their way to my tongue. I fell back into darkness.

I was not alone, but I was not with the dead from Vietnam. Faces loomed. The poacher in his earflap hat, his rotten teeth dripping with tobacco juice, turned his Gatling gun toward me. A faceless rider pointed his six-shooter at me. Dominic stared behind the stick of a fighter jet as he fingered the trigger to his missiles. Pitzer let go of the chain holding back a frothing Doberman pinscher. Edwins read from an Air Force manual. Hardiman ran under an arch made of crossed pool cues.

I could hear Pudge's drawl and Gemma's voice and November's *numu* in the blackness. The four of us walked hand in hand through a long, dark tunnel.

I will find the light and lead you out, I said.

Why should we trust you? they asked.

Then I heard more noises. First came a man's laugh and then an animal's.

Sleep tight, Coyote said. He raised his muzzle to the sky, opened his mouth, and howled.

A voice begged for one more fix. *Only one*, it said. *I promise. If I don't get it, I'll die*, it said. *I promise.*

I tried to lift my head to break the bond of frozen blood that stuck my face to the ground. A grizzly lumbered toward me on his hind legs. He was swinging a war club with his own teeth sticking out of the edge. He scooped me up and carried me to a giant canoe. He used the carved club as a paddle and spoke in bear tongue as he steered down a winding river that emptied into a giant lake ringed by broken cattails.

"Water," I groaned. "*Paa'a*."

"He is back from the spirit world now," the man said. "Listen, the old ones have taught him to speak *numu* like *numu*."

The woman touched my face again. "Only most of the way back. He still has something left to see."

"Help me," I said.

"Help yourself," the woman said.

"November? You can hear me? Tuhudda Will, is that you? Where am I?"

"The Pity Heart," November said.

"What's that?"

"You should have read the last legend," she said.

"I ran out of time," I said.

She tsked. "The Pity Heart is where the old ones went when times grew hard. No food. No water. Bad winter. It got so their time in this world was almost over. But it was not those things that brought their end near. It was their own self-pity. Feeling sorry for themselves made them weak and without will."

"Where is this place?" I said.

"The old ones built a wickiup and went inside," November continued. "They beat the drum and sang and danced for seven days and nights. And when they finished, they left their self-pity inside and set The Pity Heart on fire. And ever since, all *numu* everywhere have never felt sorry for themselves again and will be strong forever."

"This is so," Tuhudda Will chanted.

He raised his hands and pointed to the hole in the sky.

"There is another way of The Pity Heart. Once there was a band of warriors who faced a great enemy who came from across the sky. The warriors were outnumbered. Their enemy had faster ponies and more powerful bows. The great chief said, we will stand and fight, but for us to win, we must give no mercy. And so, they built a wickiup and went inside and beat the drum and sang and danced for seven days and nights. And they left their mercy inside The Pity Heart and went out and slayed their enemy. But when the battle was over, the warriors returned to The Pity Heart, for they had not burned it down. They beat the drum and sang and danced for seven days and nights to celebrate their victory and reclaim their mercy. And ever since, all *numu* everywhere have always had merciful hearts and will forever."

"This is so," November chanted. She dragged her fingertips over my eyelids. "Go and find what you must leave behind."

And again I fell into darkness.

I watched as the dead from Vietnam marched onward, comrades and enemies alike, but I did not follow them. I watched as I staggered through the front door of Walter Reed and marched out the other side.

I watched as the last two people marched out of the mist. The first wore a pilot's flight suit. I didn't recognize him and thought it must be Captain Kane, but the name on his chest was Fitzpatrick. He was Carla Donovan's Sean. Then the second person emerged from the mist and I heard a scream. It was my own.

No, no, not you! I shouted.

Carla was dressed in white. She smiled and sang her Joni Mitchell song about looking at clouds and love and life from both sides.

Why? I asked. *How?* I asked. *Who?* I asked.

Carla reached for her first love's hand, and as they marched onward together, she sang, *I've looked at life from both sides now, it's life's illusions I recall, I really don't know life at all.*

Darkness swirled as light grew stronger. I had already left my self-pity behind. Now I must leave my mercy too. I would find Carla's killer and, like Rock and Obsidian, no matter if broken and shattered, I would strike him down.

27

A beam of sunlight shining through the hole in the top of the wickiup warmed my face. I opened my eyes and tried to shield the glare with my hands, but my arms were outstretched and ropes looped around my wrists pinned me to the ground. I turned my head and saw November. She was sitting cross-legged beside a campfire and stitching tiny glass beads to the front of a small buckskin pouch. Tuhudda Will was kneeling next to her and feeding small sticks to the flames.

"Untie me, *Tsua'a Numudooa Nubabe*," I said. "Please."

"He speaks your name," Tuhudda said. "He is back from the spirit world now."

November didn't look up from her needlework.

"Did you hear me?" I said.

"How could I not? Have you learned nothing from the *nuwuddu* at your refuges? The first people know when to shout and when to whisper."

"But even Bighorn Sheep cannot remain quiet after he has eaten brittlebush," I said.

The old woman nodded. "Free him. He is back in this world now."

The old man pressed his finger against the Pendleton blanket that covered my chest. "This is so." He used a knife with a deer antler handle to slice the ropes that tethered me to four stakes pounded into the wickiup's dirt floor.

I struggled to a sitting position. I almost passed out from the effort. I put my fingers to my hairline and felt a line of stitches. My left wrist was in a cast. "What day is it?" I said.

"A day," he said.

"Where am I?"

"My family's camp."

"How long have I been here?"

"Long enough," November said. She put her needlework down. "You need soup." She lifted the lid of a cast-iron Dutch oven that was perched at the edge of the fire and spooned some of its contents into a bowl.

My stomach somersaulted at the thought of food. My muscles ached from vomiting. I held my hands out; they shook. I stunk of my own sweat. They were all the signs of having gone through withdrawal.

"I'm not hungry," I said.

November pushed the bowl toward me. "Who is asking? Now take and don't spill any."

"I can't hold it with this." I held up the cast.

"Even a robin with a broken wing can find a worm. Now eat."

I took the bowl with my good hand and sniffed. It was some kind of broth. I raised it to my lips. My teeth chattered against the rim, but I drank. When I finished, I laid my head back down. The broth warmed me from the inside, but I still shivered. I closed my eyes to keep from spinning.

Light flooded the wickiup and woke me. The tanned hide covering the doorway had been swept aside. Pudge Warbler stooped to enter. Gemma was right behind him.

"The patient lives," she said.

"This is so," Tuhudda Will said.

Gemma squatted in front of me and examined my forehead. "It's healing nicely. Those can come out soon."

"You sewed me up?"

"A cow, a horse, a man. Hide is hide."

"And this?" I held up the cast.

"Do you want me to sign it?" she said.

"A lot of damage from a pool cue," I muttered.

Her ponytail swished. "Only if it was made of lead."

"My head aches," I said. "My body too. Do you have an aspirin with you, maybe something stronger?"

"Not a chance, but I do have more rope. Do you want me to tie you down again?"

I glanced at the four stakes sticking out of the ground. "You knew I was on heroin?" She nodded. "It was that bad? I mean, I was?"

The exchange of looks between Gemma and the others told me I had given them hell. Shame washed over me.

"I'm sorry," I said. "But just so you know, I didn't relapse. They tried to kill me with an overdose."

"Who tried to kill you?" Pudge said.

"How long have I been here?"

"Four days," he answered.

Four days, I thought. The voice in my head was awfully quiet. It should be screaming, not whispering for a fix.

Gemma seemed to know what I was thinking. "I tried to wean you off it by dosing you with ketamine. It's the anesthesia I use in the field. It's also good to manage pain."

"You gave me horse tranquilizer?"

"A little bit, and less and less each day. I think what November and Tuhudda did helped you more."

"How did I get here?"

Pudge drew closer. "A Klamath brought you. He said you

were staying at his motel. He saw you leave your room at midnight and so he followed you. He found you down the street."

"Gordon Loq drove me all the way out here? The hospital in Klamath Falls would have been closer."

"That's what I said when I came outside to see who in the Sam Hill was laying on their horn in front of my house in the middle of the night. He said there was some bad business back there and he wasn't sure what end of it you were on because of an earlier visit by the Air Force police and a dead man in a wheelchair when he found you."

"A wounded veteran," I said. "A street junkie. They OD'ed him because of me."

"I warned you about sticking your nose into other people's business." Pudge puffed his cheeks. "The Klamath took you to his people first, but they said to get you out of the county fast because of the dead man. They told him the only doctor in No Mountain was a horse doctor." The deputy nodded at his daughter. "He was looking for her."

A wave of nausea rolled through me. My stomach churned. I willed myself to keep from bringing up the broth. "Sounds like there are a lot of people I need to thank," I said.

Pudge crouched as best as he could with his bum hip, so he could look me straight in the eye. "There's something I got to tell you, son, and it's bad news. As bad as it gets."

"Carla Donovan is dead," I said.

The old deputy rocked back on his heels. "Oh Lord, how could you know that?"

I gestured at November and Tuhudda. "Ask them. I saw her in here, spoke to her. Or wherever I was. Maybe I was in the spirit world, or maybe I already knew she was dead when I couldn't find her. It doesn't matter. What does is I got to go. I got to do something about it."

"Hold on. You're not in any shape to go anywhere."

I struggled to my feet. The wool blanket that had been covering me dropped to the floor. I didn't bother to cover my nakedness. "Where are my clothes?"

"Over there," Tuhudda said.

"You have a concussion," Gemma said. "Sit down before you fall down."

"It wouldn't be my first." I was wobbling and made a grab for the pile of clothes. Blood rushed to my head when I bent over, but I stayed on my feet. "My truck and gear are back in Klamath Falls. I need a lift."

"It's parked at your place," Pudge said. "When the Klamath brought you, he had a friend follow him in your rig. He didn't want to leave it at the motel and bring the law down on him and his people. It's the same reason Gemma and I brought you out here too. I've kept this off the books, but I need to sort out what's what, son."

"That's what I intend to do," I said.

"If the man in the wheelchair was murdered, then this is better left to the Klamath County sheriff."

"They don't know what's going on. I do."

"Don't make a big mistake here. You don't know the particulars."

"I know enough." I started pulling on my clothes as best I could with a cast on my wrist. It was a struggle to stay upright. My forehead beaded with sweat. "They killed Carla too."

The old lawman pushed his short brim Stetson back. "She hung herself, your nurse friend. I got a call from a young airman over there who works for the base commander. Edwins is his name. He'd been looking for you, wanted you to know about Miss Donovan."

"Carla wouldn't commit suicide. No way."

"The airman said the major got a report from the Army

Nurse Corps. It said she had a history of depression. From what she saw in the war. She'd told the major she was breaking it off and going back to Vietnam. She was waiting for a plane at Kingsley Field and it was late, and they say she must have gotten to feeling blue about everything and it all got to be too much."

Pudge looked at the ground. "They found her in a storeroom in the hangar. She'd made a noose with an extension cord, got on a stepladder, and... I'm sorry, son. Real sorry."

Gemma reached out to place her hand on me, but I shrunk away. "Don't," I said. "I don't need pity. What I need is my truck and weapons. Someone murdered Carla and they're going to pay."

I was lightheaded, but finished pulling on my boots without falling over. I tried to slide the cast through a jacket sleeve.

"Why are you so certain someone killed her?" Pudge said.

"Because I know Carla. Everything she did was for her patients. She wouldn't want someone like me to think suicide was an option. She's no more a suicide than the other deaths at Kingsley were accidents or Deeds in the wheelchair. Or me if Gordon Loq hadn't come along."

I gave up trying to put the jacket on and draped it over my shoulders. "It all has to do with smuggling heroin from Vietnam."

"Drugs?" Pudge said.

"I promised Dominic I wouldn't tell anybody, but that's what this whole thing has been about. He's been investigating it for a special department of the Air Force."

Pudge wiped his mouth with the back of his hand. "Outlaws lynched your friend?"

"Carla must have seen them unloading drugs when she was waiting for the Starlifter."

"Who are these murdering sons of bitches?"

I widened my stance to keep from falling down. "That's what I'm going to find out. Don't try to stop me."

Pudge puffed his cheeks and exhaled loudly. "Hell, son, I'm not gonna stop you. I'm gonna help you."

"You don't have to do that."

He slapped the gold star on his chest. "This says I do."

"What about your rustlers?"

"Where there's beeves, there's thieves. Always has been, always will be. Weather's turned and the rustlers have turned tail. They'll be back in the spring and I'll be waiting for them."

"Okay, then, I'll help you round them up."

"Fair enough."

The old deputy tipped his Stetson to Tuhudda and November and stooped to pass through the wickiup's opening.

Gemma said, "Come on, I'll give you a ride back to your truck. And, no, I'm not doing it out of pity. I'm doing it because I want to."

I bowed to the two Paiute elders. "I probably don't deserve what you did for me, but I do thank you."

"Take this with you," November said.

She handed me the beaded buckskin pouch she'd been sewing. A geometrical pattern of blue and yellow diamonds surrounded the shape of a wickiup made of red beads.

"What's it for?" I asked.

"For keeping whatever you don't want to lose forever close to your heart."

Tuhudda Will picked up a drum and began banging it with a stick. Girl Born in Snow closed her eyes and started to sing, and as she sang, she danced.

28

The lights of the town twinkled below the Klamath Hills. I watched them from the deck of Hardiman's house. As soon as I saw a pair of headlights making their way up the winding road, I went back inside and sat down at the table in the unlit dining room. I placed the .357 in front of me.

The front door opened. The entry hall lights turned on. Footsteps echoed in the hallway. The kitchen lights switched on next. The freezer door opened and closed. Ice clinked in a glass. Liquid poured. The swinging door to the dining room pushed open. Hardiman stood silhouetted in the doorway.

"Hello, Pete. Turn on the light and sit down," I said.

"What the hell?" He started to back up.

"Do it." I picked up the gun and cocked it.

Hardiman recognized the sound. Pilots wore sidearms when flying missions in case they got shot down. He threw the light switch. His eyes widened when he saw the stitches at my scalp line and the cast on my left wrist.

"You look sick. You're shaking and sweating. What's gotten into you?" he said.

"It's what's gotten out that you should be worried about."

"You're not making sense."

"Pity," I said.

"You've crossed so far over the line now I can't help you anymore even if I wanted to."

I jabbed the pistol at him. "Sit down!"

Hardiman plopped on a chair while holding a tumbler filled with ice and amber liquid.

"Is that the sour mash you told me you were saving for a special occasion? What are you celebrating, that you got away with murder?"

"What?"

"You killed Carla. She told you she wouldn't marry you and you couldn't take it. Maybe you tried to talk her out of leaving you. Maybe you even begged. When she kept saying no, you strangled her and then made it look like a suicide."

"My god!" He reeled backward in his chair. "So, this is what shell shock looks like. And to think Carla told me you were one of the lucky ones. She said you'd recovered. She was even proud of you."

"Don't you dare use her name in your lies."

"Lies?" Hardiman's face grew red. "Do you think I don't love her? I'm the dumb joe who asked her to marry him." He slammed the tumbler down so hard the ice cubes jumped out and skittered across the mahogany table.

"I know what you're doing," he said. "I went through interrogation training. Every pilot did. We all knew what they did to POWs at the Hanoi Hilton. Shocking you with a false accusation to get you to tell them what they really want to know is the oldest trick in the book. Forget it. You're wasting your breath."

"Prove to me you didn't kill her."

"I don't have to prove anything to you."

"Sure, you do. I'm the one with combat fatigue. I'm the one holding the gun. Let's get to the real truth, shall we?"

"What truth?"

"We both know Carla's not a suicide, so either you killed her or someone else did."

"I don't know what you're talking about."

My hand grew still. It never shook when I was going to fire a weapon. I pulled the trigger. The firing pin struck the primer, ignited the gunpowder, and sent the heavy magnum round spinning from the barrel. The slug smacked into the wall behind Hardiman's head and tore a hole in the plaster as big as a fist.

"Christ!" he shouted, leaping to his feet. "You could've hit me."

"No, but the next one will. Now, sit down."

"Dominic told me you already promised to go home and stay out of this."

"I did. But that was before someone tried to kill me using the heroin you're allowing to come in on Air Force planes. And it was before I found out about Carla. Sit down." I waved the gun. He sat.

"I swear I didn't kill her, but I can't tell you anything more," he said.

"Okay, then I'll tell it. The whole smuggling operation could've been stopped months ago at Tan Son Nhut, but somebody forgot that to kill a snake, you got to cut off its head."

Hardiman took a drink and pursed his lips.

"Why the go-slow approach?" I said.

He wouldn't answer.

"Is the Air Force so worried about its reputation that it's willing to let drugs keep flowing no matter how many bodies pile up?"

Hardiman gulped from the tumbler again and pursed his lips even tighter.

"So, that's it. You're waiting until everybody connected to it gets busted at the same time to make sure no one is left to blab that military planes were being used to ferry heroin."

I shook my head in disgust. "But you know what? I don't care about the why anymore. What I do care about is who killed Carla Donovan. I don't care how many people learn why she died. She's not getting written off as collateral damage." I pointed the gun at the center of Hardiman's chest. "Who did it?"

"You really are crazy," he sputtered.

"That's right. I can't tell what's real or a nightmare anymore, much less right from wrong. I say to hell with the rules. Who killed Carla? It has to be the person behind the smuggling here at Kingsley. Who is it? Start talking."

"I can't. It would be the end of my career."

"Or your life." I cocked the revolver. "Your choice."

"You don't scare me. You think I was scared in Vietnam? Never. Not once. I flew through more SAMs than anyone. I dropped bombs so close to the target the explosions left scorch marks on my ass."

Hardiman started whistling "Wild Blue Yonder." I shot the tumbler before he finished the second line. The sour mash splashed his uniform and a shard of glass struck his cheek. He tumbled backward and crashed onto the floor. He clasped his hands to his wet chest and licked his lips and tasted blood.

"You shot me!" he screamed. "You shot me!"

"I shot your drink."

I righted the chair and yanked him up and sat him in it.

"Tell it," I said.

"Okay, okay. It's like you said."

Hardiman started talking a mile a minute. The Air Force ordered a special investigation of the smuggling ring. Everything was by the book. Find the culprits and lock them up and shut it down. Only then the war started going badly and things back home were going even worse—antiwar protests, changing politics, and TV coverage that brought the frontlines into the living room. Then a congressional special report started making the rounds. It contended that commanders were routinely plying soldiers with amphetamines, steroids, and painkillers to help them handle extended combat. The report also documented that thousands of enlisted men had tried heroin in Vietnam or were hooked. Even more smoked pot.

"Don't you get it?" Hardiman said. "The brass had to keep the investigation out of the spotlight, knowing how it would play if taxpayers found out drugs were coming in on their dime." He struggled for air. "Trying to stop it is, well, it's war."

"Tell that to Genevieve Donovan. I'm sure she'll be real understanding when she's laying flowers on her sister's grave."

Hardiman's shoulders slumped. "No one blames themselves more for Carla's death than me." He wiped his eyes. "If I hadn't let my damn pride get in the way, I would've been in the waiting room with her. I could've protected her."

"Is that what happened, Carla saw someone offloading drugs?"

"She must have." Hardiman dabbed at the trickle of blood still seeping from the scratch from the broken glass. "If it's any consolation, we're about to snap the trap and catch them all at the same time. At Tan Son Nhut, McChord, Travis, and here too. Everything is being synchronized to the second, the same as the launch of an air strike or ground assault. It'll be over soon."

"But no one will ever know outside of the military, will they? Not the politicians or the press or the public. Bad for recruitment, bad for getting a bigger defense budget. And Carla? They'll stick to the story that she committed suicide. Her sister will never know the truth."

Hardiman shook his head. "I don't like it any more than you

do. It's the same as when that brigadier general told me I couldn't fly combat anymore. It's the way it is."

"Who's getting snapped up at Kingsley?"

"I already said I can't tell you, and I won't. I can't risk the operation and the men carrying it out. Their lives are at stake."

"Dominic wouldn't tell me either," I said.

"The captain is a good officer. He knows how to follow orders."

"He may be a good officer, but he's a lousy air policeman. He couldn't prevent Carla from being murdered."

"He would've if he could've."

"But he was there the night she was waiting for the Starlifter. Him and Pitzer."

"No, they weren't. Ever since Lieutenant Ramirez's death, I'd ordered them to stay away from the field when planes from Vietnam were coming in. We were trying to throw off the smugglers' suspicions."

"Dominic was home?"

"Yes."

"And Pitzer?"

"No doubt watchdogging his master's front door like always."

I mulled that one over. "Who found Carla?"

"A member of the ground crew. Poor kid. He's only been out of basic training a month."

"Who made the ID?"

"Me. I had to. Head of operations called the AP and AP called me. No one knew who she was. We didn't find her purse and suitcase until later."

"What about her name tag and Army Nurse Corps patch? She would've been in uniform if she was cadging a free ride on a military transport."

"Carla had ridden on cargo planes plenty of times before.

She knew how cold it gets back there." His eyes glistened. "She was wearing this white puffy down jacket she brought with her."

That prompted me to click the inside of my cheeks the same way I did when I'd ridden Wovoka.

"When is the bust going down?" I asked.

"I already told you. Soon."

"Good. I want to be sure I'm as far away from here as possible. I don't want to make a mistake and tip off Carla's killer."

Hardiman scrutinized me, but I didn't blink. "If I tell you, will you leave and not interfere?"

"You have my word."

"Okay, it's tomorrow night. And trust me, they aren't going to get away with what they did to Carla."

"I know they won't," I said.

29

I drove to a neighborhood on the other side of Kingsley Field. I found the block I was looking for, passed it, and parked on the street directly behind. I picked up the radio mike.

Pudge answered. "Where are you?"

"I just left Hardiman's."

"What did he say?"

"He confirmed what you and I talked about. The Air Force is trying to stop the smuggling on the QT."

"More like the CYA," the old lawman drawled. "Did he tell you who's involved at Kingsley?"

"No."

"Well, did you tell him we're gonna round up the punks selling dope at the bar?"

"He doesn't care. They're small fry. Are you at Smitty's now?"

"Close enough. Bust'em called his old boss at Klamath County Sheriff's and they're gonna do the arresting. I'm what you call an observer. As soon as they get here, they're going in."

"Remember, James has a red beard, but he could've shaved it

off. He had a skinny sidekick. There's a back door that opens onto the alley."

"That's exactly where I'm gonna park myself. No one is gonna rabbit on my watch." The radio fuzzed with static. "This is about the time you tell me why you're not gonna be here and what you're gonna be doing while I'm helping round up this lot."

"Getting more information."

"From who?"

"A guy."

Pudge groaned. "Don't do anything crazy, son. I can't help you if you take matters into your own hands. The law's the law and I'm sworn to uphold it. Break it and I'll arrest you myself."

"I expect nothing less in a man," I said, borrowing one of his favorite expressions.

"I'll see you back at the ranch, okay?" I didn't answer. "Okay?" he said more forcefully.

"Okay," I said.

I hung up the mike and got out of the truck. I spun the cylinder of my revolver to double-check that all the magnum rounds were unspent. I holstered it and slid the 12 gauge from the rack. I pumped a shell into the firing chamber as I walked down to the middle of the block and then ducked between two darkened houses.

Neither had watchdogs. No lights turned on either. I reached a back fence, climbed over, and dropped behind a row of untrimmed hedges. I pushed through an opening and stepped into a yard that was more weed patch than lawn. A yellow bug light shined above the back door even though it was too cold for moths and mosquitoes. The only light in the house came from the blue-gray glow of a television set.

I crept across the yard and tried the back door. It was unlocked. I eased it open. A musky, feral smell hit me, and an eerie hum came from the room lit by the television. I crept toward it and peeked in. The picture on the tube was a static Indian-head test pattern, signaling the channel had ended programming and signed off for the night.

Sallis was sprawled in a brown recliner in front of the set. His snores were almost as loud as the hum of the TV's test pattern. An oversized hardback, was clasped to his chest. It was a world atlas. I stomped down on the recliner's footrest. It catapulted him to a sitting position. He woke with a snort, but soon focused on the black eye of the shotgun's barrel.

"The bird and duck guy, right?" he said.

"The coyote, right? Telling me all of those half-truths to throw me off your scent."

"I must've dozed off. I don't usually do that."

"Because you thought I was dead after the hotshot and smack to the head. What did you use, that spanner I saw you holding the first time we met?"

"How did you find my house?"

"The phone book. You should've spent the extra fifty cents a month for an unlisted number. Who else lives here?"

Sallis showed his teeth. "I prefer my own company." He sat straighter but kept hold of the atlas.

I trained the shotgun on him. "The safety's off."

"What are you waiting for? Go on. Shoot."

"I will, but first I want some answers."

"You sure that's all you want? I saw the tracks on your arm. Man, you were into it heavy. Maybe you still are. You look pretty ragged since I saw you last. Want a little taste to take the edge off?"

"How much scag do you keep in the house?"

"So, that's it. You do want a fix. You should thank me for the one I gave you on the street. What doesn't kill you, makes you stronger, right?" Sallis snorted. It sounded like a faulty starter.

"How much?" I said.

"Enough."

"You skim the incoming and sell it locally, is that it? Give yourself a bonus for all your hard work unloading and transferring it to suitcases for sending off on commercial flights."

"Big deal. You would too, seeing you're a hype. Everybody does on down the line as soon as it leaves the cooker. It gets stepped on every time it changes hands until it goes up the vein of a junkie like you."

Despite the blue-gray glow of the television test pattern, amber reflected in his eyes. He licked his lips. "You need some, don't you? I can see it. The shakes, the sweats. Come on, what do you say? Free of charge. What do you want, a nickel, a dime? How 'bout an eight ball? It's nearly pure. It'll keep you warm and happy all winter long."

Why not? the voice in my head said. *Just a little one to keep from getting sick. Just this once, I promise.*

I thought about it long and hard. I thought about all the times I had gone out looking to score, from the back alleys off Tu Do Street to the street corners in the real world. I thought about how I traded my Purple Heart and Bronze Star for a couple of days' worth. And then I thought of Carla, how she would play "Blackbird" for me, bathe me with a cold compress when I had the shakes, and hold the bucket when I vomited while going cold turkey. I thought of Gordon Loq risking arrest, Gemma patching me up, and November and Tuhudda Will guiding me through The Pity Heart.

"I want all of it," I said. "Everything. And the money too."

"Not all, but I'm willing to make a deal. Tell you what, I'll give you half, and you let me drive out of here. It's time I was gone anyway."

I pointed the shotgun at the atlas. "Planning on going somewhere warm? Catch a flight out of Dodge and connect to another plane bound for the other side of the world?"

"Maybe."

"By the way, your local pusher, James? He's in handcuffs right now."

Sallis glanced down at the atlas. "As I said, it was time I was gone."

"I could kill you and take it all," I said.

"You could, but then you'd wind up with nothing. You'll never find the stash or the money."

"Okay, half it is."

"Now we're talking. I'll go get it."

Sallis started to get out of the recliner. I motioned him back down with the shotgun. "But first, tell me who else is in on it."

"Now you're sounding like a cop."

"I'm curious is all."

"Curiosity killed the cat."

"I'm not a cat. I'm a man with a shotgun pointed at you."

"All right, there's been another civilian contractor or two helping out at Kingsley, but they've come and gone. I work it alone."

"No, you don't."

"Sure, I do."

"No, you're hired help is all."

"Screw you."

"A boss wouldn't skim himself. When he finds out you've been stealing from him, he'll kill you."

"We'll see who kills who," he snarled.

"Did curiosity kill Captain Kane and the ground crewman?"

"You ask a lot of questions. Information is worth money. Why should I give it away?"

"Okay, I'll pay you for it."

"How much?"

"I'll shoot you once instead of five times."

"What kind of deal is that?"

"Instead of blowing off your hands and feet one by one to get you to talk, and then your head if you don't, I'll go straight for the head."

Sallis glowered. "I should've swung harder."

"You should've."

"All right, you win. The ground crewman? The package fell from the landing gear when he was checking it. Nearly hit him. What was I supposed to do? And Ramirez? Wrong place at the wrong time."

"You were going after Dominic," I said.

"Captain Voodoo does live up to his name. Pure magic to land that plane after what I done to it."

"That's another reason why I know you take orders from someone else. No way you could know the Air Force Office of Special Investigations had sent someone here, much less work out where to send the shipments on the commercial flights and arrange for them to be picked up and distributed. Who is he?"

"I give you a name, I got to change the deal. Instead of giving you half, I got to keep it all. I'll need it to get even farther away."

"You're that scared of him?" He didn't answer. "What about the nurse?" I said it indifferently and tried to bury it in all the other questions.

"What about her?"

"Did she see you unloading a shipment too?"

"She happened to walk by is all. I couldn't take a chance on what she saw or didn't. I did what I had to do. So what? She was only a nurse."

"Only?" I said.

Sallis flared his nostrils. "Oh, so she meant something to you, did she? You almost got me when you asked how I knew she was a nurse. What, you and her been going at it behind the major's back?"

"Shut up," I said.

He leered. "Want to hear what she sounded like when I choked her? What that pretty little face looked like?"

His tongue was lolling out. I jabbed the shotgun at it and shouted, "Shut your mouth."

The rush of anger blinded me. Sallis flung the heavy atlas. I had a poor grip on the 12 gauge because of the cast and fumbled for the trigger. He knocked the barrel aside. The shotgun clattered to the ground, but didn't fire. He threw himself on me, and we landed on the floor with him on top. Sallis tried to yank my revolver from the holster. I got my arms around him in a bear hug and we rolled over. Years of tossing suitcases and lifting heavy airplane parts had given him rock-hard muscles. He broke my hold, flipped me over, and pinned my arms down.

Sallis snarled and bared his teeth. I kneed him in the crotch and wrestled my arm loose. I clubbed him with the cast. Pain shot up and down my forearm and my fingers went numb, but I kept swinging. A gash opened in his eyebrow. His jaws opened wider and he snapped at my throat. I blocked him with the cast and jammed it in his mouth. He bit down, but only tasted plaster. I kept jamming the cast in deeper until the corners of his lips split. He started to choke. I shoved him off, jumped to my feet, and drew my gun.

"It's over," I said

Sallis snarled again and made a grab for the shotgun lying beside him. I pulled the trigger. And then I pulled it again.

The front door burst open as the echoes of the gunshots rang. I swung my pistol toward it. Pitzer charged in, his service weapon leading the way. Dominic was right behind him, his gun sweeping the room.

"Friendly!" I shouted. "Friendly!"

Both men took in the scene at a glance.

Dominic lowered his weapon. "Check if he's dead," he ordered.

Pitzer toed Sallis with his boot. "Two in the heart, sir." He flashed an approving nod at me. "That's some straight shooting there, Sarge."

Dominic holstered his weapon. "You shouldn't be here."

"Sallis gave me no choice." And I didn't mean that he'd gone for the shotgun.

"Now we got a problem on our hands," the captain said. "The major called me after you left his house. I had a feeling you weren't going to go away after you heard about Miss Donovan. Can't say I would have either."

He glanced down at Sallis. "Why did you suspect him?"

"A wise person told me never believe everything Coyote tells you."

Dominic cocked his head. "What's that supposed to mean?"

"His lies and laugh caught up to him. And you?"

"We knew it had to be someone on the ground crew team all along. We've had our eye on him for some time. We were waiting for him to lead us to anyone else."

"Now what are you going to do?"

"Only thing I can do. Clean up this mess and hope no one finds out about it until after we complete the bust tomorrow."

"There's another mess," I said.

Dominic sighed. "What is it?"

"A street dealer Sallis was providing with skimmings is getting busted right about now by local sheriff's deputies. He was with Sallis when they tried to OD me. They did OD another vet. A corporal with the 101st Airborne. Your operation wouldn't have looked that far down the ladder, but I couldn't let that go. Deeds served in Vietnam. He gave his leg. He deserved justice. He earned it."

The captain nodded to himself. "Street dealers get caught all the time. Hopefully, it won't get noticed."

"By the main man here at Kingsley, you mean."

"Did Sallis say something about that?"

"He didn't need to. Who's really calling the shots?"

The corners of Dominic's mouth turned downward. He motioned to Pitzer. "Secure the premises."

Pitzer took off. I could hear him scurrying from room to room, sniffing and searching.

"You don't know who it is, do you?" I said.

"We were hoping Sallis would lead us to him. Now we're going to have to wait until tomorrow night when we make the busts at all the bases along the route. Hopefully, they'll climb over each other trying to rat out the higher-ups in exchange for a shot at reducing the twenty years they're going to get at Leavenworth."

"Sallis wasn't going to give him up," I said.

"What makes you say that?"

"Because he was too scared of whoever it is." I glanced around the room. "What about me?"

"You weren't here. If I call the local authorities about this mess, I can't count on word not getting out. If I drag you back to Kingsley and throw you in the brig, then everyone will know and we'll have lost the element of surprise."

Dominic leveled his stare. "Can I trust you to stand down and keep your mouth shut?" He pointed at the grease monkey's body. "You got the man who killed your friend."

"Did I?"

"You did."

"But what about the man who gave him his orders?"

"No one ordered Sallis to kill Nurse Donovan. He did that on his own."

"That's why the AFOSI covered up what Sallis did by

spreading the story Carla killed herself." I said it more for myself than for Dominic. "It was to keep whoever oversees the smuggling at Kingsley in the game."

He nodded. "Go home, Drake. I'll call you when it's over. That's a promise."

Dominic saluted me and then turned the salute into a finger pointing toward the door. For once, I obeyed his order.

30

The moon played peekaboo as I drove east to Harney County. No log trucks were on the narrow highway. No vehicles of any kind, for that matter. The road followed a dark river coursing through a dark forest that covered dark hills. I rounded a curve and saw a buck crossing ahead. It turned toward me and froze in the headlights. A brown-eyed doe followed behind. She froze too. I braked to a stop and killed the headlights. As the moon ducked from behind a cloud, the pair shook the light from their eyes. The buck waited while the doe crossed, her tiny hooves click-clacking on the pavement. When she reached the other side, he followed. I didn't turn my headlights back on until they were safely in the forest.

I resumed driving. With each mile, the shakes and aches of having gone through withdrawal seemed to fall away. I didn't dwell on the fact that I had taken a life. I felt no pity for Sallis. He'd shown no mercy to Carla and the others he killed, and he deserved none from me. If I'd served as his judge, jury, and executioner because the Air Force had been unwilling to stop him when they first suspected him and then risked him escaping, so be it. I took no solace in his death, nor satisfaction either.

Carla was still gone, and there was still a man out there who was responsible for her death. He may not have put his hands around her neck and choked the light from her soft brown eyes, but he'd empowered Sallis, and therefore was no less guilty.

As keen as I was to get back to the lineman's shack, I still had unfinished business. I passed the turnoff to No Mountain and pressed on to Burns. I arrived at the sporting goods store where I had bought the skiff and trailer as dawn broke. I parked in the lot near the front door and dozed behind the wheel until the sounds of other cars and trucks woke me. The store manager with the white polyester shirt under a tan vest that had a row of pens clipped to the breast pocket unlocked the front doors.

"Welcome," he said. "How can I help you?"

"I need several things," I said. "Last time I was here you told me about an annual sale at the end of duck hunting season."

"It's still a week away."

"Any chance you can move that up for me?" I flashed him my badge.

"Now I remember you. You were asking about self-loaders and bought an outboard and trailer with a government purchase order. Did you ever catch that poacher?"

"Not yet. It's one of the reasons I'm here."

"And the other reasons?"

I handed him the list I'd drawn up without answering.

The store manager studied it. "That's quite a few items. I think we can give you the sales price on a lot of these, but not for the box of special ammo." He glanced at my casted wrist. "We'll carry it out to your truck for you too."

My next stop was the Harney County Sheriff's Office. Pudge Warbler was seated at his ersatz desk in the coffee room. He looked up from a report he was writing with a black ballpoint pen.

"You get any useful information from that guy you went to

see while I was busy helping the K Falls deputies arrest those little scumbags?"

"I did."

"That doper with the red beard? You were right about him going out the back door with a pool cue."

"Did he resist?"

"No. Neither did the pavement when he hit it with his chin after he elected to rabbit and I stuck out my boot and tripped him."

"And his sidekick?"

"The locals arrested him on the inside along with a couple of others. Turns out the lot of them were the candymen of K Falls. Tell me about what you found out from your guy."

I reached behind and closed the door. As soon as I did, Pudge muttered, "Oh Lord, here it comes."

I told him about Sallis. "I had to kill him."

He sucked his teeth. "Had to?"

"He went for a gun."

"Sounds like self-defense to me."

"I didn't give him much of a choice."

Pudge looked down at the Formica table that bore years of coffee cup rings and smudges from jelly donuts. After a minute or two he looked back up. "I was saying a little prayer there."

"Not for Sallis, I hope."

"Hell no. For your nurse friend."

I told him about the Air Force's plan to bust the drug smuggling operation.

"And they don't got an inkling who the big fish at Kingsley is?" Pudge said.

"They wouldn't tell me if they did, but I don't think they do. They're hoping someone will rat him out."

"They hope? That's what kids do at Christmastime. The thing about fish, the bigger they are the slipperier they are." He doodled in the margin of his report with the ballpoint pen. "But you got an inkling who he is, don't you?"

"Nothing concrete, only a feeling. And even then, it's a maybe, not a definite."

"If you can't trust your gut, who can you trust? What can I do to help catch him?"

"Nothing right now. I'm going to go home and put something together that will allow me to finally stop that poacher. Working with my hands will give me time to think. Who knows, maybe when Dominic calls later to tell me how their bust went, he'll have good news about catching the main man at Kingsley too."

Pudge squinted. "Son, that sounds like Santa Claus hope again."

THE LINEMAN'S shack was ice cold when I got there. I split some kindling with a hatchet, made a fire in the wood stove, and put a pot of water on to boil. By the time I'd unloaded my purchases from the sporting goods store, the shack was warm and the tea was steeped.

I sat at the rickety kitchen table with a knife, a hundred-yard spool of nylon cord, and a sack of four-ounce lead fishing weights. Because of the cast, it took some work to slice off a length of cord, feed an end through the eye of one of the sinkers, and make a knot. I made more until I'd used all the cord and sinkers.

As I worked, I let my thoughts drift back over the past few days. I listened to the conversations I'd had, ticked mental boxes, and lined up parallel columns of the things I knew and the things I didn't. I did the same with all the people connected to the moment Toro Ramirez plunged into Malheur Lake.

When I had all the cords and sinkers finished, I carried them outside to where I'd left ten gunny sacks stuffed with brand new duck and goose decoys. I could see my breath in the cold air as I pulled out the first decoy and tied the length of cord and lead sinker to the ring on its bottom. I set it aside and pulled out another decoy and repeated the process. When I had finished attaching anchors to all the decoys, I refilled the empty gunny sacks and placed the decoys in the front of the skiff.

I went back through my mental columns again, lining up what I knew and didn't about the murders at Kingsley Field and the shipments of heroin. I pictured the faces of all the people I'd encountered. I pictured the squadron emblem of the black bat with red eyes and outstretched wings on a yellow moon outside of Hardiman's office.

I pictured a photograph on the same wall, the one of fighter jets and the faces of men arranged in front of them—staff, ground crew, pilots, trainees, and trainers alike. I could pick out from memory Hardiman, Edwins, Dominic, Pitzer, and even Sallis. Two others in the photograph I'd never met, but I could guess who they were. There was a young, fresh-faced teen who had to be the ground crewman, and the older man with the rakish white aviator scarf and carefully tended black pompadour must be Elvis Kane.

I checked my field watch and wondered if Dominic would make good on his promise to call and let me know that the bust had gone down and whether they had succeeded in arresting everyone involved.

I opened another package from the sporting goods store. It contained boxes of ammunition for my government issue weapons. There were 12-gauge shells of varying loads from bird-shot to buckshot for the pump shotgun, a special box of high-powered, maximum weight 170 grain .30-30 cartridges for the Winchester, and two boxes of standard .357 magnum rounds for the Smith & Wesson revolver that all Fish and Wildlife rangers were given in case of a grizzly attack or, in my case, one launched by a two-legged coyote.

I thought about November's book. There were many legends about Coyote in it, more than devoted to any of the other *nuwuddu*. Coyote took on many forms and I realized that for him to have so many guises, there had to be more than one Coyote.

With everything unloaded and put in its proper place, I returned to the kitchen, poured another cup of tea, and thought about dinner. The only thing I'd eaten in days was November's broth. My appetite was coming back. I surveyed my stores. There was a bag of wild rice I'd bought from Blackpowder Smith, some canned vegetables, and a piece of chicken in the freezer. I started cooking.

The signal from the college radio station in Eugene was coming in, but the DJ wasn't in a mellow mood. He was spinning hard rock, one forty-five after another. Janis Joplin and Big Brother gave way to Jimi Hendrix, The Who followed Led Zeppelin. He played The Doors back to back. Like the come-down songs after a firefight, these were the same tunes we blasted from cheap stereos in-country to amp up before a battle. It made me think of the special congressional report Hardiman had mentioned, and I wondered if my commander had been spiking our chow with uppers too.

I finished dinner and washed the dishes, but there was still no call from Dominic. I banked the fire in the wood stove and climbed into the narrow bunk. The sheets still smelled of Carla Donovan, and I thought about the last conversation we'd had when she left in the morning for Klamath Falls. She told me she was certain that I was well on the way to recovery, that she doubted I'd ever let heroin take me prisoner again.

"But there is still something you need to do before you can ever be whole," she'd said.

"What's that?" I said.

Carla threw her arms around me and kissed me on the cheek. I didn't resist. "See, you can do it. You can let someone get close to you again. All you have to do is open your heart."

"I'll see."

"You don't have to see very far."

"What do you mean?"

Carla smiled as she got into her rental car. "The veterinarian. She practically lives next door."

31

C lear skies arrived with the morning. The snow on the ground was thin and began to be reabsorbed by the porous desert floor. I made coffee and let the grounds settle a little longer than usual after adding the cold water. I didn't have a plan of what to do if Dominic didn't call, but then the phone rang.

"I can't talk long," the captain said by way of greeting in his slight Texan twang. "I'm letting you know the special investigation team did its job last night. The AP made arrests at all the bases. There are quite a few bunks in brigs with new occupants."

"What's next?" I asked.

"Questioning and more questioning. Members of the Air Force JAG are en route to each base and will be assigned defendants. It's going to take time to sort out, but some people are going to be spending a lot of years behind bars."

"What about Sallis's boss?"

The line went silent and I wondered if we'd lost the connection. "We struck out there for now, but everyone's hopeful someone will flip and turn him in."

I thought of the poacher and his always having two escape

routes. "Even if someone does, he'll be long gone. He'll have learned of the bust by now and taken off."

"That was always a possibility," Dominic allowed, "but Major Hardiman and I are hoping he won't think he needs to run right away because his identity is a mystery to everyone."

"That's Christmas," I said.

"What's that supposed to mean?"

"A saying around here, is all."

"I got to sign off. The major left this morning for Washington DC. He and the other base commanders are giving a briefing to the Secretary of the Air Force."

"Does that mean you're in charge until he gets back?"

"Yes, but only for a couple of days or so. My reassignment came through. I'm going back to Vietnam. If this has taught me anything, it's that I'm a combat pilot, not a cop. I like it better when the enemy is in your sights and you can shoot them down. It makes things a whole lot easier."

"One other thing before you go. Can you transfer me to Airman First Class Edwins?"

"I would if I could, but he shipped out this morning. His orders finally came through too. Lucky guy, he's on a C-141 bound for Saigon. I got to go." He disconnected before I could say anything more.

I drank the rest of my coffee and swallowed my disappointment with it. The Air Force nailing everyone was always a long shot. I thought of calling Dominic back and telling him who I thought Sallis's boss might be, but then I saw an animal walk past the kitchen window.

It wasn't a coyote. It was a chestnut pony. Nagah Will was riding it bareback. I went out and greeted him.

"Good morning, Mr. Nick," he said.

"What brings you this way?"

The twelve-year-old was wearing the brown wool-lined

corduroy jacket that was two sizes too big. He looked dwarfed in it. "Uh, well, to say hello."

"It's a long ride from your camp. Cold too. Do you want to come in and have something hot to drink? I have biscuits too. They're not fry bread, but you can put honey on them."

"Okay." He slid off the pony and dropped the rope halter.

"Don't you need to tie him up?"

"He won't go nowhere until I do," the boy said.

We went inside, and he sat at the rickety table while I heated up water for tea. I put a couple of powder milk biscuits on a plate and found a jar of honey.

"Go ahead and help yourself," I said.

"Are they store-bought?"

"No, I made them. They're pretty easy."

He spread honey on one and took a bite. "Almost as good as store-bought."

"Thanks," I said. "I guess."

He added honey and evaporated milk to his tea and slurped it. I asked him about his grandfather and how things were at the camp. He told me they were settling in for a long winter, that they still needed to drive down to Catlow Valley and round up their sheep.

"When will you do that?" I asked.

"Grandfather says when we can buy gasoline for the truck."

I could tell the boy had something he wanted to say but I knew with Paiute, it was inhospitable to come straight out and ask.

Nagah Will slurped more tea and finished his biscuit.

"Have another," I said.

"No, there is only one left and it is yours."

I knew he was hungry, but I also knew it was important that I take the biscuit as a way to exchange gifts. I put some honey on it. Nagah watched carefully until I had eaten the last crumb.

"Dr. Gemma said there might be a reward for the piece of airplane that fell," he said. "Do you think they'll pay it?"

"I remember her saying that. I don't know."

"Oh." The boy seemed crestfallen.

"There might be a reward, though."

He perked up. "When would they pay it?"

"I'm not sure. I can ask. Why?"

"With a reward, we could buy gas for the truck and drive down to Catlow Valley and bring our sheep home before winter. If we don't, they might die."

"I could give you an advance on the reward."

"What's an advance?"

"It means money given before the actual reward is paid."

He shook his head. "I could not take it. That would bring shame."

"Let me explain. The Air Force is part of the government, and that means the government would pay the reward. I happen to work for the government, so if I pay an advance on the reward, it's sort of the same thing. That way you could have the money now to pay for the gas and save your sheep."

I found my wallet. It held fifty-seven dollars. I folded the bills and slid them over. "This is an advance. When the reward comes through, the government will pay me back. If there's any left over, I'll give that to you too, and everything will be square."

Nagah looked at the cash. "Do you think they would pay another reward if I found another piece of an airplane?"

"They might, but I have to tell you, it's pretty unusual for jet parts to fall from the sky, especially something like a canopy."

"But I've seen planes with a bubble on top flying around before. Maybe another bubble will fall off."

"Anything is possible."

"If I find a bubble that is smaller, will the reward be smaller too?"

"Maybe. I don't know."

"Because I saw one that is smaller. The plane is smaller too, smaller than the loud ones that flew over the lake."

The only planes I'd seen at Kingsley Field that were smaller than the F-101 Voodoo was the F-86 Sabre and the Bird Dog, but the Bird Dog didn't have a canopy. "How much smaller?"

"The size of this table."

"You mean the canopy, the bubble top?"

"Yes, it is smaller than the one that landed by the double snakehead." He slurped more tea.

"Where did you see it?"

"In Catlow Valley. I've seen the plane a few times when I'm herding sheep. I like to climb the mountain where Grandfather gave me my name."

"And you saw the small plane with the small bubble top when you were up there?"

"Yes. It is very noisy for such a small plane and does tricks. It scares our sheep."

"Tricks?"

"It flies straight up to the top of the sky and then goes round and round on the way down."

I got a pencil and sheet of paper. "Can you draw the plane?"

"I can try." Nagah grasped the pencil, held it between his fingers close to the lead, and drew with his face just inches above the paper. "Here. I'm not as good as my sister. She draws ponies and birds and can make all her letters."

I stared at the drawing. His sister had nothing on him because I could hear the roar of the souped-up engine of a P-51 Mustang and see its wings waggle.

32

P udge Warbler's roll of maps showing the cattle ranches that had been rustled rode between us in the front seat of his pickup truck. The old deputy's short brim Stetson nearly brushed the windshield. He was hunched over the wheel as if by leaning forward he could arrive at his destination that much sooner. He wasn't laying off the gas pedal any either.

"I've been a lawman a long time, and I stopped dwelling on the particulars of where I get information," he said as he kept his gaze focused on the narrow strip of blacktop that ran south from No Mountain.

We'd already sped past the Malheur Refuge and through Frenchglen where Carla and I had picnicked on the porch swing at the shuttered wayfarers inn. The thought that I may have been this close to where Sallis's boss might be hiding while Carla was still alive left a taste in my mouth more bitter than cowboy coffee with unsettled grounds.

We crested a rise and passed Roaring Springs at the head of the fifty-mile-long Catlow Valley. The rim of Steens Mountain ran along our left side. It was capped with a dusting of snow.

Farther to the southeast rose the Pueblo Mountains that crossed from Oregon into Nevada.

"I always ask myself, is it good information or is it a waste of time information?" Pudge continued. "Now, your Paiute information usually turns out to be good information, but it's information that you can't question too closely because it's always sandwiched between a slice of history and a slice of opinion and seasoned with healthy spoonsful of legend and mysticism, like your Ghost Dance religion."

He puffed his cheeks. "Now, the information you got is what I call a hybrid. You have your gut feeling, you have your facts, and you have your Paiute all rolled into one. That makes it pretty good information and not a waste of time information, and that's exactly why I hopped to it when you called me."

I was staring out the window as he prattled on. If Nagah Will was right about the P-51 Mustang and I was right about why I hadn't seen Captain Kane emerging from the mist while I was in The Pity Heart and why Sallis hadn't mentioned him when he boasted about the people he'd killed, then there wouldn't be a reward big enough that I could pay the boy. That Kane may have faked his own death to hide behind while he worked the smuggling operation made perfect sense. That he risked being exposed by stealing his prized airplane didn't. It told me if he really was alive, he had a weak spot, a weak spot I was determined to exploit.

"Tell me what else Orville found out?" I said.

"Now, his is always your good information type. That college boy is smart. I'm gonna hate to lose him to the FBI one of these days." The deputy patted the rolled maps between us. "He took a look at these and identified three landing strips that are within eyesight of the Will sheep camp. We were gonna get to those next spring as part of our plan to catch those rustlers. Anyway, Orville says one of them is particularly noteworthy."

"How so?"

"It's part of an old ranch down by the Basque Hills. They're called that because of the kind of folks who were doing a lot of the shepherding around here back when it came time to name places. Orville recalled the ranch from when he was looking at the county property records while searching for your poacher. The place changed hands earlier this year."

"Don't tell me the new owner's initials are A. J.?"

"Nope, they're not. It was bought by a business. Well, a corporation of some kind with an address in Las Vegas."

"Is there a person's name attached to the ownership?"

"There is if you consider John Smith a person. Seriously, that's who signed the paperwork, but Mr. Smith is some kind of shyster lawyer with a Vegas address too."

"What kind of ranch is it?"

"It ran cattle back in the 1800s when cattle was king in Catlow Valley, but there aren't too many of the big spreads left down here anymore. Those that have hung on have deep wells or year-round springs."

He paused as we rattled over a sizable crack in the blacktop. As far away from the Pacific Ocean as we were, Oregon's inland basin and range country was always on the move, pushed by one continental plate sliding under another. Steens Mountain was the high side of a wrinkle in the earth's crust caused by the pushing, and Catlow Valley the low spot in the fold.

"The Catlow's got a long history, that's a fact," Pudge said. "A professor was digging out here and found prehistoric campsites dating back twelve thousand years. That's even before the Paiute's time."

I tried stifling my impatience. "If it was a cattle ranch, what is it now?"

"Well, they tried sheep and that worked for a few years, but then the family up and blew away like tumbleweeds and it's been nothing ever since until this new owner, Now or Never Enterprises—that's its name—picked it up for a song."

A spark of electricity jolted me. "That *is* the name of a song," I said.

"What is?"

" 'Now or Never.' It was a big hit by Elvis Presley."

Pudge whistled. "You don't say? Well, son, I'd say your information just went from pretty good to pretty damn good."

The highway took a sharp turn to the left as it approached a gap that led to the Alvord Desert to the east, but Pudge steered the pickup onto a gravel road that headed south. We followed it for another fifteen miles. The land on either side was the color of old campfires with long stretches of desert and dunes pockmarked by dry lake beds.

"If you're looking for lonesome, you'll find plenty of it here," Pudge said.

"No real rancher would have bought an old place out here," I said. "Only someone looking for cheap land with plenty of airspace to play in and no neighbors looking over the fence."

"No telephone either. The owner must have a powerful antenna on his radio to contact the outside world."

"My guess is this is a part-time place. If it is Kane's, he probably has another place and moves between them. Maybe he spends most of his time in Las Vegas watching the real Elvis perform."

Pudge squeezed the steering wheel. "I don't like the fact that the property owner's address is down there and his shyster lawyer's too. Casinos and mobsters go together like slot machines and suckers."

I recalled what Edwins had told me about the Korean War ace, how he would always bet the other men on footraces and other competitions, how he would drive down to Reno on the weekends and come back with a showgirl. It wasn't too big of a stretch to see him gambling in Las Vegas too. Maybe he wasn't such a big winner, after all. Maybe he got in deep with loan sharks. From loan sharks to drug traffickers wasn't much of a leap. Maybe he wasn't the smuggling operation's boss at all, but organized crime's equivalent of a trucking company's area manager.

After a few more minutes of driving, Pudge stopped the pickup and brought an end to the teeth rattling, kidney jarring ride over the miles-long washboard road.

"That's the ranch road there on the right," the deputy said. "According to the map, the house and airstrip are another couple of miles in. It puts us about a jackrabbit's hop, skip, and a jump from the Nevada line. Best we look sharp. We don't know what kind of friends he might have with him."

"We'll be okay if we stick to what we talked about," I said.

Pudge gave me a sideways look. "I know that. We show him the maps with the red dots and say we're checking old airstrips being used by cattle thieves and see how he acts. But it's how you're gonna react that concerns me. The Air Force boys aren't gonna cut you a break twice if you up and plug a decorated pilot, even if he is a no-good drug smuggler."

"I'm not planning on anything."

Pudge watched as I unholstered my revolver and checked the rounds. "Oh Lord," he said. "Here we go."

We turned down the narrow dirt road that led across the desert. The outline of a house and barn appeared on the horizon with a set of treeless low hills framed behind them.

"Is that a dust devil twisting up ahead?" Pudge said, leaning even closer to the windshield.

"It looks more like it's being kicked up by a vehicle." As we drew closer, I could see a dirt airstrip running alongside the house and barn. "It's a plane."

"Is it landing or taking off?"

"It's taxiing to the far end. It's going to take off. Go, go, go!" I yelled.

Pudge stomped on the accelerator, and we tore down the dirt road as the pilot made a one-eighty and pointed the plane downfield.

"We're not gonna make it in time," he said.

"Then stop and let me out."

I turned to grab Pudge's Marlin from the gun rack behind us. Pudge didn't let off the gas as he threw his arm across my chest to block my reach.

"Hold on there. You can't go shooting any old plane you see. You don't even know who's in it. It could be a rancher who landed to talk to man about a horse."

"It has to be Kane," I said, breathing hard. The idea of him escaping made my adrenaline flow and heart pound. "Who else could it be?"

"Look again," Pudge said. "That's no P-51 Mustang. I saw my share in WW Two when they took on Hirohito's Zeroes."

The deputy was right. It wasn't a single propeller fighter; it was a twin-engine Beechcraft Baron. It raced down the airstrip and took off as we reached the ranch house. I craned my neck as it passed by.

"November One Eight Zero Zero Bravo Echo," I said, calling out its tail number.

The ranch house was weather beaten, but there were signs it was being lived in. A four-wheel drive was parked out front. Smoke curled from the chimney. A very tall radio antenna rose from the rooftop. Pudge and I both had our guns drawn as we got out of the truck.

"Same as before," he said. "You take back, I'll take front. If someone starts shooting at me, you have my permission to shoot back, Air Force be damned."

I circled the house and stayed low beneath the windows.

The back door was unlocked. As I eased it opened, I thought about the last back door I'd gone through and what I'd done afterward. If Kane was inside, I hoped he went for a gun too. He may have been a war hero, but he had forfeited all the honor that goes with it by betraying his brothers and sisters in arms for money. The deaths of the ground crewman, Ramirez, Deeds, and Carla were on his shoulders, along with all the junkies hooked on the smack he helped bring into the country.

I sniffed as I crept through the kitchen. There wasn't a feral stink like at Sallis's house, but there was a lingering smell of gunpowder. As I reached the living room, it was joined by the metallic odor of spilled blood.

A man was lying face down on a braided rug in front of the fireplace as if he'd decided to take a nap after adding another log to the flames. His black ducktail was matted with blood from a single gunshot to the back of the head. Pudge joined me. He reached down and rolled the man over. Elvis Kane's pompadour was flattened from having pressed against the floor and the lips he would make into a sensuous snarl to mimic his idol were ruined forever by the bullet that had torn through them as it exited his mouth.

"Looks like the real big fish heard of the bust and didn't want to leave any loose ends," Pudge said grimly.

Now I knew why Sallis was planning a hasty exit from Klamath Falls. He wasn't frightened of Kane. It was the mob bosses he answered to. I looked around the room. A blinking light caught my eye. It came from the front of a shortwave radio console on a table. I picked up the microphone, fiddled with the channel dial until I got reception. It took a bit, but I was soon patched through to Kingsley Field and speaking to Dominic.

"You have to trust me on this," I said. "Soldier to soldier. I'm in Catlow Valley. It was Captain Kane all along, but now he really is dead. Executed. And the ones who did it just flew off in a Beechcraft Baron. November One Eight Zero Zero Bravo Echo. It looks like the drug trafficking is linked to organized crime and the plane is headed back to Las Vegas. Can you intercept it and force it to land?"

Dominic's reflexes as a combat pilot and squadron leader kicked right in. He didn't argue, he didn't question. "Roger that," he said. "Wheels up in ninety seconds."

I could hear a siren wailing in the background. The captain had hit Kingsley Field's scramble button. I could see ground crews pulling the blocks away from the wheels of the squadron of F-101 Voodoos that were always parked on the tarmac and ready to fly at a moment's notice. Pilots were racing from the hangar to their jets and scrambling up the ladders to their cockpits. The air traffic controller was ordering commercial flights to vacate the airspace immediately. I could hear the roar of jet engines, smell their exhaust, taste the burning rubber of tires as they hurtled down the runaway, and feel the hurricane force of their takeoff as the jets shot skyward and reached supersonic speed in seconds.

"Fast thinking," Pudge said. "Those boys will be here in minutes. Even a plane with two props won't be able to outrun them."

The old lawman began searching the house while I stayed by the radio in case Dominic called back. He didn't. It wasn't long before the sonic booms of fighter jets zooming overhead shook the walls. I felt only resignation rather than a flashback coming on. The past several days had taken their toll, and I wanted nothing more than to walk out of that room with its stink of death and greed, go outside, and breathe the crisp, cleansing air of the high desert. I wanted to keep on walking—no, run—until I was no longer in the presence of evil and no longer had to mourn the dead who'd been unable to escape its reach.

Pudge rejoined me. "I just don't understand it," he said, snapping me back to the moment.

"What?" I said, not wishing to have to rehash the entire chain of events that started with a man falling from the sky and ended with a man lying at our boots.

"Vietnam and everything that goes with it. My war? It brought peace and boom times. Hell, it caused a baby boom too. Your war? Look what it's brought. Riots in the street. People burning flags. And now drugs and organized crime, right here in little old Harney County."

The deputy sadly shook his head. "Everything's changed. Nothing's ever gonna be the same again."

"Vietnam isn't only my war," I said. "It's all of ours."

Pudge sighed. "I know that, son. And that's what scares the hell out of me."

He looked at Kane's body. "The mobsters who did this? Don't think we've seen the last of them either. Not by a long shot. The flyboys may be able to force that plane down and arrest the ones in it, but there's plenty more like them. Who knows? Maybe the mob is behind all the cattle rustling around here too. I told you those thieves act different. Me and you? We're gonna have our work cut out for us, that's for sure."

"Us?"

"Who else? We've both been on the front line. Neither one of us is the kind to up and walk away from a fight. Am I right?"

He was, and so, I nodded.

"Good, because I expect nothing less in a man."

33

F all was almost over. The days were getting shorter, the nights were growing colder. It had been snowing on and off. Most of the big flocks of migrating waterfowl had already passed through. Most, but not all.

I sat in the skiff, hidden in a stand of cattails along the shore of Malheur Lake, and warmed my hands by clutching a thermos of coffee. Dawn broke and the light was silver. A large raft of ducks and geese were massed two hundred yards away, about twice the distance I had swum while clutching Toro Ramirez to my chest.

I thought about the last conversation I'd had with Pudge Warbler about Vietnam and its impact on everything. Maybe someday the war would end and the nation's wounds would heal. Maybe people would come to understand what soldiers had gone through, maybe even erect a monument to honor them, and maybe honor combat nurses with a monument too.

The put-put of an outboard making its way through the marsh punctuated the frosty silence. In time, the sound stopped and then the duck blind boat drifted into view. The poacher used the oar as a rudder and steered his camouflaged craft toward the raft of unsuspecting birds. One hundred yards. Ninety yards. Eighty and then seventy and then sixty. He put down the oar, walked to the bow, and began raking the flock with his Gatling gun.

I counted his gunshots. When he reached eighteen, I picked up my Winchester, aimed, and fired. Four times I pulled the trigger, the sound of my shots masked by the sound of his as he heartlessly emptied his murderous weapon.

The poacher's curses were louder than the echo of his gunshots when he realized no feathers were flying. The ducks and geese he thought he'd slaughtered were made of rubber and held in place by nylon cords and lead sinkers.

I hit the starter and the powerful outboard roared to life and the skiff leaped from the cattails. The poacher yanked his head around and bared his blackened teeth. He got his boat going and steered for the nearest marsh. I passed him easily and cut him off, giving him no choice but to continue straight into the jaws of the double snakehead.

It wasn't the oncoming current of the swollen twin rivers that slowed him down, but the extra weight of the water streaming through the four holes I'd punched through his hull with the heavy-grain .30-30 rounds. I steered my boat in circles around him, daring him to rush for his empty Gatling gun.

"You're lucky I didn't miss high," I said. "Though I wouldn't shed a tear if I had."

"I'm sinking," he said as he glanced down and saw the water quickly rising to the tops of his boots. "Throw me a line, neighbor, and tow me to shore."

"It's too late. You're about to sink."

"Then come get me."

"I haven't forgotten you tried to kill me."

"I was only scaring you off."

The water inside his boat reached the thwarts. He let go of the outboard's tiller and stood. "Come on, neighbor. Help me. The water's freezing."

"I'm sure it is."

I made another circle around him. The stern of his craft was inches from going under.

"I'll give up shooting forever. I promise," he pleaded. "Help me."

"I know you will because you and your gun will be on the bottom in seconds."

"You're crazy. This is murder. That's what it is. Cold-blooded murder. I thought you was a lawman."

"I am."

"Then you can't kill me. That's breaking the law."

"Not where I came from," I said.

"Where's that?"

"Hell and back."

"Ah, shit!" he cried as the river quickly poured over his gunwales. The boat, ladened with the heavy Gatling gun and chicken wire blind, sunk even faster than I thought it would.

I circled slowly around the bubbles. His greasy cap with the chewing tobacco-stained sheepskin earflaps floated up and was swept away by the current of the double snakehead. The poacher soon popped up too. He was spitting and spluttering, his arms flailing as he tried to grab hold of the sky and pull himself out of the water.

As I watched him struggle, I could feel the weight of his life grow heavy on my shoulders. He had killed countless creatures for money and deserved punishment for it. Nevertheless, I found myself feeling pity for him—not the pity of compassion, but the pity of contempt. I never wanted to see him again, but if I let him drown, his death would haunt my dreams forever.

When he looked good and tired, I swooped in, plucked him from the water and hauled him on board. I threw him facedown on the deck, yanked his arms behind him, and cuffed his wrists.

"Answer me one question, but if you lie, I'll know it and throw you overboard," I said.

"What is it?" he wheezed.

"What's your name?"

"Huh?"

"Your name."

"Able Jones."

"Well, A. J., I'm Nick Drake, and as an officer of the US Fish and Wildlife Service, it's my sworn duty to place you under arrest and haul your sorry ass to jail."

A FEW HOURS of daylight remained when I returned to the lineman's shack from the sheriff's office in Burns. I got a shovel and dug a hole within view of the kitchen window. I went inside and took all the cans of pebbles off the shelf and carried them outside. I poured out the pebbles that marked how many days I'd gone without taking heroin until the night Sallis got ahold of my arm.

Now, I had to start all over again. I'd have to fight temptation day by day because the remembrance of the warm embrace and dance on the razor's edge would not be soon forgotten. Carla had told me she believed I could kick it. She told me it was determination that made me who I am, not addiction. I'd trusted Carla when she was in this world, and that wouldn't change now that she was in what the Paiute called the spirit world.

I looked at the grave of pebbles. Two shined brighter than the rest. One was a polished nugget of igneous rock, the other a shard of obsidian. I picked up both and, rather than dropping them into one of the cans to mark my fresh start at staying clean and sober, I slid them into the beaded buckskin pouch and slipped it into my breast pocket. The rock was my memory of all the people who'd touched my life. Wherever I went, they would always walk with me. The obsidian was the future. It would poke me to embrace whatever change might come.

I covered the rest of the pebbles and went to find it.

November was sitting on the front porch wrapped in a Pendleton blanket when I arrived at the Warbler's ranch. She wasn't shucking corn like before, only sitting and staring as if waiting for someone.

"Hello, *Tsua'a Numudooa Nubabe*," I said.

"Your pronunciation makes my teeth hurt." She rubbed her jaw. "Pudge is not here. Nor is Gemma."

"I brought you a gift." I handed her a brown paper sack filled with chamomile I had collected over the summer and hung to dry for tea. She opened the bag and sniffed.

"Are you sure you did not pick death camas by mistake?"

"Pretty sure," I said.

She set the bag beside her.

I pulled the beaded pouch from my pocket. "Thank you for this."

November tsked. "You should wear it on a leather thong around your neck so it is next to your heart, otherwise you will lose it."

"I won't lose it."

"We'll see." She paused. "This will be your first winter here. Winter is very long and very cold. Maybe you will not stay."

"I'll stay."

"We'll see," she said again. "If you do, then you need to listen harder and read more. You have much to learn."

"I know."

The old woman pulled two books from beneath the blanket, and handed them to me. "Here." She disappeared inside the house, closing the door behind her without inviting me in or saying another word.

One of the books contained more Paiute legends told by shamans from different bands throughout the Great Basin. The other was Sarah Winnemucca's autobiography. I placed them on the front seat of my pickup and walked to the stable.

The two cutting horses were inside in adjoining stalls. It seemed like it had been forever since I'd ridden Wovoka. I opened the gate to his stall and held out my hand for him to sniff. A bag of oats hung in the corner. I reached in, cupped a handful, and held them out. I stroked his muzzle as he ate. A curry comb also hung on the wall, and though I'd never used one, I rubbed the buckskin's shoulders and back with it.

"You're not trying to rustle my colt, are you?" Gemma said.

I'd heard her enter the stable, but didn't turn around until she spoke. She wore her tan cowgirl hat and her hands were shoved in the pockets of a sheepskin coat.

"Your father told me what they do to rustlers in these parts," I said.

Gemma laughed. "Since you're here, let me take a look at those stitches." She ran her finger across the wound in my forehead. "How do you spell Mississippi?"

"What?"

"The state. I always mix up how many s's and i's."

I started spelling. I hadn't gotten to the second i before she plucked the first knot and pulled out the string of sutures.

"Ouch," I said.

"Works every time. Of course, cows and horses don't cry about it." She grabbed my left arm and held up the cast for inspection. "I'm not going to ask what you did to this poor thing. Are those teeth marks?"

I exchanged the curry comb for a brush with longer bristles and used it on Wovoka's black mane and tail that matched the color of his knee-high socks. "When is a colt no longer a colt?"

"If you don't geld him, when he turns four. Then he's a stallion. All horses have the same birthday. The first of January. It doesn't matter when in the year they're born."

"Will you geld Wovoka?"

"Not a chance," she said.

"Let's take them out for a ride," I said.

"Right now?"

"Right now."

We saddled the filly and colt and crossed a field of untrampled snow to the top of a rise that overlooked No Mountain. Gemma reined Sarah to a stop and turned the filly around, so they were looking back the way we'd come. Wovoka and I did the same. The breath from the horses mingled and rose in a singular column. Gemma's and mine joined it.

Looking out on the place I now called home, I could see how far I'd come since I'd ridden the Freedom Bird and how much farther I still had to go to find peace. There were no guarantees I'd ever get there, but I vowed I'd never stop trying no matter how rough the journey.

The clouds drifting overhead and the snow on the ground started to reflect the changing hue of the setting sun.

"I haven't had a chance to tell you how sorry I am about Carla," Gemma said. "I can only imagine how you must feel. I remember how much it hurt when my mother died."

I didn't say anything.

"It's especially painful to lose the ones you love," she said. When I still didn't respond, Gemma turned toward me. "You were in love with Carla, weren't you?"

The wind had picked up, and in its sighs and whistles, I could hear the Joni Mitchell tune that Carla listened to while she was in Vietnam. Like her, I'd seen both sides of life there. On one side was honor, duty, bravery, and sacrifice, on the other was death, killing, sorrow, and madness. But unlike Carla, who'd fallen for Sean Fitzpatrick, I'd only seen one side of love.

"What about it?" Gemma pressed. "Did you love her?"

I looked at Wovoka's mane. "I'm not too good at talking about those kind of things."

"Give it a try."

"I don't think so."

"Do it for Carla. Do it for yourself. Come on, it'll help."

I took a breath. "Okay, yeah, I did love her, but not in the usual sense. I mean, you can't be in a war and not love the people you serve with."

"How's that?" Gemma asked.

"It's hard to explain and probably even harder to understand if you've never been in one, but here goes. I loved Carla the same way I loved the men in my squad who'd put their lives in my hands and I in theirs. We all needed to trust each other in order to survive. It didn't matter where we came from or what we looked like or who we were. All that mattered was we trusted each other, and to do that, to give our lives over to someone else, well, it takes something that's pretty special."

"Did Carla feel the same way?"

"I'm sure she did. She trusted the nurses and doctors at the MASH because they were in a combat situation too. And she loved her patients because she asked us to trust her and we did." I paused. "Does that make sense?"

"It does, and I'd say you were all lucky to have each other."

"We were."

The horses shifted their stances, which made the saddles creak and the bridles jangle. Sarah whinnied. Wovoka tossed his head and swished his tail.

"Did I tell you I passed the test for my pilot's license?" Gemma said.

"Congratulations. Are you going to get a plane?"

"As soon as I find one for the right price."

"I know one in a barn over in Catlow Valley you could pick up for a song. It would suit you."

"What kind is it?"

"A Mustang."

"And you think the name alone makes it a good fit for a horse doctor?"

"No, I think so because the plane is a spitfire. Like you."

"Is that supposed to be some kind of compliment?"

"I suppose it is."

"You suppose?"

"Okay, it is."

Gemma smiled. "It's getting pretty cold and windy out here. Race you back?" Before I could answer, she touched Sarah's flanks with her boot heels and was off.

The music in the wind started playing louder as I watched horse and rider go. I could see chasing after Gemma and catching her by the time she reached the stable and pulling her close and telling her how I felt. I could see us putting the horses in their stalls, unsaddling them, and brushing them down, and then falling into each other's arms in a bed of hay. I could see us walking back to the ranch house and exchanging glances while sharing dinner with Pudge and November. And I could see us holding each other tight in the narrow bunk in the lineman's shack as the split logs in the wood stove crackled and the embers glowed. If not tonight, then tomorrow, or the next, or even next week or month. When didn't matter. What did was I could finally see both sides now.

Wovoka started pawing and whinnying, eager to run. I

looked out and saw Gemma and Sarah were already halfway to the stable. I clicked the inside of my cheeks.

"Come on, boy. Let's go."

The colt took off in a flash and we galloped down the rise and flew across the open. The sunset painted the snowy field below and the billowing clouds above with the same colors, and as we raced between them, I couldn't tell one from the other.

A NOTE FROM THE AUTHOR

Thank you so much for reading *The Pity Heart*. I'd truly appreciate it if you would please leave a review on Amazon. Your feedback not only helps me become a better storyteller, but you help other readers by blazing a trail and leaving markers for them to follow as they search for new stories.

To leave a review, go to *The Pity Heart* product page on Amazon, click "customer reviews" next to the stars below the title, click the "Write a customer review" button, and share your thoughts with other readers.

To quote John Cheever, "I can't write without a reader. It's precisely like a kiss—you can't do it alone."

Thanks,

Dwight Holing

ACKNOWLEDGMENTS

I'm indebted to many people who helped in the creation of "The Pity Heart."

Ben Colodzin, Ph.D. shared his expertise gained from 30 years working with combat veterans afflicted by Post Traumatic Stress Disorder (PTSD).

Sgt. Jeffrey Miller, US Air Force (ret.) provided knowledge of the USAF as well as invaluable insights as an author.

I'm especially grateful to my reader team who read early drafts and gave me very helpful feedback. Thank you, one and all, including Gene Ammerman, George Becker, Gino Cox, Ron Fox, Kevin R. LaRose, Marcia Lilley, Kenneth Mitchell, Dee Nordaby, Annie Notthoff, John Onoda, Haris Orkin, and Rhonda Sarver.

Thank you Janine Savage of Write Divas for your eagle eye and incredible grasp of English grammar.

Thank you Scott Smorra for your gorgeous photograph that graces the cover. Entitled "Frigid," it captures the Borax Hot Springs in the Alvord Desert in Harney County, Oregon. And kudos to designer Rob Williams for turning it into a stunning cover.

A special thanks to the Northern Paiute Language Project at University of California, Santa Cruz and the Burns Paiute Tribe of the Burns Paiute Indian Colony of Oregon, a federally recognized tribe of Northern Paiute in Harney County, Oregon.

Any errors are my own.

GET A FREE BOOK

Dwight Holing's genre-spanning work includes novels, short fiction, and nonfiction. His mystery and suspense thriller series include The Nick Drake Novels and The Jack McCoul Capers. The stories in his collections of literary short fiction have won awards, including the Arts & Letters Prize for Fiction. He has written and edited numerous nonfiction books on nature travel and conservation. He is married to a kick-ass environmental advocate; they have a daughter and son, and two dogs who'd rather swim than walk.

Sign up for his newsletter to get a free book and be the first to learn about the next Nick Drake Novel as well as receive news about crime fiction and special deals.

Visit dwightholing.com/free-book. You can unsubscribe at any time.

ALSO BY DWIGHT HOLING

The Nick Drake Novels

The Sorrow Hand (Book 1)

The Pity Heart (Book 2)

The Shaming Eyes (Book 3)

The Jack McCoul Capers

A Boatload (Book 1)

Bad Karma (Book 2)

Baby Blue (Book 3)

Shake City (Book 4)

Short Story Collections

California Works

Over Our Heads Under Our Feet

Made in the USA
Lexington, KY
31 July 2019